The Myth of Voter Fraud

The Myth of Voter Fraud

Lorraine C. Minnite

Cornell University Press
Ithaca and London

First published 2010 by Cornell University Press

Printed in the United States of America

Library of Congress Cataloging-in-Publication Data

Minnite, Lorraine Carol.
  The myth of voter fraud / Lorraine C. Minnite.
      p. cm.
  Includes bibliographical references and index.
  ISBN 978-0-8014-4848-5 (cloth : alk. paper)
  1. Elections—Corrupt practices—United States. 2. Political
corruption—United States. 3. Voting—United States. 4. United
States—Politics and government. I. Title.

JK 1994.M66 2010
324.6'60973—dc22
                                        2009052783

Cornell University Press strives to use environmentally responsible
suppliers and materials to the fullest extent possible in the publishing
of its books. Such materials include vegetable-based, low-VOC
inks and acid-free papers that are recycled, totally chlorine-free, or
partly composed of nonwood fibers. For further information, visit
our website at www.cornellpress.cornell.edu.

Cloth printing   10 9 8 7 6 5 4 3 2 1

Contents

Acknowledgments

In late 2001, David Callahan of the research and advocacy organization Demos asked me to conduct a study of voter fraud. After the 2000 election and calls for election reform, he and Miles Rapoport, Demos's president and a former Connecticut legislator and secretary of state, astutely saw the need for an empirical examination of the basis for claims about voter fraud that were shaping the policy debate. I am grateful to them and to Demos for giving me the opportunity to begin the research that led to the writing of this book.

Later, in 2006, Mike Slater at Project Vote asked me to write a report on voter fraud that drew on the research for this book. I thank him for his Midwestern optimism and get-up-and-go, and most of all for his deep commitment to an inclusive democracy.

My greatest scholarly debts are to Frances Fox Piven and Chandler Davidson. This book would not have been written without Frances's intellectual influence and also her gift of friendship. Chandler patiently prodded me to better develop the empirical basis for my claims, and his mentoring has made this a better book. Any shortcomings in the area of research design, of course, are my own.

My association with election reformers and voting rights advocates has convinced me of the value and integrity of engaged scholarship. At Demos, I thank David Callahan, Steve Carbò, Allegra Chapman, Stuart Comstock-Gay, Lisa Danetz, Regina Eaton, Scott Novakowski, Miles Rapoport, Tim Rusch, Tova Wang, and Brenda Wright for their expertise and friendship. At the Brennan Center for Justice at New York University Law School, Justin Levitt, Myrna Perez, Jennifer Weiser, and Wendy Weiser provoked me to extend my research by inviting me to participate in litigation. At Project Vote,

I benefitted from the work and camaraderie of Doug Hess, Jody Herman, Teresa James, Nicole Kovite, Brian Mellor, Estelle Rogers, and Mike Slater. Lillie Coney, at the Electronic Privacy Information Center and Eleanor Smith, counsel to the Leadership Conference on Civil Rights shared documents obtained through the Freedom of Information Act while I waited for the Justice Department to respond to my own public records request.

Many in the voting rights community know Carnegie Corporation U.S. Democracy Program Director Geri Mannion as a dedicated advocate of civic engagement and democratic reform. The financial support Carnegie provided freed me for a semester of the gratifying but demanding job of teaching Barnard undergraduates. Indeed, Barnard College provided a congenial setting to carry out this project. I am especially grateful to Provost Liz Boylan for her support through a family crisis and beyond, and to the many students who assisted with my research: Liz Aloi, Josh Bardavid, Nadia Bulkin, Cecila Culverhouse, Elizabeth Kraushar, Vanessa Perez, Julia Richardson, Christopher Ro, and Iris Rodriguez.

Scores of election administrators, public officials, lawyers, activists, scholars, and journalists set aside time to share their knowledge with me. I am enormously grateful for their willingness to take my calls, meet with me, answer my queries, provide data, comment on my work, or help in other ways. And spirited debate about voter fraud with an eclectic community of election junkies, law professors, political scientists, advocates, and reformers of every political stripe who populate Rick Hasen's election law listserv has helped sharpen my arguments.

Lastly, I want to thank the editors at Cornell University Press and anonymous reviewers whose comments improved the final version of this book. I am especially grateful to Peter Wissoker for his early enthusiastic response to my book proposal. To my family and friends, especially Cyndi and Steve, Barbara, Jennifer, Adrienne, David, and Manny, I hope you know how appreciative I am of your love, support, and forbearance.

The Myth of Voter Fraud

Chapter 1

Introduction

Voter Fraud and the Dynamics
of Electoral Mobilization

The 2000 presidential election was a watershed event. The candidate with
the most votes lost and the Supreme Court decided the winner. Interest in the
deadening minutiae of election administration, never before a subject de-
serving of so much spilled ink, captured the attention of the public, the
press, and academia—and remarkably continues to do so. Blue-ribbon com-
missions to study the challenges of election administration were convened
and reports issued. Thousands of pages of congressional testimony were generated by the hearings and floor debates that led to the passage of the landmark Help America Vote Act of 2002 (HAVA) dealing with the national
electoral infrastructure. Thousands more were added with hearings on a pano-
ply of election administration topics such as "what went wrong in Ohio's
2004 election," "election contingency plans," "military and overseas voting
problems," "noncitizen voting," and the National Voter Registration Act. Interest in election law, a subject once about as sexy as patent law, has ex-
ploded and the field has suddenly earned some respectability, with academic
centers, institutes, and journals all its own. Ideas percolate and debaters
hold forth in chatrooms, Internet communities, blogs, and listservs that populate this arcane field with thousands of amateurs and experts of every stripe,
computer whizzes and cyber sleuths, retired government employees and "vel-
vet glove revolutionaries." Millions of dollars in foundation money have
been poured into think tanks to fund studies on things such as residual ballots and lost votes, voting technology and software code, and Internet voting and absentee ballots, but also "a modular voting architecture ('FROGS'),"
"vertical proximity effects in the California recall election," "security vulnerabilities and problems with VVPT [Voter Verifiable Paper Trail]," and
"rational and pluralistic models of HAVA implementation."

And there has been another curious development. With so much public, media and scholarly interest in election administration, the issue of election fraud, an obsession of reformers and muckrakers in a bygone era, returned to the fore. How could it not? On the one hand, many watching the theater of the Florida recount, with the "Brooks Brothers Riot" of Republican congressional staffers shutting down the count in Miami and Republican lawyers shutting down the count in the hallowed chambers of the Supreme Court, concluded that the election had been "stolen." For others, there were plenty of examples of the rules not being followed or perhaps not being bent in the right direction. Concerns ranged from felons' illegally voting, to Democratic ballot count observers' eating chads,[1] and Al Gore operatives among Florida canvassing boards double-punching Palm Beach ballots to invalidate votes for George W. Bush or Pat Buchanan.[2] In the case of overseas military absentee ballots that lacked postmarks or did not comply with the rules in other ways, Bush operatives wanted the ballots counted anyway. To not do so would disfranchise patriotic soldiers and sailors.

The clamor over "epidemics" of voter fraud "breaking out all over" began to build. In 2002, the razor-thin majority control of the U.S. Senate by the Democrats was at stake. Heading into election day, at least eight Senate races—in Arkansas, Colorado, Georgia, Louisiana, Minnesota, New Hampshire, North Carolina, and South Dakota—were considered too close to call. In a number of these states, minority voters possessed the potential to determine electoral outcomes. The perceived Democratic advantage among these voters led to a pattern of campaign practices in key races in which the Democrats attempted to turn out their vote through registration drives, bounty programs, and transportation schemes to get voters to the polls, whereas the Republicans prepared task forces—teams of lawyers and volunteer poll watchers—to root out what they were convinced was fraud endemic to the Democrats' efforts and the electoral process itself.

In several places, Republican antifraud campaigns appeared to be directed at suppressing the minority vote and tipping the election to the Republican candidate.[3] For example, in Jefferson County, Arkansas, at the core of a Democratic district where there were highly competitive races for governor, the U.S. House, and the U.S. Senate, and where African Americans were forty percent of the population, a group of predominantly black voters who went to the County Court House to cast their votes at the beginning of the early voting period were confronted by Republican poll watchers who photographed them and demanded to see identification. One poll watcher circulated behind the counter in the clerk's office and photographed voter information on the clerk's computer screen. Democratic Party officials accused Republicans of "Gestapo" tactics to intimidate and harass likely Democratic voters; Republican Party officials accused the Democrats of committing egregious acts of voter fraud in their desperation to win and claimed Republicans were only trying to secure a free and fair election by ensuring voters were who they said they were and eligible to vote.[4]

In South Dakota, the hotly contested race between a surging Republican challenger hand-picked by President Bush to run for the Senate and a one-term incumbent Democrat mentored by Senate Majority Leader Tom Daschle (D-S.D.) focused national media attention on what was billed as a proxy race between the national parties. Between the June 4 primary and late October, 24,000 new voters registered in South Dakota, a sizable increase.[5] Approximately 4,000 of these new registrants were Native Americans, nearly all of whom registered as Democrats following efforts by the South Dakota Democratic Party, the United Sioux, and other tribes to boost registration levels on the reservations. The incumbent, Senator Tim Johnson, won his seat in 1996 by just 8,579 votes out of 324,487 cast and the Democrats believed Native American voters could be the key to his reelection in 2002.[6]

About a month before the election, local election auditors in counties on or near reservations reported irregularities in the voter registration and absentee ballot processes. The investigation centered on one woman, a paid contractor working to register new voters for the South Dakota Democratic Party. She was immediately fired by the party, which claimed it was not involved in the irregularities. The party then brought the matter to the attention of the U.S. attorney, and state and federal probes uncovered several hundred questionable voter registration and absentee ballot application forms tied to just two people.[7] Meanwhile, because of the presence of the national news media, the affair caught the attention of conservative commentators such as blogger Michelle Malkin, John Fund of the *Wall Street Journal,* and radio personality Rush Limbaugh, all of whom wrote or spoke of efforts to steal elections, "skullduggery on the Democrat side," and "a massive voter-fraud scandal" unfolding in South Dakota.[8] According to local news accounts, however, Mark Barnett, the Republican state attorney general, "bristle[d] at the idea that the two investigations are evidence of widespread voter fraud in the state. . . . 'I'm still only aware of two cases where criminal law may have been violated,'" he said, "'I just don't want the suggestion out there that there is widespread fraud when we don't have any evidence of that.'"[9] Johnson went on to win reelection in another squeaker, by just 524 votes out of 337,508 cast. Two people were arrested for alleged forgery of absentee ballot applications, but there was no fraud found in the balloting.

What happened next reveals the power of the perception of voter fraud to justify electoral and law enforcement policies that strategically advantage one political party over the other. The grip of the Republican Party on national power tightened with the 2000 election, but their majorities in Congress remained tenuously slim. Despite the Republican bluster about a mandate and a permanent majority, party operatives knew that close elections in key states were likely in elections to come and that, without real attention to key states and races, the electoral balance could tip toward the Democrats. One way Republicans tried to deal with this possibility was by embedding a campaign strategy in the voting rights enforcement routines of the U.S. Justice Department. That strategy was to aggressively investigate Democrats and their allies for voter fraud on the barest of evidence, to use the media to promote the investigations while ginning up media coverage of alleged "fraud," and to strategically time and keep those investigations open to influence elections. This later came to light in the scandal that erupted over the Bush Administration's unprecedented firing of at least nine of its own U.S. attorneys, seven of them on the same day[10] and at least two for refusing to pursue specious voter fraud allegations.

One month before the 2002 midterm elections, U.S. Attorney General John Ashcroft established a Voting Access and Integrity Initiative directed at "enhanc[ing the Department of Justice's] ability to deter discrimination and election fraud, and . . . to prosecute violators vigorously whenever and wherever these offenses occur."[11] The initiative involved the creation of task forces composed of district election officers (DEOs), who are assistant U.S. attorneys appointed by each of the ninety-four U.S. attorneys to serve in this new capacity, and Federal Bureau of Investigation (FBI) officials, whose job is to oversee "on-the-ground investigative and prosecutorial coordination" with state and local elections and law enforcement personnel, "deter and detect discrimination, prevent electoral corruption, and bring violators to justice."[12]

Federal monitoring of elections has been around since the Reconstruction period, but most often it has been directed toward defending the constitutionally protected voting rights of minority groups at the polls. What is significant about the Bush Justice Department initiative is the interpreting of voting rights as protection from corruption of the electoral process through voter fraud, despite a lack of evidence that voter fraud deserves the same level of scrutiny as racial discrimination in voting. This new understanding of voting rights is in keeping with an evolving pattern of conservative thinking and political strategy: conservatives are victimized by the liberal agenda, whites suffer discrimination more than blacks, and the rich unfairly get less from government than the poor. Nevertheless, during that first month of October 2002, DEOs implementing the Justice Department ballot security program opened just sixteen investigations into allegations of voter fraud.[13] In South Dakota, where the biggest story of alleged voter fraud of the 2002 election cycle would take place, the statewide phone number set up by federal officials to report any voting irregularities received only one call.[14]

The second way that the idea of voter fraud mattered in the wake of the 2000 election was that it was invoked as a deterrent to democratizing reform of the electoral process. Voter fraud has been the justification for the erection of much of the convoluted electoral apparatus that plagues the U.S. electoral process today. More than a century ago, the threat of voter fraud was the rhetorical rationale for the very invention of voter registration rules, and each of the major national efforts at election reform since then—from the Voting Rights Act of 1965, to the National Voter Registration Act of 1993, to the Help America Vote Act of 2002—has been seriously compromised by an organized party-based opposition warning of the dangers of voter fraud.

In 2002, arguments that the adoption of election day registration (EDR) reforms would increase fraud were crucial in defeating EDR ballot initiatives in California and Colorado.[15] In both states, antireform forces coalesced around the issue of voter fraud, arguing that eliminating the waiting period that election officials claimed they needed to verify voter eligibility would only open up the voting process to ineligible people and fraud schemes, abrogating the voting rights of legitimate voters by diluting their votes. Elections officials in California worried that the state electoral administration was not technologically advanced enough to instantaneously check for duplicate registrations.[16] In Colorado, EDR opponents warned that setting up the program would cost millions of dollars in new equipment and training, and worried that election judges, wary of lawsuits, would be chastened from vigorously questioning the authenticity of voters' identification documents.[17] Despite substantial funding to promote EDR in both states and despite early public support, opponents were able to persuade voters that the price to pay for making voting easier and more accessible was still too high.

The Myth of Voter Fraud

In this book, I show that for the vast majority of Americans committing an act of voter fraud—forging a voter registration card, stealing an identity to vote more than once, or knowingly voting illegally—is even more irrational than the individual act of voting. What would an individual voter on their own get out of committing an election crime? The incentives to cast an illegal ballot need to be pretty high to risk a felony conviction and five years in jail. This logic holds even for undocumented immigrants—the new blacks in America. Take the most likely scenario painted by those who fear a surge of illegal immigrant voters. Why would an undocumented immigrant who may have obtained a fake Social Security number in order to be paid for the low-wage labor he or she provides a U.S. employer come out from the shadows to cast a ballot that could deport that individual forever? The data revealed in the pages that follow are consistent with a logic that works against the fear that individual voters are corrupting elections. The best facts we can gather to assess the magnitude of the alleged problem of voter fraud show that, although millions of people cast ballots every year, almost no one knowingly and willfully casts an illegal vote in the United States today.

The initial research for this book began as a response to a simple question from Miles Rapoport, the director of Demos, a democracy reform research and advocacy organization in New York City. Rapoport's own efforts to lower barriers to voting when he was secretary of state of Connecticut were routinely opposed with arguments that such reforms would only open the door to more voter fraud. He wanted to know how big the problem was so that Demos could develop an appropriate agenda for electoral reform. Encouraged by Demos, I spent a number of years engaged in painstaking research, aggregating and sifting all of the evidence I could find. The results are reported in the chapters to come, but I can short-circuit the suspense— voter fraud is rare. It cannot compare in magnitude to the multiple problems in *election administration*, which present a far greater threat to the integrity of elections.

But these findings only raise more questions. Why is the specter of voter fraud recurrently conjured in U.S. electoral politics? My second major goal in this book is to explore why these allegations are made when the facts do not support them, and why they succeed in influencing electoral rules. This certainly is not the first time we have heard the warning that voting cannot and should not be made more convenient, that the rules simply cannot be simplified, or that we need to put up roadblocks to the ballot to protect it. If charges of voter fraud are not based on facts, why do we continue to believe them? These are the interesting questions, the important questions. We need a best estimate of the incidence of voter fraud, but more than that, we need to know why the myth of voter fraud can be so successfully rejuvenated in the political culture to the point that all it takes to recall it is a wink and a nod—and maybe a little bullying.

Voter fraud is a politically constructed myth. To begin, I discuss a couple of high-profile voter fraud allegations as examples that have influenced the national election reform debate, and I show how they fall apart when we interrogate them. Voter fraud politics are robust in part because they capitalize on general and widely held folk beliefs that are rooted in facts and real historical experience, notions such as corruption in party politics and government but also stereotypes and class- and racially biased preconceptions of corruption among groups long stigmatized by their marginal or minority status in U.S. society.

Fraud Allegations Examined

At the heart of my inquiry is the question of evidence. I demonstrate that the evidence proffered to support the most newsworthy allegations of voter fraud today is insubstantial and unconvincing. The United States has a fragmented, inefficient, inequitable, complicated, and overly complex electoral process run on election day essentially by an army of volunteers. It is practically designed to produce irregularities in administration: the numbers of voters signing the poll book do not exactly match the numbers of ballots cast because of the unexpected crush of citizens who wanted to vote and the fact that a poll worker's bathroom break was not covered; confused voters go here and there trying to cast their ballots in their precinct, the one they voted in eight years ago, only to find their wanderings recorded as double votes; absentee ballots do not reach their rightful destination in time, causing anxious voters to show up at the polls where they are again recorded as voting twice; John Smith Sr. on line number twelve in the poll book signs for John Smith Jr. on line thirteen and violá—another voter is ensnared in a fraud; voter registration applications go unacknowledged so voters send in duplicates and triplicates, sometimes adding a middle initial or a new last name. The list of mix-ups, misunderstandings and mistakes goes on and on. Yet the multitude of alternative explanations for any one irregularity are ignored by the media, which gets a story of fraud faxed to them in a press release by a political party and wants to avoid the gigantic public yawn sure to follow a report of simple bureaucratic failure. The press is attracted to the potential scandal, corruption, or a brewing political fight, and reporters avert their eyes from the more reasonable but boring explanation. In so doing, they become part of a party-driven campaign strategy to keep down the vote.

To get a sense of how this works, let us look at an oft-repeated allegation of voter fraud made by John Fund, *Wall Street Journal* columnist and author, who proclaimed in his 2004 book *Stealing Elections* that several of the 9/11 hijackers were registered to vote.[18] Fund asserts, "At least eight of the nineteen hijackers who attacked the World Trade Center and the Pentagon were actually able to register to vote in either Virginia or Florida while they made their deadly preparations for 9/11."[19] Fund's source for this claim is a December 22, 2002, interview he said he conducted with Michael Chertoff, then an assistant attorney general in charge of the Justice Department Criminal Division.[20] Fund provides no other corroborating evidence.

As a regular columnist for a national newspaper, Fund writes stories intended to inflame though his language is never partisan or inflammatory. The care he takes in his regular columns to appear reasonable is evident in his book, in which Fund writes that the hijackers "were actually able to register to vote," not that they *did* register to vote or *were* registered to vote. What does it mean to say someone is "able to register to vote"? Fund echoes previous statements by prominent conservatives that the hijackers or their associates *may have been registered to vote*. For example, more than a year before Fund says he interviewed Chertoff, Diane Ravitch, a senior fellow at the Hoover Institute, wrote, "Thus far, no reporter has observed that the hijackers were eligible to vote in state and federal elections, despite the fact that they were not American citizens." Of course, foreign nationals are not eligible to vote, only citizens are eligible to vote under state law. Senator Christopher "Kit" Bond (R-Mo.) picked up on the idea that our voter registration procedures are so lax that foreign terrorists can successfully apply when he asserted on the floor of the Senate that a Pakistani citizen in Greensboro, North Carolina, "with links to two of the September 11th hijackers was indicted by a federal grand jury for having illegally registered to vote."[21]

In person Fund is less careful in parsing his words. He confused what he meant by "able to register to vote" when he appeared on the CNN Lou Dobbs show on October 24, 2004, to promote *Stealing Elections.* Here is the exchange:

> DOBBS: You point out in your book that eight—eight, was it?—of the 19 . . .
> FUND: Eight of the 19.
> DOBBS: . . . 9/11 hijackers *could* have registered to vote?
> FUND: No, they *did* register to vote. [emphasis added]

Without explicitly stating it, Ravitch and Fund are referring to the fact, known within weeks of the attacks, that some of the 9/11 hijackers had obtained driver's licenses.[22] Ravitch incorrectly implies this made them "eligible" to vote because the National Voter Registration Act of 1993 (NVRA) requires that applicants for driver's licenses be presented with an opportunity to register to vote. But being presented with an opportunity to register does not make a person eligible to vote. No state creates a right to vote or establishes voter eligibility through possession of a driver's license. By linking the 9/11 hijackers to the "motor voter" law, one of the very first bills signed into law by President Bill Clinton, over the objection of congressional conservatives, both Ravitch and Fund are talking in code, reinforcing the idea held fervently by right-wing partisans that the NVRA has corrupted democracy by opening the door to voter fraud.

To register to vote through a driver's license agency in Virginia or Florida during the time the hijackers were in the United States, any applicant would have had to affirmatively assert citizenship. In Florida in 2000 and 2001, an individual applying for voter registration through a driver's license agency had to verbally confirm to agency personnel that she was a citizen, and sign her name on a card preprinted with the same information submitted to obtain the driver's license. In Virginia, applicants were presented with a carbon-copy form; the top part served as the application for a driver's license, and the bottom half was used for voter registration. More recent efforts to confirm Fund's allegation that some of the 9/11 hijackers were registered to vote in either Virginia or Florida have failed to turn up any supporting evidence at all. According to Philip L. Edney, a public affairs specialist at the FBI, who spoke to "someone actively involved in investigating this allegation," the hijackers were not registered to vote in either state.[23]

Fund provides no evidence from Virginia or Florida elections officials confirming the registration status of any of the hijackers, but we may never know for sure.[24] Could the 9/11 hijackers have used aliases? In October 2006, the BBC reported that the FBI was confident it had positively identified all nineteen hijackers, but many Arab names are similar and when transliterated into English can be spelled a variety of ways. Arabic naming conventions, which incorporate honorifics and extended family or tribal identifiers, are unfamiliar to non-Arabic speakers. For example, the Palestinian president and leader of the Fatah Party, Mahmoud Abbas, is also known as Abu Mazen, or "father of Mazen," Abbas's eldest son.[25]

The 9/11 Commission found that some of the hijackers used passports "manipulated in a fraudulent manner," made detectable false statements on their visa applications, and gave false statements to border officials to gain entry to the United States. So it is possible that some of the hijackers either registered to vote when they obtained driver's licenses or state ID cards (which some did in four states: California, Florida, Maryland, and Virginia), although the motive for their doing so is not immediately obvious. The point is that those claiming that the hijackers were registered to vote have yet to provide any evidence that they were. In June 2007, Virginia elections officials were unable to confirm or deny that any of the hijackers had registered to vote. None of the hijackers had a Virginia driver's license, but eight did acquire Virginia ID cards, most of them fraudulently.[26] Valarie Jones, acting secretary for the Virginia State Board of Elections, said that the veracity of the claim that any of the hijackers voted could not be investigated because poll books in Virginia are retained for only two years after an election.[27] At my request, the Broward County Governmental Center in Fort Lauderdale reviewed the Florida statewide database for all the names and aliases used by the hijackers and found no identical matches on names and addresses.[28] Nor was any evidence concerning the voter registration status of the hijackers presented to the National Commission on Terrorist Attacks Upon the United States or unearthed by any of the congressional inquiries that reviewed the FBI investigation of the attacks. I conclude from these findings that, in the absence of any affirmative evidence from state elections or federal law enforcement officials, it is highly unlikely that any of the hijackers was registered to vote.

Fund's allegation about the 9/11 hijackers was widely circulated and has had a surprisingly long life given that it is poorly documented and very likely false. For example, in protests on the floor of the House over various border security provisions stripped from the Intelligence Reform and Terrorism Prevention Act of 2004, U.S. Representatives Ed Royce (R-Calif.), Steven King (R-Iowa), and Sam Johnson (R-Tex.) all repeated Fund's allegation that eight of the nineteen hijackers were registered to vote.

The lack of scrutiny of voter fraud charges and the ease with which partisans have been able to insert them into the public discourse means that arguments based on demonstrably false information, or no information at all, are entered into the congressional record, sway lawmakers, and are cited by Supreme Court justices as fact. It means pundits who relish the charges and their whiff of scandal will continue to manipulate public understanding. On the evening of the November 2006 congressional elections, John Fund was a guest on Glenn Beck's CNN syndicated talk show. Two years had passed since the publication of his book, and because he has yet to be upbraided for any of the misleading information he provides there, Fund must have felt it was safe to again repeat the provocative charge that eight of the nineteen 9/11 hijackers were registered to vote:

BECK: OK. To put this into perspective on how bad and out of control our system is—and I don't think the Republicans or the Democrats really want to fix it—explain how many of the 9/11 hijackers were registered to vote.

FUND: Eight out of the nineteen 9/11 hijackers were registered to vote in either Virginia or Florida. They could have easily voted if they'd wanted to.

BECK: And how did they do that?

FUND: Well, we have something called the motor voter law. You can go into any government office building, any transaction you conduct with them, driver's license, unemployment, whatever you get the check off, [sic] do you also want to register to vote?

All the registrations are on a postcard. There's no question as to whether you're a citizen. There's not [a] question as to whether or not you're a real, live human being. You're automatically registered.

Our registration rules have a lot of people on there who are dead, don't exist or registered many times over.[29]

This is a good example of what I call *voter fraud politics*, the use of spurious or exaggerated voter fraud allegations to persuade the public about the need for more administrative burdens on the vote. I frame my analysis and case studies to explore the politics of fraud allegations—to ask who are the actors, who are the targets, what are the tactics deployed, and what are the factors that account for their success in maintaining barriers to the vote that disproportionately affect certain Americans?

Fraud politics is about the behavior of partisans and their allies and is therefore a different phenomenon than the alleged criminal behavior of the voters that partisans implicate. The levelers of politically motivated allegations have far greater influence on electoral policy than the behavior of the average voter. John Fund is an influential opinion-maker, not a criminal voter. Through his widely circulated, national syndicated newspaper columns, his book, and his many appearances on cable news and radio programs, he has a wide audience and appears to speak with authority when he says our voting system is so porous that eight young men from the Middle East who allegedly hate us for our open democratic system and our freedoms, were actually registered to vote right here in the United States. How might the power that John Fund wields to influence public opinion compare to that of our mythical criminal voter? Contrast the incentives to the individual voter to commit fraud to those which appear to motivate baseless voter fraud allegations on the part of a political opponent. Who stands to gain the most? Committing voter fraud is a crime, falsely accusing someone of it is not.

A second example of influential voter fraud claims that collapse when scrutinized is the 2005 report of a now-defunct nonprofit organization called the American Center for Voting Rights (ACVR) created by Republican Party operatives that same year. On March 15, 2005, Robert Ney (R-Ohio), chairman of the U.S. House Administration Committee, held a field hearing in Ohio on election administration and balloting problems during the Ohio 2004 election. Mark F. "Thor" Hearne, II testified that voting problems in Ohio were the result of the National Association for the Advancement of Colored People (NAACP) paying people with crack cocaine to get them to register to vote. Hearne was identified as the general counsel for the ACVR and "a longtime advocate of voter rights."[30] But, according to Murray Waas, writing in the *National Journal*, the ACVR was founded by Hearne, "with encouragement from [Karl] Rove and the White House."[31] Hearne himself has impressive Republican Party credentials going back to an early stint in the Ronald Reagan administration Department of Education. He worked as a lawyer and observer for the Republicans on the Florida recount, and as an adviser and national counsel for the 2004 Bush-Cheney campaign. He was a delegate to the Republican National Convention, a delegate to the Missouri State Republican Convention, and chairman of the Missouri Republican Platform Committee, as well as a member of the national Republican Platform Committee. In 2003 and 2004, he chaired the National Election Law "School" of the Republican National Lawyers Association. Hearne also played a role in the 2000 election in Missouri when he represented the Republicans in a successful lawsuit appealing a St. Louis court order to keep the polls open two hours after closing time. Pervasive administrative failures in that election resulted in long lines, denying some voters the opportunity to vote before the close of polls, so the Democrats who expected to reap the benefits went into court to keep the polls open. The Republicans continue to see this move as evidence that Democratic voters committed fraud in that election.[32]

Three days after Hearne's appearance before Representative Ney's committee, journalist Brad Friedman reported that the address of the organization was a U.S. Post Office box in Dallas, Texas, shared with another fund set up by the law firm of former Secretary of State James Baker, the leader of the Bush-Cheney 2000 recount team.[33] That address, which Friedman obtained from the Internic record for ac4vr.com, the ACVR's Internet domain name, was 8409 Pickwick Lane 229, Dallas, Texas 75225. The records were quickly made private after they were discovered, so Friedman called Jim Dyke, who was listed on the Internic record as both the administrative and technical contact for the ACVR. Dyke, too, was a Republican Party operative. He had worked as the communication director for the Republican National Committee (RNC) during the 2004 election and is a protégé of Ed Gillespie, the former RNC chair. He told Friedman that the address on the Internic record was for the company that had designed the ACVR website, a company whose name he could not recall. The address—8409 Pickwick Lane in Dallas, Texas—is actually for a UPS store.[34] According to Sourcewatch, a project of the Center for Media and Democracy, the user ID and password needed to access the fundraising page for the ACVR Legislative Fund, an affiliated 501(c)4 organization, belonged to eDonation.com, a member of the Donatelli Group, a consulting firm "that has raised campaign funds for the Republican National Committee, Republican National Convention, Bush-Cheney '04 Inc., John McCain, the NRA [National Rifle Association], and an exhaustive list of Republican members of the U.S. Senate and the U.S. House of Representatives, as well as other political organizations." The Donatelli Group also created the RNC website and the website of another Republican Party front group, Swift Boat Veterans for Truth.[35]

Within six months of bursting on the scene, the ACVR Legislative Fund released a self-commissioned report, titled "Voter Fraud, Intimidation and Suppression in the 2004 Presidential Election," that professed to be "the most comprehensive and authoritative review of the facts surrounding allegations of vote fraud, intimidation and suppression made during the 2004 presidential election." Analysis of its many claims, however, shows it to be little more than a pile of poorly scrutinized newspaper articles sensationalizing election shenanigans allegedly instigated in all but two instances by Democrats, who were accused of far more voter intimidation and suppression than Republicans. In other words, it is a piece of political propaganda produced by Republican Party operatives who veiled their work as civil rights advocacy. The report identified five "hot spots" for voter fraud. Four of these were cities with substantial black populations (Philadelphia, Milwaukee, St. Louis, and Cleveland), plus Seattle, which rounded out a roster of key Republican swing states—Pennsylvania, Wisconsin, Missouri, Ohio and Washington—in the 2006 election.[36] Table 1.1 summarizes the findings of the report and shows that, among the more than one hundred cases cited of alleged voter fraud implicating nearly 300,000 potentially fraudulent votes in the 2004 election cycle, only about 185 votes could be confirmed as possibly tainted by fraud.

Over the course of its brief two-year life, the ACVR achieved remarkable influence, promoting the idea that U.S. elections are riddled with voter fraud.

TABLE 1.1

American Center for Voting Rights, voter fraud allegations versus actual incidence of fraudulent votes, 2000–2004[a]

			Total number of votes affected by alleged fraud[c]	
	Total number of cases[b]	Total number of states	Alleged or implicated in	Confirmed by other
Type of fraud	mentioned	involved	ACVR report	sources
Registration fraud	57	10	275,000+	0[d]
Voting by ineligibles (i.e., felons and noncitizens)	12	5	16,400+	9
Double voting	15	5	3,052–3,652	10
Vote buying	28	5	Unknown[e]	Unknown[e]
Absentee ballot fraud	4	3	256	29[f]
Total	116	15[g]	294,708–295,308+	48+

Source: American Center for Voting Rights, Legislative Fund, "Vote Fraud, Intimidation & Suppression in the 2004 Presidential Election," Washington, D.C., August 2005; for details, see, appendix 1.

[a] The American Center for Voting Rights (ACVR) report claims to be "the most comprehensive and authoritative review of the facts surrounding allegations of vote fraud, intimidation and suppression *made during the 2004 presidential election*" (ACVR report, 3; emphasis added;). It includes, however, allegations of voter fraud in the 2000 and 2002 elections, and cites a few media reports about fraud in certain places going back as far as 1988.

[b] Measurement of the number of individuals or votes involved in any one allegation of fraud made in the ACVR report is difficult because the data presented lack the necessary detail. To tackle this problem, I adapt the concept of a "case" from the case study method commonly used in social science (see Alexander L. George and Andrew Bennett, *Case Studies and Theory Development in the Social Sciences* (Cambridge, Mass.: MIT Press, 2005). A *case of voter fraud* is a hybrid measure of individuals and incidents. It can involve multiple individuals alleged to have committed fraud, officially charged with fraud, or convicted of voter fraud, or it can refer to an incident in which the number of individuals is not specified. An *incident* refers to the alleged commission of a specific form of fraud in a discrete place and time. For example, consider an incident of voter registration fraud allegedly committed in the 2004 presidential election in fictional "Happyland, New Jersey" that involved the submission of fraudulent voter registration applications. As described in news stories, several types of voter registration fraud were involved, for example, the submission of forms for dead or fictitious people and the submission of forms that inexplicably changed the party registration of people who were already registered to vote. Each is counted as a separate incident in this example because, although the fraud was committed in one election and one place, three different forms of voter registration fraud were allegedly committed. It is worth distinguishing among these types of fraud because they involve different techniques and expose different vulnerabilities in election security. Therefore, the number of *cases* counted in this example is three. In sum, number of cases measures alleged incidents of distinguishable forms of fraud occurring in single elections and specific places where the number of individuals and votes may not be known.

[c] Stories about election irregularities, like other newsworthy events, unfold. The "Alleged" column counts the number of votes allegedly affected by the potential, alleged, or actual voter fraud reported in the news stories serving as the sources for the incidents mentioned in the ACVR report. For example, a news organization's comparison of voter registration records against tax or other records may produce a number of records in which addresses do not match. In some cases, news stories have reported on these findings as "potential" evidence of voter fraud. "Potentially" fraudulent votes estimated in this way are counted as allegations. The "Confirmed" column counts the number of actual illegal votes arising from each allegation of fraudulent registration or voting made in the ACVR report, as confirmed by a second or government source. See appendix 1 for a description of the allegations and the facts surrounding each case.

[d] As confirmed by other sources, across the states and examples presented in the ACVR report, at least 5,650 fraudulent voter registration forms were collected and, in some cases, submitted by 24 people prosecuted for voter registration fraud in six states—Colorado, Florida, Minnesota, Missouri, New Mexico and Wisconsin—during the 2004 election cycle. There is no evidence that any of these fraudulent registrations resulted in illegal or fraudulent ballots.

[e] The usual standard for a criminal showing of vote-buying does not require a full accounting of the number of votes sold. Neither the ACVR report nor the news stories cited as sources for the report's discussion of vote-buying cases estimate or make allegations about the number of votes tainted by vote-buying conspiracies. In the absence of such evidence, we can count the number of people prosecuted and convicted for vote-buying. In the cases identified in the ACVR report, there were 26 people convicted of various crimes related to vote-buying in the 2000, 2002, and 2004 elections in Illinois and Kentucky, and elections going back to 1990 in West Virginia.

[f] See appendix 1, case 6.1a, the September 14, 2004, Greensboro, Alabama, mayoral run-off election, in which 162 illegal absentee ballots were identified in an investigation conducted as part of an election contest. At least 22 of these ballots are counted as fraudulent because a number of voters testified at a hearing that they had sold their votes, which they cast as absentee ballots.

[g] Multiple forms of voter fraud are reported for most states in the ACVR report; here states are only counted once.

In 2005 and 2006, the group successfully advocated for strict, government-issued photo identification requirements, although their victory was incomplete. Thor Hearne, their leader, attorney, and political operative, served as an expert witness before the Republican-dominated Congress and other government bodies on the need for voter photo identification requirements, entering into the record testimony that mirrored the ACVR report and using unverified allegations to make his case. Over and over again, Hearne hammered home the message, repeatedly relying on anecdotes and misleading news reports that wildly overstated the problem of voter fraud. The ACVR also supported upholding the earliest possible voter registration book closing dates in all states, a one-week turnaround time for the return of voter registration forms by volunteer groups, and more stringent list-maintenance procedures during the last month before an election.

The ACVR was a Swiftboat-style organization that incorporated as both a tax-exempt nonprofit "educational" corporation and as a commonly controlled "legislative fund" that served as a vehicle for initiating litigation. The tax-exempt entity appeared and disappeared swiftly enough to evade the federal reporting requirements that might have revealed the true sources of its revenue.[37] It cloaked its partisan interests in the language and mantle of voting rights, and with the help of a few congressional Republican allies, exercised an outsized influence by invoking the specter of voter fraud. Even though the organization may have disappeared, its report leaves fingerprints. I take up an analysis of the scene of the crime in chapter six, where we examine more specific examples of fraud politics.

To summarize the argument so far, spurious voter fraud allegations by media figures such as John Fund and "nonprofit" front groups for political parties such as the ACVR confuse the public debate about fraud. It is not uncommon for politicians and partisans to hurl accusations of "fraud!" at one another when elections are close. The accusations make great copy for journalists who sometimes purposefully, but also unwittingly, contribute to the confusion when they fail to address the allegations with any skepticism. They simply repeat and sometimes sensationalize the accusations, most of which turn out to be false (as documented here), instead of investigating and clarifying the issues for their readers.

But we cannot lay this problem solely at the feet of the press. Election administration is intricate and arcane, and *voter fraud* has multiple meanings. Considered abstractly, the term is tied to competing notions of the proper exercise of the suffrage and the meaning of the right to vote. Fraud could be anything that corrodes the operation of elections. In a democracy, the popular will should shape the allocation of political power through the mechanisms of elections. "Such elections are instruments of democracy to the degree that they give the people influence over policy making."[38] Distortion by fraud, therefore, is intolerable. But if we think of election or voter fraud as corrosive of the suffrage, it can take many forms, depending on our theory of the suffrage and the meaning of the *right to vote.* I take up these disputed meanings in later chapters. For now, let us make the question of voter fraud more precise by distinguishing voter fraud from the other manifold ways in which electoral democracy can be distorted. I am searching for a definition that dispels the clouds of political scandal and permits empirical investigation. To do that I turn to legal concepts and the social science literature on elections.

In the first attempt to bring together the "scattered adjudications relating to the law of elections" in the United States, George W. McCrary's *A Treatise on the American Law of Elections,* penned in 1875 and revised in later years, presents an early treatment of fraud as an election crime.[39] McCrary states that *election fraud* is

> *any* act on the part of such an [election] officer, by which a legal voter has been designedly and wrongfully deprived of his vote; or by which an illegal vote has been purposely and unjustly received; or by which a false estimate has been imposed upon the public as a genuine canvass, is fraudulent. Fraud, however, cannot be predicated of a mere emotion of the mind disconnected from an act occasioning an injury to some one. There must be a fraudulent transaction, and a party injured thereby.[40]

McCrary reviews cases involving the application of various state election laws in the prosecution of fraud and concludes that, as a general rule, ignorance of the law does not dismiss culpability but that ignorance of the facts does. Moreover, the fraud must be evident either in the ballots or in other discrepancies in the election records. As an example, McCrary cites the case of *Littlefield v. Green,*[41] in which evidence was presented in an election contest that some 2,820 ballots were cast and counted in a jurisdiction of approximately 450 legal voters. Most of the names of voters in the poll book were recorded in alphabetical order. The court rejected the entire return because it had no way of separating the legal from the illegal ballots.[42] But discrepancies alone are not evidence of fraud. Elections are presumed to be faithfully and honestly administered, so fraud must be *shown.* In *Judkins v. Hill,*[43] a New Hampshire court made no inference of fraud from the single fact that there were twenty-seven more votes than voters counted in an election. Nevertheless, fraud can be deduced from the right kind of circumstantial evidence. In yet another case cited by McCrary, *Covode v. Foster:*[44]

> a return was rejected, upon proof that a hat and a cigar box were used, instead of the regular ballot boxes; that they were placed in or near the window, through which the votes were received; that persons other than members of the board were permitted in the room where the votes were received, and were near the boxes, and were passing in and out at pleasure during the day; that

there was great noise and confusion in the room; that whisky was kept in the room, and members of the board drank to intoxication; that challenges were disregarded; and when the votes were counted, there were six ballots in the box over and above the number of names on the tally list. These facts . . . were regarded . . . as furnishing good ground for rejecting the return. But misconduct which does not amount to fraud, and by which no one is injured, does not vitiate the poll.[45]

McCrary's approach anticipates my own preference for a legalistic definition of *fraud* that requires the establishment of intent and evidence of injury.

In *Modern Democracies* (1921), James Bryce, a British observer of U.S. society, suggests a different approach. He proposes a broad classificatory scheme that defines *election fraud* as resulting from activities that violated the expression of reason at the ballot box: "The rational will which the citizens are expected to possess and to express by their votes may be perverted in three ways: by Fear, when the voter is intimidated; by Corrupt inducements, when he is bribed; by Fraud, when the votes are not honestly taken or honestly counted."[46] Bryce's thinking about fraud reflects what Walter James Shepard calls the "ethical theory of the suffrage" prevailing at the time, the notion that voting is a means for the development of individual human character.[47] Howard W. Allen and Kay Warren Allen, however, note the problem with using "perversion of reason" at the ballot box as an indicator of fraud.[48] Coercion to vote a certain way that stops short of a physical or economic threat and "corrupt inducements" (such as money offered to cast a ballot for a particular candidate) does not always violate a voter's rationality as expressed through his or her vote choice. The coercion can impose order on that rationality by bringing the coercer's and the voter's minds together in a harmony of mutual self-interest, as when a husband and wife discuss their differences to the point of resolving them. Because of the secrecy of the ballot, money can be given and received for a vote that would have been cast for the payer's candidate anyway, regardless of the favor the inducement was meant to purchase. Vote-buying is nevertheless widely accepted as a form of election corruption and was so when Bryce made his study of U.S. democracy.[49]

Plan for the Book

The best definition of *voter fraud* is the legal one, as a crime. It is not that "mere emotion of the mind" that sees fraud lurking behind an unusually high number of absentee ballots or a bus parked near a polling place with out-of-state license plates. As McCrary states, "there must be a fraudulent transaction." But what kind of crime is fraud? Voter fraud, because it distorts the operation of "free and fair elections" violates a core constitutional commitment, and therefore, it is a political crime, an intolerable violation of democratic norms.

Defining voter fraud as a crime, however, immediately runs into difficulties. The first problem is that, as a crime, *voter fraud* is not precisely defined in law, even though there is an abundance of law at the federal and state levels that criminalize behavior we call voter fraud.[50] In fact, there is no single accepted legal definition of *voter fraud* because we have fifty state electoral systems and fifty state criminal codes governing the administration of elections, plus a federal code that applies in national elections—there is no uniform standard.[51] This legal incoherence contributes to popular misunderstandings.

Chapter 2 takes up the definitional problems, constraining the meanings of *voter fraud* to legal concepts and the forms of corruption that can be committed by voters given their limited access to the electoral process overall. A scholarly study should begin with definitions, and a good definition of a crime should distinguish among actors, motives, and means. In common parlance *voter fraud*, and *election fraud* are used interchangeably; I distinguish them. As W. Phillips Shively notes, "if political [science] research is to be useful, a minimal requirement is that its results should mean the same thing to any two different readers."[52] Shively urges analysts to strive for indivisible concepts and unidimensional words; otherwise they run the risk of enlisting poor communication with the reader, and of encountering difficulties in measurement and theoretical understanding.[53]

In chapters 3 and 4, after a discussion of the academic literature on voter fraud, I turn to the empirical evidence drawn from my research using national and state and local sources to assess whether U.S. elections are threatened by criminal voting. These chapters show empirically that voters rarely corrupt the electoral process by knowingly, willingly, and deceitfully registering or casting illegal ballots. Chapter 5 supports this evidence with a theoretical discussion of rational motives and shows that, although it may be irrational for individual voters to attempt to cast illegal ballots, it is rational for *parties* to allege voters are doing it. Chapter 6 argues that voter fraud allegations construct a political myth about U.S. elections and use this myth to justify rules believed to favor one political party over the other. Competitive elections present the prime conditions for elevating voter fraud myths, which tap into not only the colorful history of U.S. political corruption but also darker cultural attitudes toward racial minorities and the "discordant voter," and into a less than robust commitment to the right to vote. This is the political work of the myth of voter fraud. Chapter 7 concludes with an examination of one important consequence of the myth—voter identification laws. As motivated, instrumental, political acts, unfounded fraud allegations are sometimes used in the context of a campaign to sway the outcome of a particular election. More important, however, they can be deployed to institutionalize a partisan advantage through the piling on of more and more rules to encumber the vote and keep the barriers to "our most sacred right" as high as possible. In this way, the myth of voter fraud contributes to political inequality and misshapes democracy.

Chapter 2

What Is Voter Fraud?

Before we take up an analysis of the contemporary evidence of voter fraud, the subject of the next two chapters, we must define the term. Most popular meanings boil down to cheating at elections. Voter fraud, vote fraud, and election fraud are blurred in the popular mind and the media, and all evoke the general notions of political corruption, rigged elections, and winning with deception to subvert the rules. There is, however, an important but usually neglected distinction to be made between fraud committed by voters and election fraud committed by officials. Individual voters on their own are not capable of stealing elections, whereas election, party, and campaign officials are in a position to rig or manipulate electoral outcomes by virtue of their organizational capacity and their access to the machinery of the electoral process, two resources voters do not have.

The association of fraud with corruption explains why fraud allegations can generate what one anthropologist has called a "Rashomon effect," after a famous 1950 film by Akira Kurosawa.[1] Losers in close elections see fraud, but winners see a squeaker. Journalists see a story with legs, but readers shake their heads with resignation, their confidence that politics is a dirty business reaffirmed. Conservative Republicans believe they have unveiled a left-wing criminal conspiracy to subvert democracy, but liberal Democrats see a familiar racist campaign to suppress the vote. These are contradictory views that leave us with muddled meanings. The media, election officials, and even disinterested experts mistake a confused voter who mails in a ballot and then shows up at the polls to vote again because he or she is not sure the mailed ballot got counted, with an organized conspiracy to stuff a ballot box. Both are called fraud. Popular accounts mostly ignore the difference between a temporary, part-time voter registration worker forging a signature and a party official authorizing and paying a private firm to jam the phone lines of the opposition's get-out-the-vote operation. Both are called voter, vote, or election fraud. Inconsequential mischief, such as registering a dog to vote, is equated with breaking into an election board to steal ballots. *Fraud* therefore means too many things. Important differences among possible perpetrators of fraud—whether they count the votes, prepare the ballots or cast them, their motives and the nature of the corruption—are either misunderstood or ignored. Without the distinctions between types of fraud and types of perpetrators, we misdiagnose the disease and do harm by finding costly remedies for problems that do not exist.

A Broad or Narrow Concept?

Contemporary academic definitions of *election fraud* usually lump it together with other activities that corrupt the electoral process, so that the terms *voter fraud* and *election fraud* are used interchangeably. For example, Robert Goldberg writes, "Election fraud, or vote fraud as it is commonly called, may be defined as any activity that has the effect or intent of subverting the rights of voters to cast ballots free of intimidation or improper influence and to have their votes accurately counted without dilution by illegal ballots."[2]

Following on from this definition, Goldberg identifies four forms of election fraud: vote buying, fraudulent registration (often to facilitate multiple voting by "repeaters"), fraudulent use of absentee ballots, and falsification of election counts. His definition is a wide-ranging amalgam of concepts that are analytically separate: *election fraud* and *vote fraud* are synonymous; effect and intent to subvert voting rights are given equal weight; intimidation is classified as a form of fraud, as is coercion ("improper influence"); and anything violating the right to an accurate and equally weighted vote could be considered a form of fraud. This definition is overly inclusive, even if Goldberg narrows the forms that an act of election fraud can take.

Nevertheless, some argue for expansive definitions of *election fraud*. In 2005, the U.S. Elections Assistance Commission (EAC) commissioned a baseline study to make recommendations for defining *voting fraud* and *voter intimidation*. Their final report concluded that these terms were unwieldy because they were so widely applied as to encompass "almost any bad act" associated with an election. Oddly, for purpose of future study, the EAC instead adopted *election crimes*, subsuming vote fraud and voter intimidation beneath an equally generic term. According to the EAC report:

> The phrase "voting fraud," is really a misnomer for a concept that is much broader. . . . Election crimes are intentional acts or willful failures to act, prohibited by state or federal law, that are designed to cause ineligible persons to

participate in the election process; eligible persons to be excluded from the election process; ineligible votes to be cast in an election; eligible votes not to be cast or counted; or other interference with or invalidation of election results. . . . Election crimes can be committed by voters, candidates, election officials, or any other members of the public who desire to criminally impact the result of an election. . . . The victim of an election crime can be a voter, a group of voters, an election official, a candidate, or the public in general. . . . Election crimes can occur during any stage of the election process, including but not limited to qualification of candidates; voter registration; campaigning; voting system preparation and programming; voting either early, absentee, or on election day; vote tabulation; recounts; and recalls. . . . [3]

For more than two-and-a-half pages the report goes on to list, without prioritizing, specific acts constituting election crimes. This is hardly a recipe for future studies that will shed light on the corrosion of the electoral process.

Similarly, R. Michael Alvarez, Thad Hall, and Susan Hyde, the editors of a 2008 collection of conference papers on domestic and international election fraud, endorse the search for a universal definition that can apply across space and time. They complain that a simple legalistic concept of election fraud does not provide "a complete understanding of electoral manipulation," pointing out how procedures that are legal may not translate the voters' will into electoral victories, and that legal means, like protest, may be used to disrupt election administration in ways that similarly distort outcomes. They argue that a legal approach to defining *election fraud* would miss these important ways in which elections can be manipulated.[4]

I take a different position. I think the legal framework is the best way to define *voter fraud* for purposes of studying it empirically. *Fraud* is a generic term; it lacks meaning outside specific cultural, legal, and historical contexts. If we want to find it, study it, and understand it, a broad cross-cultural, translegal, and transhistorical definition of the kind called for by scholars does not get us very far. Folding it into another generic term such as *election crime* will not mitigate the confusion. Searching for universal definitions will only return us to unworkable generalities and unusable measures. If fraud is fraud in part because it corrupts a thing (say, voting procedures or electoral outcomes), we can know what it is only by understanding what and how it corrupts. What it corrupts controls the context that gives the term meaning. This is different from saying that the thing itself, for example the rules structuring the electoral process, can be corrupt or manipulated, which is what Alvarez, Hall, and Hyde say when they advocate that such rules and their manipulation be included in the definition of *fraud*. It may well be the case that certain election rules and laws distort the democratic voice of the people, but are rules that violate normative concepts fraud or something else?

I vote for a more modest approach that anchors the definition of *fraud* to its legal meaning. Fabrice Lehoucq, too, prefers a legalistic definition of *fraud*, but introduces other political criteria for judging fraudulent behavior. He suggests we think of electoral fraud as "clandestine efforts to shape election results," noting that "an activity is fraudulent if its perpetrator wants it hidden from the public gaze."[5] In addition, "an act is fraudulent if it breaks the law."[6]

Lehoucq correctly notes that the advantage of a legal definition of *fraud* is the distinction it permits between what is morally repugnant or socially unacceptable in political activity and what is merely legally possible. Nevertheless, his wide-ranging review of empirical research on electoral fraud in the Americas, Asia, and Europe over the last century takes us no closer to the kind of taxonomy that can organize empirical phenomena like the one I have in mind. Perhaps because it is a synthetic analysis of the literature, Lehoucq's discussion of electoral fraud ranges over a variety of forms of electoral corruption, broadly defined but mostly concerned with ballot rigging by politicians, election, and party officials and with vote buying.[7]

Thus, the line between legal and illegal is relevant to empirical social science because it provides at least a measure of observation, and social science starts with observation. Other measures such as whether an electoral system is more or less democratic, or open to manipulation, or secure and transparent are fine, and I join the call for more systematic and empirically grounded research on election administration that contributes to our understanding of the laws of democracy.[8] But we do not need to fold these concerns into a definition of *election fraud*. In fact, doing so only contributes to the confusion.

We need a place to start. My argument for restricting rather than widening a definition of *election fraud* is an effort to make it useful to the social scientific enterprise and to the cause of democratic election reform that the social scientific enterprise can serve. A definition in this sense must help us observe and measure. All definitions are no doubt imperfect where there is conceptual disagreement. But that does not mean that a working definition cannot be reasonable. What makes a definition reasonable is a clear rationale for the decisions made about where to set the boundaries around a term or concept. Let us start with a basic proposition: because voter fraud in the United States is a crime in both federal and state law,[9] a legalistic definition is best because it gives us a means of measuring fraud. Whatever else voter or election fraud is—myth, legend, historical reality, or cross-national phenomenon of developing nations and mature democracies alike—it is also a crime in the United States, and the legal framework provides our best opportunity for grounding a definition of fraud in something we can observe.

Some who seek a more universal definition argue that tortious acts causing civil harms and civil rights violations should also be included under an umbrella definition. I disagree.[10] All violations of the laws of democracy are egregious, but voter fraud has a special place in the history of election reform in the United States. Allegations of voter fraud have been used to justify electoral rules, such as voter registration, that impose unequal burdens on the right to vote among different classes of eligible voters, however laudable their other administrative functions.

In fact, allegations of fraud justified some of the earliest efforts of self-proclaimed reformers to enact registration laws. In 1836, Pennsylvania ratified its first registration law, but applied it only to the city of Philadelphia. It required city assessors to compile a list of qualified voters and prohibited anyone whose name did not appear from voting. Supporters claimed the law was needed to prevent the "gross election frauds" that prevailed in the city. But at the constitutional convention the following year, the law was assailed as a partisan move aimed at cutting down the Democratic vote in Philadelphia and cutting out the poor and the laboring classes. James Madison Porter, a delegate from a prominent political family and later founder of Lafayette College, stated:

> The effect of this law is to restrain and restrict the right of suffrage. It is not to be disguised, for the fact is unquestionable, that one of the leading characteristics of distinction between the two great and leading political parties of this country, when we had parties formed on principle, was the fact that the federal party was for restraining the right of suffrage . . . while the democratic party was for giving the largest extent to the exercise of the right of suffrage. . . . This act was . . . passed to carry out the sentiments of those who do not wish the right of suffrage extended to all. . . . It was got up for political purposes, to produce political results that could not otherwise be attained.[11]

Porter was an old-fashioned federalist, a strong supporter of Henry Clay aligned with the Whig Party. He nevertheless opposed the new registration law on the principled grounds that it discriminated against the poor.[12] He went on to say, "Its effect is to give advantages to the rich and the knowing, to the prejudice of the poor laborer, who, toiling for his daily bread, has not time to run after these registering officers and their lists, and may not have information enough to study out the complicated provisions of this law; and thus it tramples under foot the rights of the poor and the humble."[13]

In the nineteenth century, the property and tax-paying requirements that impeded the right to vote established the rationale for the scattering of registration laws on the books at the time. They also provided the means (the tax rolls) for compiling names of eligible voters. But by the 1850s, these had mostly been eliminated. The modern two-party system began to take shape, and the era of mass politics began. Rapid economic change, shifts in the social structure, and the diffusion of democratic ideas shaped electoral contests and swept voters into the maelstrom of electoral politics that characterized the age. The closing decades of the nineteenth century saw the highest rates of voter turnout in U.S. history. Turnout began its long and precipitous decline, however, with the introduction of election reforms such as the secret ballot, direct primaries, and personal voter registration requirements.

Scholars continue to debate whether the decline in turnout associated with reform was intended by its proponents or simply was an unfortunate by-product (this debate is discussed in more detail in chap. 3). In the nineteenth century in the North, when Republicans dominated the state houses they frequently passed registration laws applying only to the largest cities, where the Democrats were stronger. When the Democrats regained control, they abolished the laws, only to see them return with a revival of Republican rule. Sometimes Democrats became supporters of registration because they worried about future Republican chicanery or, as was the case with Irish-dominated machines in a number of cities, because they had little interest in mobilizing the new immigrants from southern and eastern Europe flooding into the cities by the end of the century.[14] Registration requirements, promoted by partisans and adopted piecemeal in the decades after the Civil War, were a principled means by which the parties attempted to restrain a surging electorate.[15]

It took more than half a century before voter registration laws covered not just the big cities, with their teeming immigrant enclaves and transient populations, but also rural counties of landowning whites. For example, New York, which first adopted compulsory registration in 1840, but only for the city of New York, did not impose mandatory statewide registration until 1965. Similarly, Ohio resisted statewide registration until 1977.[16] The histories of these developments from the liberal reform perspective take official justifications at their face value and explain away the uneven application of onerous registration requirements with the argument that registration was (and is) simply a response to the problem of election fraud as much as it was a modernizing administrative development.

Race also matters in the history of voter registration procedures. Richard Valelly argues that African Americans are the only people in the modern history of the West who were legally enfranchised only to be legally disfranchised, all within a generation.[17] If violence and terror were the most immediate means by which blacks were prevented from voting in the late nineteenth century, voter registration rules became the official means by which black voting rights were eviscerated. J. Morgan Kousser reports that new statutory restrictions on black voting rights were passed as soon as Democrats gained even temporary control of state legislatures in the South.[18] For example, between 1875 and 1889, state legislatures in Alabama, Mississippi, Texas, and Tennessee enacted statutes empowering local governments to erect strict registration ordinances to provide, in the words of historian William Harris, "an excellent means for local Democrats to reduce Negro voters to a manageable proportion—an opportunity many seized upon immediately."[19] The poll taxes, long residency requirements, re-registration requirements, and literacy tests invented by white supremacists after the collapse of Reconstruction were designed specifically to circumvent the Fifteenth Amendment. These taxes and tests were incorporated into the procedures by which state officials and local registrars worked to eliminate the black vote in the South after 1875. African Americans who held on to the memory of what had once been won struggled to regain what was lost.[20] Ordinary people caught up in the Civil Rights Movement enacted a direct confrontation with racism in the local registrar's office where, before the great marches and speeches that came to define the movement, they went, one by one, to try to register to vote.[21]

Despite the overwhelming evidence compiled by historians that voter registration requirements were designed and used to block voting by certain groups of people, the alternative story about the evolution of voter registration requirements largely ignores the significance of racial conflict.[22] The liberal reform version of the story anchors the origins of voter registration requirements in the reputedly "massive" election fraud of the industrial era. To cut down the number of alleged "repeaters," "floaters," and votes from the grave, registration-in-advance was instituted to give officials more time to verify voters' qualifications and compile lists of legal voters. The lists became the means of securing the "purity" of the ballot, and reformers promoted their necessity as a safeguard against corruption once election judges no longer knew their neighbors.[23]

The notion that registration-in-advance is simply a good government reform that protects the integrity of the ballot, not a mechanism for shaping the electorate, is the one that prevails today. Arguments for restrictive voter registration laws continue to turn on the question of fraud. For some, the ballot is in near-constant jeopardy of being corrupted by illegal votes and fraudulent voters intent on stealing elections; registration rules should be stringent and strictly enforced. For others, voter registration rules, because they establish the gateway to the ballot, are a battleground where Americans continue to fight over the right to vote—what it is, what it should be, and who should have it. For them, the registration process should impose no undue burden on this right.

In the next section, we search for a definition of *voter fraud* in the context of federal voting rights law. This is followed by a brief overview of the treatment of voter fraud in state laws.

Legalistic Definition

Voter Fraud as a Criminal Fraud Concept

Voter and election fraud are forms of criminal fraud, but what is criminal fraud? If voter fraud is criminal fraud, it should share some family traits with other forms of criminal fraud. Ellen Podgor, an expert on white-collar crime, notes that fraud is the focus of many white-collar criminal offenses but that in U.S. law it is not a crime with clear boundaries: "In the federal system, there is no indictment or conviction for fraud. Rather, as in English law, the term 'fraud' is a 'concept' at the core of a variety of criminal statutes."[24]

The idea of deceit is fundamental to the concept of fraud in criminal law. There is no fraud without deceit. In fact, the word *fraud* derives from the Latin *fraus*, which means "deceit." *Black's Law Dictionary* defines *fraud* as "a knowing misrepresentation of the truth or concealment of a material fact to induce another to act to his or her detriment."[25] And in criminal law the deceit must be intentional and cause harm. This seems straightforward— but it is not. Podgor notes that *fraud* is not so easily defined and that meanings shift depending on the statute in which the word appears, the nature of the harm inflicted, whether the fraud is alleged to stem from conduct or state of mind, and the prosecutorial theories pursued in criminal fraud cases.

The elusive character of fraud extends to the treatment of voter fraud in U.S. law. There is no single statute outlawing something called "voter fraud" or, for that matter, "election fraud." The laws regulating crimes that violate electoral integrity when federal candidates are on the ballot are not confined to the criminal code but are sprinkled throughout the U.S. Code.

On the other hand, the Supreme Court, in numerous decisions dating back to the post-Reconstruction era, has clearly recognized the authority of Congress under the Constitution to regulate activity that exposes federal elections to harm.[26] By the 1970s, the Court had elevated electoral integrity to the status of an enforceable, constitutionally protected voting right. In a 1974 case dealing with ballot box stuffing called *Anderson v. United States*, the Court said, "Every voter in a federal . . . election, . . . whether he votes for a candidate with little chance of winning or for one with little chance of losing, has a right under the Constitution to have his vote fairly counted, without its being distorted by fraudulently cast votes."[27] Perhaps because it is the people as a whole, rather than identifiable individual voters, whose legal votes might be "diluted" or canceled out by "illegal" votes, federal criminal statutes consider voter fraud a form of public corruption, a serious crime that carries fines, lengthy prison terms, and, in the case of illegal voting by noncitizens, deportation.[28] Election fraud as a crime (rather than a tort or a civil rights violation) is usually treated as a crime against the state.

Voter Fraud as Defined by Federal Enforcement Practices

Podgor suggests a number of methodologies for narrowing the diffuse concept of criminal fraud. One of them is to trace the consequences of enforcement decisions and to use federal judicial workload statistics to break down the concept of criminal fraud by specific types of offenses.[29] We might follow a similar strategy. The modern federal role in ensuring free and fair elections is institutionally divided between enforcing laws that prohibit discrimination against minority voters protected by the Voting Rights

Act of 1965, as amended, and enforcing federal campaign finance and criminal fraud statutes. The Civil Rights Act of 1957 created the Civil Rights Division of the Justice Department and granted it authority to bring civil suits to address racial discrimination in voting. But the mild innovations in voter protections of the 1957 Act and the two civil rights laws that followed in 1960 and 1964 failed to erect a muscular defense of black voting rights, especially in the face of intransigent Southern white supremacy. The 1965 Voting Rights Act addressed these failures and "dramatically relies on administrative enforcement," shifting the locus of enforcement from the judiciary to the attorney general.[30] Voting rights, of course, are obstructed when deceit, trickery, and intimidation are used to prevent eligible citizens from registering and voting, but as a matter of practice, most criminal election statutes, including some enacted as part of the Civil Rights Acts, the Voting Rights Act, and the National Voter Registration Act of 1993, are enforced by lawyers in the Justice Department Criminal Division.[31] We turn to the enforcement policies of that division for further guidance on defining the conceptual boundaries of voter fraud.

Let us take as our guide the election crimes training manual for U.S. attorneys prepared by the Justice Department Public Integrity Section. This manual can be read as a policy statement. It defines *election fraud* as involving "a substantive irregularity relating to the voting act—such as bribery, intimidation, or forgery—which has the potential to taint the election itself."[32] Federal election law is an amalgamation of statutes, some of which expressly apply to elections and voting and others, such as those prohibiting mail fraud, that have been used to prevent and punish voter fraud.[33] Most federal statutes apply only to federal or mixed federal-state and local elections. For election crime to rise to the level of federal prosecution, there must be a "specific federal interest," such as the registration of voters for federal elections; the protection of voting rights of racial, ethnic, and language minorities; or the protection of the federal election process against corruption.[34] Only a handful of federal statutes apply to purely state or local elections.[35]

Federal election law as it pertains to fraud can be divided into two categories: anti-intimidation and antitrafficking laws. Anti-intimidation laws have their origins in the Enforcement Acts passed by the post–Reconstruction era Congress. These laws significantly expanded the federal role in policing the electoral process in the states, but were largely repealed in the 1890s after the Democrats briefly returned to national power.[36] What remained is codified today as Section 241 (the Conspiracy Against Rights Act) and Section 242 (the Deprivation of Rights under Color of Law Act) of Title 18 of the U.S. Code (1988). Section 241 makes it a felony to conspire to "injure, oppress, threaten, or intimidate any inhabitant of any State, Territory, or District in the free exercise or enjoyment of any right or privilege secured to him by the Constitution or laws of the United States or because of his having exercised the same." Section 242 provides for criminal punishment of anyone who deprives another of federally secured rights in acting "under color of law" in a nonconspiratorial setting.

Federal prosecutors have used Section 241 to litigate election crime in federal elections for over a century. Such prosecutions depend on the finding of a "definite and certain" federal right.[37] The Supreme Court has found a constitutionally guaranteed right to vote, and Congress has passed legislation to protect this most fundamental of all rights. There is debate, however, about whether the Constitution guarantees a right to vote in purely state and local contests—here the judicial record is inconsistent. Federal prosecutors, therefore, avoid investigating fraud allegedly committed in these elections.

Anti-intimidation laws protect a citizen's right to vote. They outlaw the use of superior physical, economic, or political force either to prevent a voter from voting or to compel a voter to cast his or her ballot for a candidate he or she does not prefer. Antitrafficking laws, on the other hand, restrict a citizen's right to vote by prohibiting the offering, making, soliciting, or receiving of payments in return for voting or withholding a vote. For example, Section 1973i(c) of Title 42 of the U.S. Code makes it unlawful in a federal election to pay, offer to pay, or accept payment for registering to vote or for voting, or to conspire with another person to vote illegally. Penalties include a fine of up to $10,000 and five years in jail. The Justice Department, as a matter of practice, does not prosecute voters whose only involvement in voter fraud is in compromising their votes, nor does it prosecute isolated instances of vote buying because "isolated incidents do not implicate federal interests sufficiently" to warrant federal interference in what is traditionally a state function. It appears that the majority of vote-buying schemes prosecuted involve small amounts of money and occur in low-income neighborhoods.[38]

Other federal statutes make it unlawful to station "armed men" at the polls, coerce voting among military personnel or political activity from federal employees, vote more than once, or vote "illegally" by knowingly participating in a conspiracy to cast a vote despite ineligibility. The National Voter Registration Act of 1993 included a new criminal statute aimed at extending the reach of federal prosecutors by reinforcing laws against voter intimidation and safeguarding against fraudulent registration and voting. Earlier laws against false information were limited to false information involving only name, address, or period of residence. The new statute, subsection 1973gg-10(2)(A), applies to any false information that is material to state registration requirements. For example, although the Constitution does not require that qualified electors be citizens, all states do, so falsifying citizenship on a voter registration application is now a federal felony.

Voter Fraud in State Law

Within the constitutional framework for regulating the electoral process, the states vary widely in how they administer elections. For example, they differ in who they disenfranchise among those lacking constitutional protections (i.e., noncitizens, misdemeants, felons, and ex-felons); in the number of days an individual must be registered prior to an election in order to be allowed to vote in that election; in the way in which voters cast ballots, diverging on matters related to absentee and mail-in balloting; in how long the polls are kept open; in the manner in which votes are validated; and in who counts the ballots, who challenges ballots, who contests elections, and who decides the outcome of such disputes.

Such idiosyncrasies extend to state laws governing election crime. (See appendix 2, which presents summaries of state statutes and case law governing voter fraud for ten diverse states from all regions of the country. It gives a sense of how the states vary in their treatment of election fraud— beyond criminalizing the basic acts of voter fraud, and including illegal voting, multiple voting, and vote buying.) Because of the historically parochial manner in which states administer elections, the way they handle the problem of criminal voter fraud also varies. All states have prohibitions against falsifying voter registration information, voting more than once in an election, impersonating another voter, intimidating or coercing voters, and bribing voters or buying votes. Most of these crimes are classified as felonies and carry fines and prison sentences. In some states, a person convicted of voter fraud can permanently lose the right to vote. State election laws allocate the responsibility for ensuring free and fair elections to various agencies and officers, giving them responsibility for administering and monitoring the electoral process and ensuring that it is free of corruption. Although it is incumbent on state officials to bring criminal charges where appropriate, all states also empower private citizens to bring civil suits to contest election results, making the burden of rooting out fraud not entirely a state function.[39] Likewise, the NVRA (Sec. 11(b)) provides a private right of action to any person aggrieved by a violation of the act.

Voter Fraud and the Electoral Process

Criminal law frames our definition of *voter fraud*. But is this enough? Any workable definition of *voter fraud* should also respect the ordinary meaning of the terms *voter* and *fraud*. We strive, as Shively would have it, for unidimensional words and unambiguous meanings. For social science, a good definition of voter fraud should be broad enough to capture the sense of fraud as an act of deceit and willful corruption, and narrow enough to help us distinguish the different forms of corruption that might plague the electoral process. We need a way of sorting out differences between the malcontent who registers his dog to vote and rogue election officials who conspire to stuff the ballot box. Which kinds of problems are more likely to occur, and which are more serious to securing the vote?

There are several good reasons why the term *voter fraud* should apply only to the behavior of *voters*. The most important one comes from historical experience: as already noted—election reforms adopted in response to generalized threats of voter fraud and taking the form of electoral rules have disproportionately burdened the right to vote for various racial, ethnic, and socioeconomic groups of eligible voters. Guarding elections from fraud means erecting procedures to ensure that for any one election only qualified voters vote and vote only once. Rules are needed to ensure a qualified voter's vote counts equally among the ballots cast by other qualified voters and is not diluted by fraudulently cast ballots. In a big, complex, modern and highly mobile society such as our own, the procedures for preventing fraudulent votes will encumber the process of voting because we do not know one another. The identity of voters cannot be stored in the heads of election workers. So we need other means of keeping track of voters and their votes. The procedures we put in place to track identity and votes should be carefully tailored to maximize security and minimize the burdens on those for whom the costs of voting are highest (see the next section). To evaluate the rules using these criteria, we need to understand how voters could corrupt the process so that we can judge the appropriateness of fraud-prevention procedures that restrict access. We need to distinguish, therefore, between general forms of electoral corruption and the forms of corruption available to voters (actual *voter fraud*).

If we want to understand how voters might corrupt the voting process by committing fraud, we need to first identify which parts of the voting process are corruptible by voters. For voters, casting a ballot is basically a two-stage process. First voters register, and then they vote. The diagram in figure 2.1 outlines the voting process.

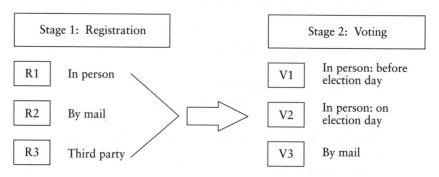

Figure 2.1   Stages in the voting process.

Registration

Voters register to vote in three basic ways: in person before the local registrar or some other authorized state agency such as a Department of Motor Vehicles (R1), by mail (R2), or through the activities of third-party groups conducting voter registration drives (R3). The NVRA expanded the opportunities to register by requiring states to ask people if they wanted to register to vote when they obtained or renewed a driver's license or interacted with other designated state agencies and by mandating that states accept a national voter registration form or equivalent state form by mail. Third-party groups obtain voter registration forms from local registrars and distribute them through registration drives. More often than not, groups assist voters in filling out the forms, collecting and returning them to local authorities for processing.

To commit voter registration fraud, individuals must lie about their identity or intentionally provide other false information on their registration form. If they are registering in person at a local board, they must commit forgery or perjury by standing before the authorities and lying about who they are; where they live; or whether they are a U.S. citizen, a felon, a parolee, or a probationer. If they are registering by mail or through a third-party voter registration drive, they must submit false information on the registration form. In all cases, intentionally providing false information on a voter registration application is a crime; if that information is transmitted through the mail, it is a federal offense. In all states, voter registration is regulated by law to prevent the registration of ineligible or fictitious people. Under federal law, local elections officials may design nondiscriminatory and reasonable list-maintenance programs to verify address information. In most cases, these programs involve sending all registered voters a letter or informational document about an upcoming election. If the mailings come back as "undeliverable," voters may be moved to "inactive" lists and registrars may require further identification if the voters in question turn up at the polls on election day. As chapter 3 shows, there are episodic problems with voter registration fraud in the United States today, but in the infrequent instances when it has resulted in fictitious or ineligible people being registered to vote, there is almost no evidence that such people actually cast ballots.

Critics of the NVRA and others who believe that it is easy to register fictitious people sometimes forget that local registrars, the state agencies that supervise them, and state and local law enforcement agencies responsible for enforcing state election laws all have a responsibility for ensuring that voter registration lists are accurate. The media have focused on a handful of absurd cases of voter registration fraud, such as forms submitted in the name of "Mary Poppins," in the names of people's pets or children, or with an address belonging to a vacant lot or an airport hangar. Personal registration systems, such as those in place in nearly every state, put the burden of registering on the voter. That means that people who want to exercise their right to vote must first take the initiative to register to vote. In other advanced postindustrial democracies, the government assumes the responsibility of ensuring that eligible citizens are registered to vote. In the United States, private groups can and do get involved in campaigns to register citizens to vote, acting as intermediaries between voters and the state bureaucracies responsible for maintaining the lists. When such groups register people who are already registered to vote, when they fail to ensure that the forms they collect in their drives are filled out completely or accurately, or when they file forms in the wrong jurisdiction, they may add to the burden of local registrars to compile and verify accurate lists of eligible voters. The inefficiency is the price we pay for a personal registration system. Because voters must come into contact with the registration system, registration records and the registration process can be corrupted by voters.

Voting

The second stage of the voting process is to obtain, mark, and cast a legal ballot. There are fewer ways to vote than there are to register. Voters cast ballots in person (V1 and V2) or through the mail (V3). Private, third-party groups are mostly barred from intervening directly between the voter and the casting of ballots or from handling ballots the way they are permitted to handle registration forms. Most in-person voting still occurs on one day in an election cycle (V2), but the trend is to extend the time people can cast ballots by opening up "early voting" periods before election day (V1). How might a voter corrupt the process of obtaining, marking, and casting ballots?

Eligible Voter versus Qualified Voter

Before turning to the basic methods that voters use to cast ballots, we need to further define our terms in the context of our generally legalistic concept of voter fraud and to consider the difference between an eligible and a qualified voter. To be a legal voter, an eligible voter must be qualified by the state to vote. The centuries-long struggle for the franchise in the United States established a common law right to vote and constitutional bans on voter discrimination by race, color, gender, or age (over the age of eighteen). The lack of an affirmative right to vote in the Constitution and the delegation of authority to the states to determine voter qualifications and oversee election administration are peculiar features unique to U.S. democracy among democracies of the world. The Constitution explicitly grants the states the power to set voter qualifications, reserving authority to Congress to regulate only "the times, places and manner of holding elections for Senators and Representatives."[40]

Eligible voters are those whose age and citizenship status, and in some cases absence of a felony conviction, allow them to be credentialed, or qualified, by the states as legitimate or legal voters. *Qualified voters*, therefore, are those eligible voters who complete a state's procedures for casting a legal ballot.[41]

Because the Constitution vests power to qualify voters in the states, as long as they do not unconstitutionally discriminate against people by race, color, gender, or age, the states may make different rules for qualifying voters, and they do. This is why the definition of a *legal vote* varies across the states, especially with regard to residency and felony disqualification rules. Consider, for example, the ballot of an otherwise eligible and qualified voter with a felony conviction who is no longer under state supervision. If that citizen lives in Maine and registers to vote by or on election day, his or her vote counts as a legal ballot. But if that citizen lives in Florida (where a felony conviction eliminates the right to vote until clemency is granted) and votes, he or she can be prosecuted for casting an illegal ballot. A formal, robust, and constitutional right to vote would not permit state residency to determine whether the vote of an eligible citizen was legal or illegal.

In fact, states make a lot of rules for qualifying voters. The most important is the requirement that all eligible voters register. All states except North Dakota require eligible voters to register before casting a ballot.[42] Thus, all states except North Dakota qualify eligible voters by requiring them to meet certain conditions in order to register their names on the rolls of legitimate or valid voters. Voter registration, therefore, is a means of voter qualification, and in nearly all states, otherwise eligible voters must be registered properly or the vote they cast is illegal.[43] In addition, ineligible voters, such as those disqualified by state law because of a felony conviction or because they do not possess U.S. citizenship,[44] could register to vote either mistakenly or by deceit, thus appearing on the voter rolls as qualified voters despite their ineligibility. Their votes would be treated as legal votes when, in fact, they would be illegal.

There are a few known cases in recent years of ineligible individuals such as noncitizens making it on to the voter registration rolls due to a misunderstanding about who has the right to vote in U.S. elections or to mistakes made by elections officials who misinformed such applicants or failed to note their lack of citizenship. One is the case of Usman Ali Chaudhary. In 1988, Chaudhary left his native Pakistan to attend the University of South Alabama in Mobile. A few years later, he applied for a change in his student visa to a nonimmigrant status, but it is not clear whether Chaudhary ever succeeded in adjusting his status.[45] He moved to Florida and opened a jewelry store in Tallahassee. In 1996, he obtained a driver's license. Over the years, he successfully applied for a Florida identification card, and then in 2002 a driver's license and a business loan. Along the way he married and had a daughter; both his wife and daughter were U.S. citizens.

The original six-count indictment against Chaudhary, dated November 9, 2004, charged him with falsely representing himself as a citizen of the United States to obtain a Florida driver's license and the business loan. It did not charge him with any voting-related violations. Perhaps the intensified scrutiny of immigrants after 9/11 and enhanced voter registration and voting database matching capabilities led the government to file a superseding indictment in January 2005. This time, Chaudhary was charged with "knowingly and willfully falsely represent[ing] himself to be a citizen of the United States, when in fact the defendant was not a citizen of the United States . . ." when on or about April 3, 2002, "he registered to vote and completed a voter application form."[46]

Charged with a violation of Title 18, Section 911, with making a "false claim of citizenship," Chaudhary was now faced with a felony crime, a deportable offense. Before the case went to trial, the government dropped five of the seven charges. Chaudhary told the *New York Times* that when he went to renew his driver's license, the clerk behind the window turned out to be a customer of his at the jewelry store. She assumed he was a citizen, and because the NVRA requires motor vehicle agencies offer customers the option of registering to vote, the clerk encouraged Chaudhary to fill out a registration form. He was too embarrassed to admit he was not a citizen and complied. This is how Usman Ali Chaudhary became a registered voter in the state of Florida. The incriminating evidence was his voter registration form, which, because it asks applicants to indicate whether they are U.S. citizens, can be used in a court of law to establish an intent to deceive. Chaudhary was convicted of impersonating a citizen and, despite the fact that he never voted, was deported to Pakistan. "We're foreigners here," he told a reporter who tracked him down living in Lahore, and his daughter, who speaks only English, cries everyday.[47]

Voters have limited access to the electoral process, but when they do interact with it, they confront an array of different rules depending on where they live. The more rules and restrictions, the more stumbling blocks voters face when trying to cast legal ballots. For example, in Pennsylvania, where voters must qualify with an excuse when applying for an absentee ballot, it is illegal to vote that ballot if their plans change and they remain physically present at their residence (barring a disability that prohibits voters from visiting the polling place).[48] Voters must apply for an absentee ballot a full week before election day.[49] What happens if their plans change or the business trip gets canceled and the voters are present on election day after all? If a voter then mails in the ballot instead of standing in line at the polling place, that voter is breaking the law in Pennsylvania. But can we not imagine that a voter not intending to break the law would make things easier for themselves by dropping the ballot in the mailbox? The more complex the rules regulating voter registration and voting, the more likely voters and election clerks will make mistakes,[50] and mistakes—or what I generically refer to as irregularities—are the manna of voter fraud allegations.

TABLE 2.1
Voter eligibility, voter registration, and legal balloting

Voter	Registered	Voter is	Vote is cast	Ballot
Eligible	Yes	Qualified	Properly	Legal
			Improperly	Illegal
	No	Not qualified	Properly or improperly	Illegal
Not eligible	Yes	Improperly qualified	Properly	Illegal
			Improperly	Illegal
	No	Not qualified	Properly or improperly	Illegal

Eligible voters may nevertheless fail to qualify as legal voters because they fail to register properly. Usually, their ballots will be considered illegal. Illegal ballots, however, may also result from qualified—or properly registered—voters failing to follow the rules for casting a ballot under state law. As table 2.1 suggests, the multiplying rules create more ways to cast an illegal ballot than a legal one. Table 2.1 also summarizes the concepts and relationship between eligible and qualified voters.

Let us consider how voters might commit fraud in the voting process.

By Mail

There have been a number of cases of absentee ballot fraud in recent years. Absentee ballots have been issued to people who are ineligible to vote and to intermediaries who have tampered with the ballots. Compared to voting in person, official scrutiny of the marking and casting of ballots is relaxed. On the one hand, voting by mail and absentee balloting take place over an extended time period, which means local elections officials have more time to verify the qualifications of the applicants for ballots both before and after election day. On the other hand, more of the voting process occurs without the direct observation of election officials, which some believe encourages fraud. To commit fraud when voting by mail, a voter must commit perjury and or forgery, and because the U.S. Postal Service is usually involved, absentee ballot fraud can result in the commission of a federal felony. To obtain ballots for dead people whose names may still appear on the list of registered voters, a person would need to know the names and addresses of such people, how to forge these people's signatures, and that the registrar is unaware that the dead people are on the list.

In Person

Voting in person involves showing up before local election authorities, obtaining a ballot, and marking and casting it. More and more, states are authorizing "early voting" periods of a week or even a month, when voters may complete this process before election day, but the process is exactly the same as occurs on election day itself. For voters to commit fraud when voting in person, they must commit perjury or forgery to hide their identity if they are ineligible to vote (i.e., if they are underage, not U.S. citizens, do not live in the jurisdiction, or are under some form of state supervision) or to impersonate a legitimate voter if they are trying to cast more than one ballot or vote in a legitimate voter's name. The same is true if they have committed voter registration fraud and seek to vote in the name of a person who shows up on a list of registered voters but who, in reality, does not exist. Stories about voter fraud in the 2004 election describe voters double-voting by casting an absentee ballot and then showing up on election day to cast a second ballot. It is difficult to understand why a person would walk into a polling site to commit a crime under the watchful eyes of precinct workers. This is akin to a mugger walking into a police station, grabbing the handbag of a woman in line to talk to a desk officer, and signing the visitors' logbook with their real name before fleeing. It is more likely that these cases of so-called double-voting fraud are not cases of fraud but of people trying to make sure that their ballots were received and that their votes will be counted. Given what we now know about the mismanagement of the vote count, and the large numbers of ballots that go uncounted in national elections for one reason or another, their skepticism about government efficiency is not unwarranted.

We need a basic definition of *voter fraud* that cuts through the confusion without violating the way voter fraud is diversely treated in state and federal law. I want to keep it simple and straightforward to start. Voter fraud is a category of election fraud, which is a form of criminal fraud. Therefore, *voter fraud* is the intentional, deceitful corruption of the electoral process by voters. Intent to commit fraud is essential; it distinguishes fraud from error. This definition covers both knowingly and willingly giving false information to establish voter eligibility and knowingly and willingly voting illegally or participating in a conspiracy to encourage illegal voting by others.[51] Apparent acts of fraud that result from voter mistakes or isolated individual wrongdoing or mischief making not aimed at corrupting the voting process should not be considered fraud, although sometimes these acts are prosecuted as such.[52] All other forms of corruption of the electoral process and corruption committed by elected or election officials, candidates, party organizations, advocacy groups, or campaign workers fall under the wider definition of *election fraud*. With our concept of voter fraud in hand (the intentional corruption of the electoral process by voters), I turn now to the evidence we have to answer the question, are contemporary U.S. elections vulnerable to voter fraud?

Chapter 3

Are U.S. Elections Vulnerable to Voter Fraud?

In the aftermath of the contested 2000 presidential election, the theme of electoral corruption returned to U.S. politics. Once again, the colorful lore of voter fraud was featured in the press, invoking the mythic exploits of unscrupulous characters from the past, figures such as William Marcy "Boss" Tweed and the Tammany Ring thugs called the "Short Boys," who had stuffed ballot boxes, threatened election workers, and intimidated voters.[1] Allegations of illegal aliens swarming over the Mexican border to cast ballots or busloads of college students infiltrating sleepy New Hampshire hamlets from Massachusetts to fraudulently vote recalled the notorious nineteenth-century exploits of "repeaters" and "floaters," who voted multiple times, and of "colonizers," whom the party bosses moved around from place to place to inflate the vote. Could it be that the infamous electoral corruption of the past had never been vanquished?[2]

In fact, present-day allegations pale in comparison to those storied days; but if we call on the ghosts of Election Day Past to interpret contemporary facts, those facts seem much worse. Raise a question about why the poll book count does not match the machine count and then cast your mind back to the days of Huey Long, the Louisiana "Kingfish," and his 160 percent turnout rates in New Orleans.[3] Or what about the infamous Precinct 13 from rural Alice, Texas, where 202 out of 203 voters politely lined up in alphabetical order to sign the poll book and vote for the young Lyndon Johnson in 1948; those voters in Alice helped put Johnson over the top and launched his Senate career.[4] And everyone has heard of the exploits of Richard J. Daley, the legendary Chicago Democratic party boss, and his alleged vote stealing in Chicago in 1960 for John F. Kennedy.[5] Past episodes of election fraud fuel popular suspicion that U.S. elections are hopelessly corrupt.

Some scholars agree. Tracy Campbell, a historian, calls endemic election fraud the product of a culture of corruption that has infected U.S. politics from the beginning: "What makes this culture so enduring is that the participants did not perceive their deeds to be assaults on the democratic process. Rather, they internalized a powerful rationale that considered cheating part of a game that one has to practice in order to counteract one's equally corrupt competitors."[6] Larry Sabato and Glenn Simpson argue that U.S. politics is much cleaner today than it was in the days when politicians accepted bags of cash behind closed doors and voters were intimidated, beaten, and, in the South, sometimes killed as they tried to vote. But they, too, insist that a culture of corruption persists, periodically uprooted by reform efforts, only to reassert itself: "The result is that wave upon wave of corruption washes over American democracy, despite all attempts to erect a seawall sufficiently strong to prevent it. Corruption is truly a staple of our Republic's existence, and its durable, undeniable persistence in the face of repeated, energetic attempts to eradicate it is darkly wondrous."[7]

In academia, however, these views are more often the exception. The scholarly study of U.S. elections and voter turnout assumes the official tallies are an accurate picture of what Walter Dean Burnham calls "the American voting universe."[8] The vast field of U.S. electoral behavior is built on an almost religious faith that the count is free not only of fraud but also of (nonfraudulent) irregularities large enough to put the results in question.[9] There is little academic research on the scale of fraud or the extent of irregularities in the count either today or in the past. As a consequence, the use of official numbers by professional political scientists presumes that the votes cast are those counted, that the count is accurate and reflects the will of the voters, that each vote cast is legitimate and of equal weight, that the voting process is free of bias, and that all who want to vote are able to do so. Yet if we have learned anything since the 2000 election, it is that these assumptions now stand challenged.

That said, the dearth of literature on election fraud and election administration means the question of fraud will remain open for some time to come. What work has been done provides little guidance for how we should evaluate it today. There are at least three lines of research in the academic literature that contribute something to our understanding of election fraud. One flows from the investigations of political historians into election fraud perpetrated on black voters during the Redemption period that followed the passage of the Fifteenth Amendment, when Southern Democrats used both terror and newly devised legal stratagems to strip blacks of the vote. This was a kind of organized fraud perpetrated not *by* voters, per se, but *on* voters by elites, officials, and mobs. In its organization and magnitude it stands in stark contrast to what is even alleged today. The story is well known, and there is a rich literature on this subject, much of it stimulated by the work of C. Vann Woodward and following the pioneering work of his student, J. Morgan Kousser.[10] A proper review of the contributions of historians of Southern politics to political science, however, is beyond the scope of this study.

In political science, we can draw on an early literature critical of the urban political machine and the immigrant working classes produced by scholars working in the emergent field of public administration in the 1920s. And third, something can be learned about election fraud from a later debate between Walter Dean Burnham and other scholars led by Philip Converse. This debate stretched over a twenty-year period and addressed competing theories of electoral behavior, electoral rules and institutions, and party development during the Gilded Age. I discuss the relevant strands of research in the political science literature in what follows.

Political Science and the Question of Voter Fraud

When I began my inquiry into the question of election fraud in 2001, there had been no new empirical research published on the subject for almost two decades.[11] Moreover, notwithstanding the prominent exception of Frances Fox Piven and Richard A. Cloward's book, *Why Americans Still Don't Vote and Why Politicians Want It That Way*, the question of fraud today is usually considered only in passing in the literature on electoral rules and turnout. In the debates among policymakers and advocates of one reform or another restrictions and rules governing access to the vote are often robotically defended as necessary measures to prevent fraud. The same assumptions about rampant fraud that underline arguments against the relaxation of the rules governing access to the vote today are present in the scholarly debate over what caused the decline in turnout at the end of the nineteenth century. In that case some scholars believe fraud inflated late nineteenth-century returns by as much as 40 percent. Others continue to argue that these historical claims are simply unsupported by the available evidence or misleading in the absence of a deeper understanding of the rhetoric of nineteenth-century politics. They contend that the intent behind a rhetoric of fraud was to justify rules that disenfranchise or dissuade and discourage participation by minority, immigrant, or lower-class groups in the electorate.

In fact, both the rhetoric and the research about contemporary voter fraud in political science have failed to go much beyond the earliest empirical studies that addressed it.[12] These studies are remarkable for what they reveal about how problems with election administration and the partisan debates about the rules today are frozen in time.

Voter Registration Rules versus Fraud

In two volumes written for the Brookings Institution in the late 1920s and early 1930s, Joseph P. Harris, a young public administration reformer, explored in scrupulous detail the history and workings of voter registration systems and the state of election administration in the United States. The purpose of his research was to systematically document how badly elections were run and to improve election administration by drawing on the best practices to create an ideal system. Phillip Converse, a political scientist, has called Harris a "godson" of the earlier Progressive movement because of his firm belief in rational, scientific solutions to political problems.[13] Harris's work on voter registration evolved from a doctoral dissertation written under the supervision of Charles Merriam at the University of Chicago to a 390-page survey of "the practical workings of existing registration laws," from which Harris would "deduce . . . the principles of sound administration."[14] The problem of election "frauds" featured prominently in this work, as it did in his later examination of election administration. In fact, Harris believed, although he never convincingly demonstrated, that fraud had been widespread. He also clearly identified corrupt politicians and partisan election officials, people with power and authority over the electoral process, not average voters fingered by today's partisans, as the prime source of the problem. We learn from Harris' work that this is an important distinction. Harris was quite confident that the culprits, the corrupt political and election officials and the machine party bosses, could be toppled by the science of government. Thus, he argued strenuously for administrative modernization in the form of procedural and code reform, professionalization, the implementation of better auditing and accounting systems, and the removal of the machinery of electoral operations from the hands of party workers. Harris remained true to his administrative-reform roots and his conviction that political machines were the source of election fraud when in the 1950s he invented the Votomatic Vote Recorder, or punch-card voting machine, which he hoped would reduce the risk of fraud by removing ballot counting from the hands of precinct workers.[15]

But it was the fraud-palliative function of voter registration that captured Harris's early attention. "Voter registration," he wrote, is "one of the most important safeguards of the purity of the ballot box."[16] For him, the origins and purpose of voter registration were to reduce fraud, and none too soon. Corrupt practices in elections, Harris claimed, "have prevailed throughout the greater part of our political life as a nation." Conjuring the ghosts of elections past, and sounding much like the *Wall Street Journal* today, he told lurid tales of chicanery and "voter colonization" infecting the electoral process:

> Hoodlums were rounded up and lodged for a night or so in various lodging houses and cheap hotels and then registered from all of them. On the day of

the election, gangs of "repeaters" were hauled from precinct to precinct and voted under different names. Sometimes the same persons would vote several times at each precinct, changing coats or hats between times. The early registration list were often padded with bogus names or the names of persons who had died or moved away, and these names were voted by "repeaters" on the day of election or were checked off and voted by the corrupt precinct election officers without the necessity of providing "repeaters." Before the enactment of the personal registration law for Philadelphia in 1906 it was a common saying that all of the signers of the Declaration of Independence were still regularly voted in that city.[17]

When he published his landmark study in 1929, a number of states had not yet adopted permanent personal registration systems, although some form of voter registration existed in every state except Arkansas, Indiana, and Texas. Unlike the rules in place in other industrial democracies, personal registration systems put the onus on the citizen to register rather than on the state to enroll voters, despite early experience with such state-initiated voter registration systems in the United States. In 1800, Massachusetts passed the first registration law in the nation. Property qualifications to vote were common then, and the Massachusetts law drew on the precedents of the colonial era, which limited the suffrage to owners of real estate valued at 20 pounds or more. A 1742 law had required the assessors of each town to provide the town clerk with a copy of their land assessments for use in connection with elections. The 1800 law required town assessors to draw up "correct and alphabetical" lists of qualified electors annually, submit them to selectmen, and post them for review prior to an election. The lists were not final; they could be revised up until the morning of election day when the selectmen or assessors met to hear applications for registration. Thus, the first voter registration law in the United States required the government to enroll qualified voters and allowed voters to register on election day.[18]

There was little extension of registration beyond several of the New England states until after the Civil War. At that time, U.S. election law charted a new direction toward a path begun by New York in 1866. The New York law transferred the burden of registering voters from election officials to the voters themselves, who were required to appear in person before a registry board prior to *each* election to prove that they were qualified to vote. As property qualifications fell away, and as black men won the vote, new forms of discriminatory rules governing access to the ballot emerged, many of them operating through the mechanism of registration. Permanent personal registration systems were an improvement over those requiring voters to re-register before every election. During the 1920s, a movement for permanent registration was active in promoting the idea in more than a dozen states. Delaware, Idaho, Indiana, and Kentucky adopted laws in their 1923 and 1925 legislative sessions; New Jersey enacted such a law for cities of over

15,000 population in 1926; the following year, Ohio, Wisconsin, Iowa, and Washington adopted permanent registration laws; and campaigns were active in Pennsylvania, Missouri, California, and New York.[19]

Harris hoped to influence the reform debates of his day. He argued that the removal of property qualifications for voting, the granting of universal manhood suffrage, and the influx of immigrants "have given votes to a large number of persons without political experience, education, or ideals."[20] This burden and corrupt party control over electoral rules and the mechanics of running elections contributed to the creation of electoral bureaucracies that were more badly managed than those in just about any other area of public administration. "Our elections," he lamented, "have been marked by irregularities, slipshod work, antiquated procedure, obsolete records, inaccuracies, and many varieties of downright fraud."[21]

Generations later, the administrative explanations of the 1920s for why elections were so badly mismanaged continue to resonate. From this perspective, the main problems stem from inept partisan control of electoral administration ("Too often the election office is the dumping ground for incompetents who could not be placed elsewhere," Harris wrote[22]); a lack of effective state supervision of local election offices (Harris noted that "In many states the precinct officers are practically a law unto themselves"[23]); and a lack of policy research on the problem of fraud.

The Complexities of Election Laws

Harris also bemoaned the proliferation of needlessly complex electoral laws. "The election statutes are so detailed that the precinct officers cannot know the law," he observed. "The election laws are being constantly changed, but without any fundamental revision or improvement." The result was an accumulating mess, a "patchwork upon patchwork" of conflicting and uncertain rules that bulked out election codes to hundreds of pages. Yet, Harris argued, electoral bureaucracies were still primitive, hardly changed in form, function, or operation since the 1890s. Because they simply could not cope with their mission, local officials were left to operate in "a highly irregular manner." In other words, they improvised:

> The records are not kept as required by law; the tally sheets are marked up at the close of the count, instead of while the counting is being conducted; the ballots are not counted one by one as is generally provided by law; the numerous required signatures, supposed to be made at the close of the day, are made during the day; the voters are permitted to mark their ballots upon the wall and outside of the voting booth; voters are permitted to confer with each other while marking the ballot; the precinct officers fail to sign each ballot; sometimes the election officers may go outside of the polling place to receive the vote of a person unable to come to the polls; outsiders are permitted to participate in the conduct of the election, particularly in the count; some of the

precinct officers are absent for long periods of time; no record is made of challenges and many other formalities are not complied with. . . ."[24]

Fraud could thrive in this environment. To uproot it, the whole system needed to be reformed from top to bottom. For Harris, the solution lay in scientific, nonpartisan (not bipartisan), and professional public administration principles and techniques. If fraud was the *raison d'etre* for voter registration, then voter registration is the *raison d'etre* of modern election administration. If ballots are simple enough, counting them can be done by school children—as long as the process is transparent (and they get nap time). But voter registration is where the professionals come in as the gatekeepers of the franchise. For the rationalist administrator, the questions were settled long ago: the massive fraud of the big-city boss era was a fact, voter registration is a necessity, and professionals should be nonpartisan. The outlook of the early public administration scholars, whose work contributed much to the development of political science as an academic discipline in the United States, casts rule-making as a natural rational process. Ironically, their commitment to a science of government ignores the role of politics in shaping electoral procedures such as voter registration. But politics featured prominently in the other strand of scholarly research in political science that touches on election fraud.

The Decline in Voter Turnout Debate

The question of motivation behind the electoral rules changes of the Gilded Age played an important role in a lively debate about what caused the significant decline in voting that followed. The debate was touched off by the publication in 1965 of a seminal article by Walter Dean Burnham.[25] In the pages of the *American Political Science Review*, Burnham attacked the scholars who relied most heavily on survey research to explain voting behavior. Surveys could tell us little about why Americans have an anemic attachment to voting. He called for a political and historical sociology of voting that better explained the larger structural conditions underlying voting behavior. To make his case, Burnham conducted a statistical analysis of changing U.S. voting patterns in the 1896–1932 era. Burnham believed that the characteristics of the modern mass electorate, the declining rates of voting, and the crisis of the party system that it signaled were decisively formed during this earlier period. He argued that "revolutionary contraction in the size and diffusion in the shape of the voting universe" after the 1890s was due in large measure to the heavily sectional party realignment of 1896 and the collapse of party competition that followed the rise of industrial capitalism.

Burnham further contended that the nineteenth-century U.S. political system was incomparably the most thoroughly democratized of any in the world. Indeed, prior to large-scale industrialization in the United States, working men were widely enfranchised. This was not the case in Europe, where the struggle for the suffrage was part of the struggle against rising capitalist exploitation. Thus, U.S. industrial elites probably felt themselves more vulnerable to democratic resistance than their European counterparts. This "crisis of vulnerability" peaked in the 1890s. Burnham claimed the electoral reforms that led to massive voter demobilization within a generation were promoted by political and economic elites in their search for stability and political order. The collapse of party competition after 1896, coupled with institutional changes in the voting process, eroded the political universe of an agrarian past "so sharply different from the one we all take for granted today that many of our contemporary frames of analytical reference seem irrelevant or misleading in studying it."[26]

The question of voter fraud figured prominently in an influential critique of the Burnham thesis.[27] Philip E. Converse, a distinguished student of voting behavior,[28] spent most of the first half of a long essay on political change attacking Burnham's assumption that high turnout levels of the late nineteenth century were accurate. He argued that the wide-ranging political reforms of the Progressive era, in particular, the introduction of the "Australian," or secret, ballot and the gradual implementation of personal registration systems across the states were more directly responsible for reshaping the electorate than were the political factors associated with the destruction of party competition identified by Burnham.

Like Harris before him, Converse saw the legal reforms of the electoral process as politically neutral. In fact, he reasoned, they decreased the certainty in the vote that both parties preferred. To push his point, he argued that the "advocates of clean democratic process" behind the reforms did not intend to depress turnout but were, instead, simply more concerned about the intimidation and fraud that occurred with the use of the nonsecret ballot. "If anything," he wrote, "they were more alarmed by the fraudulence that ran rampant in the voting process due to lack of control over the identity of individuals arriving at the polling place on Election Day."[29] Converse was convinced that fraud was rampant, even though he acknowledged that the literature on the subject of voter fraud is "everywhere anecdotal."[30] Nevertheless, he concluded, "All told, accounts of malpractice were sufficiently dense and colorful for this period that the oblivion into which they seem to have fallen from the point of view of modern scholars working on nineteenth-century voting data is remarkable in itself."[31]

Significantly, the debate turned on the empirical question of the extent of nineteenth-century voter fraud. If the high turnout rates critical to the Burnham thesis turned out to be an artifact of fraud, the decline in voting after 1900 was less stark and other explanations could be offered. Converse's view was that, whatever negative effect electoral reform in this era had on turnout, it was "almost prototypic of 'unintended consequences.'"[32]

The debate over fraud in the nineteenth century remains unresolved.[33] Even the definitions of *fraud* remain disputed, and a systematic survey of the empirical evidence is daunting because much of whatever evidence there once was probably no longer exists. Some scholars took up the call for more empirical research on fraud,[34] but none attempted a systematic survey of the primary evidence. Most of this work confirms Burnham's claims that voter fraud in the nineteenth century was marginal and episodic, sometimes flagrant, but not endemic to U.S. elections, as Converse and others have asserted.[35] The most comprehensive review of the literature on U.S. electoral corruption concluded that "there are reasons to doubt the reliability and accuracy of many generalizations which have been made about vote fraud in American politics," namely the indiscriminate lumping of a variety of forms of corrupt practices together under the name of "vote fraud" and the characterization of hard-driving political tactics to mobilize the votes of "undesirables"—techniques that were then or are now unscrupulous or illegal—as "fraud."[36] The vast gap in this understanding of the character of electoral democracy in the past remains. This is regrettable because knowledge of the nineteenth century would be useful in shedding light on the contemporary hysteria over voter fraud.

The Contemporary Evidence

Law Enforcement Efforts and Federal Government Prosecutions

The best source of data on federal law enforcement efforts to combat election or voter fraud should be the U.S. Department of Justice itself. This is especially the case for the George W. Bush Justice Department, which made the investigation and prosecution of election fraud a top law enforcement priority, "outranked only by crimes involving terrorism and espionage," according to the director of the Justice Department Election Crimes branch.[37]

Five months after the 2000 Florida election debacle, the Justice Department announced a new initiative to fight election fraud.[38] Given the wide publicity on the myriad ways that qualified Florida voters had been both intentionally and unintentionally confused and obstructed by Florida election administrators so that their ballots were voided or they were kept from casting them, the concern about voter "fraud offenses" and "violators" was bizarre. Some 180,000 votes (out of approximately 6.1 million) were "lost" in that election, meaning that they were cast by eligible voters but not counted because the ballot-counting technology failed or because the voter abstained or spoiled the ballot. A review of discarded ballots in Palm Beach County by the *Palm Beach Post* found that Al Gore, the Democratic candidate, lost 6,607 votes, more than ten times the Republican's winning margin, when voters marked more than one name on the county's "butterfly ballot."[39] Upward of 27,000 votes, or 9 percent of all ballots cast, were tossed in Jacksonville, Duval County, after voters were confronted with the unfamiliar "caterpillar" ballot in which candidates names weaved up and down one page and on to the next. A study of the statewide overvote problem by *USA Today* and Knight Ridder suggested that Gore lost at least 2,600 votes in Duval County due to ballot-design problems. Secretary of State Katherine Harris's infamous felon purge of the Florida voter rolls certainly contributed to the confusion. A study by Allan J. Lichtman commissioned by the U.S. Commission on Civil Rights found disproportionately high ballot rejection rates for black Floridians. Lichtman estimated that if black and white voters had experienced similar ballot-rejection rates, more than 50,000 additional ballots cast by blacks would have been counted in the 2000 election in Florida.[40]

At a press conference in early March 2001, called to announce the intent of the Justice Department to pursue "a new ethic" of voting rights enforcement, John Ashcroft, the new attorney general, demonstrated little knowledge of why the new "voting integrity" initiative was needed. A movement conservative from Missouri, Ashcroft was a true believer in the notion that fraud plagued U.S. elections even if he did not know the facts. He shared the obsession of the Republican Party with what Republicans say is a wide-scale conspiracy on the part of the Democrats and their allies to win elections by committing fraud.

> REPORTER: I was wondering if you have any idea what the record of this division is on prosecuting voter fraud. How many people have been charged with it recently or convicted? Have there been any indictments or charges as a result of the Florida situation? And also a second part: Will this initiative include funding for things like training voter boards, the people who man the polls, and maybe even new voting machines?
>
> ATTY GEN. ASHCROFT: First of all, I don't have a rack up of voter fraud prosecutions. And that—there would be times where the Civil Rights Division in some of those settings would be conferring with the Public Integrity Section of the department in order to get that done. I don't have—frankly I don't have the history of the department in terms of numerics in either of those areas, either in voter access or voter fraud, but those are two primary thrusts that we are going to be working on prospectively.
>
> The second part of your question escaped me."[41]

The new initiative later took the name the Ballot Access and Voting Integrity Initiative (BAVII).[42] It brought together experienced attorneys from the Justice Department Civil Rights and Criminal Divisions to train U.S. attorneys and other designated personnel at annual seminars convened to teach them how to recognize, investigate, and prosecute voter fraud and voter intimidation.[43] The BAVII also upgraded the Justice Department election day operation by designating district election officers (DEOs) in each U.S. attorney's office and publicizing their availability to receive complaints from the public about possible incidents of voter fraud, as well as allegations of voter intimidation. From this day on, the Justice Department repeatedly insisted that "under the ongoing initiative, election crimes are a high law enforcement priority of the Department."[44]

My Alice-in-Wonderland quest for the federal data on election crimes is detailed in appendix 3. As noted there, during a June 2006 U.S. House hearing on non-citizen voting, a case list of ninety-five indictments for "election fraud" brought by the Justice Department during the first three years of the BAVII was quietly entered into the congressional record. The list contains the court of jurisdiction, case name and number, charges and number of individuals charged, year, status, and a brief description of each indictment. As I explain in appendix 4, I cross-checked the Justice Department case list against the final data set of "election law violators" that I derived from the Federal Court Cases Integrated Database (FCCID), which provides an "official public record of the business of the federal courts."[45] The FCCID data combine records from several federal criminal justice agencies and from ninety-four district and twelve appellate court offices throughout the United States for the 1996–2005 period (federal fiscal years). A third, or thirty-five of the ninety-five indictments on the Justice Department list, were not coded as election law violations in the FCCID and so were missed in searches using the Administrative Office of U.S. Courts coding system.[46] So even with the improvements offered by the FCCID, it is not possible to identify all cases of election crime using the available coding and charge data alone.

Figure 3.1 displays the final results of analysis of the FCCID by year. Beginning in 2003, we see the results of the decision at the Justice Department to increase its enforcement effort against alleged election fraud. Table 3.1 shows how the record of fraud indictments compares with indictments for other kinds of fraud. Notable here is that in both (federal fiscal years) 1996 and 2005 federal prosecutors indicted far more people for violations of the nation's migratory bird laws than for election fraud, despite the announced prioritizing of election anti-fraud enforcement after 2002.[47]

Without knowing more about the specific nature of the other forms of fraud presented in table 3.1, we can still see that in general they share features with election fraud. For example, Social Security fraud can involve impersonation and false claims about eligibility; counterfeiting can involve forgery and false claims of identity; tax evasion can involve false claims of residence; and mail fraud statutes have been used to prosecute voter fraud. The number of individuals indicted for these types of fraud in any one year further suggests that the claim against a methodology relying on measures of law enforcement to assess the threat of voter fraud to the integrity of U.S. elections is of little merit.

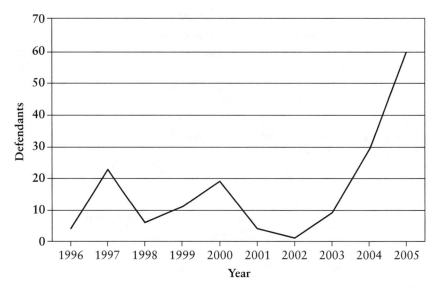

Figure 3.1 Total defendants in federal criminal election fraud cases, FY 1996–2005.
Source: Election Fraud Defendants Database, derived from Federal Judicial Center, *Federal Court Cases: Integrated Database*, 1996–2005 [computer file], conducted by the Federal Judicial Center, ICPSR08429, ICPSR03415, ICPSR04059, ICPSR04026, ICPSR04348, ICPSR04382, Ann Arbor, Mich.: Inter-University Consortium for Political and Social Research [Producer and Distributor]; author's calculations.

TABLE 3.1
Defendants charged in federal criminal election fraud cases compared to other crimes: Prosecutorial effort, FY1996 and FY2005

Criminal charge[a]	FY1996	FY2005	Change (%)
Election fraud violations	4	60	+1,400.0
Other fraud violations			
Citizenship fraud	243	776	+219.3
Social Security fraud	764	1,980	+159.2
False claims and statements	4,169	6,658	+59.7
Counterfeiting	2,078	3,161	+52.1
Postal, Internet, and wire fraud	6,369	6,929	+8.8
Tax evasion	916	781	−14.7
Other			
Migratory bird law violations	167	207	+24.0
National park violations	357	290	−18.8
Total criminal defendants	112,346	183,284	+63.1

Source: Federal Judicial Center, Federal Court Cases: Integrated Database, 1997, 2005 [computer file], conducted by the Federal Judicial Center, ICPSR04306, ICPSR04382, Ann Arbor, Mich.: Inter-University Consortium for Political and Social Research [producer and distributor]; author's calculations.
[a] At least one of the top five filing charges for each defendant falls into crime category.

The Fight for the Forty-Sixth Congressional District Seat

In his pathbreaking analysis of partisanship in contested House and Senate elections over the whole of U.S. history, Jeffrey Jenkins argues that the partisan strategy of using (and deciding) election contests has lost whatever potency it once had.[48] But this does not mean that partisan motives have disappeared from modern election contests. We turn now to an examination of one recent contested election to explore how spurious fraud allegations can be used as a political tool. Fraud charges figured prominently in a disputed House election in California in 1996. Orange County, California, is the fifth largest county in the United States, with 2.9 million people, one-third of them Latino. The population of the county has doubled twice since 1960 and has been transformed in recent decades by immigrants from Mexico, Latin America, and Asia. The Forty-Sixth Congressional District is nestled in the heart of Orange County and includes centers of Latino concentration; Santa Ana, the county seat; and most of Garden Grove and Anaheim, giving the Forty-Sixth District a population that is nearly two-thirds Latino. Crafty redistricting by Democrats in the California state legislature has facilitated political change in Orange County as well. Orange County was once a Republican stronghold, a core constituency for the Republican Party in presidential elections because it could swing California to the party.[49] As late as 1988, voters in the Forty-Sixth District gave 62 percent of their votes to George H.W. Bush. By 2000, however, a 24 percent Republican margin in presidential elections had been replaced by a 12 percent Democratic margin when Al Gore won the Forty-Sixth District with 54 percent of the vote to 42 percent for George W. Bush. The advancing ability of new immigrant and Latino voters to define Orange County politics and the growing Democratic vote set the stage for an explosive case of alleged voter fraud in 1996.

Perhaps better than any other contemporary example, the 1996 contest for the House seat in the Forty-Sixth District, between Robert K. Dornan, the nine-term Republican incumbent, and Loretta Sanchez, a little-known businesswoman, lays bare the politics of voter fraud controversies today. The contested election involved a blizzard of allegations of registration fraud, noncitizen and illegal immigrant voting, double-voting, voting from nonresidential addresses, illegal inducements to register and vote, voter intimidation, ballot box tampering, and absentee ballot fraud, all under the canopy of a bitter and protracted partisan battle that quickly bled into the national political scene.

One day after the November 5, 1996, election Dornan led Sanchez by 233 votes, but 12,000 absentee and provisional ballots had yet to be counted. A week later, with approximately 3,000 ballots still left to tally, the Associated Press called the election for Sanchez, who had moved into the lead with a 929-vote margin. As the count proceeded, Dornan repeatedly raised the specter of noncitizen voter fraud and vowed to take his reelection fight to the floor of the House of Representative if he lost. He added that his Republican colleagues were looking for a case to use in challenging the recently implemented NVRA, signaling the likely entry of national political forces into the fray.[50] Dornan specifically charged that a well-known Latino rights group and the Democratic Party signed up illegal voters in a drive he argued may have led to "the first case in history where a congressional election was decided by non-citizens."[51] His lawyer later called the case "what we think is the single largest example of voter fraud in a federal election in the last 50 years, and yes, maybe in this century."[52]

On November 22, 1996, the Orange County registrar of voters certified Loretta Sanchez the winner by 984 votes,[53] and a fourteen-month rancorous battle to deny Sanchez a seat in the House was joined. State electoral and law enforcement agencies were the first to open investigations into the alleged election irregularities. Indeed, the Orange County District Attorney's Office had opened an inquiry several weeks before the November 5 election when a complaint from a registrar of voters in Santa Ana was lodged with the office regarding the improper registration of a noncitizen by an organization named Hermandad Mexicana Nacional. Immediately after the election, when the Dornan campaign provided its own preliminary documentation of the alleged voter fraud, the Secretary of State's Office opened an inquiry. Both state and local inquiries were converted into full investigations in December, and Hermandad, a forty-five-year-old Latino rights organization with offices in a number of California cities, Chicago, and New York, quickly became the central focus of the probes. It is important to point out that California Governor Pete Wilson, a Republican, crested to reelection in 1994 partly on the strength of his anti-immigrant rhetoric. Wilson strongly supported Proposition 187, which would have barred the children of undocumented immigrants from enrolling in public schools and required everyone to prove their citizenship or legal status to receive public benefits. Once he came out in support of Proposition 187, Wilson's poll numbers shot up from a 15-point deficit to a 20-point lead.

Hermandad, like numerous immigrant rights groups around the country, ran an Immigration and Naturalization Service (INS)–sponsored citizenship program that helped prepare approximately 2,000 immigrants per month for naturalization. Applicants were offered citizenship classes, and Hermandad would arrange for large groups of those completing the classes to receive INS citizenship interviews on-site. According to evidence presented by the Orange County District Attorney's Office to a California grand jury in fall 1997, those who successfully completed the INS citizenship interview were then escorted to tables and asked to sign voter registration cards. They were also given official letters from the INS that began, "Congratulations, your application for citizenship has been approved," even though most applicants were not scheduled for swearing-in ceremonies for another two to three months. The district attorney's case to the grand jury claimed that Hermandad staff encouraged applicants to sign their names to the voter registration cards and told them that, once they had been sworn in, the other information on the card would be filled in for them and the card processed. Nativo Lopez, the Hermandad executive director, produced evidence to show that he had informed staff that only those who had been sworn in as new citizens were eligible to vote. But the misleading letter from the INS to applicants congratulating them on being "approved" for citizenship, and the apparent misunderstanding by some of the Hermandad staff regarding California eligibility requirements for voter *registration*, likely resulted in the premature registration of some noncitizens coming through the Hermandad citizenship program.

Just how many noncitizens were prematurely registered remains disputed, as do nearly all the numbers of "illegal" votes alleged in the protracted election controversy, which employed use of unprecedented legal tactics and involved previously untested provisions in the Federal Contested Elections Act of 1969 (FCEA) governing election contests in the House. On January 14, 1997, at 7:30 in the morning, state and county investigators raided the offices of Hermandad in Santa Ana, stationing a dozen armed guards outside the building, and encircling it in yellow police tape used to mark the scene of a crime. Police served a search warrant on the lone maintenance worker inside.[54] Twelve hours later, the investigators carted away fifteen boxes of documents and computer hardware with the records of the Hermandad membership base, financial dealings, services, and clients. The criminal investigation of Hermandad dragged on for a year, during which time Hermandad lost its funding to conduct the INS citizenship classes and had its motions for the return of its property repeatedly denied by local judges. But in December 1997, with the district attorney's case involving evidence gleaned from over 300 interviews conducted by 40 investigators and a review of 33,000 documents before it, a grand jury declined to bring a single indictment. This closed the criminal investigation of Hermandad and severely undermined the veracity of Dornan's allegations that hundreds of noncitizens had fraudulently voted in Orange County.

Meanwhile, national political forces were being drawn into the dispute. On December 26, 1996, Dornan formally requested that the House of Representatives investigate the election. This was within his prerogative and the constitutional authority of the House under Article 1, Section 5, Clause 1, which provides that each house of Congress shall be the judge of the "elections, returns and qualifications" of its members. Under the rules of the FCEA, the review is first made by the Committee on House Oversight (the Committee), which conducts its own investigation, and then by the whole House, which disposes of the contest by resolution or majority vote. In the 105th Congress, the eight-member Committee was chaired by Representative William M. Thomas, a Republican from Bakersfield, California, and dominated 5–3 by Republican members. Thomas created a three-person Task Force composed of Vernon Ehlers (R-Mich.) and Robert Ney (R-Ohio), and later Steny Hoyer (D-Md.), to conduct the investigation and recommend a course of action to the full Committee. Like the Orange County district attorney and the secretary of state investigations, the House Committee investigation took a full year and produced, in the end, a disputed finding of fraud that was too insubstantial to convince the Republican-dominated House to reverse Sanchez's victory. On February 12, 1998, the House voted 378–33 to dismiss Dornan's contest.

The Task Force investigation of the contest was unprecedented in the thirty-year history of the FCEA. Prior to the Dornan-Sanchez contest, under the FCEA the House had considered twenty-nine requests to use its constitutional authority to make the final decision in settling a disputed election for one of its seats. In no previous contest did the Committee deny the contestee's motion to dismiss, as it did when it rejected Sanchez's motion. No prior Committee had decided to grant the contestant subpoena power or proceed with its own investigation after the contestant failed to meet the substantial burden of showing "credible" evidence that the election result was erroneous or that the state was wrong in certifying the winner as mandated by the FCEA, as it did in the Dornan-Sanchez case. The denial of Sanchez's request to dismiss the case set the investigation in motion and also set the Committee off into uncharted waters. According to the law, Dornan was required to make specific claims showing that there were enough disputed votes to reverse Sanchez's victory. He spelled out his allegations in a February 7, 1997, letter to the Committee outlining several categories of tainted votes that he argued overcame his margin of defeat. His claims were directly controverted by the Orange County registrar of voters, who within two months of the elections conducted her own internal review of the registration and voting records administered by her office. As the registrar's report indicates, most of Dornan's claims were unsubstantiated and based on his own sloppy data-gathering methods.[55] For example, one of Dornan's claims alleged that as many as seven hundred votes were "suspect" because they were cast by large groups of voters who shared common addresses. This list of voters was derived from a simple analysis of the voter files that generated a subset of 127 addresses where more than six people were registered to vote. The *Los Angeles Times* interviewed people at sixty of those addresses and found "no evidence of illegal or nonexistent voters at any of them."[56] When Joyce Georgieff was contacted by the newspaper and told she, her husband, daughter, two sons, and another family member who all reside at her North Santa Ana home were "suspect" voters, she exclaimed, "We're a family, for Pete's sake! I used to be a Republican, but Dornan frustrates the crap out of me. His blustery antics get tiresome after a while."[57] Doan Bui, a Vietnamese American who shares a home with five other family members and said he was a Dornan voter, nevertheless expressed his outrage at making the Dornan list. Using an obscenity, he groused, "Just because we live in Santa Ana doesn't mean we're all . . . illegal." The addresses challenged by Dornan also included the St. Francis Home, a facility for the aged and infirm in Santa Ana, whose eighteen Catholic nuns made the list; apartment complexes, mobile home parks, and the Marine Corps Air Station in Tustin where seventeen active-duty Marines, all registered Republicans, were, according to Dornan, "suspect" voters "that must be thoroughly investigated."[58]

Other Dornan claims involved the allegation of thirty-eight cases of double-voting, and thirty-nine cases of people illegally voting outside their home precincts. The *Los Angeles Times* investigated these charges and found them "of little merit."[59] Among the thirty-eight people alleged to have voted twice were twins, such as Joanne and Jeanne Acker, who told the *Times*, "If the Dornan people really wanted to know [if Joanne and Jeanne were the same person], they could have called"; fathers and sons with the same name, such as Clarence H. Hoon Jr. of Anaheim and his son, Clarence Hoon III; and people who were mistakenly registered twice but who voted once, such as Cecilia Jurado, who told the *Times*, "I have no idea why my name was on there twice." The records show that when Jurado went to vote, she crossed out the second registration and voted once. As for the "documented" cases of voters registering to vote from nonresidential addresses, a violation of California's election code, the *Times* concluded that Dornan's list "appears to be almost entirely inaccurate." The list included people such as Maricela Zarate, registered to vote from a business address, Angela's Beauty Salon in Santa Ana. Zarate, however, does not work at the salon; instead, she lives in an apartment at the back. In addition, Dornan's list included U.S. war veterans living in a homeless shelter for former servicemen and the animal curator at the Santa Ana Zoo, Constance Sweet, who lives in a trailer behind the zoo's monkey cage. When contacted by the newspaper about the charge that she was illegally registered to vote, Sweet complained, "I've been hounded about this to the Nth degree. If this isn't good enough for everybody, too bad. It's a part of my job."[60]

The Task Force Minority analysis of Dornan's original allegations based on the registrar's internal review led them to conclude that the case should have been dismissed in February 1997 for lack of "credible" evidence that there were enough tainted votes to overcome Sanchez's margin of victory. The Majority disagreed, scheduled a hearing in Orange County, and began searching for a means of evaluating Dornan's most serious challenge—one that he had been publicizing for months but had actually failed to substantiate in any way, including in his formal submission to the Committee prior to its decision to proceed—that significant numbers of noncitizens had registered and voted in the November election. This quixotic journey led the Task Force into the woolly world of complex records management and the impossible quest for matching often imprecise, incomplete, and sometimes inaccurate records kept by state and local bureaucracies with similarly flawed records maintained by large federal agencies, specifically, the INS.

The final determination of the Task Force that it had found "documented evidence of illegal non-citizen voting" involving 624 voters, a claim the Minority strenuously disputed, was ultimately based on a records match performed by the Task Force using multiple INS databases and the Orange Country voter registration file.[61] The INS records, however, as INS officials repeatedly informed the Committee, do not track citizens and would prove enormously difficult to work with because they segregated people into numerous files with the potential for duplication and were not routinely updated with information from the INS field offices. INS databases include the Central Index System (CIS), Naturalization Casework System (NACS), Refugee, Asylee and Parolee System (RAPS), and the Student and Schools System (STSC). In a letter to Chairman Thomas dated May 1, 1997, the INS wrote,

> INS databases are not organized for this purpose [to prove citizenship status] and there are inherent limitations on their use to match against lists of registered voters. For example, with only two common identifiers name and date of birth there is a potential for false matches and duplicate matches for a single registered voter. Also the INS does not typically update files of individuals after they are naturalized. In addition, automated databases do not necessarily contain records pertaining to individuals who naturalized prior to 1973. Therefore, records of long-time naturalized citizens would not necessarily be easily retrievable from INS databases. Finally, the INS does not, of course, maintain records on native-born United States citizens.[62]

This last point meant that any native-born U.S. citizen listed on the Orange Country voter registration rolls and sharing a name and date of birth with a person in the INS, CIS, or NACS databases would turn up as a match using the methodology adopted by the Task Force for rooting out noncitizen voters.

The CIS central database alone contained more than 45 million names and some 500 million individual records of everyone who had dealt with the INS over the last twenty-five years. But the central database also was notoriously out of date with respect to information regarding naturalization. INS officials testified at a May 15, 1997, congressional hearing before the Committee that, because the central database was not uniformly updated, the only way to know for sure whether a foreign-born resident was a citizen was to manually check the person's paper files for a naturalization certificate.[63] In fact, the INS later told the Committee that there was more than a 50 percent error rate in its computerized files, meaning more than half of the people missing a naturalization date in the database were likely to be citizens.

Through a protracted months-long process of whittling down an initial roster of 504,572 names that had made it on to the Task Force "suspect voter" list when the imperfect INS data were matched against the 1.3 million-person Orange County voter registration file by surname and date of birth, the Task Force developed a list of 4,023 possible noncitizen voters living in the Forty-Sixth Congressional District. These records, along with approximately seven hundred more that turned up from various other sources, were then manually reviewed in the Los Angeles field office of the INS and elsewhere for evidence of naturalization.[64]

As the manual review continued, the Task Force searched for other sources of evidence of noncitizen voting. It obtained records from the Orange County Superior Court of individuals dismissed from jury duty when they claimed noncitizenship. The Superior Court informed the Task Force that these records had a 33 percent error rate. The Task Force aided the Secretary of State's Office in its targeted investigation of 190,456 people who registered to vote on forms signed out to over 1,500 third-party organizations by the Orange County registrar of voters, most of them immigrant rights groups, good government groups such as the League of Women Voters, labor unions, and Democratic Party campaign organizations. This investigation concluded that 5,087 registered voters in Orange County were "potential noncitizens."[65] The Task Force requested copies of registration affidavits from the Orange County registrar of voters and approached the INS for signatures contained in its files in order to attempt signature matches with the registration records using handwriting analysis.

The work dragged on throughout summer and fall of 1997 as calls for the Task Force and Committee to conclude their investigation began to mount among Democrats in the House.[66] Public pressure to end the probe had been building for months. In November, the *New York Times* editorialized that "The House Oversight Committee's investigation into the election of Rep. Loretta Sanchez, a Democrat, has become a costly farce that should come to a quick end."[67] And protests by Latino rights groups in California and throughout the nation threatened to tar and disable Republican Party efforts to incorporate any significant segment of the Latino electorate for a long time to come.

The deeply divided Task Force concluded its work with a report to the Committee that it had uncovered "documented evidence" that "624 persons registered when they were not citizens."[68] The Minority disagreed, stating, "To be charitable, this is a gross mischaracterization," pointing out that about half that number were citizens at the time they voted in the 1996 election, although their registration appeared to be in question because it was processed before they were officially sworn in. The Minority continued,

> In fact nothing definitive can be concluded about most of these people with respect to their citizenship status and right to vote, either because the INS has not been able to locate a signature in its records that can be compared to the signature provided by the Orange County Registrar, or because the INS has not located in its various computer databases and paper files a naturalization

date for these individuals. Without a legible signature from both agencies, a signature comparison cannot be conducted to determine whether the voter in Orange County is likely the same person as the one in the INS file. Without a naturalization date, it is impossible to determine when or if the "suspect voter" became a citizen.[69]

Finally, the Orange County registrar had voided 124 absentee ballots that did not conform to the letter of California's absentee ballot law.[70] This brought the total number of votes in question to 748, 231 short of Sanchez's margin of victory.[71] The contest ended in February 1998 when the Task Force recommended to the full Oversight Committee that the case be dismissed, the Oversight Committee voted 8–1 to dismiss and the full House agreed.

The Dornan-Sanchez electoral dispute fits squarely what Benjamin Ginsberg and Martin Shefter call "politics by other means"—the use of legal strategies and the courts, revelation, prosecution and investigation, and the media to win elections. According to Ginsberg and Shefter, "During the political struggles of the past decades, politicians sought to undermine the institution associated with their foes, disgrace one another on national television, force their competitors to resign from office, and, in a number of cases, send their opponents to prison. Remarkably, one tactic that has not been so widely used is the mobilization of the electorate."[72]

In an era when the cost of mobilizing voters is only going up and party system is unstable, politics by other means has replaced the full use of the electoral arena by politicians as they compete for leadership in government. Classes of voters such as African Americans, Latinos, and new immigrants once on the margins of the U.S. electorate, voters who have struggled for inclusion and a political voice, are cast in suspicion by voter fraud allegations that suggest their votes are "illegal" or that they are prone to subvert the rules—in other words, cheat—to overcome their minority status in a majoritarian system. Thus, voter fraud allegations that taint the votes of these groups are useful to politicians engaged in politics by other means. The Dornan-Sanchez race was a watershed election for California politics and for Latino politics nationally. Sanchez was called a "giant-killer," and her victory was considered an irrevocable advance for Latinos as a growing force in U.S. politics. The fraud allegations and subsequent fourteen-month investigations by state, county, and federal government agencies cost U.S. taxpayers over $1.4 million.[73] In the end, very little voter fraud was convincingly substantiated. On April 29, 1998, the California secretary of state announced that the people identified by the Task Force as illegal, noncitizen voters in the Forty-Sixth Congressional District election of 1996 would not be prosecuted for voter fraud, concluding that they had registered in error and not from criminal intent.[74]

Chapter 4

Evidence from the States

The findings from my research into cases of voter fraud in non-federal elections are consistent with the conclusions we can draw from the federal court data. This chapter describes and analyzes various types of records obtained from four states—California, Minnesota, New Hampshire, and Oregon. The evidence illuminates that the states lack uniform policies for handling, investigating, and prosecuting voter fraud complaints, but at the same time, as discussed in more detail below, it strongly suggests that criminal voter fraud is episodic and rare relative to the total number of votes cast in a given year or election cycle.

California: Election Fraud Investigations Unit

The Election Fraud Investigations Unit (EFIU) of the California Secretary of State's Office handles complaints of criminal violations of the California elections code from victims, voters, parties, and elected officials.[1] Investigators conduct a preliminary analysis of complaints and, if they find them justified, refer them to the Attorney General's Office, a district attorney, or U.S. attorney, depending on the nature of the potential code violation. Prosecutors then decide whether to file charges.[2]

In May 2007, I obtained a file of all election fraud complaints referred to the Secretary of State's Office dating back to 1994. For each complaint, the records include the year the complaint was made; the nature of the allegation; and final action taken, including whether the case was referred to a law enforcement agency. The data do not tell us any more about who may have committed the alleged violation[3] (nor does it tell us anything about

58   *Chapter 4*

who lodged the complaint), so I matched the allegation code to the section of the state election code to which it appears to apply and grouped the complaints into three categories based on whether violations were likely to have been committed by (1) voters; (2) election officials; or (3) organized political groups or campaigns, elected officials, or candidates. Table 4.1 presents the number of cases for each of the three types of alleged perpetrators by the year the complaint was made.[4]

Allegations of voter fraud are by far the largest group, accounting for seven of every ten complaints filed over the thirteen-year period. Table 4.2 breaks down the complaints against voters by whether the alleged violation concerned the registration or voting process and by the outcome or final status of the allegation. The table reveals several important insights. First, the data show that investigators do not refuse or fail to investigate allegations of voter fraud, an important claim made by those who dismiss crime

TABLE 4.1
California election fraud complaints by type of alleged perpetrator, 1994–2006

	Voters[a]	Election officials[b]	Candidate, party, campaign, or other organizations[c]	Unknown	Total[d]
1994	71	16	42	4	133
1995	165	6	25	4	200
1996	124	11	63	6	204
1997	143	2	33	8	186
1998	188	10	45	4	247
1999	48	4	25	1	78
2000	79	7	35	4	125
2001	125	7	16	2	150
2002	172	5	68	2	247
2003	80	4	25	4	113
2004	338	8	89	11	446
2005	114	4	34	1	153
2006	87	2	69	2	160
Total	1734	86	569	53	2,442

Source: California Secretary of State's Office, Election Fraud Investigations Unit, Sacramento, Calif.
[a] *Voters* includes complaints about "absentee ballot requirements," "double voting-absentee," "double voting-precinct," "fraudulent absentee voting," "fraudulent voter registration," "fraudulent voting," "non-return of absentee ballot application," "non-citizen registered," "non-citizen voting," "residency," "selling/trading votes on eBay," and "voter registration after 54th day."
[b] *Election officials* includes complaints about "alteration of election returns," "ballot offenses," "consideration for voting," "handling of ballots," "neglect to perform official duties," "secrecy of ballot," and "tampering with voting devices/secrecy of ballot."
[c] *Candidate, party, campaign, other organization* includes complaints about "alteration of voter registration card," "consideration to become or withdraw as candidate," "charging fee for registration," "corruption of voters," "electioneering," "failure to file nominating papers," "failure to maintain records on paid personnel," "failure to surrender petition," "falsified petitions," "fictitious name on nomination petition," "holding voter registration card more than 3 days," "intimidation of voters," "mass mailing penal provisions," "misleading of voters," "misuse of signatures on petition," "misuse of voter rolls," "no declaration of candidacy," "payment for signatures," "payment for voting," "printing of simulated sample ballots," "suppression of nomination paper," "threats to a circulator," "vandalism of political signs," and "verification of signatures."
[d]Total excludes 17 complaints coded "no violation."

TABLE 4.2
California election fraud complaints: Allegations against voters and final status of complaint, 1994–2006

| | Final disposition | | | | | | |
| | No criminal violation found | | | | Violation found | | |
Type of voter fraud	Insufficient evidence, unable to identify or locate suspect, statute of limitations expired	Declined to investigate, dismissed, or no action taken	No violation	Lack of intent	Administrative action	Convicted or pled guilty	Total
Registration							
Fraudulent voter registration	263	53	157	15	101	52	641
Noncitizen registered	42	7	8	101	1	2	161
Residency	8	1	4	0	0	0	13
Voting by mail							
Nonreturn of absentee ballot application	1	0	3	0	0	0	4
Absentee ballot requirements	1	1	2	0	0	0	4
Double voting: absentee	84	90	61	39	0	14	288
Fraudulent absentee voting	3	1	3	0	0	1	8
Voting in person							
Double voting: precinct	130	61	80	37	1	8	317
Noncitizen voting	14	5	7	0	0	2	28
Fraudulent voting	25	13	41	6	22	4	111
Selling/trading votes on eBay	6	5	1	0	0	0	12
Total	577	237	368	198	125	83	1,588
	(36%)	(15%)	(23%)	(13%)	(8%)	(5%)	

Source: California Secretary of State's Office, Election Fraud Investigations Unit, Sacramento, Calif.
Note: Complaints whose final status could not be determined are excluded from the analysis. This includes ten complaints turned over to law enforcement and 136 complaints whose status was either pending (N=78) or unknown (N=58).

or law enforcement statistics as relevant to measuring the incidence of fraud.[5] Even if we take the categories "declined to investigate," "dismissed," and "no action taken" as cases in which the California EFIU failed or refused to investigate—and this may *not* be what these codes actually mean, but for the moment we will err on the side of assuming that these election fraud complaints were not investigated—we find that only 15 percent of some 1,588 complaints about voter fraud were not investigated, for reasons unknown. But, of course, finding no intent to commit a crime or no violation does not mean that the complaint was not investigated, as is sometimes implied by critics of law enforcement efforts against voter fraud.

Second, we find that about one-third of the allegations of voter fraud referred to the California Secretary of State Office's EFIU could go no further because they lacked evidence or the investigators were unable to identify or locate the suspect or because the complaint was made too long after an election or alleged commission of the crime. For another third of all complaints made and resolved between 1994 and 2006, no violation was found or investigators determined that the person against whom the complaint was brought lacked any intent to commit a crime. Of those complaints that resulted in some kind of violation (approximately 13 percent of all complaints), 126 of a total 208 were not serious enough to warrant criminal penalties. About one-third of all those found to have committed a violation—or 83 voters out of nearly 1,600 potential cases of election fraud over a period of more than a decade—were convicted of a crime in California. Most of these were convicted of crimes related to fraudulent voter registration (only twenty-nine were guilty of some kind of fraudulent voting).

Other patterns evident in the California election fraud complaint data are instructive of how procedural complexity can lead to voter error. Take, for example, the complaints about noncitizens registering and voting. Evidence from federal prosecutions of illegal non-citizen voting and from the example of the Dornan-Sanchez contested congressional election that occurred during the same period covered by the California complaint database (see chap. 3) suggests ways in which ineligible noncitizens may mistakenly become registered to vote. And, in fact, in California, where the noncitizen population at 5.6 million[6] dwarfs that of any other state, we find that fully one-third of the complaints made regarding alleged noncitizen voter registration were dismissed because investigators could not find an intent to commit the crime.

Alleged violations of residency requirements provide another example of the same phenomenon. Redistricting and routine administrative reassignment of polling places within jurisdictions means that for voters, especially those who may vote only in presidential elections, poll sites can move from one election to the next. The problem can be made worse by the relatively high rates of residential mobility and the changing residential property landscape in recent years, which can add hundreds, if not thousands, of new residential units to a voting jurisdiction. Election administrators must adapt to the redistribution of the population between elections, and they do so by redrawing administrative boundaries and changing polling locations. The California voter fraud allegation data, with a meager thirteen complaints about residency, nevertheless shows that none was a case of voter fraud.

Finally, it is interesting to note that there were more complaints of in-person or precinct-based voter fraud than absentee or mail ballot fraud. It is a commonplace among those on both sides of the voter fraud debate to assert that voter fraud is most likely to be committed with an absentee ballot. The California data are not definitive on the question, but we do not see a spike in complaints about mail balloting compared to other methods by which voters might corrupt the electoral process. As noted above, the largest category of complaints, as well as the largest number of guilty suspects (those convicted or who faced administrative action), concerns fraud in the registration, not the voting, process. Still, at 156 people, or twelve people per year over the thirteen-year study period, the evidence of registration fraud from this data is underwhelming.

Keep in mind that more than 75 million votes in statewide elections were cast in California during this same period.

Minnesota: Help America Vote Act Complaints and News Reports

In response to my request for records of voter fraud complaints, the Minnesota Secretary of State's office provided a CD-ROM containing all complaints made to that office through a complaint mechanism established to meet mandates of the HAVA.[7] The records are for a two-year period, September 2004 to September 2006.[8] Although these complaints were collected by the same state-level elections administrative office as in the California example—the Secretary of State's Office—the Minnesota complaints are restricted to alleged violations of Title III of the HAVA, which pertains mainly to voting machine standards, the posting of voting information, and voter registration procedures and records. In California, HAVA complaints are subsumed under the same complaint procedures.[9] Because of its specific and restrictive scope, the HAVA complaint procedure, which all states receiving federal funds through HAVA must establish, is of limited use to us as a source of information about alleged voter fraud, except perhaps in Minnesota where county attorneys are required by law to investigate complaints of voter fraud at risk of losing their jobs.[10] I supplemented the analysis of the HAVA complaints with a review of news reports of voter fraud and a survey of local prosecutors.

Of 161 HAVA complaints made to the Secretary of State's office over the two-year period, 14 expressed a concern about the potential for voter fraud (see table 4.3). For five of the complainants, the records made available to

TABLE 4.3
Minnesota HAVA and other election law complaints, September 2004-September 2006

	2004–2005	2005–2006	Total
Registration problems or issues	25	8	33
Poll worker practices	22	5	27
Polling place problems or complaints	16	6	22
Complaints about ballots or candidates	14	5	19
Complaints about possible fraud	8	6	14
Witnessed failure to comply with ID	4	0	4
Want more stringent ID	4	0	4
Electioneering/intimidation	3	3	6
Campaign finance complaints	2	0	2
Unspecified or other	13	17	30
Total	111	50	161

Source: Minnesota Secretary of State's Office, St. Paul, Minn.

Note: Included are election complaints not processed as Help America Vote Act of 2002 (HAVA) complaints. These include complaints referred to county attorneys under Minnesota election law, incomplete complaints, and instances in which the complaint form was used to offer suggestions and comments, or to make other inquiries. Copies of complaints were not maintained by the Secretary of State's Office until 2004; 2005–2006 combines fiscal years 2006 and 2007, the latter of which was incomplete at the time of my request to the secretary of state, ending in September 2006. Minnesota law incorporating Title III of HAVA and describing the state's complaint process reads:

200.04 HELP AMERICA VOTE ACT COMPLAINTS.
Subdivision 1. Procedure. The secretary of state shall establish a procedure for the review of complaints regarding the administration of Title III of the Help America Vote Act of 2002, Public Law 107–252, including complaints about voting system standards, computerized statewide registration lists and equipment, voter registration requirements, and other features of state implementation of that act. The secretary of state shall provide a complaint form that requires the signature of the complainant, an affidavit and notarization, and the attachment of any supporting documentation. The form must indicate that any election judge, while serving, is deemed a notary public for purposes of Public Law 107–252, section 402.
Subd. 2. Political subdivisions. (a) The procedure in this subdivision applies if a complaint under subdivision 1 pertains to a town, city, school, or county employee or official.
(b) The secretary of state must provide the town clerk, city clerk, school district clerk, or county auditor with a copy of the complaint within three business days of receiving it.
(c) The town clerk, city clerk, school district clerk, or county auditor has 20 days to either reach an agreement with the complainant or file a written response to the complaint with the secretary of state.
(d) The secretary of state shall provide the complainant with a copy of the response and an opportunity for a hearing on the record.
(e) If a hearing on the record is requested, the town clerk, city clerk, school district clerk, or county auditor must be given notice and the opportunity to participate.
(f) The secretary of state shall issue a final determination, and, if necessary, a remedial plan, no later than 90 days after the filing of the complaint. If the secretary of state fails to issue the determination within 90 days, the secretary of state must provide alternative dispute resolution for the disposition of the complaint. That process must be completed within 60 days of its commencement.
Subd. 3. Secretary of state. (a) The procedure in this subdivision applies if a complaint under subdivision 1 pertains to the secretary of state.
(b) The secretary of state must forward the complaint to the Office of Administrative Hearings within three business days after receiving it.
(c) The secretary of state has 20 days to either reach an agreement with the complainant or file a written response to the complaint with the Office of Administrative Hearings.
(d) The Office of Administrative Hearings must provide the complainant with a copy of the response and an opportunity for a hearing on the record.
(e) If a hearing on the record is requested, the secretary of state must be given notice and an opportunity to participate.
(f) The Office of Administrative Hearings must issue a final determination and remedial plan if necessary no later than 90 days after the filing of the complaint. If the Office of Administrative Hearings fails to issue the determination within 90 days, it must provide alternative dispute resolution for the disposition of the complaint. That process must be completed within 60 days of its commencement.
Subd. 4. Application of chapter 14. Proceedings under this section are not subject to chapter 14.
Subd. 5. Appeal. A determination made under subdivision 2 is not an agency determination subject to appellate review. Either party may initiate an appeal from the secretary of state's final order in the district court in the county where the town, city, or county employee or official is employed.
Subd. 6. Review. A determination made under subdivision 3 is subject to appellate review.

me do not divulge the details of their concerns.[11] Of the other nine, however, none convincingly claimed to have witnessed potentially fraudulent behavior by voters or poll workers. A Minneapolis man reported that when he voted he noticed that the poll book did not indicate the fact that his wife had voted an absentee ballot. This mysteriously led him to worry about registration fraud. Elections Division staff explained to him that in Minnesota it is not illegal for a voter who requests an absentee ballot to vote in person instead. For that reason, at any time on election day, the poll books reflect whichever happens first: the arrival of an absentee ballot or a voter in the flesh. Absentee ballots are delivered to the precincts in which they are to be counted by the last mail delivery on election day. If a voter shows up to vote after his or her absentee ballot has been delivered and accepted by the election judge, he or she is not permitted to vote again.

Another voter wrote a letter to the secretary of state to express concern that the receipt given to voters entitling them to a ballot could be used as a vehicle to commit fraud. According to the acknowledgement letter prepared in response, this voter "suggested that an 'unscrupulous' individual could pocket a receipt, leave the polling place, and then mass copy it, to be distributed and used to obtain ballots in other polling places." Minnesota election officials assured the man that this was an unlikely scenario because the form and content of the receipts varied across the election districts of the state.

A complaint forwarded to the Hennepin County attorney for further investigation appeared to be based on little more than paranoia. A Mr. John Heath reported that on his drive from Eden Prairie to Bloomington he noticed a young Asian man driving a small car "with 50 to 100 John Kerry bumper stickers on it." Heath followed the car into a polling place. He observed the young man removing an "I Voted red sticker" and overheard him give "a story about moving [and] waiting for his new drivers license in the mail for the last three months." The speed at which this young man then registered and filled out his ballot ("in less than 10 seconds") aroused Heath's suspicions even more. "Mr. Heath contends the gentleman voted 'too fast to be right,'" states the county attorney's letter explaining why prosecution could not go forward. Heath followed the young man out of the polling place, but "lost him" before he could get the man's license plate number. Given the lack of information about the alleged perpetrator and the fact that the prosecutor could find no law specifying a minimum time period a voter must take in completing a ballot, the case was closed.

Finally, five voters in a small farming community registered various complaints alleging abuse of absentee ballot and residency laws. A group of concerned citizens petitioned the secretary of state with complaints about several other voters they believed had moved into their community just before a local election in order to vote in favor of a multimillion-dollar school bond issue. The county attorney and county auditor investigated and found no wrong-doing; instead, they concluded that several absentee ballots were mistakenly given out on election day but then withdrawn and not counted once the problem was identified. In the whirl of activity at one polling place, a man whose residency was challenged by another voter was given the wrong form to fill out by an election judge, who later explained, "There were so many people, we were so busy at the time." The man was able to vote without confirming his residence (792 ballots were cast, and the bond issue passed by a margin of 106 votes). The prosecutor concluded there was no intent to rig the election and closed the matter.

A separate search of Lexis-Nexis news databases for Minnesota covering a six-year period from 1999 to 2005, turned up a similarly sparse record of individual voters committing fraud. There was one incident, however, that suggests how conspiracies to commit fraud are often not difficult to detect.

The case involved a conflict between Richard J. Jacobson of Prescott, Wisconsin, and the residents of the rural Minnesota town of Coates (population 163). Jacobson was the owner of Jake's Gentlemen's Club, a strip club in Coates which is located in Dakota County, about thirteen miles south of St. Paul. The building that housed the club at 15981 Clayton Avenue, a former bar, was painted hot pink, causing one reporter to remark that it looked "as out of place in Coates as a giant conch shell on a Minnesota beach."[12]

By 2002, the dispute with what the flamboyant thirty-two-year-old Jacobson called "a small town run amok, with a Nazi mayor and a bunch of sheep as councilmen" had dragged on for eleven years.[13] As soon as he had arrived to open his nude-dancing establishment, the town fathers passed a series of zoning, liquor, and other ordinances to regulate "sexually-explicit" establishments and put Jacobson out of business. Adult businesses were defined in the ordinances as including seminudity or full nudity, a cover charge, and the sale of beverages. To get around the regulations, Jacobson dropped his cover charge and made his patrons drink their "pop" in a parking lot across the street. He put up a tent and had the dancers strip under the big top instead of inside the club. Jacobson was a self-proclaimed "ordained minister," and he later told the press he had been considering calling Jake's a church and passing a collection plate instead of charging admission.[14]

A federal court soon ruled the adult business ordinance unconstitutional, so the town revised it in 1994, giving Jake's two more years to shut down. Jacobson appealed and was finally ordered again to shut the club down by May 2002. He complied, but re-opened a month later with bikini-clad dancers. On October 4, 2002, U.S. District Judge Donovan Frank upheld the revised town regulation of sexually explicit businesses and ordered Jake's closed. Jacobson was found in contempt for violating previous court orders, fined $68,000, and required to pay legal and other fees. The order included a provision that Jacobson pay his fine by certified check, and for good reason. The previous August, Jacobson had hired a truck driver to deliver two tons of pennies to the city council. Jacobson and some of his strippers dumped the 600,000 coins in a fit of pique at council members, who had won a court order mandating that Jacobson reimburse Coates $6,400 in legal fees. The town had to pay to collect the pennies and turn them in. Meanwhile, Jacobson used some of his profits from Jake's to open up another strip club, Fat Jack's Cabaret (rumored to be named after Coates Mayor Jack Gores) in neighboring Bock (population 105), where residents organized a vigil at the Lutheran church to pray for him to leave. As the townspeople prayed, eighty-nine voter registration cards, all bearing the same address for the applicants, 15981 Clayton Avenue, were dropped in the mail to the Dakota County auditor one day after Judge Frank's order. The address belonged to Jake's Gentlemen's Club.

Mayor Gores and two city council members who were strongly opposed to Jake's were up for reelection that year. They faced an unusually tight race. Tiny Coates cast just seventy-nine votes in the 2000 presidential election, and local officials usually had little trouble remembering every voter by name. Gores told a reporter he suspected something underhanded when his opponent, an ally of Jacobson's, started bragging about all the people backing him.[15] Carol Leonard, the Dakota County treasurer-auditor, said that her staff, too, became suspicious when the cards from 15981 Clayton Avenue came in. Coates was not known to have any apartment buildings. Police searched the premises of Jake's and found no beds or signs of residential occupation, but in Jacobson's car they did find thirty-nine blank voter registration forms, two completed applications, and a copy of the state law on voter eligibility. None of the first twenty-five people on the voter registration cards and interviewed in the police investigation lived in Coates. Jacobson's lawyer told the press that he saw no grounds for a violation. He said the county auditor was responsible for sending out notices to verify the legitimacy of voter registration applications. "It only becomes a crime," he opined, "if you vote after you receive the notice."

Jacobson was charged with felony conspiracy to commit forgery and with felony conspiracy to commit forgery for promoting a vote fraud scheme in which ninety-four other people, mostly employees and patrons of the nude dancing establishment, fraudulently registered to vote using Jake's Gentleman Club as their legal address. The matter was treated seriously because it seemed clear that Jacobson was trying to steal an election. Election administrators did their job and caught the fraud before he could do that, although we might concede the fraud was about as hard to miss as that hot pink building.

The indictment cast Jacobson's favored challengers under a cloud. Nearly the entire town (eighty-three of the eighty-six registered voters) showed up to vote for the incumbent mayor and the two city council members who had been most vocal about shutting down the club. "It's victory for the Constitution, a victory for the right to vote, a victory for this town," said Mike Bohn, owner of House of Coates, the town's only restaurant.[16] Todd Tubbs, one of the embattled councilmen winning reelection, said after the town's great victory he hoped that all the hoopla would die down. Two weeks before the election, he was in South Dakota, 300 miles from home, when someone recognized him in a restaurant. "They looked at me and said, 'I know you—you were on TV.' I told them who I was, and everyone piped up, 'Hey, look! We got a celebrity here!'" Tubbs was content and satisfied with the results. "This was democracy at its finest."[17]

None of the fraudulent registrants charged with felony forgery actually voted, so most were offered a deal to pay a $240 fine and plead guilty to a misdemeanor.[18] Several later claimed they had been duped and intimidated into signing the cards. Carol Finlay, a former Jake's dancer, told a reporter that she had initially refused to sign a false registration card but that later, at a meeting with five other dancers, the bar manager told them all to sign or lose their jobs.[19] Nineteen-year-old Rachel Auge said she was approached in a Wisconsin bar and asked to sign a card to keep Jake's open. "If I would have known that's what it was [a false voter registration card], I wouldn't have done it," she said.[20] In February 2004, the Eighth Circuit Court of Appeals overturned the ban on clothed lap dancing and Jacobson's fine, but left the ban on nude dancing in place.[21]

But this was not the end of the saga of Coates and the strip club impresario. Jacobson's legal troubles continued for another three years. He fought on, battling the charges and appealing decisions that prohibited him from using certain defenses, such as that he had received bad legal advice about what constituted a crime under the Minnesota election laws. In March 2007, Jacobson was vindicated on a technicality. A Dakota County jury found him not guilty of conspiracy to procure unlawful voting and conspiracy to commit forgery on the theory that, even though (as his new lawyer admitted) Jacobson masterminded a "cockamamie scheme" to have his patrons and employees vote illegally in Coates 2002 town election, he had a right to rely on the erroneous advice of his previous lawyer.[22] As the only egregious case of voter fraud that turned up in my research on Minnesota for the 1999 to 2005 period, the Jacobson case lends support to the argument of this book: that voter fraud is episodic and relatively rare; that organized voter fraud is not impossible to detect; and that individual voters, even when they are enmeshed in the schemes of partisans and others intent on corrupting the electoral process, can make mistakes that violate the rules because they do not fully understand registration and voting procedures.

New Hampshire: Attorney General's Office Investigation

Like Minnesota, New Hampshire permits its residents to register to vote on election day. And also like Minnesota, it has a sparse record of voter fraud.

Contacted by me in 2004, long-time New Hampshire Secretary of State William Gardner said, "we haven't had much fraud up here in New Hampshire" in the past thirty years. First elected in 1976 and continuously reelected by Democrats and Republicans in the state legislature to serve as the chief elections officer of the state, he would know. But in the important 2004 presidential election, New Hampshire officials "made a major effort" to enforce the election laws against fraud.[23] Were state officials spooked by the case of Mark Lacasse? The Lacasse incident is the only case of voter impersonation I have found in my intensive search of federal, state, and local records since 2000. But was the Lacasse incident really a case of voter impersonation?

The scene is Londonderry High School, January 27, 2004; the legendary New Hampshire presidential primary is underway. Lacasse, a seventeen-year-old honors student accompanied his teacher and classmates to the polling site located in his school to observe the voting process. The civic-minded teacher encouraged students to vote if they were eighteen years old. Lacasse took at least some of that advice to heart. He later lied to poll workers about his identity, claiming to be his father (who has the same name), so that he could vote his father's ballot. The father was away on business, and the son knew the father wanted to vote for George W. Bush (who was running unopposed). A teacher overheard the underage Lacasse admit to friends that he voted, saying he had "subbed" for his father. Lacasse's illegal voting was discovered after the teacher turned him in to an elections moderator. To avoid a felony charge, Lacasse agreed to serve eight hours of community service and make a speech to his class about voting.

Capitalizing on general fears of fraud, Republican opponents of the New Hampshire election day registration system have maintained a campaign to repeal it since it was adopted in 1994.[24] In the heat of the tight 2004 election, the Attorney General's Office thus undertook a broad investigation into whether voter fraud was a problem in New Hampshire. According to its report, "attorneys and investigators from the . . . [o]ffice and specially trained Deputy Sheriffs were either positioned at polling places or were traveling around the State checking polling places and responding when complaints were received."[25] Staff also set up and monitored a toll-free number to receive complaints and, after the election, met with concerned citizens who suspected fraud might have occurred on election day. The state legislature held a hearing at which several people testified about suspected fraud in the November election. Overall, the main concerns focused on election day registration, multiple voting, and voting by people who were not legally domiciled in New Hampshire. The biggest concerns came from places such as Keene and Dover, cities with large college populations. The Attorney General's Office actively encouraged people who had made complaints on election day and at the subsequent state hearing to submit any evidence of wrongful voting, but "only a very few of those raising concerns provided the Attorney General's Office with any information about their concerns."[26]

Each specific complaint or allegation that the attorney general could identify was investigated. This involved combing through a database of over 40,000 registration records, checklists, and copies of identity documents, a tedious examination of voting records and other "nonpublic information," cross-checks with the Department of Motor Vehicles as well as state and law enforcement agencies, and interviews with local election officials and the people under investigation. The records review resulted in follow-up investigations of approximately 240 people, most of whom had registered to vote on election day. This case of alleged double-voting in Keene is instructive.

> Based on testimony before the Election Law Committee that individuals were listed multiple times on checklists for the City of Keene, an investigation was conducted. It was established that while seven people with identical names, but different dates of birth and different addresses, had registered and voted in Keene on November 2, 2004, only one person was found to have his name listed on the checklist as having voted in two different wards in Keene. Based on interviews of the election officials and the voter it was determined that: 1) This individual reported to ward 4 to vote and was sent home to get identification when he was unable to prove his identity; 2) The individual is a local person who graduated from Keene High School, but is not a student at the college; 3) The individual had been licensed to drive in New Hampshire, but did not have his driver's license available for identification because of court action; 4) The individual returned to ward 4 with identification, registered and got almost all the way through the process when an election official determined that he was at the wrong polling place. Based on his residence, he was required to vote in ward 5. The voter registration form was voided, but his name was inadvertently not voided on the checklist. The individual was *not* allowed to vote in ward 4; 5) The individual went to ward 5 and lawfully registered and voted.[27]

In other words, the suspect was not a criminal; he was an eligible, registered voter who did not have his driver's license on him when he went to vote. He was also the victim of an election administration mistake.

In the end, all but six of the more than two hundred people investigated by the attorney general were found not to have committed fraud but were in fact legal New Hampshire voters. The suspect six were people who had provided false information when they either registered or voted. Four who registered to vote on election day provided recent but no longer accurate addresses on their registration forms. Three of these four still lived in New Hampshire and were prosecuted for providing a false address; by the time of the investigation, the fourth had moved to another state and an warrant was issued for his arrest. Of the remaining two, one was the young Mark Lacasse, who had "subbed" for his father in the January primary, and the other was a man who signed a nominating petition twice, once using his name and a second time using the name of a relative. Both of these individuals were caught and reprimanded. The attorney general found no evidence that anyone in New Hampshire voted more than once in an election in which more than 375,000 ballots were cast.

Oregon: State Election Division Records

Like California and a small number of other states, Oregon has a state-level agency that handles complaints or allegations of voter fraud. In Oregon, state-level monitoring is a consequence of the fact that Oregonians have chosen to vote by mail in all elections. To protect the process from fraud and shore up public confidence, state officials have developed procedures for checking the signature of every voter against registration records and have kept more detailed information on the nature and outcome of complaints than any other state I know of. Their record-keeping efforts go beyond those in California, Minnesota, or even New Hampshire. Signature-matching administrative requirements produce data useful in documenting evidence of the incidence of voter fraud because they produce records of local inquiries about the validity of voters' signatures and then channel those records into a central investigations unit inside the Secretary of State's Office where they are compiled and screened. Thus, the data made available to me by the Oregon secretary of state provide another source that might help us estimate the incidence of voter fraud. These data are particularly useful because the method of voting in Oregon—by mail—is one that is believed to be more vulnerable to fraud.

Oregon began experimenting with voting by mail more than twenty years before it became the first state in the nation to conduct a presidential election entirely by mail in 2000.[28] Turnout increased by 11 percent over the previous presidential election.[29] And, as we will see, evidence of voter fraud in Oregon is negligible, suggesting that with proper safeguards and ample time for voters to become accustomed to voting by mail this method of casting ballots can increase participation without sacrificing ballot security.[30]

Vote-by-mail got its start in Oregon in Linn County, a blue-collar area where turnout in local elections was dipping as low as 10 percent; the local elections clerk asked for permission to run an election by mail to try to increase electoral participation.[31] The Oregon legislature approved a test program in 1981, turnout in Linn doubled, and the legislature moved to make vote-by-mail permanent for local and special elections. The first vote-by-mail special statewide election was held in 1993, and another was held two years later. In response to the growing popularity of absentee voting—votes in all elections in Oregon increasingly were being cast absentee—the Republican-controlled legislature attempted to expand vote-by-mail to all elections but were blocked by the Democratic governor who wanted more study of the issue.[32]

A larger experiment in vote-by-mail sneaked in through the back door when a special election was called to replace Senator Bob Packwood who, after becoming embroiled in a sexual harassment scandal, had resigned from the U.S. Senate. The secretary of state in Oregon, not the governor or the legislature determines the format of any special election, and the Oregon secretary of state at the time was a strong supporter of vote-by-mail.[33] Oregon experienced another first in 1996, liberalizing its voting format by becoming the first state to conduct an election completely by mail in a statewide primary, and then in a statewide general election for federal office. Three more special elections conducted entirely by mail were held over the next two years, but the legislature resisted converting all elections to vote-by-mail. By May 1998, 41 percent of registered voters in Oregon were permanent absentee voters (Oregon has "no excuse" absentee balloting). Turnout plunged to 35 percent in the 1998 federal primary election, but two-thirds of all ballots cast were absentee and the turnout rate among absentee voters was double the turnout rate at the polls, demonstrating voter preference for the mail-in method of casting ballots. In November, voters bypassed legislative and executive resistance to vote-by-mail by overwhelmingly (69 percent) approving a ballot initiative to expand it to all elections in Oregon.[34] In the first federal primary election to be conducted entirely by mail, turnout in Oregon increased 16 percent, reversing a twenty-year trend in declining primary voting; the general election followed and 80 percent of registered voters mailed in their ballots.

Opponents of vote-by-mail system have expressed a number of concerns: the problem of buyer's remorse, the potential delay of election results, the loss of national community, and the possibility of voter intimidation and voter impersonation. Critics worry that early voters cast ballots without the full benefit of information about the candidates and issues that often comes out in the closing weeks of an election;[35] they also worry that the extra procedures involved in counting mail ballots could unacceptably delay reporting the outcome. They are concerned that what one critic called a "diffusion of mobilization" might contribute to the loss of national community that comes from all Americans voting on the same day.[36] Another critic, who brought an unsuccessful federal civil rights suit against the state of Oregon on grounds that the state's vote-by-mail system violated federal voting laws, worried about the opportunities for voter coercion and the loss of the secret ballot:

> [J]ust imagine the chicanery possible when a stack of mail ballots arrives at a nursing home, union hall or church. It wouldn't take long for "ballot parties" to be planned, where members of a group bring their ballots to the hall and "vote the right way" in return for a free meal, entertainment or other

rewards. Remember, with voting by mail, there is no more secret ballot, so the voter's current right to vote his or her conscience in the polling booth would be lost.[37]

And examples of coercion of vulnerable people living in group or nursing homes certainly suggest the possibility for abuse.[38] Moreover, some states permit political parties to handle absentee ballots in a variety of ways, including applying for absentee ballots on behalf of voters, picking up the ballots and delivering them to voters, and collecting ballots and mailing them or dropping them off on behalf of voters. It is easy to see why some may be concerned.

Thus, the most common complaint about early and absentee voting has to do with the opportunities it allegedly presents for fraud. John Fund, a critic of absentee balloting, makes the point succinctly: "Simply put, absentee voting makes it easier to commit election fraud, because the ballots are cast outside the supervision of election officials."[39]

The evidence of voter fraud since Oregon adopted vote-by-mail, however, is practically nonexistent. In 2000, before the state integrated its county registration lists under the mandate of the HAVA, the Republican Party claimed that 1,204 Oregon voters had registered in more than one county and had voted twice. But an investigation by the Secretary of State's Office found only a handful of people registered in two places and found none who had cast more than one ballot.[40] In November 2004, the Republicans said they found six voters who had cast ballots twice, and again, an investigation by the Secretary of State's Office found that only one person had cast two ballots but that second ballot was flagged by a computer scan and was not counted.[41]

Fraud detection begins at the local level with the clerks of thirty-six Oregon county boards of elections. The state maintains a vigorous signature-matching process for qualifying mail-in ballots. Approximately two and a half weeks before election day, local registrars mail ballots and instructions for returning them to all registered voters in their jurisdictions. Ballots that are undeliverable are returned to the county elections office by the post office; they are not forwarded to new addresses. Voters mark their ballots and place them in "secrecy" envelopes, which are then sealed in return envelopes that the voter signs. Ballots must be returned by mail to county election offices or delivered to special secure drop boxes established by the county registrars by 8 p.m. on election day. Teams of election workers verify each signature against computerized records of registered voters and pass to the county election clerk any ballots whose signatures do not match the files. Clerks review problem ballots for which they do not think signatures match and take a number of actions to challenge the voter and resolve the problems. If a signature is missing, the ballot is not counted; if there is enough time, it is sent back to the voter to sign, and if there is not enough time for the ballot to go out and come back by election day, election clerks call the voter to come to the office to sign the ballot. If a signature does not match the signature on file for the voter, the clerk may try to contact the voter to have the person come in to the office to re-sign the ballot in the presence of an election official. It is not uncommon for a person's signature to change over time, and many of the ballot signature-match problems appearing in the Oregon data indicate this to be the case. A signature for a voter who does not appear on the registration list is investigated by the clerk, who attempts to contact the voter or, if the voter's county can be determined, forwards the ballot to the appropriate county.

If the clerk determines that a voter has voted more than once, the voter is contacted; if fraud is suspected, the case is referred to the Secretary of State's Office for further investigation. Also, if the clerks get no response from voters notified of signature problems, county election clerks send the case to the Secretary of State's Office. The Election Division conducts an investigation. Officials send a letter of inquiry, and if they receive a reasonable explanation, they admonish and advise the voters to take steps such as re-signing their voter registration card to update their signature. If voters inform the Election Division that they voted their own ballot but allowed someone else (such as a spouse) to sign it, they are advised that this is not allowed and their ballot is not counted. If no response is received by the Election Division, officials send second and third inquiries via certified mail and attempt to call the voter. If there is still no response, the Election Division refers the case to the attorney general for prosecution, along with any other positive cases of potential fraud.[42]

Among the states, Oregon appears to have the best system for keeping records of election law complaints. State election officials also are willing to share this information with researchers. Complaints are channeled from county election officials up to the Secretary of State's Office and over to the attorney general for further investigation and, if warranted, prosecution. The Election Division of the Secretary of State's Office keeps investigation logs of all election law complaints, except for those stemming from alleged campaign finance violations. The logs record the case number; date received; complainant information; the county; a description of the allegation the state statute(s) allegedly violated; a coding scheme for identifying the type of allegation—a cross-statute classification system that reflects the fact that a complaint may involve violations of multiple laws, including laws that do not speak specifically to the nature of the corruption; whether the case alleges a civil or criminal violation; the date the case is closed; and a summary description of the case disposition, which is updated to reflect developments in the investigation and/or prosecution of a violation. All cases referred to the attorney general are reported back to the secretary of state so that the case records and logs can be updated and closed.

According to Norma Buckno, compliance specialist in the Elections Division, between 1991 to October 2006, there were 6,605 election law complaints (other than campaign finance report–related matters) filed with the Oregon Secretary of State's Office. "These include complaints involving general election laws (such as 'undue influence' and allegations of false statements in required election documents); candidates and political parties; conduct of elections; initiative, referendum and recall petitions; public employee restrictions on political campaigning; voter registrations; voters' pamphlet; and voting, ballot and polling place prohibitions."[43] Investigations into these 6,605 complaints found several hundred technical violations caused by administrative or voter error in which there was no criminal intent, but only fifteen people who were eventually criminally prosecuted for voter fraud (all pled or were found guilty)—an average of one criminal voter per year.

To conduct my analysis, I reviewed the Secretary of State's Office election law complaint logs for this period and extracted cases involving complaints or allegations of violations of the laws governing the registration and voting processes, excluding all others pertaining to political parties, candidates, initiative, referendum and recall petitions, the printing of sample ballots, electioneering and potential crimes that did not implicate voters. Only complaints regarding voter registration fraud committed by voters, "non-qualified" voting, violations of voting and polling place prohibitions, ballot signature problems, double-voting, and sale of the ballot were analyzed.

The problems the analyst confronts in estimating the incidence of fraud from the record of statutory violations of federal law, also are present even in the current best state systems for identifying voter fraud. Measurement of fraud depends on how statutes are constructed and applied. Precision is elusive. A general false swearing statute can be used in different ways to charge alleged violators with what we have defined as voter fraud, that is, knowingly and willfully falsely claiming voter eligibility. Double-voting may or may not implicate false swearing of eligibility on a registration card, so false swearing may or may not be charged, depending on the evidence and any of the variables that get sifted in the exercise of prosecutorial discretion. For example, a prosecutor might charge an egregious case with all possible violations but a first-time violator who votes more than once with only the lower-level crime of false swearing. In the latter case, the double-voting would not get picked up in an analysis that looked only at statutory violations.

After sorting through the records and categorizing the 6,605 cases of election law complaints to groups of cases related to intentional voter fraud registration and various forms of illegal voting (excluding, for example ballot referenda and initiative petitioning violations), I reviewed each individual case to distinguish potential violations of the law by voters from violations by all other sorts of perpetrators (candidates, voter registration workers, etc.) and from complaints by voters about registration or election procedures or reports of their own mistakes. The results are summarized in table 4.4.

TABLE 4.4
Oregon election law complaints: Allegations against voters and final status of complaint, 1994–2006

| | Final disposition | | | | |
| | | Violation found | | | |
Type of voter fraud[a]	No criminal violation found	Administrative action taken[b]	Convicted or pleaded guilty	Unknown	Total
Registration[c]					
False statement or swearing by voter on registration card	6	9	4	27	46
Noncitizen registration	4	4	1	0	9
Voting by mail					
"Non-qualified" voting	3	0	1	5	9
Ballot signature problem	2,625	1,616	15	473	4,729
Double voting	117	407	5	74	603
Sale of ballot	0	0	0	1	1
Miscellaneous prohibitions on voting (betting on election outcome, non-citizen voting, unqualified voter)	3	0	0	0	3
Total	2,758	2,036	26	580	5,400

Source: Oregon Secretary of State's Office, Elections Division, Salem, Ore.

Notes: Ms. Norma Buckno, compliance specialist, Elections Division of the Oregon Secretary of State's Office supplied the data presented here. In her letter of October 10, 2006, accompanying the data, Ms. Buckno notes that between 1991 and October 2006, there were 6,605 election law complaints filed with her office, covering a range of possible violations of laws contained in ORS Chapters 246–260, some classified as civil and some as criminal. This number includes non-voter fraud election-related violations such as initiative, referendum and recall petition violations not analyzed here. Moreover, the investigation logs provided by Ms. Buckno for violations related to voter fraud dated back only to 1994.

[a]*Type of voter fraud* refers to categories of violations associated with sections of Oregon's election code: "False statement of swearing by voter on registration card": ORS 247 and 260.715(4); "Non-qualified voting": ORS 260.695(4); "Ballot signature problem": ORS 260.715(1); "Double voting": ORS 260.715(3); "Sale of ballot": ORS 260.715(8); and "Miscellaneous prohibitions on voting and the balloting process": ORS 260.665, 260.635(2), 260.695(5) and 260.715(1).

[b]Determined to be voter or administrative error, with no intent to commit fraud. Administrative action usually consisted of sending the voter an admonishment letter, canceling a duplicate or erroneous voter registration record, or sending a new registration card so that the voter could update his or her signature.

[c]One case of voter registration fraud also involved double voting. The case was counted twice, in both categories as prosecuted (case #99–133). Also, two of the registration fraud cases are double counted as nonqualified voting; one is counted twice among "Unknown" (#2000–08) in both categories and the other among those convicted or pleaded guilty (#2003–432).

Several interesting findings stand out. First, there is a large number of requests on the part of county election officials for assistance from the Secretary of State's Office in verifying ballot signatures. Equally striking is the almost equally large number of requests for investigations by the Election Division that result in findings of no criminal intent. The logs reveal a number of common problems regarding voters who unintentionally but technically broke the law by allowing others to sign their ballot envelopes. Mostly these cases were not treated as criminal matters, and ballots with signatures that do not match registration records are not counted in Oregon. In case after case of this type, notes recorded by the Election Division staff indicate a variety of voter errors that likely resulted in voters forfeiting their ballots. For example, "wife signed as he had broken finger"; "let his parents sign, admonished, not prosecuted"; "said her father signed but she voted her own ballot"; "husband signed the ballot"; or "no violation found; signed the ballot envelope in the car on the lap."[44]

Early critics of vote-by-mail warned of the dangers of voter impersonation inherent in procedures that permit voters to fill out their ballots beyond the watchful eyes of election officials. Their fears appear to be unwarranted. Instead of ballot thievery and willful attempts to steal voters' identities or impersonate eligible voters, the data actually reveal how balloting procedures and the voting process itself shape the kinds of violations that can mar the process. Vote-by-mail systems work best with voters who are literate and are able to follow written instructions—much more so than traditional polling place systems. Thus, vote-by-mail systems are bound to experience some problems with voters who are not literate or who do not pay enough attention to the rules on how to fill out and sign a ballot. Therefore, we should expect a larger number of ballot signature problems in voting systems that require voters to sign their ballots before mailing them in than in systems in which the mode of voting takes some other form.

According to Oregon election officials, verifying the signatures of every ballot before that ballot is opened and counted helps prevent fraud better than most procedures used in polling place elections.[45] The record of prosecution of election law violations pertaining to voter fraud bears them out. The log of prosecuted criminal election law complaint cases for Oregon for the period 1991–2006 records just fifteen cases of voter fraud. Appendix 6 describes these cases (see table A6.1) and the ten cases of alleged fraud involving noncitizens (see table A6.2) forwarded to the Election Division over the same fifteen-year period.[46]

The rigorous Oregon signature-matching procedures are key to the success of vote-by-mail. County registrars go to great lengths to run a flawless verification operation because they know the state is under a microscope and that ballot security is of utmost concern. Moreover, the Oregon Secretary of State's Office believes that, due to the frequency of elections in

Oregon, where referenda and ballot initiatives proliferate, the state has the cleanest registration lists in the country. Because voters receive three or four nonforwardable ballots a year, they are forced to keep their registration current and the county boards of elections are forced to clean the rolls.[47]

Chapter 5

Would the Rational Voter Commit Fraud?

Our working definition of *voter fraud* combines the legalistic concept of criminal fraud with the idea that the context is controlling in tying the meaning of *voter fraud* to the stages of the electoral process exposed to voters. If voter fraud is a crime, the next question is: What is the motive for committing it? If we understand why voters might be motivated to commit voter fraud, we can anticipate the behavior and design procedures that protect the voting process against it.

Rational Choice Models of Voting

Rational choice theorists ask why people decide to vote or not to vote. The individual decision-making process is central to rational choice concerns, although the theory of voting developed from this perspective does not purport to predict why any one particular individual will vote or not. Rather, it offers us a perspective that presumes people think before they act and that human action can be understood as a response to incentives that outweigh the known or knowable costs of acting. The theory predicts that voters will choose to vote after they estimate the benefits and costs of going to the polls and perceive the benefits to be of greater value.[1]

Rational choice models of voting continue to fascinate political scientists. The calculus of voting model appeared in the 1950s and presented researchers with a problem that they have been grappling with ever since: it predicted no rational person would vote.[2] The early models of "economic voting" were based on the following reasoning. Let R equal the reward in "utiles" (a unit of utility) that an individual voter receives from his or her act of voting; let B equal the differential benefit in utility that an individual voter receives from the success of his or her more preferred candidate over the less preferred one; and let P equal the probability that the citizen will, by voting, bring about the benefit B. Probability is calculated as a positive value between zero and one, $0 \leq P \geq 1$. Let C equal the cost to the individual of the act of voting. The basic or Downsian economic model of voting is:

$$R = (BP) - C \qquad (1)$$

A rational voter will vote if the benefit received by voting for the winner as a product of the probability that the voter will receive the benefit is greater than the opportunity costs of voting. If the reward from the act of voting (R) is less than or equal to zero, it is irrational to vote. As the number of voters participating in an election increases, the probability that any one voter will receive a benefit from voting for the winner decreases. More recent research estimating the probability that any one vote in a national presidential election will "matter" in this way estimates the odds at one in ten million.[3] The smaller the probability, the larger the benefit must be if the reward from the act of voting is going to be positive because the cost, even if small, is always larger than zero.

Anthony Downs calculated the benefit of voting for the winner (B) as the expected utility ($E(U)$) of voting for Candidate 1 for a particular time period over the expected utility of voting for Candidate 2 over the same time period, where Candidate 1 was the preferred candidate:

$$B_i = E(U^1_{t+1})_i - E(U^2_{t+1})_i \qquad (2)$$

The benefit is always positive because the expected utility of the favored candidate is, by definition, larger than the expected utility of the disfavored one.

The problem with these initial theories centers on the inclusion in the basic model of a probability term to represent the rational part of the decision-making process. That is to say, the calculus that rational people use to decide whether to act does not simply add and subtract estimated benefits and costs but evaluates the estimated benefits as a product of the likelihood that the action will actually bring that benefit about. Borrowing heavily from neoclassical economic theories of human nature, rational choice theory presumes that people are hardwired to seek the highest possible return from their decisions and actions. They think about whether to act in terms of the consequences of their actions, and they decide whether to act by evaluating the likely returns on their investment. This means that the individual decision to vote is not simply an estimation of costs and benefits—voters will also think about the probability of their vote being decisive in the election and calculate the benefits that will accrue to them by voting for the winner as a product of the probability that their one vote will "matter." Otherwise, why bother? If the probability of influencing the outcome is zero, so, too, will be the benefits; and because there are always opportunity costs to acting, rational people will do the math and stay home.[4]

Fifty years of thinking about the paradox of rational choice models of voting have produced a voluminous literature on voting, elections, and political behavior. I do not take up a critical review of that literature here, except to acknowledge that researchers have amended the model in several important ways that have improved it and that they continue to test its validity with real-world data.[5] Some are satisfied that we can keep the basic assumptions of the formal rational choice model of voting and improve on the conceptualization and measurements of the benefit, cost, probability, and reward terms of the equation to produce better predictions of the conditions under which people will decide to vote. The most important revisions of the basic model partition the benefit term (B) into two portions: one that is instrumental and directly dependent on the person voting for the winner, and the rest, which is usually described in terms of psychic gratification that is independent of the individual voter's instrumental decision to vote and his or her vote choice. We can think of the former as an "investment" benefit that accrues only if the voter engages in the act of voting and votes for the winner and of the latter as a "consumption" benefit that accrues to the voter from the simple act of voting. William Riker and Peter Ordeshook label consumption benefits D.[6] In most accounts, the positive effects of D are summarized as "satisfaction"—satisfaction with complying with one's ethics if one is raised with an ethic of civic participation, with affirming allegiance to the political system, with affirming a partisan preference and standing up for one's belief in the preferred candidate and what he or she stands for, and with affirming one's efficacy in the political system.[7] Consumption benefits can be individual or particularistic benefits of this sort, or as Carole Uhlaner, Rebecca Morton, and others argue, voters also may be motivated by their participation in or identification with a group whose goals are indirectly related to the individual or investment benefit that the voter expects.[8] In other words, individuals can be motivated to overcome the costs of voting (which, even if small, almost always outweigh the individual benefits that a voter expects from voting for the winner) by the consumption benefits he or she anticipates as a member of a group mobilizing its stake in an election.

These considerations revise the original Downsian formula with the addition of the D term:

$$R = (BP) - C + D \qquad (3)$$

Note, $R = D$ when $(BP) = C$; that is, when the costs of the act of voting equal the product of the benefits of voting for the winner and the probability of bringing about that benefit by voting, the reward is simply the satisfaction that comes from exercising the right to vote. Most of the time we disregard the benefits of voting for the winner and the probability of bringing about the benefits by voting (B and P) because they are tiny when the electorate is large; this suggests that the calculus for voting is different depending on the jurisdiction, office, type of election, and turnout. Where those factors produce small electorates, the calculus of voting changes and BP is more likely to be larger than usual because P is higher; in other words, in certain types of elections BP is an effective incentive to vote.

But problems abound because turnout is usually higher, not lower, in elections with larger electorates. Moreover, these formulations verge on tautology because just about any rationale can be used to explain the decision to vote, and models that explain everything explain little. There have been several other important amendments to the rational choice or calculus of voting models aimed at eliminating the tendency toward tautology; I draw no conclusions of my own here about how successful these revisions are. Instead, given the powerful influence of rational choice theory on the study of voting behavior, I accept the basic model as revised to include a consumption benefit and ask: If it is ever rational to vote, under what conditions is it rational to commit a felony to vote?

A Rational Choice Model of Voter Fraud

Let us examine the rational choice voter model in the context of the two basic forms of voter fraud: (1) illegal voting that results in what sometimes is called overvoting (the casting of or attempt to cast multiple ballots by a single voter), and (2) vote buying and selling. First, *overvoting* is the term popularized by the various ways that voters in 2000 presidential election in Florida accidentally marked more than one vote choice or made multiple markings for the same candidate, disqualifying their ballots. In the context of voter fraud, illegal votes are a kind of overvoting because they attempt to register votes that should not be counted. Fraudulent overvoting results from various illegal forms of multiple voting, voting by ineligibles, and impersonating legal voters.

Using a calculus of voting logic to model illegal overvoting and vote selling requires we adjust the parameters in different ways. We can guess that the individual or investment benefits of casting a fraudulent or second ballot are probably higher than they might be for the first (legal) vote cast, especially if the voter is to receive money for committing the crime.[9] But even if no exchange of money is involved, a rational person willing to subvert the security controls over the voting process in order to cast a fraudulent ballot may be motivated by a more intense feeling of loyalty to his or her candidate, party, or cause. Both the B and D terms, his or her investment and consumption benefits, might be represented by higher values than they would be for the average legal voter casting only one ballot. For the rational voter casting an illegal second or multiple ballot, the probability of that vote's influencing the outcome of an election is also incrementally higher than it would be for the average legal voter if we assume the second or multiple ballots are cast for the same candidate as the first legal one. The probability of one illegal vote, such as one cast by an ineligible voter—a person who is not a U.S. citizen who has a felony conviction in a state disqualifying ex-felons from voting, or who is not properly registered to vote in a local jurisdiction—being decisive is the same as it is for one legal vote. But the probability of two or more illegal ballots being decisive in an election must be more than the probability for one. Although the benefits and probabilities for casting decisive votes in the calculus of illegal overvoting and illegal vote selling might take different values in the rational voter model, we can nevertheless assume that, for both, the *BP* term is likely to be higher than it is for the legal voter casting one vote. In other words, if the cost of casting an illegal vote is the same as the cost of casting a legal vote, it is probably more rational to cast an illegal vote.

But we know that the cost of casting an illegal vote is higher. What distinguishes illegal voting from legal voting in the calculus of voting is *C*, the opportunity cost of voting. Although the benefits of illegal voting may be higher than the benefits of legal voting, the cost of casting an illegal vote is exponentially higher because illegal voting is treated as criminal behavior by statute and is, in every state, punishable by prison sentences, monetary fines, and deportation for those who are not citizens. The cost of casting an illegal vote can be partitioned into two segments. The first is equivalent to the opportunity cost of casting a legal vote, so we will continue to call it *C*. The second part of the cost, C_f, is composed of the criminal penalties for illegal voting and the public shaming that comes from being convicted of a crime. So the total cost for casting an illegal vote is $C + C_f$. A rational illegal voter, however, might also consider the probability of getting caught. C_f, therefore, should be multiplied by the probability, P_c, to reflect the rationality of committing a criminal act. The new total cost for casting an illegal vote is $C + C_f P_c$, and the model for estimating the various forms of illegal overvoting and vote selling is:

$$R_f = (B_f P_f) - (C + C_f P_c) + D \qquad (4)$$

where R_f is the reward for casting an illegal vote, B_f is the investment benefit that the illegal voter enjoys in casting an illegal vote for his or her preferred candidate, P_f is the probability that the illegal vote will be decisive, C is the opportunity cost of voting, C_f is the consumption cost or penalty for casting an illegal vote, and P_c is the probability that cost will be imposed. Despite the logic we have noted that the illegal voter's motivation to take on risk to cast an illegal vote could inflate his consumption benefit (*D*), in the calculus of illegal voting there are other reasons why we should zero it out (the term is left in eq. 4 for consistency with eq. 3). The consumption benefit of voting has been defined in a number of ways, but the general idea is that it reflects something like satisfaction in performing one's civic duty or in fulfilling one's moral obligation in a democracy. What might the consumption benefit be for breaking a rule or committing a crime? If the illegal vote changed the outcome of the election, the person who cast it might feel good about taking the risk, but he or she also might be afflicted with guilt. Either way, we cannot conceptualize D in the same way. The rule of law is a central feature of any democracy, and violators bear a psychic penalty, the opposite of something like the satisfaction gained from conforming to social norms by voting. If it is ever individually rational to vote, it is individually rational to commit a crime to vote only if the investment benefits are higher than the costs.

Here is where those who think that there is a lot of voter fraud in elections today make their best case. They agree with the assumptions of the rational choice model of illegal voting that I have sketched here—that for some people the potential benefits and the probability of influencing the outcome of an election are higher than they are for legal voting. This reflects the notion that rule-breaking is motivated behavior. But they insist the costs are not real costs unless they are actually imposed and that the probability of those costs being imposed is next to zero. This is what they mean when they assert that voter fraud crimes are not investigated by the authorities.[10] If the cost of illegal voting is calculated only when it is multiplied by the probability that it will be imposed and the probability that it will be imposed is negligible, the rewards and therefore the incentives for illegal voting go up and the motives for some are intensified.

If we include a cost probability term in the calculus of committing voter fraud, there is no evidence to suggest that probability term itself will be so small that it will cancel out the actual cost of fraudulent voting. In the final calculus, the costs of committing voter fraud will far outweigh the benefits that might accrue to the individual voter. Let us throw some numbers into the equations to see how this might work. The numbers are meaningless except to show how the same rational thinking that might lead a person to vote would also cause him or her to avoid casting an illegal vote.

Assume that the value for the reward gained by voting ranges from zero to one ($0 \leq R \leq 1$) and that for our purposes $R = 1$. We use a familiar formulation from equation 3, in which the total benefit as a product of the voter's investment benefit and the probability that by voting the person will bring it about (BP) is equal to the opportunity cost of voting (C). It is rational to vote if there is any consumption benefit (D) to be gained.

$$R = (BP) - C + D \qquad (5)$$

We can substitute the following arbitrary values: $B = 2$; $P = 1$; $C = 2$; and $D = 1$. Then $R = (2 \times 1) - 2 + 1$, or $R = 1$. For illegal voting (R_f; see eq. 4), I have argued that $B_f > B$, $P_f > P$, $(C + C_f P_c) > C$, and $D_f = 0$. Again, for the sake of the presentation, we assign arbitrary values: $B_f = 2.5$, $P_f = 1.5$, $C = 2$,

$C_f = 2$, $P_c = 1$, and $D = 0$. Under these modest terms, the calculus of illegal voting suggests it is irrational for the average voter to cast an illegal ballot; $R_f = (2.5 \times 1.5) - [2 + (2 \times 1)] + D$, or $R_f = -0.25$.

When it may be rational to vote, for the individual voter who is the object of our inquiry, it will almost always be irrational to cast an illegal vote.

The Logic of Making Voter Fraud Claims versus Committing Fraud

In chapter 1, I discussed the difference between the act of committing voter fraud and a spurious allegation that voter fraud has been committed. Simple enough. But there is also a way in which the two are similar. So far in this chapter, I have argued for a more analytically rigorous, reasonable, and straightforward definition of *voter fraud* as a crime and used a rational choice framework to examine under what conditions the average voter might be motivated to commit it. But what about allegations of voter fraud? What should we make of them? If it is so unlikely that the average voter would be motivated to commit a crime to vote, why all the fuss? In the absence of evidence that any fraud has been committed, the allegations themselves are political acts (see chap. 6), just as the act of committing voter fraud is a political act. And as political acts, how might the logic of rational choice apply to these allegations?

Let us substitute a collective partisan interest for the individual voter and work through the logic of making an allegation of fraud versus committing the act itself. Fraud allegations, after all, are made in the context of elections, just as votes are cast to influence electoral outcomes (they are not cast simply to be cast). Voter fraud allegations are motivated acts, like voting, and here we assume they are motivated to influence the outcome of an election.

We could argue that this assumption is wrong, that spurious allegations of fraud are not all political acts or that, when they are made by other than losing candidates, they are nonpartisan efforts to influence election administrators or to influence public opinion to build public support for new electoral rules needed to curb fraud. But there are good reasons for rejecting this hypothesis. At least in recent national elections, allegations of voter fraud have been made by the supporters, partisans, and operatives of only one party while being denied by the other (see chap. 1). They have been made in defiance of the views, claims, and explanatory statements of election administrators, who deny that the irregularities forming the basis of the allegations are caused by fraud. And they have been made in conjunction with arguments in favor of new voter identification rules that are likely to burden some voters more than others. It defies the obvious to claim that the voter fraud allegations of the past several election cycles are the cry of nonpartisan reformers concerned about ballot security.

To examine the political logic of making voter fraud allegations, we do not have to specify which party or candidate is supported by the partisan interest, only that one party or candidate is favored over the other, just as we do when we analyze the calculus of voting for the individual voter—we assume that the voter is deciding to vote for a preferred candidate and that the desire to express a vote choice is the same as the desire to vote. For a partisan interest to receive a reward (R_p) from the act of alleging fraud, the benefits must be greater than the costs. Let B_p equal the differential benefit in utility that a partisan interest receives from the success of its more preferred candidate over its less preferred one; let P_p equal the probability that the partisan interest will, by making the allegation, bring about the benefit, B_p; and let C_p equal the opportunity cost to the partisan interest of making the allegation. The same Downsian equation 1 then applies.

What distinguishes this calculus of influence from the individual voter's calculus of voting is the conceptualization and estimation of the probability term, P_p. For the voter, the probability of his or her vote determining the outcome of the election is trivial, diminishing indirectly with the size of the electorate. For the partisan interest, the size of the electorate probably works in the same way, but the electoral arena in which the allegations are made— public opinion, influence with the media, popular notions or understandings about electoral integrity, and the securing of election machinery and procedures—is different (for the voter, the electoral arena in which he or she acts is the electorate). Thus, for the partisan interest, the context for estimating the likelihood that its behavior will bring about the desired benefit is also different. Unlike voters, partisan interests making allegations of voter fraud can influence electoral outcomes only indirectly through their influence on ideas, the media, and even policymaking. They are not casting ballots so much as they are seeking to influence whether ballots get cast. The inputs into rational decision making about when, where, and how to make fraud allegations are different from those going into the individual decision to vote.

What about B_p, the benefit term? In our rational voter model, recall that B was partitioned in two, with one part an instrumental "investment" benefit quantity and the other a "consumption" benefit independent of any instrumental value (D). But because partisan interests reflect collective rather than individual behavior, the calculus of influence benefit to be derived from the act of making fraud allegations is purely instrumental. There is no state of mind we can investigate when we analyze group rather than individual behavior. Therefore, something like a consumption benefit, which Riker and Ordeshook cast as psychic gratification, does not exist for a group. There is no need, then, to factor in a D term; the benefits should be estimated for their instrumental value given the group's interest in influencing the victory of one candidate or one party over the other.

What is the opportunity cost C to a partisan interest for making a voter fraud allegation? It is hard to see how it could be very high. It is not illegal to allege voter fraud without showing any evidence that it exists. There are no fines or penalties from regulatory agencies to worry about. To spread the idea that voter fraud is a serious problem, an organization can send out a press release, hold a press conference, or prepare testimony for a congressional hearing, activities that require resources but that are usually factored into the routine business of organizations that want to influence public opinion or decision makers. Or, if you are the Republican Policy Committee of the U.S. Senate, you just issue a report stating that voter fraud is out of control.[11] If we use our examples from chapter 1, John Fund's book *Stealing Elections*, or the report of the ACVR (all of which we have shown to be full of misleading statements, anecdotal evidence, and factual inaccuracies), we might try to calculate the costs of producing those documents. I have no information about Fund's financing, but we do know from Internal Revenue Service (IRS) filings that the ACVR raised $903,902 in 2005 and spent $944 on "research," a pittance in comparison to the organization's other expenses, most of them hundreds of thousands of dollars in fees to Republican-connected law firms and political consultants.[12] For this organization, at least, the opportunity costs for misleading the public were negligible.

Thus, unlike the calculus of illegal voting, which suggests that the benefits of committing voter fraud for the rational voter will be largely abstract or emotional (because the costs and the infinitesimal probability of affecting electoral outcomes wipe out any instrumental benefits to be gained by committing this crime), the benefits to a partisan interest group of alleging voter fraud where none exists are quite likely to be positive and instrumental.

Chapter 6

The Political Work
of Fraud Allegations

In this chapter, I develop a theory about partisan voter fraud allegations and about why they are effective; I then test the theory using material drawn from four case studies of voter fraud politics.

The Strategic Uses of Voter Fraud Allegations

In the debates over the extent of fraud in the late nineteenth century, Peter Argersinger argued that a focus on the incidence of fraud is misplaced. "And while [a claim of] 'massive fraud' injects distortion into any analysis," he noted, "the reality of election fraud [in the Gilded Age] was its *strategic* not *massive* nature."[1]

Gary Cox and J. Morgan Kousser extend Argersinger's insight to examine how partisans as rational actors decide not only to break the rules, but how to break the rules. In an illuminating study of rural corruption and election fraud from the late nineteenth and early twentieth centuries, Cox and Kousser suggest that electoral laws governing the voting and vote-counting processes influence the strategic alternatives and therefore the form of fraud deployed by partisans to win elections.[2] Specifically, drawing on a case study of the impact of the secret ballot on rural election fraud in New York State, they hypothesize that the method by which fraud is committed reflects changing opportunities yielded by modifications in rules and regulations imposed to protect against fraud. They analyze turnout data and accounts of fraudulent electoral practices recorded in a variety of newspapers and find that the adoption of the secret ballot in New York in 1890 caused a change in the methodology of rural fraud. Once voters could protect their ballots from the prying eyes of party agents, who were no longer assured that they were getting what they paid for, the methodology of fraud shifted from "inflationary" forms such as vote buying, to "deflationary" forms of vote suppression, such as paying people to stay home.

Factors Affecting Politically Motivated Uses of Fraud Allegations

Today, after four decades of electoral reforms that have lowered barriers to the vote and weakened the power of parties to manage the electoral process, some of the strategic opportunities of the kind identified by Cox and Kousser have dried up. Within this environment of shrunken opportunity, the use of spurious fraud allegations to contest election outcomes and promote the erection of new rules, such as more stringent voter identification requirements that aim to reduce voting among marginal voters, take on greater weight. Opportunities to deploy fraud allegations are shaped by three factors: institutional electoral arrangements, electoral competitiveness, and what Argersinger called an "indulgent" political culture. I add to Argersinger's list the existence of marginalized subjects within the political culture whose presence alone stands in as the evidence of the alleged fraud. Let us consider each in turn.

Electoral arrangements are institutionalized in the party system and in election law. The incentive structure in a two-party plurality system influences the dynamics of electoral competition, which in turn, presents the candidates, parties, and campaigns with options for choosing whether to stimulate turnout among supporters, demobilize the opposition's voters, or do both. As we argue in *Keeping Down the Black Vote*, suppressing the opposition's votes is often a more attractive strategy than mobilizing new voters. This is because vote suppression leaves a party's electoral coalition intact, whereas mobilizing new voters can destabilize the coalition by incorporating new groups that usually come with new demands that may be at odds with those already in the coalition.[3] Because the winner in a two-party plurality system needs only one vote more than the loser, the smaller the margin between the two candidates the greater the strategic incentive for the loser to shift just enough votes to win. In other words, tight elections produce the biggest pay-off for the smallest shifts in vote share. The value of any one vote increases when elections are close, and winner-take-all rules heighten the effect. Where 50.5 percent of the vote wins 100 percent of the representation, criminal conspiratorial behavior to fraudulently capture even just a small number of votes may appear rational. These are the conditions under which politically motivated allegations of voter fraud are most likely to succeed in influencing electoral contests or electoral policy.

But there is more than this to the strategic use of allegations. The mid-twentieth-century civil rights movement shattered the old order of racial and political subordination and ushered in a new regime of electoral rules.

By doing so, it created a new challenge—the incorporation of millions of African American voters into the party system. The Democrats hesitantly moved toward blacks, and as they did, the Republicans seized the opportunity to capitalize on the antagonism toward blacks among some of the Democratic Party base. Party elites on the Republican side understood the problems that the changing racial dynamics of the civil rights and post–civil rights era inflicted on their opponents. To take advantage of emerging strategic opportunities, Republican Party elites have long cultivated a politics of resentment to mobilize whites, including those defecting from the Democratic Party, into Republican ranks.

A new partisan realignment, most evident in the sectional realignment of the South, unfolded gradually within an emerging arena of election law, where more democratic rules came to govern the game. The new rules were enshrined in the Voting Rights Act of 1965 and the Twenty-Fourth Amendment, which outlawed the poll tax.[4] Together they opened up the U.S. electoral system to wider participation, making the long-relied-on methods of racial discrimination in electoral politics illegal, and more firmly embedding the doctrines of free and fair elections in U.S. law. Since the great victories of the civil rights movement, it has no longer been easy or acceptable to suppress voting through the use of terrorism or violence, or with poll taxes or literacy tests.

Enforcement of what we might call the voting rights rules regime (and what others have called the Second Reconstruction[5]) has eliminated some of the crudest forms of vote suppression, but it has not removed other long-standing opportunities for suppressing the vote through legal means, namely the opportunities embedded in the complexity of state election laws erected ostensibly to prevent voter fraud. Instead, it has privileged these means. Today, vote-suppression strategies are pursued through subtle forms of intimidation and obstruction that take on the mantle of law and order. The strategy involves exaggerating the fraud threat to justify the complexity of the electoral system, a complexity created and compounded by the layering of more and more rules to deter fraud. The more complex the electoral rules, the more difficult they are to implement and enforce, and the more likely the occurrence of inadvertent or technical violations by the weakest links in the overly bureaucratized machinery of the electoral system: the poll workers, administrative clerks, and voters. Given the number of poll workers, administrative clerks, and voters there are in any given statewide or federal election, and given the increasing complexity of election rules, technical violations are simply inevitable.

The voting rights rules regime has been constructed from the wreckage of a electoral and administrative system that legally stripped blacks of the right to vote, subordinating them to second-class citizenship. Administrative complexities justified as race-neutral necessities for deterring voter fraud are also opportunities for administrative error that have come to replace opportunities for vote suppression by other means. This is the context for the proliferation of unsupported fraud allegations today. The allegations shrewdly veil a political strategy for winning elections by tamping down turnout among socially subordinate groups. It is the most vulnerable voters, those with the least education or the least experience in operating the machinery of the electoral process, that are most in need of the simplest rules and the easiest access. Thus, it is these voters who stand in for the criminal voters conjured up by spurious voter fraud allegations and imagined by the U.S. cultural myth of voter fraud.

Partisanship and Suppression

Marginalized Americans—racial minorities, immigrants, and lower-income groups—are strongly identified with the Democratic Party. New research on the social bases of partisanship locates the sources of political party attachment in the social group imagery associated with the parties and outside rational or programmatic evaluations of policy positions. Donald Green, Bradley Palmquist, and Eric Schickler, for example, argue that partisanship is a genuine form of social group identification:

> Social identification involves comparing a judgment about oneself with one's perception of a social group. As people reflect on whether they are Democrats or Republicans (or neither), they call to mind some mental image, or stereotype, of what these sorts of people are like and square these images with their own self-conceptions. In effect, people ask themselves two questions: What kinds of social groups come to mind as I think about Democrats, Republicans, and Independents? Which assemblage of groups (if any) best describes me?[6]

Thus, the inclusion of African Americans, Latinos, and other socially subordinate groups, or "discordant" voters (as Richard McCormick might have put it),[7] in the base of the Democratic Party has meshed with Republican efforts to tar the Democrats with politically motivated fraud allegations in order to suppress the votes of their most vulnerable voters.

This represents a substantial revision of the Southern strategy. Republicans once manipulated white distaste of blacks by tarring Democrats as being concerned mainly with "black" issues such as affirmative action, welfare, and liberal criminal justice policies. But the success of the Republican Party (with help from some Democrats) in reducing the salience of these issues by eliminating the programs and reversing the policies that supported the Great Society agenda has weakened the effectiveness of the electoral strategy that brought them to power in the first place. Racial peace inside the Democratic Party has created new challenges for the Republican Party as well.

In search of a new electoral strategy to keep them in power, Republicans operatives resorted to tapping into cultural myths about voter fraud. Invoking fraud, this new Southern strategy plays on both the historical memory of Southern Democratic Party corruption after the Civil War and also on big-city political machine vote stealing. If the blogosphere is any indication, the reddest base of the Republican Party has been energized by the tarring of Democrats as cheaters and the association of Democrats with a racialized crime-prone underclass.

Voter fraud allegations thus work for a variety of reasons. They are a kind of culturally produced and indulged code. They announce to the players that the team is on the field and then signal the play. They lay out the path to victory by justifying tactics such as voter caging and challenging strategies and by requiring specific forms of voter identification that are meant to discourage voting among the opposing teams' players. As code, the strategic use of voter fraud allegations is well understood by the partisan elites who deploy them. For the public at large, they function as myth and therefore do not have to be proven to be accepted. They justify a "legitimate state interest" in measures to ensure "ballot security" against potentially criminal voters. The allegations are effective because they encode deeper unresolved conflicts about the myth of democracy in the United States.

Myth as Ideology

We live by myths. They challenge the explanatory power of facts and are a convenient, even comforting replacement for a lack of knowledge about how the real world works. Stories about who we are, where we come from, and why we do what we do structure everyday life in hidden ways. Claude Lévi-Strauss writes that we create myths to make sense of the random and chaotic data of life and nature.[8] He argues all myths have an elementary structure of binary opposition and are extensions of the nature of human intelligence that forces the data of life into dualisms resolved only by the emergence of new contradictions. "We are split creatures literally by nature," writes Wendy Doniger, summarizing Lévi-Strauss's view, "and we organize data like a simple digital machine. Our common sense is binary; the simplest and most efficient way to process experience seems to be by dividing it in half, and then to divide the halves in half, reformulating every question so that there are only two possible answers to it, yes or no."[9] Myths find unity in opposing dualities. If Lévi-Strauss is correct, they are powerful because they give meaning to human beings in ways that mirror the workings of the human mind.

Americans, like all people always, make myths about themselves, and one of the more powerful of these is the myth of American democracy. Following Lévi-Strauss, we can break that myth down into its opposing elements, its competing celebratory and cautionary narratives. One glorifies U.S. origins, individual freedoms, and "our most fundamental right, the right to vote."[10] U.S. exceptionalism extols the Constitution as a work of genius that ushered on to the historical stage a new age of freedom and equality. Indeed, in its telling and ritual retelling, the celebratory story takes on the luster of divine right. This is a purity myth like those that prop up the idea of a city on a hill or a chosen people or white supremacy.

Its binary opposite is a myth of pollution, of the corrosion and corruption that comes from without and threatens the chosen people's democracy. Our democracy is pure and therefore sacred precisely because it self-consciously excludes the impure, those lacking in qualities deemed necessary to the enjoyment of the privilege of citizenship, of being an American. Thus, democracy is reconciled with exclusion, and the contradictions between the real and the ideal are obscured.

As myth, the story of American democracy sifts, rearranges, condenses, and omits our actual, complex, and heterogeneous experience, weaving the sweep of history into a simple tapestry of good and evil, the pure and the corrupt. It is a religious myth, zealously guarded. It grips the popular mind and will continue to do so for as long as the democratic promise of equality, inclusion, and social justice is unfulfilled. It reorganizes the complex and tension-filled politics of an imperfect democracy into the categories of the sacred and the profane. And in so doing, it imposes order on some of the most fundamental contradictions of American democracy, a constitutional democracy forged through the conquest and genocide of native peoples, the contradictions of freedom and slavery sanctioned by the Constitution and chiseled into the tablets of U.S. law, and the contradictions of equality and a continuing disfiguring racism. Only the fulfillment of American ideals, when the ideal and the real actually become one, can displace the myth of American democracy, and then we will awake from a dream—or nightmare, depending on which part of the binary myth you believe.

In the celebratory story that finds democracy in a parchment encased in glass, there is no room for the actual struggles for inclusion, justice, and equality by people who have been shut out. The celebratory myth is always threatening to erase the troubled history of democracy's unfolding, even as struggles for inclusion continue under the blind eyes of the enfranchised and the entitled today. If certain people were not deemed worthy by the framers and, therefore, are not reflected as equal citizens in the intelligent design of their Constitution, what makes them truly worthy now? By promoting a sanitized version of the country's origins that justifies forms of political exclusion, the myth of American democracy is "ideology in narrative form."[11]

The myth of voter fraud succeeds in its political work when it taps into this larger framework of mythmaking. Even though it is no longer acceptable to voice the view that certain people among one's fellow citizens do not deserve to vote, many ordinary Americans do in fact share this idea and can take comfort from the fact that some elites do, too. For example, disdain for the inept lower classes was evident in a well-publicized comment by Justice Sandra Day O'Connor, blurted out during oral argument in the *Bush v. Gore* case that determined the winner of the 2000 presidential election. The justices asked respondent's lawyers what the standard should be for identifying the intent of Florida voters who failed to completely punch out their ballot chads. O'Connor quickly became exasperated. As one of the lawyers laboring below her gaze began an explanation of the painstaking process involved in accurately counting ballots, O'Connor cut him off and griped, "Well, why isn't the standard the one that voters are instructed to follow, for goodness sakes? I mean, it couldn't be clearer."[12] In other words, "it couldn't be clearer" that inept voters with their dimpled and hanging chads do not deserve to have their votes counted, even where state law provides for it.[13] The incredulity that a ballot not properly marked for reading by a machine could possibly be a legal vote is echoed in Chief Justice William Rehnquist's concurring opinion, which called unreasonable the Florida Supreme Court finding that state law required machines to be capable of correctly counting votes.[14]

And here we have another example: the comments of Sue Burmeister, the Georgia legislator who sponsored the controversial Georgia photo identification legislation in 2005 (HB 244) remind us again of the sentiment that to protect the integrity of the ballot some people should not be encouraged to cast one. In this example, however, it is not just ineptitude that disqualifies, it is the reputed criminal tendencies of blacks. According to a leaked U.S. Justice Department Voting Section staff memorandum objecting to the bill's new restrictive identification requirement,[15] Representative Burmeister told Justice Department officials that the attacks of September 11 caused her to reflect on how easily the terrorists had obtained IDs once inside the United States. She said that she was aware of vote buying in Georgia and had read John Fund's book, *Stealing Elections*, which argues elections are easily and routinely stolen in the United States through vote-buying schemes (see chap. 1). According to the memo, Burmeister said "that if there are fewer black voters because of this bill, it will only be because there is less opportunity for fraud. She said that when black voters in her black precincts are not paid to vote, they do not go to the polls."[16]

Allegations of voter fraud routinely invoke and strengthen racist stereotypes and unsupported narratives such as this one. They simultaneously celebrate deep-seated myths about the purity of American democracy while casting out the unworthy—the inept who cannot follow arcane, arbitrary, even nonsensical instructions and do not do what bureaucrats tell them to do. Or they exclude African Americans, who some still believe are endemically prone to criminality. Myths of voter fraud have power today, four decades after the winning of the vote by African Americans and the passage of the Voting Rights Act, because they are a part of the master narrative of American democracy itself.

Case Selection

The foregoing analysis suggests there are at least two important analytical problems for the study of voter fraud in contemporary U.S. elections: the problem of measurement and the problem of understanding why electoral policy responds to false or distorted allegations of fraud by incorporating excessive safeguards that entangle less educated and lower-income Americans in rules making it harder for them to vote. The first is a problem of empirical research. How can social scientists detect, observe, and measure criminal voting behavior, which by its nature is designed to be concealed from view? And related to this, if there is no fraud, how can positive science detect, observe, and measure the absence of it? The second analytical problem involves disentangling the empirical study of criminal voting behavior (or its absence) from the powerful ideological narrative of corruption invoking the popular myth of American democracy. In other words, concealed criminal voting behavior and the story told about it are related but distinct phenomena presenting the researcher with different analytical and empirical problems that require alternative modes of analysis.

In chapters 3 and 4, I addressed the first problem of measuring criminal voter fraud by analyzing statistics and other data on the incidence of fraud produced by the law enforcement process directed against it, treating the definition and measurement of voter fraud as problems similar to those found in the study of any other form of (concealed) criminal behavior. Having established voter fraud as a type of crime, the question of motive then becomes relevant. As shown in chapter 5, we can understand motive as the logic of casting an illegal ballot, applying the calculus of voting or rational choice approach to the costs and benefits of illegal voting for the individual. In the abstract, at least, the individual voter's motive to commit fraud turns out to be even weaker than it is for casting a legal ballot because the costs are potentially much higher in the absence of a strong D term (the supplement to the benefit of voting). Extending the model by substituting the partisan group for the individual voter and substituting the spurious voter fraud allegation for the vote allowed us to work out a similar cost-benefit analysis for understanding why partisan groups engage in voter fraud politics. By this kind of strategic reasoning, the spurious voter fraud allegation is a virtually cost-free tactic that carries the potential for a very large payoff to the party group making the charge. This explains in part the large gap we see between the proliferation of spurious voter fraud allegations in recent elections and the reality of a small amount of individual criminal fraud, as observed in the tiny fraction of investigations, prosecutions, and convictions obtained against fraud.[17]

Here, I address the second analytical problem—the stories told by partisans about voter fraud in their efforts to influence electoral outcomes. My cases consist of recent significant instances of voter fraud politics. Relying primarily on news accounts, court records, government reports, and personal interviews I have constructed the cases from the behavior of the actors and events as they unfolded in specific times and places. But, although the places, actors and events are empirical matters, the cases themselves are not treated as units of measurement; rather, they have been chosen for theory-building. In fact, the stories presented here are all cases of the same phenomenon; they are all instances of voter fraud politics, and if I were interested in predicting the partisan use of spurious voter fraud allegations, I would be guilty of selecting on the dependent variable. But this is not my purpose. I am most interested in why voter fraud politics works, not the conditions under which it will be tried. We can assume that partisans make fraud allegations to gain leverage in electoral contests or to influence electoral policy in ways they perceive will work to their benefit. In any given instance, the failure of this strategy does not erase the fact that it was tried. By studying these multiple instances that share common characteristics as cases of the same thing, we can identify the theoretical significance of the several political, cultural, and institutional factors that explain why spurious allegations of voter fraud succeed in doing their work—making voting harder for certain groups.

Overview of the Case Studies

The cases discussed here are drawn from four states—Florida, Missouri, Wisconsin, and Washington—during the 2000–2004 period, in which the pattern of spurious voter fraud allegations now prominent in the campaign rhetoric of U.S. national elections began to emerge. First, we look at an early altercation in Florida between the Association of Community Organizations for Reform Now (ACORN), a national community organizing and advocacy organization, and the Republican Party–dominated conservative coalition of pro-business groups that have vigorously attacked ACORN during the past few election cycles, prompting state and federal investigations of the ACORN voter registration activities. The second case analyzes voter fraud politics in St. Louis during the 2000 presidential election season. The third case examines the record of federal voter fraud prosecutions in Milwaukee following the 2004 presidential election, and the fourth assesses the question of fraud in the 2004 Washington state gubernatorial election. All four cases share the following characteristics: (1) the allegations of voter fraud implicated marginalized populations or their advocates, specifically African Americans, people with prior felony convictions, or low-income Americans; (2) the allegations were made in the context of close elections and appear to have been timed to influence electoral outcomes; (3) the allegations were demonstrably false; and (4) a political party or allies with financial or other evident ties to the party were the source of the allegations.

The cases differ in a number of ways. First, they exhibit regional varia-
tion because they occurred in states with different political cultures, legacies
of political conflict, and electoral traditions and systems.[18] With respect to
region, two cases occurred in the South, in the Southern or border states of
Florida and Missouri, and the other two occurred in the North, in upper
Midwest state of Wisconsin and in Washington state in the Pacific Northwest. Both Florida and Missouri were slave states and supported plantation
economies into the nineteenth century. Florida, a former Confederate state,
and Missouri, a deeply divided border state during the Civil War, have complex histories of racial strife and partisan conflict. Florida is one of the few
states in the nation to require government-issued identification to vote, and
Missouri also enacted a strict voter identification law (later found invalid
under the state's constitution).[19] As reform states, Wisconsin and Washington embrace their political cultures of tolerance and political independence. Their openness to political participation is reflected in numerous
features of their election codes. For example, Wisconsin has permitted election day registration since the 1970s, and voters in Washington now vote
almost entirely by mail.

Second, although the cases were selected because they represent instances
in which spurious voter fraud allegations had an impact on electoral mobilization and election rules, there are some important differences in the outcomes. When voter fraud allegations are evaluated for their short-term success in winning specific elections, we find that efforts in this direction were
largely unsuccessful. It is in the question of the longer-term impact on electoral outcomes through the manipulation of electoral rules where we see
some differences. In Florida, the campaign to smear ACORN was aimed at
undermining the ability of the organization to get a living-wage referendum
on the 2004 ballot. ACORN's work not only contributed to the referendum's winning ballot status but also to the overwhelming electoral support
for the initiative. John Kerry, the Democratic presidential candidate, lost
Florida in 2004 by 381,000 votes (5 percentage points), but the living-wage
referendum passed by a whopping 71 percent. But this was only the beginning of ACORN's troubles with groups allied with the Republican Party.
Florida lawmakers soon enacted some of the most restrictive rules in the
nation governing the participation of advocacy and civic groups in voter
registration drives.

In Missouri, the scandal of the 2000 election in St. Louis prompted a
federal investigation, which found that the St. Louis Board of Election
Commissioners had improperly purged eligible voters from the rolls, disfranchising thousands. Nevertheless, the senior Missouri U.S. Senator, Christopher "Kit" Bond, effectively misrepresented the St. Louis election as a case
of voter fraud and gained a spot on the Senate-House conference committee for what became the Help America Vote Act of 2002 (HAVA). In last-
minute backroom negotiations with other lawmakers, he managed to slip a

voter identification requirement into the bill and threatened to derail reform if it was removed. Once enacted, the HAVA created a federal voter identification requirement for the first time in the history of federal election law.

In Washington, spurious allegations of voter fraud were not significant in the 2004 gubernatorial election until the end of the courtroom battle, and then failed in their purpose of winning judicial support for a revote. But the mere specter of fraud was enough to persuade state lawmakers to subsequently enact new protections against it.

The longer-term outcomes of the Milwaukee, Wisconsin, case are more ambiguous than the other three cases. As in Florida, Missouri, and Washington state, Republican Party–sponsored allegations of voter fraud in Milwaukee were not enough to change the 2004 outcome in favor of the party's interests in the specific election in which they were raised. However, the fraud issue was not enough to change electoral rules. Despite repeated efforts to pass a strict voter identification law, the Democratic, veto-wielding Wisconsin governor has avoided sending the state down this path. Instead, voter fraud politics in Milwaukee helped spur an experimental effort by the U.S. Justice Department to root out ostensible fraud. Nevertheless, the effort resulted in fraud convictions for only a small number of individual voters. The Justice Department did revise its election fraud manual for U.S. attorneys, which serves as the department policy statement on the matter, but it is not clear that this had an impact of any consequence on the few prosecutions that followed. Instead, under the Obama administration, the department appears to have returned to its previous long-standing policy of pursuing organized election fraud involving elected officials, party operatives, or election administrators engaging in conspiracies to corrupt the voting process and steal elections.

Florida: An Early Attack on ACORN and the Mobilization of the Poor

One important example of how the politics of fraud claims are used to manipulate the public is the political pillorying of ACORN for alleged widescale registration fraud, which emerged as an organized effort in 2004 and built to a crescendo in the run up to the 2008 presidential election.[20] ACORN is the largest community-based organization of low- and moderate-income people in the United States.[21] It organizes locally and, in addition to coordinating large-scale multistate voter registration drives that have helped to register hundreds of thousands of new voters, has developed ballot campaigns for a range of issues such as campaign finance reform and raising the minimum wage. This is a story of one such campaign. It is a useful early example of the strategies used in later campaigns to exploit missteps in which temporary canvassers hired by ACORN, in violation of ACORN policies and training protocols, fabricated or otherwise mishandled voter registration applications.

As in later instances, the campaign began with spurious allegations of voter fraud against ACORN. These allegations created the cover for an organized campaign by groups opposing ACORN efforts to influence employment laws in the state of Florida through the ballot box. The campaign against ACORN, promoting voter fraud allegations that were false, relied on two tactics: (1) a media disinformation campaign to spread rumors, amplify the theme of fraud, and mobilize the base and (2) a law enforcement strategy to demand that the authorities investigate ACORN's alleged criminal behavior, the evidence of which was produced by the media campaign. The pattern of creating events to draw media attention and plant stories in the press, which then unwittingly or not creates the poorly scrutinized record of fraud allegations later used to make the case that fraud is occurring was repeated throughout the 2004–2008 period by Republican Party operatives and strategists.[22] Criminal investigations, of course, take time, and the truth of any allegation leading to a formal investigation by government agents cannot be known nor can incriminating evidence be disclosed until the investigation is over. Thus, open investigations keep the issue of alleged voter fraud open to political manipulation.

A politically motivated campaign to undermine ACORN's ability to collect the hundreds of thousands of signatures needed to get minimum wage referenda on ballots in a number of states in 2004 spurred accusations of voter fraud, leading to independent criminal investigations and then litigation—in which ACORN was exonerated of any wrongdoing.[23] The case in Florida involved a disgruntled former employee named Mac Stuart, who for awhile became a cause célèbre of ACORN's enemies and the pundits who fuel the fraud paranoia. The Mac Stuart affair is instructive because it illustrates the politics that constructs much of the contemporary fraud debate.

In November 2003, Mac Stuart was hired by Florida ACORN and was put to work as a petition gatherer collecting signatures supporting the placement of a Florida minimum wage amendment on the 2004 ballot. When Stuart was fired a few months later for suspicion of his involvement in an illegal check-cashing scheme, he filed a Florida whistleblower lawsuit against ACORN claiming the organization engaged in a variety of illegal practices. He was represented by a major Republican law firm with ties to the Chamber of Commerce and other business interests opposed to raising the state minimum wage. In the course of petitioning for signatures, ACORN workers ascertained whether signatories were registered to vote and conducted voter registration activities. Stuart's lawsuit claimed that canvassers were paid an additional $2.00 for each completed registration card collected, that ACORN illegally copied the voter registration cards its workers collected and sold its lists for a profit, that ACORN committed fraud by failing to deliver registration cards for people who designated "Republican" as their party affiliation, and that it collected cards from ineligible individuals such as convicted felons. Stuart claimed that in July 2004 he refused to participate in these illegal activities and was fired in retaliation under the pretext that he had attempted to cash another person's check.[24]

ACORN countersued Stuart for defamation of libel and slander. After Stuart was fired, he contacted television and print news reporters claiming that "[t]here was a lot of fraud committed" by ACORN, asserting the organization knowingly submitted thousands of invalid registration cards while storing away cards for people designating their party affiliation as Republican. Stuart's allegations were immediately picked up by news organizations such as the *Washington Times*, the *Florida Times-Union*, and other Florida newspapers, and the stories began to spread on right-wing Internet blogs. In fact, for a while Stuart's assertions were taken as fact and repeatedly reported as evidence that ACORN routinely engaged in fraud to promote its "radical political agenda."[25] That is, until the real facts about Stuart came to light and his case collapsed in court. ACORN denied and Stuart failed to prove that canvassers were paid by the card to collect voter registration applications. ACORN's copying of voter registration applications was an element of the organization's quality-control program and well within the bounds of Florida law.[26] Finally, ACORN denied and Stuart failed to produce any evidence that the organization prejudiced Republican voter registration applicants or misleadingly solicited registration cards from ineligible applicants. On December 6, 2005, the matter of *Mac Stuart v. ACORN* was dismissed with prejudice by Judge James Lawrence King (a Richard Nixon appointee), exonerating ACORN of any and all wrongdoing.[27]

The problem is that the end of this story has received considerably less media attention than the baseless claims of organized voter fraud on the part of ACORN. Opponents of ACORN continued to spread false rumors that as a policy ACORN engages in voter fraud. For example, the Employment Policies Institute (EPI), an organization associated with a firm that lobbies on behalf of the hotel, restaurant, alcoholic beverages, and tobacco industries, and opposed to ACORN's efforts to raise the minimum wage in Florida and elsewhere, routinely issues press releases and "reports" attacking ACORN. As late as July 2006, EPI was still claiming that ACORN engaged in a "pattern and practice" of voter fraud, citing the Mac Stuart affair as more evidence of ACORN's "widespread practice of fraud."[28] In April 2009, a search of the EPI website for "ACORN" resulted in sixty-two hits, most of them press releases or other documents attacking the organization and its voter registration campaigns.[29]

With ACORN under a cloud, Florida passed a law that carried stiff penalties for organizations failing to turn in voter registration applications later than ten days after they were collected. Supporters justified the law in ways that tracked the allegations made by Mac Stuart and ACORN opponents. The reporting requirements of the law were so draconian that the League of Women Voters (temporarily) ended seventy-seven years of voter registration activity in the state because it feared it could not comply and would be bankrupted if there were problems with just sixteen registration forms collected by its volunteers.[30] Labor organizations such as the American Federation of Labor and Congress of Industrial Organizations (AFL-CIO) and the Service Employees International Union also ceased their voter registration activity until Judge Patricia Seitz (a Bill Clinton appointee) later blocked the implementation of the law as unconstitutional.[31]

Missouri: How Local Party Competition Influences National Reform

The case of St. Louis, Missouri, a majority black city with budget problems, shows how the mishandling of voter registration and elections procedures can be misrepresented as fraud. There is little doubt that in the past St. Louis experienced some election fraud and public corruption. St. Louis politics were long organized by political machines, and fraud has a storied past in that city that for some, condemns the politics of the present.[32] In 2000, the historical memory of fraudulent elections, bribery, conspiracies, ballot tampering, and voting from the grave colored the rush to judgment when administrative mismanagement and shockingly poor record-keeping by the city's election bureaucracy combined to produce troubling election irregularities.[33] Before the irregularities could be sorted out, they were seized on by partisans, including Christopher "Kit" Bond, Missouri senior Republican senator, who claimed the problems were evidence of a Democratic Party–driven "major criminal enterprise designed to defraud voters" instead of what a federal probe later determined them to be—procedural incompetence and official failure to abide by the law.[34]

For many voters attempting to cast ballots in the 2000 presidential election, election day in St. Louis was a chaotic mess. Many long-time voters were told that they were not registered to vote when they showed up at polling sites where they had cast ballots in the past. To reestablish their legitimacy, many of these rejected voters were told to go down to the St. Louis Election Board headquarters at 300 North Tucker Boulevard and cast a ballot there because the phone lines to the elections board were jammed and election judges staffing the polling sites were unable to establish whether such voters' names had been moved to an inactive list of registered voters.[35]

It was this controversial inactive list and the failure of the St. Louis Elections Board to comply with the NVRA that later formed the basis for a federal lawsuit alleging that the elections board "denied or significantly impaired the voting rights" of thousands of city voters before the election.[36]

The St. Louis Elections Board has had problems maintaining accurate voter registration rolls, and leading up to the 2000 election, there were still no clear rules for specifying when a voter should be dropped from the rolls.[37] Between 1994 and 2000, the elections board had conducted a series of mail canvasses of its voter registration rolls, none of which complied with the requirements of the NVRA.[38] Based on these improper canvasses, the elections board removed more than 50,000 names of voters who had been on the rolls in 1996 and "made no effort to notify inactive voters that their registration status had changed, that their names would not appear on the voter registration lists provided to election judges in each voting precinct, or that they would face additional administrative steps on election day before they would be permitted to vote."[39] This number represented roughly 40 percent of the total number of votes cast in St. Louis in the 1996 election and was about twice the national and state averages for the proportion of inactive voters on the rolls.[40] Moreover, for all elections that it conducted after 1994, the board failed to provide precinct election judges with a list of any of the voters it had designated as "inactive," setting up the mass confusion at polling sites that many legitimate voters faced when they showed up to vote and were told they were no longer registered.[41]

In the days leading up to the November 7, 2000, election, the unprecedented administrative reclassification of thousands of active voter registration records in the overwhelmingly Democratic city was seen by Democrats, including national party officials with the Gore-Lieberman campaign, as an illegitimate Republican party–sponsored effort to restrict Democratic voting. When he spoke at a Gore-Lieberman campaign event, Democratic congressional hopeful William Lacy Clay Jr. told supporters not to "let anyone turn you away from the polls" and warned, "If it requires leaving the polls open a little longer, we're going to get a court order to do it."[42]

In fact, this is exactly what happened. Voters stood in line for hours. First, they had to check in with precinct workers; then, for those whose names were not on the precinct voter registration lists anymore, they stood in another line to plead their case before the sometimes single election judge present at many of the city's precincts.[43] When many of these officials were unable to confirm their registration status with headquarters because they could not get through to elections officials at the elections board, these same voters were sent down to the board's office to try to resolve the problems on their own. According to news reports, "It made for a wild hour at Board's downtown office, where hundreds of voters turned away from the polls because they were not registered or had problems voting filled the lobby throughout the day. By early evening, the lobby was shoulder to shoulder with people who wanted to vote."[44]

In the afternoon, the Democrats and the Gore-Lieberman campaign filed suit in a state circuit court requesting the polls remain open for an additional three hours to accommodate voters victimized by the inaccessible and inaccurate inactive list. St. Louis Circuit Judge Evelyn Baker complied, but her order was overturned within forty-five minutes of the regular poll closing time (7 p.m.) by a three-judge appeals panel. The St. Louis City Board of Elections, joined by Mark F. "Thor" Hearne representing the Bush-Cheney campaign, successfully argued that she lacked jurisdiction to change state law. Elections officials estimated that only approximately one hundred extra people had been permitted to vote by Judge Baker's order. But Republican officials charged there may have been a "preconceived plan" to misuse the judicial process to keep the polls open longer than their statutorily mandated closing time, as well as an "organized campaign" (by the Democrats) to abuse the procedure by which voters obtain court orders to vote, resulting in voter fraud and the casting of hundreds of illegal votes.[45] Senator Bond said the order to keep the polls open until 10 p.m. "represents the biggest fraud on the voters in this state and nation that we have ever seen."[46]

In a fifty-one-page report, Republican Secretary of State Matt Blunt outlined the possible violations of law committed in the City of St. Louis by alleged illegal voters. He referred to an unspecified conspiracy "to create bedlam so that election fraud could be perpetrated"[47] and to corrupt election judges put in place to manipulate the results of the election. The report claimed that (1) 342 people obtained court orders to vote even though the information provided by them on affidavits suggested they were properly disqualified from voting; (2) sixty-two convicted federal felons and fifty-two Missouri felons voted in either the City of St. Louis or St. Louis County; (3) fourteen votes were cast in the names of dead people; 4) there was a high probability of multiple voting by dozens of people; (5) seventy-nine votes were cast by people registering to vote from vacant lots; and (6) forty-five election judges were not registered to vote and therefore disqualified to serve.

Many of Blunt's allegations have been significantly weakened or outright debunked by the discovery of major records management problems at the elections board resulting in grossly inaccurate voter rolls. The *St. Louis Post-Dispatch* conducted a canvass of over 2,000 alleged vacant lot addresses from which thousands of St. Louis voters were supposedly registered and found buildings on virtually all of them. The lots had been misclassified by the city assessor or misread by elections officials. They concluded that "most of the 79 people on the state's suspect voter list from last fall probably shouldn't be on it," including the city's budget director, whose ten-year-old condominium was mislabeled as a vacant lot.[48] The claim that more than one hundred felons may have illegally voted is also unreliable because the data on which it was based were inconclusive, as the report itself admits.[49] Later investigations by the state auditor did find that three years after the 2000 election fiasco, the St. Louis voter rolls still included the names of over 2,000 felons prohibited by state law from voting or registering to vote. But the auditor found no conspiracy to commit voter fraud on the part of voters and questioned instead why the elections board had failed to remove the names from its lists when it had been provided with monthly and quarterly felony conviction reports from state and federal authorities. Like the Blunt Commission, the state auditor also found thousands of duplicate records of voters registered to vote in St. Louis and elsewhere in the state, but found only twenty-eight instances across three recent election cycles in which a voter *may have voted* more than once. Without further investigation, it is impossible to know whether these twenty-eight cases represent actual illegal behavior or are the product of clerical errors in the board's voter registration files.

Throughout the months following the election, Republicans and Democrats both called for a federal investigation, each side charging the other with fraud or with suppressing the vote. Both sides expected to be vindicated. The federal investigation provided a decisive end to the Blunt Commission allegation that corrupt election judges allowed hundreds of patently unqualified voters to vote. After an FBI investigation that involved subpoenaing *all* of the registration and voting records from the St. Louis Elections Board for the months before the election, the Justice Department made a surprise announcement. It told the elections board that it was planning to sue it for violating the NVRA and threatening the voting rights of thousands of eligible voters in St. Louis by erroneously purging their records from the active voter file. The board was forced into a consent decree that stipulated how it would change the procedures for maintaining accurate registration records to comply with federal requirements for notifying voters of their status on the list, and for handling voters whose names are not on the active voter list on election day.

Four years after the St. Louis Elections Board signed the consent decree acknowledging these failures,[50] Thor Hearne, the influential Republican activist and St. Louis attorney, submitted Senate testimony in his capacity as general counsel for the American Center for Voting Rights (see chap. 1) that included citations to materials he produced after 2002 that ignored the election board's culpability and simply repeated the misleading allegations of voter fraud in St. Louis.[51]

Wisconsin: Swing-State Politics

In 2000, Vice President Al Gore won Wisconsin by just under 6,000 votes out of more than 2.5 million cast. Heading into the final months of the 2004 presidential campaign, candidates George W. Bush and John Kerry were neck-and-neck in the polls in Wisconsin, and the race was once again projected to be razor close. As a battleground state, Wisconsin attracted attention from the national campaigns and a host of third-party nonprofit and political-consulting organizations that poured money, staff, and volunteers into the state to increase voter registration before election day. By September, the voter registration drives and heightened national interest in Wisconsin as pivotal in the election of the next president led Kevin Kennedy, state elections director, to report that elections officials across the state had been swamped by an unprecedented increase of over 200,000 new registration applications submitted by mail.[52] Wisconsin's swing-state status and the closeness of the presidential contest also led to outside voter registration groups flooding their volunteers into the state.[53]

Preelection news coverage in Wisconsin focused on three controversies: (1) problems associated with some of the voter registration drives, (2) a dispute between county and city officials over the number of ballots to be printed and provided to the city of Milwaukee, and (3) a flap over thousands of alleged "bad addresses" on Milwaukee's voter registration list. Procedural breakdowns and discrepancies in the voter registration records were associated with what Kennedy called "volume" problems, but they helped create a climate of suspicion about the quality of record-keeping at the Milwaukee elections commission and the ability of the commission to run a "clean" election.[54] The preelection disputes repeatedly invoked the language of voter fraud, although no evidence was ever produced that voters were intentionally committing fraud. The climate of distrust made it difficult to see clerical mistakes, illegible handwriting, and workload problems leading to backlogged voter registration applications as human error or problems related to resource issues. Instead, foul-ups and mistakes were assumed to be evidence of fraud perpetrated by partisans trying to "steal elections."

Voter Registration Problems

Intensified political competition and the influx of outside organizations, campaign workers, and volunteers into Wisconsin in the months and weeks before the election contributed to an inevitably flawed voter registration process. Duplicate registration cards, improperly filled-out cards, and cards from people who are not eligible to vote or who do not live in the district in which the cards are submitted are not uncommon in the chaotic preelection atmosphere of an intense political campaign. Imperfect voter registration drives and simple human error, however, are not the same as voter fraud, nor do they inevitably lead to fraudulent voting. As the Milwaukee case demonstrates, however, these deficiencies can be easily exploited by partisans.

As stories of potential voter registration fraud circulated in the press, a partisan fight erupted in Milwaukee. In October, the chief elections official in Milwaukee asked the county elections board for 260,000 extra ballots in anticipation of a record turnout. Under Wisconsin law, counties print and pay for all ballots for their localities. Milwaukee county elections officials rejected the request, with County Executive Scott Walker writing in support of the county board decision to give Milwaukee roughly the same number of ballots it had received in the previous presidential election. In 2000, the number of ballots on hand exceeded the eligible voting population in

Milwaukee by at least 200,000. But in planning for the number of ballots needed, local officials must compensate for the fact that, to scan and count the ballots after they are cast, a bar code is assigned that prevents ballots from being counted outside the ward in which they are issued. In other words, unused ballots cannot be moved around from ward to ward to cover shortfalls. Estimating the probable turnout involves estimating the turnout in each ward rather than citywide. This could have the effect of inflating the overall estimated number of ballots needed citywide. In 2004, Milwaukee requested 938,000 ballots for a voting population of approximately 424,000. The county board agreed to give the city 679,000 ballots, and a firestorm of protest erupted when County Executive Walker defended the decision by suggesting that he was concerned about potential voter fraud and did not want people to be able to "grab" extra ballots at the polling site.[55]

Milwaukee Mayor Tom Barrett accused Walker of trying to foment chaos at the polls and suppress the central city vote. Barrett is a Democrat and served as a state co-chair of John Kerry's campaign, whereas Walker is a Republican and served as state co-chair of George W. Bush's campaign. In press reports, the dispute was repeatedly referred to as "ugly," generating partisan recrimination on both sides. On the morning of October 14, about a hundred protesters, including students, elected officials, and union activists, stormed Walker's office while he was meeting with municipal election clerks, chanting, "Let the people have their voice!" and demanding that Walker issue the extra ballots to Milwaukee. Wisconsin Governor Jim Doyle intervened by asking the state elections board to help resolve the dispute and offered state aid to pay for the extra ballots. The next day, Walker and Barrett held a joint press conference on the steps of Milwaukee City Hall to announce a compromise between the city and county: the county would supply the extra ballots, giving the city the 938,000 ballots it had originally requested, and the city would split the cost, estimated at about $40,000, and promise to return all unused ballots to the county election commission to ensure that all ballots were accounted for.[56] Approximately 665,000 unused ballots were later returned to the county board of elections.[57]

At 4:57 p.m. on Wednesday, October 27, 2004, three minutes before the legal deadline for filing a complaint with the city elections commission, the state Republican Party challenged the validity of 5,619 names on the city voter rolls. Rick Graber, state Republican Party chairman, said, "This is a black eye on the city of Milwaukee and the state of Wisconsin. These 5,600 addresses could be used to allow fraudulent voting. Whether it's deliberate or not, something's wrong when you have people from addresses that don't exist."[58] First, the local elections board voted 3–0 when the board's lone Republican appointee joined the two Democrats in finding that the challenge lacked sufficient evidence. Grant Langley, the Milwaukee city attorney, conducted a review that he said in a letter to the city elections commission executive director casts "doubt on the overall accuracy" of the list supplied by the state Republican Party.[59]

Then, just four days before election day the state Republican Party demanded that Milwaukee city officials require identification from 37,180 people that it said its review of the city voter rolls turned up as living at questionable addresses. The list, which was produced using a computer program to match data from the city's voter database with a U.S. Postal Service list of known addresses, the same methodology used to provide the first list of 5,619 names, included 13,300 cases of incorrect apartment numbers and 18,200 cases of missing apartment numbers. City Attorney Langley, a nonpartisan officeholder, called the Republican Party request, "outrageous," adding, "We have already uncovered hundreds and hundreds and hundreds of addresses on their (original list) that do exist. Why should I take their word for the fact this new list is good? I'm out of the politics on this, but this is purely political."[60] Langley's review did find some addresses that did not appear to exist, and the *Milwaukee Journal Sentinel* did its own limited investigation, finding sixty-eight questionable addresses. "Others, though," it said, "were likely to be clerical errors."[61]

By Monday, officials from the state Republican Party and the City of Milwaukee worked out an agreement about how the registrations of voters with addresses challenged by the Republicans would be dealt with at the polls. The list of 37,000 was pared back down to 5,512 and the city agreed to provide poll workers with the names of people in their wards from the list whose addresses appeared to be incomplete or inaccurate. Those people would be flagged if they showed up to vote and asked to show identification and/or re-register to update their records.[62] At the time, Wisconsin law did not require preregistered voters to show identification to vote at the polls; they needed only to state their names and addresses to receive ballots.[63] The compromise deal with the Republican Party imposed on people who found themselves on the party's list an identification requirement not mandated by law.

The *Journal Sentinel* reviewed the Milwaukee voting records. The most troubling finding from the detailed computer analysis made by the newspaper was that as many as 1,242 votes, three-quarters of them cast by people registering on-site on election day, appeared to have come from invalid addresses. Another 1,305 registration cards with discernible flaws, such as missing addresses or missing names, were accepted on election day from voters who were then allowed to vote.[64]

The newspaper opined on its own investigation and reporting: "Republicans are quick to jump on the discrepancies, real or imagined, in voting data in Milwaukee as proof of widespread fraud in the big city. In their minds, the *Journal Sentinel's* findings fit that pattern. A more plausible explanation, however, is that the findings reflect the unfortunate tendency of voting systems throughout America to err."[65]

By the end of January, the mayor had appointed an internal task force to review the city's electoral procedures, and federal and county law enforcement agencies began a joint investigation into whether breakdowns in procedure, poor record-keeping, human error, or fraud explained the discrepancies. On February 10, the bipartisan Joint Legislative Audit Committee of the state legislature voted unanimously to direct auditors to review the voter registration and address verification procedures. All these investigations produced clear evidence that the Milwaukee Board of Elections was overwhelmed by its own incompetence and understaffing on election day, resulting in massive record-keeping problems. Poll workers failed to follow procedures; the number of votes cast in Milwaukee failed to match the number of people recorded as voting; same-day registration cards were not filled out properly, and follow-ups were not performed when postregistration address verification efforts identified address discrepancies; and some voters were allowed to register to vote in the wrong ward.

The scrutiny from federal, state, and local law enforcement and elections officials produced several reports, an intensive review of voter registration practices in a number of Wisconsin cities, many recommendations for improving election administration and voter registration procedures, several later-vetoed photo identification bills in the state legislature, a variety of other legislative proposals, and very little conclusive evidence of voter fraud. For example, a state audit of 150 Wisconsin municipalities found "105 instances of potentially improper or fraudulent voting in the November 2004 elections" in six jurisdictions. The irregularities were only identified in the audit—they were not confirmed, and they were overwhelmingly cases of potential illegal felon voting.[66]

The Wisconsin felony disenfranchisement laws are more restrictive than those in twenty other states.[67] Individuals with felony convictions are barred from voting while in prison, on probation, or on parole.[68] Yet widespread ignorance among the public and elections officials alike of the seldom-enforced Wisconsin felony disenfranchisement laws accounted for the hundreds of cases since 2000 of ineligible felons' voting that postelection audits and reports found. Because 60 percent of those convicted of felonies in Wisconsin do not serve their sentences in jail, an ineligible felon voter can register and vote if officials allow it.[69] Alleged illegal felon voting constitutes nearly all of the "voter fraud" reported by the media in Wisconsin since 2000. Over two federal election cycles, from 2002 to 2005, only ten cases of felon voting in Wisconsin were prosecuted by the federal government, and only five people were convicted or pled guilty. Moreover, Wisconsin election crime laws require the establishment of a willful effort to defraud. Most of those identified as ineligible have not been prosecuted because they were never informed that they lost their voting rights until they had completed their *entire* sentence, meaning were released from probation or parole.[70]

As election officials in the city and state struggled to meet the challenges of fixing the Milwaukee election system, the city, unbeknownst to its elected officials, was designated by the U.S. Justice Department for a pilot program for prosecuting individuals for voter fraud.[71] This was new territory for the Justice Department. According to the 2006 U.S. Election Commission (EAC) report, *Election Crimes: An Initial Review and Recommendations for Future Study*, under the banner of the Ballot Access and Voting Integrity Initiative of the attorney general, the Justice Department designed three pilot programs "to determine what works in developing the cases [referring to the prosecution of individuals not involved in conspiracies] and obtaining convictions and what works with juries in such matters to gain convictions."

> Since 2002, the department has brought more cases against alien voters, felon voters, and double voters than ever before. Previously, cases were only brought against conspiracies to corrupt the process rather than individual offenders acting alone. For deterrence purposes, the Attorney General decided to add the pursuit of individuals who vote when not eligible to vote (noncitizens, felons) or who vote more than once.[72]

The head of the Elections Crime Branch of the Criminal Division Public Integrity Section told the EAC researchers that the pilot projects focused on (1) felon voters in Milwaukee, (2) alien voters in the Southern District of Florida, and (3) double-voters in a variety of jurisdictions.[73] The Justice Department record of indictments fits this description—thirty-five of the forty voters indicted between October 2002 and September 2005 are among the three groups targeted by the pilot projects. This includes ten alleged felon voters in Milwaukee; sixteen alleged alien voters in the Southern District of Florida; and nine alleged double-voters, including four people in Milwaukee and five people in Missouri and Kansas.

The pattern of prosecutions is troubling. Over the last several federal election cycles, Wisconsin, Florida, and Missouri have been key swing states for the Republicans. We have seen how Republican activists and their allies in these states leveled exaggerated and even false allegations of voter fraud; how they capitalized on the bureaucratic failures of election administration that have produced irregularities, mismatched numbers, and registration problems; and manipulated the chaos to their partisan advantage. And what have been the consequences for some of those ensnared in the web, the people targeted for all those investigations? As shown, the record of actual federal prosecutions is feeble. Worse, it is marred by troubling signs of racial targeting. Most of the forty people prosecuted for voter fraud are racial minorities;

only a third were found guilty of the charges, and some of those convicted have maintained that their convictions were for actions they did not know were illegal.

The stories of two of the Milwaukee residents prosecuted under the Justice Department pilot project are enlightening. In summer 2007, I interviewed Marvin Smalls, whose case was dismissed before it went to trial, and Evelyn Robinson, one of the five people convicted out of the total fourteen Milwaukee residents who were charged with voter fraud.[74] Both Smalls and Robinson are African Americans, as are eleven of the other twelve people indicted.

Marvin Smalls

Marvin Smalls remembers sitting on the couch in his aunt's tiny wooden frame house in Milwaukee. It was November and cold. That day, election day, November 2, 2004, he had come back a little tired from his job hauling junk to a local scrapyard and was resting when his aunt returned from voting wearing a big yellow sticker that said, "I Voted!" "You better get yourself on over there, Marvin, and vote," she told him, "they're about to close the polls. Take an ID and something showing you're living here now and hurry up." Marvin, a high school graduate in his late forties, was a regular voter, casting his first ballot at the age of eighteen and voting in every presidential election since, until a felony conviction on a state drug charge sent him to prison. Serving out the rest of his sentence on probation, this was the first presidential election he thought he could vote in since he had been released from prison.

"OK, I'll go," he says he remembers thinking, "but what kind of ID can I use?" He did not own a car so he did not have a driver's license. He remembered that he had kept the ID card they gave him while he was in prison. He rifled through his things and fished out the plastic card he wore while incarcerated. It was issued by the Wisconsin Department of Corrections; it had his picture on it; his name and date of birth; and indicated his height, weight, eye and hair color. "That ought to do," he thought. It also said "OFFENDER" in big, thick, heavy lettering. In fact, no text on the card was larger or stood out more than that word, "OFFENDER," which appeared above his prison identification number and his name. He grabbed a letter from his state probation officer that was addressed to him at his aunt's house as further proof of who he was and where he lived, and walked over to a local school to vote.

When Marvin got there he had to wait in line. The poll worker asked him if he was registered to vote. Because he had moved since the last time he voted, she told him they would fill out a new registration card for him. The poll worker asked him a couple of questions—name? address?—which she filled in for him on a green City of Milwaukee On-Site Registration Card, checking off "New Voter in Milwaukee" and writing in his district and ward. Marvin handed her his prison ID card, and the clerk filled in the prison identification number on the line labeled "WI Dept. of Transportation—issued driver's license or identification card number." She then filled in the last four digits of Marvin's Social Security number even though the instructions on the card said it was required only if the person did not have a Wisconsin driver's license or state ID. Marvin attested that he was a U.S. citizen and that he was at least eighteen years of age by signing his name on the bottom of the card. He says no one at the polling place told him that as a probationer he was ineligible to vote in Wisconsin, and nowhere on the voter registration card did it indicate that a person still under state supervision for a felony conviction was prohibited from voting. Marvin later said that he saw no sign on the wall of the polling site with this information and that during his entanglement with the prison and criminal justice systems if anybody had ever told him that he could not vote while he was on probation, he did not remember it.

He cast his ballot and went home.

On a morning in July, eight months later, Marvin was eating his breakfast when two detectives approached the house and knocked on the door. A family member answered the door and yelled that the police were there for him. Marvin looked up from his plate and saw the two law enforcement officers standing there. "My appetite was shot," he later recalled. The detectives told him he was facing five years in the federal penitentiary for voting. "For voting?" he asked. They told that him he was going to get a summons in the mail and he had better pay attention to it. Then they left. Marvin says he could not eat for three days. When he finally got the summons in the mail he went down to the federal courthouse for his arraignment. That is when he met Nancy.[75]

Nancy Joseph is a tall, striking woman with an open face, an easy smile, and a determined quiet confidence that you feel as she walks toward you. She had been an attorney for fourteen years when she first met Mr. Smalls (this is how she always addresses him).

For the past eight years, she had worked for Federal Defender Services, Inc., of Wisconsin, a nonprofit legal organization providing legal services to people accused of federal crimes who lack the means to hire a private defense attorney. On the eve of Marvin Smalls's trial, Jones discovered that he had registered to vote using his Wisconsin prison identification card and a letter from his state probation officer addressed to him at his current residence. Yet Marvin was being charged by the federal government for having "knowingly and willfully deprived, defrauded, and attempt[ing] to deprive and defraud the residents of the State of Wisconsin of a fair and impartially conducted election process by casting a ballot that he knew to be materially false and fraudulent under Wisconsin law."

Once the fact became known that Marvin Smalls had registered to vote presenting an identification card that should have raised questions about his eligibility, the charges against him were dropped by the U.S. attorney.[76] But in my interview with Mr. Smalls and his attorney, he asserted that because of this experience he plans to never vote again. Nancy Joseph has told me that she was taken aback by Mr. Smalls's statement, and in fact, when he made the statement to me in her presence, Joseph reminded him that it was his right to vote. But Mr. Smalls remained firm; he said he would not put himself in a situation like that ever again, distrustful that the government was going to "change the rules" on him one more time.

Evelyn Robinson

Evelyn Robinson was indicted by the federal government for voter fraud in fall 2005. She had been charged with the same crime as Marvin Smalls, a violation of Title 42 Section 1973gg-10(2)(b) of the U.S. Code (ironically, since both voters are African American, an amendment of the Voting Rights Act of 1965) and Title 18 Section 2, for voting while on probation for a felony battery charge.

"That [battery charge] was my first case," she told me when I interviewed her in summer 2007. "I'd never been arrested before. I was with a guy. We were in a car and coming from a party when we got into a fight. He was choking me, so I grabbed a bottle and hit him over the head. I'm the one who called the police." When the police arrived they found Evelyn with the man's blood on her hands and clothes. They arrested her for battery and took her to jail where she stayed for about a week before she was released. Upon her release she was processed, given some papers to sign, then sent to another office where she signed the same papers again. She then met with a probation officer.

Evelyn had decided not to contest the battery charge. She did not hide the fact that she had struck the man, but she knew she was the victim and she had hit him in self-defense. An evaluation by a domestic violence counselor later found this to be true. Nevertheless, she pleaded guilty. She did not want to go to trial because she could not afford to lose any more time from her job as a machine operator. She had already lost time over the week that she had been detained. For the past fourteen years she had worked at a factory that makes electrical parts for all kinds of machines, airplanes, engines, and elevators—"you name it, we make it," she said. It was a good job and she needed the money because she is single mother of four with two teenagers still at home.

On election day, November 2, 2004, a friend of Evelyn's picked her up at the factory at the end her shift. The friend was wearing a bright yellow "I Voted!" sticker and asked Evelyn if she wanted to be dropped off at the polls so that she could vote. Evelyn was tired and she really did not feel like standing in that line, but she usually voted in presidential elections and she thought, "well, OK, I'll vote." She walked into her polling place, waited in line, and when it was her turn, the poll worker behind the table helped her fill out a new voter registration card. The worker asked Evelyn her name and address, and whether she was a citizen; then she pushed the card toward her for her signature. Evelyn did not read the card; she figured the poll worker knew what she was doing. She signed the card, and the poll worker wrote a ballot number on it and handed Evelyn the ballot. She voted and went home.

Months passed. Evelyn kept every appointment with her probation officer. She violated none of the many rules she had agreed to abide by every time she met her probation officer and signed yet another set of forms. Then one day in September 2005, her probation officer came to see her at home. He had a copy of the newspaper in his hand. He asked her if she had something she wanted to tell him. Evelyn wondered why he was standing in front of her asking her such an odd question. "No," she said, she did not have anything she wanted to tell him. "Are you sure?" he asked again. "You don't have anything you want to tell me?" "No, no, I don't have anything I want to tell you," she answered. The probation officer handed Evelyn the newspaper. "Look," he said, "look there," and pointed to a story about people being indicted for voter fraud in the City of Milwaukee. In big black letters was her name.

"I was blown away," Evelyn remembered. "I mean, wow. I looked at my probation officer, and I asked him, is this serious? Do I have something to worry about?" He told her yes, this is serious; this is very serious, and you do have something to worry about. He wanted her side of the story, and he wanted it in writing. So Evelyn wrote out a short statement saying that she did vote but that she did not know that she was not permitted to vote. She did not know she had done anything wrong. The probation officer told her that some time soon the police would come to take her down to the station to fill out papers. Two or three weeks later, the sheriff delivered a letter to her door. One of her kids answered the door and gave Evelyn the letter. It informed her that she was being indicted and that she was to call a number for more information. She called and was told when and where to show up for her arraignment.

The trial lasted two days. Evelyn testified, repeating what she had told her probation officer: that she voted, but that she did not know that she was not permitted to vote while on probation for the battery charge. The jury convicted her.

I was blown away, I was just kinda shocked when they came back guilty. I don't sugar-coat things. I don't have any reason to lie about voting. I wasn't going to pretend I didn't vote, I just didn't know I was doing anything wrong. I didn't see any sign saying if you are on probation you are not eligible to vote, but even if I did I still would have voted because I didn't classify myself as a felon. I never went to jail so I didn't think of myself as a felon.

Evelyn was sentenced to four months of house arrest and fourteen months of probation for casting a fraudulent vote. She had used her real name and her real address, and she had voted only once, but because of the felony battery charge, in Wisconsin Evelyn Robinson had committed voter fraud. House arrest meant she could leave her house only to go to work, except for four hours every Saturday when she was allowed out of the house to do her shopping and errands. Throughout the four months of house arrest, Evelyn wore an ankle bracelet that monitored her whereabouts. "That part was nerve-wracking," she later said, "I had to get everything I needed to get done in those four hours." But otherwise, she did not let the confinement bother her too much. "It's not like I ever went out to bars or hung out. My time was always limited because I'm a mother and I have to work."

I asked Evelyn how this episode made her feel about voting. "I'll never vote again," she replied, "never."

> Because going through this trial, my name being in the paper for everybody to see—not once, but twice—first with the indictment, and then when they convicted me, another article with my name in bold print, it was humiliating. I had never heard of anybody who's ever been prosecuted for voting. It was a shock to me to read my name in the paper. I had no say so. No reporter ever called me up for my side of the story. I felt like scum, like I was a really bad person when I thought what I was doing was my God-given, constitutional right. No, I'll never vote again.

On the day that I interviewed Evelyn, her probation had finally come to an end. "If you hadn't called," she told me, "this being my last day of probation, I never would have thought about all this again." She was just happy to be free. "Yes, I'm happy now because I can leave town. All my family is in Chicago. I might just go there this weekend, just to get out of here."

The prosecution and conviction of Evelyn Robinson was a travesty of justice. Nancy Joseph had wide knowledge of all fourteen cases of alleged voter fraud in the Eastern District of Wisconsin and said she would have brought all of them to trial. Her colleague at the Federal Defenders Services, Chip Burke, credited Nancy with uncovering the troubling pattern of prosecutions and with convincing her colleagues that the indictments were aberrant and may have been politically-motivated. Another attorney, Tom Erickson, who represented one of the Milwaukee voters charged with double voting (she was acquitted by a jury after less than an hour of deliberation),[77] said that in twenty-one years of practice, he had never seen such a flimsy, circumstantial case brought by the federal government. Indeed, the thirty-six percent conviction rate obtained in the Milwaukee prosecutions is a strikingly low record for the Justice Department.[78]

Washington State: The Best Election Administration in the Nation?

The 2004 Washington state election was the closest gubernatorial election in U.S. history.[79] This case reviews in some detail how errors in election administration—inevitable because they are practically engineered into the intricate electoral system—produce the fodder for spurious voter fraud allegations. The scrutiny of electoral procedures that accompanied the two recounts following the Washington election and the subsequent judicial contest exposed what can go wrong in any jurisdiction and any election, even in the absence of fraud.

The campaigns for the open governor's seat in Washington began more than a year before the election, and by November 2004, both parties had spent record amounts of money, blitzing the state with advertising, mailings, and calls as the election approached. Public opinion polling heading into November suggested that Christine Gregoire, the Democratic candidate and three-term state attorney general, would win.[80] But Dino Rossi, her scrappy Republican opponent, a former commercial real estate agent and state senator, was the most attractive gubernatorial candidate fielded by the Republicans in years. Washington state has a fractious political history and long ago voters there started splitting their tickets before the practice became more widespread throughout the rest of the country.[81] For example, in 2004, Washingtonians voted for Democrats John Kerry for president and Patty Murray for U.S. Senate, and for Republicans Sam Reed for secretary of state, Rob McKenna for attorney general, and Cathy McMorris to fill an open congressional seat. The 2000 U.S. Senate race between Slade Gorton, the incumbent Republican, and Maria Cantwell, his Democratic challenger, was decided only after a month of counting absentee ballots and a recount (Cantwell won by just 2,229 votes). Despite Kerry's eventual 7-percentage-point advantage, Gregoire and Rossi were locked in an epic battle.

Election Day to Certification: November 2–17, 2004

As the ballot counting got underway, Gregoire opened up a 15,000 vote lead, erasing an earlier Rossi lead of 1,000. And by midnight on election night, with 88 percent of all precincts counted, Gregoire was up by about 7,000 votes. By morning, after rural counties reported their mail ballot tabulations, Rossi took the lead, only to lose it by afternoon after King County reported some of its absentee ballot counts.[82] Foreshadowing a pattern that would keep Washingtonians from seating their next governor for two more months, Gregoire's lead shrank and disappeared over the next week of wild fluctuations in the vote count. By November 10, Rossi had surged ahead by 3,500 votes, sending the Democrats to court to challenge the vote-counting procedures being used in King County.

Vote counting is a drawn-out affair in Washington compared to other states because laws give voters much latitude, for example, allowing "no-excuse" absentee voting and the mailed ballots to be postmarked up to and on election day.[83] The state's election laws and political institutions reflect its political culture, which encourages participation. As the county auditor November 17 certification deadline approached, Rossi continued to hold his lead, but by this time, the bulk of the uncounted ballots were provisional ballots, about a quarter of them cast in heavily Gregoire-leaning Seattle, King County. The Democrats wanted county elections officials to release the names of voters whose provisional ballots were rejected when the signatures on the ballots failed to match the signatures in the county registration records. Under state law, the parties have access to the names of absentee voters whose ballots are rejected for similar problems (those voters are given until the afternoon of the certification day to correct problems with their ballots). But Dean Logan, King County elections director, refused to release the names of provisional ballot voters, citing the HAVA, which he thought prohibited him from doing so.

So the Democrats launched the first of nine lawsuits ultimately filed by both political parties and by voters over a variety of election law disputes.[84] King County Superior Court Judge Dean Lum ruled that the county had misinterpreted the HAVA and ordered elections officials to release the names of 929 people whose provisional ballots were rejected, finding that signature problems on provisional ballots should be treated the same way that signature problems on absentee ballots were treated; in other words, voters using provisional ballots should get a chance to correct their mistakes, as did absentee ballot voters.[85] Moreover, nothing in state law prohibited third parties from helping voters correct the mistakes.[86]

The Democrats were overjoyed. "We'll go door to door to make sure they come to the courthouse to defend their votes," vowed Paul Berendt, Democratic Party chairman.[87] Chris Vance, Berendt's Republican counterpart warned, "I'm now becoming very worried that the Democrats are going to try to turn this into Florida. They're losing, and now they're grasping at straws."[88] Democratic campaign workers and volunteers worked over the weekend to contact those voters and others whose absentee ballots were problematic, screening out people who may not have voted for Gregoire.[89] By Monday, they had delivered approximately four hundred affidavits from voters attesting to their eligibility to vote and had promised another two hundred by the Wednesday deadline.[90] That sent the Republicans back to court for an injunction to stop King County from counting these now-challenged ballots. But their case was weakened by the fact that they had scurried to match the Democrats in contacting likely Rossi supporters among the problem provisional and absentee ballot voters. Because the vote in King County swung heavily to Gregoire, the Republicans did not find many problem Rossi voters there,[91] so they wanted the court to challenge the validity of the "voter-signed documents" brought in by third parties and to order that the 929 signature-problem provisional ballots could not be counted unless the voter him- or herself came into the King County Elections Division to clear up the problems. Judge Lum's ruling against the Republican request for a temporary restraining order came down the day after Rossi's lead had evaporated to just nineteen votes.

Meanwhile, on the same day that the Democrats delivered the affidavits of rejected provisional ballot voters, King County discovered it had 10,000 more ballots to count than previously reported. Elections officials explained the discrepancy by noting that they had verified more provisional ballots than expected and absentee ballot turnout was higher than originally projected.[92] Bloggers and Rossi supporters were suspicious of the sudden appearance of thousands of uncounted ballots, calling them "magical mystery ballots," as if they had appeared out of thin air.[93]

Bloggers would come to play an increasingly important role in shaping the perceptions of the legality, fairness, and impartiality of the elections officials, and therefore the outcome of the election, and ultimately in shaping the myth of voter fraud. Intrepid "citizen journalists" obtaining data and documents through open records requests frequently scooped the mainstream newspapers while providing expert analysis of vote counting and other procedural controversies.[94] One of the most talented of the bloggers to emerge from the Washington governor's race was Stefan Sharkansky, a computer software consultant and founder of the conservative state watchdog blog Sound Politics. It was Sharkansky (or "the Shark," as he became known to his fans for his analytical ability; data deftness; and incisive, often devastating commentary), who named the discovered ballots "magical mystery ballots."[95]

Commentators on the Sound Politics blog were sometimes as well-informed as the regular bloggers. One, Jim King, who claimed thirty years of Republican campaign experience in Washington, offered this response to the mystery of the missing ballots:

> The unreliability of the counties' "ballots remaining to be counted" numbers is no surprise to those who have followed elections for some time—some smaller counties have in the past used a number that reflects every unreturned ballot at that point in time even knowing that many ballots were not going to be returned. Thus an "old" conventional wisdom was that the estimates were high. The provisional ballots introduce new problems—they are voted in one county and often counted in another—counties have no clue how many are coming to them until they arrive—many counties did not include provisionals—even those produced AND counted in their own county—in their estimates UNTIL they had been verified. King County is not the first to find new ballots—it was happening on a smaller scale in other counties late last week—but this was clearly the single largest batch.[96]

Later, as mistakes, flaws, and administrative snafus produced a series of irregularities in the count, the early recognition of these problems as management failures rather than intentional fraud committed by Democrats was forgotten. At the outset, however, even those who later demanded a new election after a second recount reversed Rossi's victory, mostly avoided the conclusion that fraud explained the irregularities. For example, on the "magical mystery ballots," Sharkansky reported that an anonymous King County vote count observer "reports that the last of those 'extra' ballots seem to be legitimate. According to the observer many of the ballots had signature problems of some variety and had been put aside awaiting resolution such as follow-up verification from the voter. Others were from the canvassing board where they had been sent for a decision on the voter's intent in marking, or mis-marking the ballot."[97]

At the end of the counting period, with Washington's dozens of counties finalizing their counts, and with bloggers tracking their every move and noting every discrepancy,[98] the vote differentials between Gregoire and Rossi seesawed back and forth at a dizzying rate. After the Democrats had frantically collected and turned in hundreds of affidavits from disqualified provisional ballot voters, correcting their mistakes, and the King County Elections Division began counting their newly discovered ballots, Gregoire reversed Rossi's near-week-long position in the lead, moving ahead of him by 158 votes. Three days later, on November 17, the day that counties were required to file their final tallies with the secretary of state, Sharkansky reported the numbers every half hour or so (see fig. 6.1). As the day wore on, the lead again shifted up and down between the two candidates like stock prices on a wild day of trading.[99] Washingtonians were transfixed and local bloggers were the first to call the election for Rossi, based largely on Tim Goddard's and Stefan Sharkansky's spreadsheets projecting the outcome of the uncounted absentee and provisional ballots.[100] Rossi emerged 261 votes ahead of Gregoire and was certified the winner by the county auditors.

The First (Machine) Recount: November 20–30, 2004

The question of whether fraud marred the 2004 election was only hinted at in the blogosphere before Rossi's reported victory. For example, one of Sharkansky's readers questioned the wisdom of King County Superior Court Judge Lum's decision to allow third parties (i.e., the Democrats) to collect new registration documents from people whose ballots had been rejected for signature-matching problems:

The problem from [sic] third party collection of new registrations resides with persons who illegally voted for another using a provisional ballot. The signatures may not match because the person signing the ballot isn't the person registered with the county. If third parties come to an address listed on the

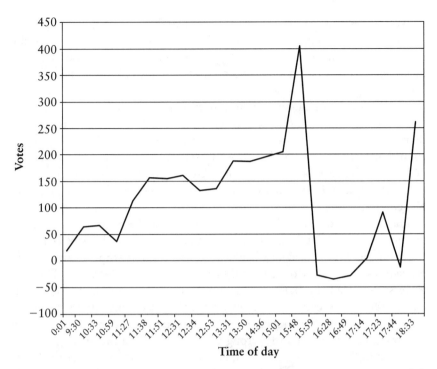

Figure 6.1   Rossi's fluctuating margin, November 17, 2004 as Washington's counties certified their results.
Source: Stefan Sharkansky, "Wednesday Vote Count," Sound Politics Blog, November 17, 2004, available at www.soundpolitics.com.

provisional ballot there is no guarantee they will be contacting the actual voter registered with the county or there is the possibility that fraud was committed but that the actual voter was complicit in the fraud or will be afterwards. A family member may not legally vote a provisional ballot for another family member but may be motivated to do so if they know that the inconvenience of voting will deter the real voter. If the family member is asked to cure an illegally voted provisional ballot by supplying a new signature, and the new registration signature is not compared to the old registration signature a fraud will have been accomplished. Similarly a fraud artist could vote many provisional ballots for persons who, from polling lists obtained late on election day, it was apparent would likely not be voting, and could list a different address on the provisional ballot. When approached by third parties, the fraudulent voter could fill out many new registrations with a signature that corresponds to the provisional ballot and the real voter would not discover the error until it was too late to affect the election.[101]

Perhaps. Procedures in which third parties intervene between the voter and elections officials are potentially less secure and more open to manipulation than those that simplify and streamline registration and voting transactions between voter and official. But because the activity suggested in this passage is criminal and subject to penalties and fines, it will not occur unless it is motivated and it will not affect an election unless it remains concealed, two qualifying factors that must be incorporated into any calculus of actual voter fraud.

Washington law mandates an automatic machine recount of the vote in a statewide race if the margin of victory is under 2,000 votes and is also less than one-half of 1 percent. If the difference is less than 150 votes, the recount must be done by hand.[102] Once Rossi was first certified the winner by 261 votes, the secretary of state ordered the counties to prepare for the mandated machine recount, which began in most counties on Saturday, November 20.

The Washington State Republican Party wasted no time in seeking to protect their candidate's tiny lead by filing an emergency lawsuit in federal court on the day the recount began to challenge and stop certain recount procedures that they worried would tip the balance to Gregoire. The controversy involved the handling of undervotes by King County, or ballots that could not be read by the county optical scan voting equipment. When the optical scan machine kicks out a ballot as unreadable because the voter has mismarked it or used the wrong color pen to fill in the ovals for candidate choice, Washington law requires election workers to inspect the ballot to see if the voter's intent is clear.[103] "If we look at it and there's clearly an indication from the voter that they intend to vote for one of the candidates for governor, it's enhanced or duplicated" so that it can be read by the optical scan machine, said Dean Logan, county elections chief.[104] The rules for "ballot enhancement" allow election workers to mark up spoiled ballots or fill out new ballots that can be read by machines when the voter's intent is obvious. For example, if a voter circles an oval instead of filling it in, an election worker may fill in the oval and send the ballot back through the machine. If election workers cannot figure out what the voter's intent is, ballots are sent to the county canvassing board for review.[105]

The Republicans wanted the court to force King County to stop counting ballots rejected by optical scan ballot counting machines. Using the same troubling logic sanctioned by the Supreme Court in *Bush v. Gore*—that procedural differences in the handling of *ballots* are analogous to constitutionally impermissible unequal treatment of *voters*[106]—they asserted that the King County "ballot enhancement" procedures "trampled" the equal protection rights of "hundreds of thousands of Washington voters." "In a process reminiscent of Florida 2000," the lawsuit alleged, elections officials—especially those in Democratic-leaning King County—were abusing voters' rights by second-guessing vote-counting machines and using human intelligence to "divine" the voters' intent.[107] Reviewing ballots rejected by the counting machines, argued the Republicans, amounted to a manual recanvassing of those ballots instead of the simple machine recount provided for in state law, giving King County voters a greater chance to have their votes counted than other voters living in counties using punch-card ballots for which ballot enhancement procedures did not apply. At an impromptu news conference on the steps of the federal courthouse, Diane Tebelius, Republican party attorney, explained, "We believe all votes should be counted equally."[108]

U.S. District Judge Ricardo Martinez ruled that the Republicans had to wait until the recount was complete before they could get a hearing on their complaint. He set a hearing date for November 30.[109] Meanwhile, on Sunday, November 21, U.S. District Judge Marsha Pechman denied the Republicans' request for a temporary restraining order to halt the recount. King County assured the judge that, in accordance with the uniform standards for conducting a recount under state law, it was keeping track of all ballots duplicated or "enhanced" for better machine reading. Lawyers for the Elections Division said that it could subtract them from the count should the court rule in favor of the Republicans. Counsel for the Democrats (who intervened in the litigation) denied the Republicans had a *Bush v. Gore* complaint, pointing out that that case involved a question of unequal treatment of the *same* type of ballot, the punch-card ballot. Here, the complaint alleged unequal treatment of *different* types of ballots. Treating different voting technologies as if they were the same would be the real violation of equal protection, argued Dave Burman, the Democrats' lawyer. Based on these arguments and assurances, Judge Pechman found no possibility for "irreparable harm" inflicted by King County, making way for the recount to continue.[110] Out of some 300,000 recounted polling ballots, and about 22,000 undervotes in all, King County eventually added 710 formerly rejected ballots to its final count.[111]

The recount revealed unsightly imperfections in the counting process. A number of counties found previously uncounted ballots and added them to the count. Snohomish County discovered 224 previously uncounted ballots originally overlooked by election workers when someone put an empty tray on top of the tray containing the ballots, concealing them from view.[112] The Republicans amended their complaint and filed affidavits from election observers that, contrary to what the lawyers for King County and the secretary of state had told Judge Pechman, King County was not following the rules for ballot enhancement. "We don't believe King County," said Chris Vance, Republican state chair. "Our observers have watched. Ballots are being altered. And we don't believe they are being set aside."[113] Indeed, a number of Republican election observers made troubling claims. They reported that machine-rejected ballots were not being preserved in their original state when election workers marked them up to trigger the machines to read them; that ballots rejected by the machines as overvotes because they appeared to record votes for both Gregoire and Rossi were being indiscriminately processed (in some cases, alleged the Republican poll watchers, election workers covered over the oval for Rossi and fed the ballots back into the machines to record a vote for Gregoire; in others, the elections supervisor referred the ballots to the King County canvassing board; and in still other cases, the ballots were simply rejected and not counted or referred); and that ballots were not being stored securely (in one case, the receipt for an improperly unsealed box recorded two fewer ballots than were counted after the box was retrieved from the vault; in another case, 88 ballots appeared to be missing from a precinct until the ballots were later found in a bag that Logan said a poll worker had used because the ballots would not fit into the box).[114] Cowlitz County was the only county to report counting seventy fewer votes in the recount. Asked by the (Tacoma) *News Tribune* to explain the difference, County Auditor Kristina Swanson said, "We're not real sure yet. If I were to make a wild guess, it would be that we ran some of those ballots twice."[115]

The ever-vigilant blogs covered the recount better and more immediately than did the establishment press. As the deadline for the counties to finish their recounts approached, Rossi maintained his lead. It would all come down to King County, which counted 1,053 more ballots than had been tabulated the first time around.[116] Sound Politics called the gubernatorial race for Rossi at 2 p.m. on Wednesday, an hour and a half after King County reported its results.[117] Rossi held on and won the recount by forty-two votes. Reed signed the canvass report on November 30, setting up Rossi's certification by the state legislature on January 10.[118]

The Second (Hand) Recount: December 1–23, 2004

But the story of the 2004 Washington gubernatorial election was far from over. State law permits anyone to request a second and final recount—if that person pays for it, 15 cents per ballot to recount the ballots by machine and 25 cents per ballot to recount them by hand. The money must be deposited upfront; if the outcome of the election changes, the state picks up the bill, but if the outcome is the same, the party requesting the recount is responsible for covering the counties' costs. For a moment, the Democrats faced a strategic dilemma, whether to ask for a full recount or for a recount in only those counties likely to produce a net gain for their candidate. Rossi had won thirty-one of the state's thirty-nine counties, whereas Gregoire's support was heavily concentrated in King County, where she garnered nearly 60 percent of the vote. The discrepancies between the first and second machine counts were most pronounced there. Only 208 net votes were added to either Rossi or Gregoire in all counties outside of King County. But in King County, which makes up one-third of the electorate in Washington, Gregoire had a net gain of 245 votes, more than the rest of the state for both candidates combined. To be even more precise, Gregoire's base in King

County was Seattle; outside the city, she actually had lost the rest of the county to Rossi by a slim margin, some 685 votes.[119]

If the Democrats asked for only a partial recount, and the election outcome changed as a result, the state would be obligated to continue with a manual count of the rest of the counties. Widely seen as a critically strategic mistake, the decision of the Gore campaign to request only a partial recount of pro-Gore counties in Florida in 2000 was still fresh in the minds of many Democrats. Asking for a partial recount now, would not preclude a full statewide manual recount if the partial count in pro-Gregoire counties gave Gregoire the lead. But it would look bad because the Democrats and the Gregoire campaign had picked up the mantra of the Gore campaign in Florida. As the counting and recounting dragged on, Gregoire's supporters demanded that election officials "count every vote." Chanting the rallying cry, they held a candlelight vigil outside of Rossi's victory party.[120] The Republicans let it be known that they were ready to go toe to toe with the Democrats and to request their own manual count in counties that voted for Rossi. Nevertheless, failing to learn the lesson, the Democratic National Committee told the Washington party it would pay for only a partial recount, and the Washington party was broke. "We budgeted to end on November 3rd," Kirsten Brost, a spokeswoman for the Democrats told *The Seattle Post-Intelligencer*. "We now have a week in which to raise $700,000."[121]

Rossi supporters warned that if a third count reversed Rossi's victory, it would be due to Democratic fraud or shenanigans inside the King County Elections Division. And it is the belief that King County elections officials or workers participated in fraud to ultimately swing the election to Gregoire that is at the core of a lingering bitterness among Rossi's supporters. John Carlson, the Republican nominee for governor in 2000, wrote a column for the *Seattle Post-Intelligencer* in which he claimed that the only reason Dino Rossi's margin had slipped from 261 to 42 votes between the first and second counts was because King County was allowed to "enhance" votes rejected by the machines.[122] Dan Evans, former Republican governor, told a columnist for the (Tacoma) *News Tribune* that "I think there is no way that Gregoire can recount herself into the governor's chair without a large share of our population thinking the election was stolen."[123] And the growing specter of fraud soon attracted national attention as well, with John Fund for the *Wall Street Journal* wondering, "Florida Northwest: Will Democrats Steal the Washington Governorship?"[124]

The big tab for a hand recount proved to be a challenge, and it sent the Democrats scrambling back to donors already bled dry by the most expensive gubernatorial election in Washington history. Gregoire had faced an unexpectedly tight race in a state that had voted by healthy margins for John Kerry and sent Maria Cantwell back to the U.S. Senate. The Democrats got a boost when Representative Adam Smith approached his friend

John Kerry and persuaded him to contribute $250,000 of unused campaign contributions to Gregoire's recount fund. By Thursday, December 2, one day before the Democrats needed to meet a 5 p.m. deadline with a deposit, they had collected an additional $135,000 in online contributions from more than 10,000 contributors and had commitments from the Democratic Governors' Association and Emily's List. With twenty-four hours to go, they needed to raise another $100,000. Gregoire tried put a stop to the speculation about whether her party and campaign would ask for a partial or full statewide manual recount. "My request of the state Democratic Party is simple: Count the entire state or don't count at all," she said in a statement released by her campaign office. "Counting every vote is the only right thing to do."[125] But the party wanted to hold on to the possibility of a partial recount. When Gregoire said that she would concede to Rossi if the Democrats failed to raise the money for a full recount, Paul Berendt, party chair said, "That would be irrelevant. Concessions have no legal standing."[126]

Meanwhile, with their candidate the putative winner of the race, the Republicans dropped their lawsuit in federal court.[127] But the Democrats picked up the Republican complaint and wrote a letter to the secretary of state urging him to investigate what they believed were irregularities across the state in the way ballots were counted. They wanted Reed to make clear in his hand-recount guidelines that ballots previously rejected should be reviewed again.[128] Reed had said that only ballots counted in the initial count should be included in the hand recount. Ballots disqualified by county canvassing boards would stay disqualified. Sounding like their Republican counterparts just the week before, it was déjà vu all over again for the Democrats. Their letter to Reed alleged that the counties were inconsistent in how they evaluated the validity of a ballot. Provisional ballots were rejected out of hand for signature problems in some counties, alleged the Democrats, whereas in others election officials did not even bother to check signatures. In King County alone, 2,478 absentee or provisional ballots were not counted because voters failed to sign them or their signatures did not match those on the registration file.[129] Deadlines for updating signatures varied from one county to the next, and one county was hours late certifying its results from the recount. David Burman, the lawyer for the Democrats who sent the letter, alleged that if the certification deadline had been enforced, that county's votes would not have been accepted and Gregoire would have won. Gregoire claimed she knew nothing about the letter.[130]

The Republicans were outraged that the Democrats were threatening litigation even before the recount had begun. For the first time in what was already a protracted period of recounting and acrimonious litigation fueled by allegations of cheating and deceit, the Republicans began to invoke the specter of fraud. Chris Vance, the party state chair, was adamant that the Democrats were "flat-out trying to steal the election with illegal votes."[131] A spokeswoman for Rossi complained, "It sounds like they [Gregoire and the Democrats] want to make Florida look like a tea party. . . . We are not going to let this stand. We will not let her try to steal this election."[132]

The minor rift opening up between Gregoire and the state party closed quickly Friday night when the Democrats announced that they had raised the money to request a full manual recount of the state. At the last possible moment, donors flooded the state party with enough money to reach their goal and the Democrats paid a $730,000 deposit to launch an unprecedented hand recount of Washington's more than 2.8 million ballots. Contributions came in from the DNC, Moveon.org, organized labor, Emily's List, Native American tribes, and supporters of Howard Dean, the former presidential candidate who had appealed to contributors through his online networks.[133]

At the same time, the Democrats opened up a second flank in their tactical war to win the governorship by filing a mandamus action in State Supreme Court against Reed; King County and its election chief; and Franklin, Pierce, and Pend Oreille counties.[134] The action sought to compel the court to order Reed and the counties to recount previously disqualified ballots that may have been rejected in error.[135] Republicans called this move "a nuclear bomb" dropped by the Democrats to "blow up our election system in Washington state."[136] Chris Vance, the Republican Party state chair, ratcheted up the fraud rhetoric when he said, "By filing this lawsuit, the Democrats are flat-out trying to steal this election."[137] On the other hand, Reed, an independent and pragmatic Republican, understood the game pretty clearly: "The party that's behind always wants to have more ballots counted. The party that's ahead wants to have less ballots counted," he flatly explained to the press.[138]

On Monday, December 13, as lawyers for the two parties prepared to argue before the court, according to news reports "a buzz went through the courtroom."[139] Election officials in King County revealed a new problem— elections workers had incorrectly disqualified 561 ballots. The problem surfaced over the weekend when King County Councilmember Larry Phillips discovered his name on a list of absentee ballot voters whose ballots were not counted. He had gone to the Elections Division to pick up materials for a day of canvassing voters whose absentee ballots had been rejected. "I went through the first page or two," he said, "and No. 10 on the list was this very familiar guy: Lawrence R. Phillips. That's me."[140] Phillips's ballot was among a pile of absentee ballots that were initially rejected because there was no match in the computer system for signatures on the ballot envelopes. Workers are supposed to pull the paper files for each voter to manually check their signatures. This was not done. Instead of being set aside for further review, these ballots were stuck in a pile of rejected ballots and forgotten.

The day after the hearing, the State Supreme Court unanimously rejected the Democratic Party petition, ruling that the court had no authority to order the secretary of state to establish standards for recanvassing ballots already rejected. They found that "under Washington's statutory scheme, ballots are to be 'retabulated' only if they have been previously counted or tallied. . . ."[141] By evening, King County elections officials revised the number of incorrectly uncounted absentee and provisional ballots to 573. Then, in the process of retrieving polling machine equipment from the county's 540 polling places, another 22 uncounted ballots were discovered unsecured in the units' side bins. These ballots should have been logged on election night and returned to election headquarters in sealed bags. That did not happen.[142] The State Supreme Court decision had no bearing on the counting of King County's rolling number of uncounted ballots because it applied only to ballots previously rejected. The newly discovered ballots had not been counted or rejected, they were only partially canvassed, lost, and then found, and state law permits canvassing boards to revise their tallies to correct for mistakes and discrepancies on the part of county election administrators.[143]

The manual recount exposed problems across the state that were not caught the first two times, when the ballots were counted by machines. In Whatcom County, seven unopened ballots were discovered stashed in the wrong pile; in Mason County, three punch-card ballots were wrongly rejected because voters wrote X's on the cards instead of punching out their chads and another twenty ballots were mistakenly not counted because voters had not fully punched out their chads (under state rules they should have been counted); in Skamania County, four ballots lightly marked in pencil were erroneously not counted; in Pend Oreille County, Rossi picked up two votes from ballots that had stuck together the first time they were run through the ballot counters; and in Grays Harbor County, several ballots were not counted because voters failed to circle the oval for their choice, drawing arrows to candidates' names, writing in an X, or circling the party designation instead of the candidate's name. Sometimes, the errors ran in the other direction—the machines were right and the human beings were wrong. In Jefferson County, for example, with four people observing the recount in one precinct, ballot counters still made mistakes in the tallies and had to recount the ballots all over again.[144]

Rossi maintained his lead throughout most of the three weeks it took county elections officials to hand-count the state's more then 2.8 million ballots. After all but King County had completed their hand recounts, Rossi had picked up eight votes, expanding his margin over Gregoire to fifty votes. The tables turned, however, when King County elections officials started finding improperly disqualified ballots that had not been counted the first or second time because election workers made mistakes or did not follow procedures. A cascading set of events tumbled into a Keystone Cops–like fiasco, with King County election administrators turning up yet another 150 ballots that should have been counted but were not, and the two parties running to court to force the canvassing board to count or not count the disputed ballots. One week and two more court cases later—one slapping a temporary restraining order on King County to stop the counting, the other lifting it—Christine Gregoire was determined the winner by 129 votes.[145]

Gregoire's election was certified by the secretary of state on December 30, 2004, and she was sworn in to office on January 12, 2005.

The Aftermath

But Gregoire's victory remained under a cloud until June, when an election contest brought in state court by the Rossi for Governor campaign and seven voters was dismissed and her certification was confirmed. In that case, the court found that 1,678 illegal votes had been cast. These included 1,401 ballots cast by people with felony convictions whose civil rights had not yet been restored, 19 ballots in the names of deceased voters, 6 double-voters, 175 provisional ballots cast by people whose qualifications to vote could not be determined, and 77 more ballots than voters.[146] Judge John Bridges was clearly disapproving of the ineptitude, careless mistakes, and deficiencies in the electoral process highlighted in the legal proceedings that allowed hundreds, if not thousands, of illegal ballots to be counted.[147] "Almost anyone who works in state or local government knows exactly what this culture is," he said. "It's inertia. It's selfishness. It's taking our paycheck but not doing the work. It's not caring about . . . the public we are supposed to serve."[148] We can only wonder what more he may have said if he had been asked to consider the number of citizens whose legal ballots were not counted, but their disfranchisement was not at issue in this case.

What the judge emphatically did not find was voter fraud.[149] In Judge Bridges's words, "The Court concludes that, having neither pled nor disclosed . . . fraud [it] cannot now be claimed and that to the extent that it was claimed, neither the act of fraud nor the causation arising therefrom were proved by the higher burden of proof of clear, cogent and convincing."[150]

The bitterness of the 2004 governor's race lingers. A task force on election reform established by Governor Gregoire shortly after she took office conducted public hearings, solicited public input over the Internet, and made recommendations to the governor and state legislature for changes in state law. One of the recommendations called for requiring some form of voter identification. As the task force noted, "Because voters are not currently required to produce proof of identity at polling sites, some members of the public believe that there is an ability to impersonate others and thus vote illegally. . . . A majority of those testifying at the Task Force meetings feel that requiring identification to be presented at the polls will reduce the potential for voter fraud."[151]

To make symbolic amends and restore public confidence, in 2005 Washington enacted a large package of electoral reform initiatives that included a polling place voter identification requirement. What failures in voter identification have to do with all of the other administrative problems revealed under the microscope of a close election remains unclear.

Later, in December 2006, John McKay, the U.S. attorney for the Western District of Washington, was quietly asked by a high-ranking official in the Justice Department to resign. He was not told the reason for his dismissal, which quickly became, along with the dismissals of at least eight other U.S. attorneys, a cause célèbre for critics of the Bush administration. But the rumors swirling around his firing suggested that McKay was being let go for, among other reasons, failing to launch investigations and prosecutions of voter fraud in the 2004 governor's race.[152] In hearings before the U.S. Senate and House Judiciary Committees on March 6, 2007, McKay described receiving a call from Ed Cassidy, the chief of staff of U.S. Representative Richard "Doc" Hastings (R-Wash.), in late 2004 or early 2005. Cassidy asked for information about any action being taken on the part of McKay's office regarding the controversial election. "I related to him the information that was publicly available at the time, which was that the Seattle division of the Federal Bureau of Investigation was taking any information that any citizen had about election fraud or election crime and, in fact, that my office, in consultation with the voting rights section, had done the same, so that anyone with information should report it to the bureau."[153]

McKay explained that he had cut off the conversation with Cassidy, whom he believed was calling at Hastings's request, to prevent Cassidy from violating ethics rules prohibiting the lobbying by elected officials for information about open investigations.[154] Representative John Conyers (D-Mich.), the committee chair, asked McKay about a *Seattle Times* story that reported on a Building Industry Association of Washington (BIAW) newsletter column written by Tom McCabe, the executive vice president of the home builders' lobbying group, and entitled "Good Riddance." BIAW supported Rossi in the 2004 election and were long at war with Christine Gregoire, who had once headed the state Department of Ecology where she presided over environmental regulations that are anathema to the BIAW.[155] In the column, McCabe said McKay "had a disastrous six years as U.S. Attorney. Two years ago, he steadfastly refused to investigate voter fraud despite overwhelming evidence." McCabe also said he "urged President Bush to fire McKay."[156] McKay responded, "I was aware that I was receiving criticism for not proceeding with a criminal investigation [of alleged voter fraud]. And, frankly, it didn't matter to me what people thought. Like my colleagues, we work on evidence, and there was no evidence of voter fraud or election fraud. And, therefore, we took nothing to the grand jury."[157]

TABLE 6.1
Voter fraud politics case studies

Case studies	Apparent strategic intent of fraud allegations	Votes cast	Voter fraud committed	Election administration errors committed	Association of fraud with discordant voter	Policy consequences
Florida: 2004 living-wage campaign	To smear a working-class advocacy organization leading a coalition of groups to raise the state's minimum wage	7,295,665	No	No	Yes (multiracial, immigrant, low-income working class)	More stringent regulation of private third-party voter registration organizations
Missouri: 2000 St. Louis presidential election	To call into question the validity of the results in St. Louis and to justify the imposition of more stringent voter identification requirements	124,752	No	Yes	Yes (African Americans)	HAVA voter identification requirement for first-time voters registering by mail, and a new mandate for the use of provisional ballots when polling places are kept open beyond normal closing times by court orders
Wisconsin: 2004 Milwaukee presidential election	To shift the state to Bush and the GOP in the election	277,535	5 people found guilty of voting while on probation or parole for a prior felony conviction	Yes	Yes (urban "underclass")	DOJ pilot program to test what works with juries in the prosecution of individual voters
Washington: 2004 gubernatorial election	To smear election administrators and persuade the court to order a revote	2,810,053	7 people found guilty of voting for deceased relatives; 1 person found guilty of double voting	Yes	Yes (felons)	Adoption of new polling-place voter identification requirements

Sources: Florida Department of State, Division of Elections; Missouri Secretary of State's Office; City of Milwaukee Election Commission; Washington Secretary of State's Office.
Notes: DOJ, U.S. Department of Justice; GOP, Republican Party; HAVA, Help America Vote Act of 2002.

In the absence of cooperation from White House political operatives, after an investigation into the firing of McKay and eight other U.S. attorneys, the inspector general of the Justice Department was unable to come to a conclusion about the role of voter fraud allegations in the firing of John McKay.[158]

Voter Fraud Politics

The four case studies reviewed here are all instances in which spurious voter fraud allegations played a strategic role in party combat. Table 6.1 summarizes the findings. The case studies support the claim that spurious voter fraud allegations were exaggerated to serve strategic partisan functions by raising public fears about voter fraud and presenting lawmakers with a rationale for imposing new rules to make it harder to vote.

Both the new rules and the manipulation of public opinion have consequences for electoral participation, even when they do not improve the immediate electoral fortunes of those making the allegations. Three of the cases demonstrate that myriad problems in election administration create the fodder for spurious voter fraud allegations in the form of inaccurate voter registration lists, mishandled voter registration applications, mismatched records, polling place log books that do not match the number of ballots cast, violations of polling place procedures, mistakes in the handling of ballots, and the like. The complexity and proliferation of regulations and, especially, the churning out of new regulations with each election cycle make errors inevitable. And these routine errors are then seized on by strategic party actors alleging fraud. Finally, it is important to point out that, without the presence of marginalized voters, those with the lowest turnout rates to begin with, the myth of voter fraud loses its power to persuade.

Chapter 7

Voter Fraud Allegations and Their Consequences

Why should political scientists who study U.S. elections and voting rights care about voter fraud? I have established here that fraud itself is a relatively rare event. Rather, the problem is the *myth* of fraud that can influence the vote count and, more important, shapes the rules that erode voting rights. In this chapter, I examine some recent consequences of the politics of voter fraud and offer suggestions for how we might dispel the myth.

Unfounded fraud allegations influence electoral politics in two different ways. In the immediate context of specific contests, fraud allegations justify voter-challenge campaigns that can lead to voter intimidation or trigger a judicial intervention in electoral recounts and disputes, which can flip elections and undermine public confidence in the integrity of electoral outcomes. Over time, unfounded fraud allegations influence voting policy by shaping voting rules and procedures in ways that inhibit the democracy-expanding potential of voting rights movements. The new policy changes stay in place long after the particular partisan battles that inspired them. They are the hidden cost of spurious voter fraud allegations. By justifying the rules that encumber access to the vote, the myth of voter fraud obscures how administrative practices combine to depress turnout in the United States.

In this book, I have documented the political use of the myth in the post–*Bush v. Gore* electoral period by showing that there is good evidence to support the conclusion (1) that voters rarely fraudulently register or vote; (2) that protections against voter fraud are sufficiently provided for in federal and state law; and (3) that from a cost-benefit perspective this makes it irrational for voters to cast fraudulent ballots. But using that same calculus, we find rational reasons why parties and their allies might seize on the imperfect mechanics of electoral administration to *allege* voter fraud. A selection of cases in which voter fraud allegations were used to influence electoral outcomes or shape election law are discussed in chapter 6. Throughout the period covered by this study, we can see efforts at the federal and state levels to up-end election laws, some of them long-standing rules to which regular voters and election workers were well adapted (see table 7.1). The legislative upsurge has been accompanied by a troubling increase in election law litigation[1] that has only further spurred the politicization of election administration. At the root of all this is the myth of voter fraud.

The Thicket of Election Legislation

The accretion of rules entangling voters and making it harder for some (if not all) to vote involves a process we might call "death by a thousand election laws," whereby the production and reproduction of laws and procedures stifles the sovereign exercise of the right to vote.

U.S. election codes are hardly models of legal elegance; and in a Weberian sense, the state agencies created to implement them are practically prebureaucratic. Election officials in charge of running elections do not make the election laws; they only implement them, and they do this through the promulgation of more rules and procedures. When election laws are changed, procedural rules, mandates, and codes must be adapted undermining a principle of modern bureaucratic administration—that of a fixed and stable structure. A second way U.S. election administration is prebureaucratic is in its weak authority over line workers—the poll workers—who provide the link between the voter and a counted ballot.[2] Thorough training of all personnel across the organizational hierarchy, specialization across a division of labor, and expertise acquired by routines of work and practice—these are all hallmarks of a modern bureaucracy. Often they are not found in the administration of elections in the United States. As Max Weber notes, "the reduction of modern office management to rules is deeply embedded in its very nature. The theory of modern public administration . . . does not entitle [regulation] by commands given for each case, but only . . . abstractly."[3]

But this is not how we regulate elections. The piecemeal accretion of fragmentary rules is actually the failure of bureaucratic administration. The convoluted, sometimes even contradictory election codes in place today are the product of electoral competition carried into the legislative arena. Election codes reflect the efforts of dominant parties to institutionalize their electoral advantage. We can think of them as embedded party strategies. The years pass, the circumstances and temper of partisan conflict changes, but the rules—being laws and, therefore, institutions—remain on the books.

The 2000 election set off an explosion of state legislative activity in the area of election law. In the first nine months of 2001 alone, nearly 1,800

TABLE 7.1
Total number of election reform bills in the states, 2001–2008

	Total introduced or carried over from previous session[a]	Enacted	Vetoed	Failed
2001	1,997	303	14	908
2002	1,477	171	7	1,266
2003	1,677	324	21	702
2004	1,437	144	7	1,090
2005	1,838	219	17	940
2006	1,275	140	5	909
2007	1,967	246	16	892
2008	1,913	171	20	1,622
Total	13,581	1,718	107	8,329

Source: National Conference of State Legislatures, Database of Election Reform Legislation (accessed June 2009), available at http://www.ncsl.org/default .aspx?tabid=16588. The National Conference of State Legislatures Election Reform database uses the following categories to code election-reform legislation in the states: Absentee Voting, Absentee Voting—Application for, Absentee Voting—Distributing Ballots, Absentee Voting—Early Voting/In-Person Absentee, Absentee Voting—Eligibility, Absentee Voting—Military/Overseas, Absentee Voting—No-Excuse, Absentee Voting—Permanent Status, Absentee Voting—Returning Ballots, Appropriations, Audits—Post-Election, Ballot Access—Candidates, Ballot Access—Parties, Ballots—Format and Design, Candidates—Qualifications for Office, Candidates—Resign-to-Run, Candidates—Withdrawal, Candidates—Write-in, Canvass, Challenges to Voters, Contests, Cost of Elections, Counting Votes, Dates of Elections, DREs—Paper Trail, Election Crimes, Election Data—Collection/Retention of, Election Day Holiday, Election Officials—Campaign Activities, Election Officials—County/Local Election Officials—Statewide, Election Results, Electioneering, Electoral College, Election College—NPV, Emergencies/Disasters, Exit Polling, Fusion/Dual-Party, HAVA Compliance, Instant Run-Off, Internet/Electronic Voting, Mail Voting, Office—Method of Filing, Political Parties, Poll Watchers, Poll Workers, Poll Workers—Compensation, Poll Workers—Selection/Qualifications of, Poll Workers—Training, Poll Workers-Youth, Polling Places—Arrangement of/Procedures at, Polling Places—Disabled Access/Assistance, Polling Places—Hours, Polling Places—Locations, Polling Places—Vote Centers, Precinct Definition, Primaries—Dates, Primaries—General, Primaries—Presidential, Primaries—Run-offs, Primaries—Types, Provisional Voting, Recall, Recounts, Registration Drives, Registration—Application Form/Content, Registration—Centralized Voter List, Registration—Deadline, Registration—Election Day, Registration—Electronic, Registration—General, Registration—ID Required, Registration—List Maintenance, Registration—Preregistration, Registration—Sale/Distribution/Use of Lists, Registration—Universal, Robo-Calls, Run-Off Elections, Sample Ballots, Special Elections, Straight Ticket Voting, Task Forces/Study Commissions/Interim Committees, Vacancies, Voter Education/Information, Voter ID—All Voters, Voter ID—New Voters Only, Voter Info Pamphlets, Voter Intent, Voters—Absence from Work, Voters—Age, Voters—Convicted Felons, Voters—Disabled, Voters—Miscellaneous Qualifications, Voting Equipment/Technology, Voting System Standards/Testing/Security, and Weekend Voting. DRE, direct recording electronic (voting machine); HAVA, Help America Vote Act of 2002; NPV, National Popular Vote.
   [a] Includes Carried Over, Enacted, Vetoed, Failed, and Pending legislation; the total number of bills introduced over the eight-year period still pending by June 2009 was 182 (not shown).

election reform bills were introduced in state legislatures across the country, and some 250 of these were signed into law.[4] Over the next eight years, the struggle to gain competitive advantage by manipulating electoral rules did not abate. For an example of the process, let us look at what happened in one important swing state, Colorado.[5]

Colorado is like many states in that, after a decade in which hardly any new election rules were passed or changed, its Republican-dominated legislature awakened to the political opportunities that the HAVA presented for re-engineering election law. Of course, Democrats are no less opportunistic when it comes to manipulating election laws, but it is the party in power that has the upper hand. The HAVA required all states to pass implementing legislation, thus creating new opportunities at the state level for gaining partisan advantage. Colorado Republicans seized the opportunity, amending the state election code in every session after 2002. This included passing and repealing the same sections of the code over the course of just three years. Guiding them was the growing concern that Colorado voters were shifting toward the Democrats during the 2000–2007 period.[6]

Administrative rules issued by the secretary of state and recent legislative changes to the Colorado Uniform Election Code now combine to mandate the following: all voters must show identification,[7] unless they vote by mail, except if they also registered by mail, in which case they must include a copy of any of the forms of identification allowed for voting in person[8]—unless they previously voted in Colorado,[9] but not if they are entitled to vote by absentee ballot under the federal Uniformed and Overseas Citizens Absentee Voting Act, or are provided the right to vote otherwise than in person under (b) (2) (B) (ii) of the federal Voting Accessibility for the Elderly and Handicapped Act.[10] If a voter shows up at a polling place but does not show identification, or if that voter's qualification or entitlement to vote "cannot be immediately established upon examination of the registration list . . . or upon examination of the records on file with the county clerk and recorder," the voter is "entitled" to cast a provisional ballot.[11] In 2004, Colorado voters "entitled" to cast provisional ballots cast 12,461 ballots that were not counted.[12]

If a voter who applies for a mail-in (absentee) ballot in Colorado and spoils it or never receives it in the mail then tries to vote in person and is willing to swear under oath that he or she "has not or will not cast the mail-in ballot," a provisional ballot awaits.[13] But Colorado administrative rule 26.23(B) provides that provisional ballots will not be counted if the voter applied for an absentee ballot. If the voter fails to sign the provisional ballot, it will not be counted unless that voter pays a visit to the county clerk no later than eight days after the election.[14] The eight days are more like four or five because the election officials have two days after the election before they are required to send out letters notifying voters of the problem. If a voter goes to the wrong precinct and somehow manages to vote, the ballot will not be counted, except that votes cast for president or vice-president will be counted, but not if the voter also applied for an absentee ballot.[15]

Could the impenetrable logic and administrative problems associated with these confusing rules have anything to do with why in 2004, according to the EAC Election Day Survey, Colorado managed to count 271,524 more absentee ballots than were returned?[16]

Voters who move into Colorado are not spared the confusion. "A person who moves to Colorado from another state no later than the thirtieth day before an election but fails to register to vote before the close of registration may cast a provisional ballot, but the ballot shall not be counted."[17] Colorado requires all voters to register by the twenty-ninth day before an election— why would the state allow an unregistered person to cast a provisional ballot only to then not count it? Given the many ways a regular ballot can morph into a provisional one, it is not surprising that nearly 5 percent of all ballots cast at polling sites in Colorado were provisional ballots, twice the national average. Of course, as we might expect, "A person who moves to Colorado from another state in the twenty-nine days before an election may cast a provisional ballot, but the ballot shall not be counted."[18] But why would it be counted? It would take a miracle to cast it in the first place.

In the end, what gets counted comes down to the county clerk and recorder's ability to figure it all out: registered/not registered?; registered by mail, but voted in Colorado before?; "active"/"inactive?"; right form of ID/wrong form of ID?; right precinct/wrong precinct? Then there is the small matter of a system that is dependent on the perfect efficiency and accuracy of the U.S. Postal Service because failing to respond to notices from election officials can get a voter "purged" from the rolls.[19] Finally, even if a voter manages to stay within the undulating bounds of the law, assuming he or she knows what those bounds are, he or she still is not in the clear. A Colorado voter can be challenged as ineligible by a fellow citizen "watcher" or even "any eligible elector of the precinct" on the challenger's belief—no substantiating evidence is required—that the voter is not eligible to vote.[20] If the challenge is disputed, the voter must answer questions, sign the challenge form, or take an oath,[21] and "the person shall be offered a provisional ballot."[22] And we can close the circle because we are back to the ability of the county clerk and recorder to keep perfect records and successfully puzzle through this mess. A voter and even an election official might be tempted to stash a flask of whiskey in her purse or his pocket just to get through the ordeal of election day. Be forewarned, however: "It is unlawful for any election official or other person to introduce into any polling place, or to use therein, or to offer to another for use therein, at any time while any election is in progress or the result thereof is being ascertained by the counting of the ballots, any intoxicating malt, spirituous, or vinous liquors."[23]

E. E. Schattschneider had a fundamental insight into the workings of modern electoral and party politics. In an oft-quoted passage, he once said, "In politics as in everything else it makes a great difference whose game we play. The rules of the game determine the requirements for success."[24] The power of the voter fraud myth is its power to justify electoral rules that competitive parties and politicians create to "keep down the vote" and gain advantage over their opponents.[25] The victims are the most vulnerable voters who lack the resources, educational background, or experience to resist being expunged from the electorate by the culminating effect of these rules.

Partisan Tactics as Law: The Voter Identification Hoax

At the time, the 2000 election debacle in Florida generated strong public interest in election reform. Liberal civil and voting rights groups sought redress in a broad federal law that at a minimum would prohibit certain administrative practices and the use of the most error-prone voting equipment believed to be partly responsible for the Florida election day meltdown. Then, the 9/11 attacks distracted lawmakers and the public alike from this goal. Following nearly two years of attending to other pressing concerns, and the deliberate efforts by some to avoid reform, Congress passed and the president signed the Help America Vote Act of 2002 (HAVA).[26] The law is sometimes elevated into the pantheon of federal voting rights laws,[27] but it is not concerned with traditional voting rights issues such as full and nondiscriminatory access to the ballot and should not be considered a voting rights law. As the Bush Justice Department repeatedly asserted in legal briefs supportive of the restrictive application of the law's provisional balloting requirements, HAVA does not establish any new individual rights.[28] Instead, the HAVA is an election administration law that addresses some of the more egregious problems highlighted by the Florida debacle by outlawing the punch-card voting machine and requiring the states to permit qualified voters facing registration problems at the polls to cast provisional ballots.[29] The HAVA appears to tackle these problems, but it does not expand the meaning of the right to vote, nor does it address the corruption of election administration by partisanship, simplify the voting process, or do anything significant to assure us that our votes will be more accurately recorded and counted.[30]

The HAVA also addressed an alleged problem that did not surface in Florida—voter fraud and the need for more stringent voter identification rules. Indeed, Florida already had a voter identification law on its books, and all Florida voters had to present identification in the presidential election that year. There were no known cases of voter impersonation in the 2000 election in Florida or elsewhere that needed to be addressed by federal legislation. Yet the HAVA became the first federal election law that requires the states to collect official identifying information from citizens when they register to vote. Moreover, voters registering by mail who are unable or unwilling to provide a driver's license number or the last four digits of their Social Security numbers must present documentary proof of their identity the first time they vote in a jurisdiction.

The HAVA voter identification requirements were contested, and the dispute nearly derailed passage of the bill. The House version, which garnered bipartisan support by wide margins, contained no new voter identification requirements.[31]

In the Senate, however, Christopher "Kit" Bond (R-Mo.) was almost single-handedly responsible for keeping the voter identification requirements in the final Senate version of the bill.[32] Bond's obsession with voter fraud was inflamed by the 2000 election, when the Missouri Republican Party lost all of its statewide races except for secretary of state.[33] He mounted a relentless campaign to promote the idea that the election results in Missouri were illegitimate. On the floor of the Senate and to any reporter who would listen, Bond pounded home the notion that voter fraud and cheating by Democrats were major threats to U.S. elections. Bond alleged that "brazen," "shocking," "astonishing," and "stunning" fraud was committed, with dead people registering and voting from the grave, fake names and phony addresses proliferating across the nation's voter rolls, dogs registering, and people signing up to vote from vacant lots. In short, a "major criminal enterprise designed to defraud voters" was underway.[34] Bond became known for saying that he wanted to "make it easier to vote and harder to cheat," even though on states rights grounds he opposed outlawing the punch-card voting technology that had bedeviled Florida voters, and which experts identified as responsible for a truly "astonishing" number of "lost" votes.[35] Allegations of a "premeditated effort" in St. Louis, an "overwhelmingly Democrat-controlled city," to stuff the ballot box in a federal election were casually thrown around on the floor of the Senate. Bond implied that a residence where eight registered voters lived was a "drop site" involved in a "common form of absentee ballot fraud," where "individuals . . . register, usually by mail, multiple names at one address and then request absentee ballots for all their new roommates, phantom though they might be, and they vote all of the ballots coming in to those invisible roomies."[36] He made snide comments about voters who had to get court orders to vote on election day in St. Louis because the city's Republican-appointed Board of Election had illegally purged them from the rolls.[37] And ever in search of a laugh line, Bond employed cartoonish language about how he liked dogs and had respect for "the dearly departed, but I do not think we should allow them to vote."[38] One dog—Ritzy Meckler—became the most famous Springer Spaniel registered to vote in world history.[39]

Corruption versus Inefficiency and the National Voter Registration Act of 1993

Bond also played to his far-right base, blaming the epidemic of voter fraud on the NVRA, a Clinton-era voting rights law designed to move the country toward a European-style universal voter registration system in which government plays a more active role in ensuring all eligible citizens are registered to vote.[40] To trash the NVRA is to speak in Republican Party code. The law was passed during a brief period when Democrats controlled both Congress and the presidency (1993–1995) and came to be identified with Bill Clinton, the target of so much ideological fury for hard-core, right-wing partisans. Congressional Republicans almost uniformly opposed the bill on the grounds that it was an unconstitutional exercise of congressional power and an intrusion on states rights. They also objected to what they believed was another unfunded federal government mandate on the states and railed about how the law's restrictions on purging and mail-in registration requirements would increase opportunities for voter fraud. An earlier version of the "motor voter" bill was vetoed by President George H. W. Bush on the eve of the Fourth of July, 1992, because, he said, it exposed the election process to "an unacceptable risk of fraud and corruption."[41]

Perhaps to the chagrin of its critics, and despite a slow start, the NVRA has been responsible for adding millions of new voters to the rolls. The increase in access to the franchise, however, has provoked the old saw that greater access inevitably leads to more voter fraud. Bond is a principal proponent of this unfounded theory. For example, he charged in a *Washington Post* opinion piece that "the National Voter Registration Act of 1993, aka 'motor voter,' not only *caused* sloppy voter rolls, it actually facilitated organized vote fraud" in the 2000 election in Missouri.[42] According to Deborah M. Phillips, another critic of the NVRA and founder and chair of the Voting Integrity Project (a defunct national organization concerned about voter fraud), "the National Voter Registration Act has tied the hands of election directors to protect the rights of legitimate voters from the dilution of vote fraud."[43] John Samples, the director of the Center for Responsive Government at the conservative Cato Institute, added his voice to the chorus of conservative opponents of the NVRA when he testified before the Senate Rules and Administration Committee that the NVRA encouraged lax registration requirements (through the use of mail-in registration forms) that "have left the voter rolls in a shambles in many states," breeding mistrust in the electoral process and "foment[ing] 'the appearance of corruption,' that has, fairly or not, done real damage to American government." Because NVRA "has made it difficult if not impossible to maintain clean registration rolls," Samples said, NVRA was responsible for some of the decline in trust in government observed by political scientists over the past four decades.[44] At the same hearing, Todd F. Gaziano, a senior fellow in Legal Studies and director of the Center for Legal and Judicial Studies at the Heritage Foundation, and later a G. W. Bush appointee to the U.S. Civil Rights Commission, testified that, "Regardless of the intent of the Motor Voter law, it has helped create the most inaccurate voting rolls in our history. Citizens are registered in multiple jurisdictions at the same time, and very few states have effective procedures to ensure that those registered even are citizens. . . . you can almost guarantee that illegal voting may provide the margin of victory in a close contest."[45] Fueling these views, one of the most vociferous critics of the NVRA, the *Wall Street Journal*, published at least four editorials lambasting the NVRA in 2001, as the Congress deliberated over election reform bills, claiming voter fraud was out of control.[46]

One way that the NVRA has increased access to voter registration is by increasing the number of physical sites where citizens may submit voter registration applications, including motor vehicle agencies and state agencies administering services to the indigent, elderly, and disabled. The NVRA requires state officials at these sites to inform clients about voter registration opportunities. If state officials follow the law, people who visit motor vehicle agencies and welfare offices more than once stand a good chance of being asked on more than one occasion if they would like to register to vote. Moreover, multiple registrations can occur if a registrant submits updated information using a new application form. It is not difficult to understand why a person might fill out a duplicate application, given the common experience with bureaucratic inefficiency.

Local election officials must spend time and resources checking new registration applications for duplication. For example, a 2001 Government Accounting Office (GAO) report on election administration found that 99 percent of voting jurisdictions nationwide routinely checked for multiple registrations.[47] One local official complained to the GAO about the way the NVRA created multiple avenues to the voter registration rolls and what he saw as a needless duplication of work: "You can ask any county clerk in the state and they will tell you that the biggest problem is motor voter. Residents can register at the welfare office, the health department, the motor vehicle authorities, and they do, time and again. This results in tons of registrations which are costly and time-consuming to sort through and check against records."[48]

On the other hand, other election officials told the GAO they supported the motor vehicle authorities' policy to encourage citizens to reapply if they had any reason to believe they might not be registered. Another pointed out that duplicate registrations rarely convert to multiple votes, commenting, "We were even on *60 Minutes* in 1998 with our 16,000 fraudulent voter registrations. . . . However, we did track those. We did not have a single one of those people vote."[49] Statewide voter registration systems now mandated under the HAVA reduce the potential for multiple registrations by auto-matically flagging duplicates or canceling a registration at an old address when a new address is submitted.[50]

Critics of the NVRA rules for list purging (and the costs associated with purging) point to the considerable amount of "deadwood," or ineligible vot-ers, on voting rolls. Deadwood is presumed to be fodder for voter fraud—names of voters no longer living in a jurisdiction, dead, or otherwise in-eligible to vote but whose names can be voted by those willing to commit fraud. Indeed, as the states came into compliance with the NVRA list main-tenance requirements and its constraints on purging, the number of "inac-tive" registrants significantly increased from 1.6 million in 1994 to over 18 million in 2000, or 11 percent of the total number of registered voters. Moreover, before the HAVA forced the states to consolidate their locally administered voter registration lists, purges became more costly. In some places, the number of registrants grew to outnumber the voting-age popula-tion because local or county registrars failed to keep their lists up to date.[51]

The NVRA permits the maintenance of inactive lists, or lists of voters who have failed to respond to address verification notices sent by the voter registrar. Inactive lists are a measure of the churning produced by combin-ing a voter registration system tied to territorially based eligibility criteria with high voter mobility.[52] It is important to note that voters do not stay on inactive lists indefinitely; they may be deleted from inactive lists after failing to respond to mailings sent to verify residency and failing to vote in two successive federal elections. "Inactive" voters, therefore, may be left on such lists for as little as two-and-a-half years before they are purged entirely from the rolls.

Contrary to the claims of NVRA critics, for about half of the forty states that purged voters for failure to vote prior to the enactment of the NVRA, this represents a *decrease* in the length of time a voter could remain inactive under prior state law before being deleted entirely from the rolls.[53] More-over, the NVRA list maintenance provisions, which were crafted to balance voter protections against the arbitrary power of local registrars to knock eligible voters off the rolls,[54] permit deletions from the rolls in eight states that did not purge for nonvoting before the NVRA.[55] In the 1999–2000 cycle, five of those states purged 1,888,795 names from their new inactive lists, names that prior to 1993 could have remained on state and local voter registries.[56] Also, they removed an additional 719,761 voters from their ac-tive lists. A number of high-profile cases of election fraud involving the manipulation of "deadwood" voter registration records (mostly through absentee ballot fraud) gave critics' arguments some weight. But the misman-agement of voter registration lists involving the erroneous removal of voters from active lists used at the polls has always been a more significant prob-lem, one that emerged in the 2000 presidential election and that was com-pounded by the failure of elections officials to observe the NVRA fail-safe provisions to provide opportunities for those voters to vote.[57] In sum, NVRA, properly administered and enforced, is responsible for significantly tightening up, not loosening, list maintenance requirements in many states.

Several states resisted the initial implementation of the NVRA. All the lawsuits brought to challenge the legislation's constitutionality raised concerns about voter fraud.[58] None of the federal courts hearing the challenges, however, found the evidence convincing or the concerns legitimate.[59] Today, states reporting problems in maintaining accurate voter registration lists mostly complain about the cost of complying with the mailings required in the state implementation of the NVRA; none has raised the issue of voter fraud among the implementation problems. The NVRA requires the states to clean their voter registration rolls by deleting voters who have moved out of the jurisdiction or died; it requires voters to sign their names attesting to their eligibility to vote under penalty of perjury, and deportation for noncitizens. It does not prohibit states from requiring mail-in registrants to vote in person the first time they vote, nor does it prohibit states from checking individuals' identification prior to registration, as some critics of the NVRA have alleged.[60] Finally, the NVRA actually strengthened the enforcement provisions against fraud.[61] Properly implemented and adequately funded, the NVRA helps guard against the possibility of voter fraud.

Protection by Exclusion: The Help America Vote Act

On February 27, 2002, Senator Charles Schumer (D-NY) introduced a measure to gut the identification requirements that Senator Bond proposed for inclusion in the Senate election reform bill that became the HAVA. Schumer would have allowed first-time voters who registered by mail to affirm their identity at the polls with simply a signature, the way all voters do in New York. Schumer estimated that only half of his voting-age constituents had driver's licenses,[62] and for those millions of New Yorkers with roommates, utility and phone bills were often in others' names.

But Bond was unrepentant. "Sending in a signature," he quipped, was "not going to cut the mustard." A spokesman for Bond explained, "The rolls are bloated with deadwood, *literally*. It's a joke! That's why Kit is demanding voters show ID—to restore integrity to the system."[63]

The Republicans put pressure on Schumer and accused him of bargaining in bad faith. They put up posters around the Capitol featuring "a balding, deer-in-the-headlights" Schumer and this warning: "WANTED FOR KILLING ELECTION REFORM IN THE SENATE. CONSIDERED EXTREMELY QUOTABLE AND DANGEROUS TO BI-PARTISAN DEALS."[64] They then led a filibuster against the Schumer amendment, and Senator Tom Daschle, Democratic Senate Majority leader, failing to find sixty votes to shut down debate pulled the bill from the floor.[65] Schumer and the Democratic leaders held a meeting with civil and voting rights groups to discuss what to do. They worried about a voter backlash in the upcoming midterm elections that would blame the Democrats for holding up the reform measure.

The advocates wanted to hold firm while Schumer wanted to compromise, which he did after meeting with Bond by withdrawing his amendment. The two of them agreed to make clear that nothing in the final bill was intended to override existing civil or voting rights laws. To accommodate senators from Oregon and Washington who worried that the voter identification requirements would inhibit their states' vote-by-mail systems, language was added to the bill that would allow voters to simply write their driver's license number or Social Security number on their registration application or mail-in ballot. The Democrats and Republicans worked out a compromise during conference to reconcile the two versions of the bill. Instead of requiring first-time voters to present photo identification to vote, acceptable forms of identification could include a copy of "a current utility bill, bank statement, government check, paycheck, or other government document that shows the name and address of the voter."[66]

The final version passed the House 357–48 and the Senate 92–2, with the only No votes cast by New York senators Hillary Rodham Clinton and Charles Schumer. A number of civil rights groups representing people of color, such as the NAACP, the National Urban League, and National Council of La Raza were furious, calling the measure "an exercise in intimidation."[67] Referring to the inclusion of new voter identification measures, Marisa J. Demeo, director of the Washington office of the Mexican American Legal Defense and Educational Fund, said, "We are in a state of shock that at least the Democratic members of the conference committee signed off on these Republican proposals."[68] Later, even though they continued to oppose the identification requirements, the NAACP and the Congressional Black Caucus reluctantly endorsed the bill because they believed that in the end it was the best they could get.

In practice, the HAVA voter identification requirement has proved largely uncontroversial, perhaps because it applies to only a fraction of the electorate. Those most likely to be affected are not randomly drawn; they are a vulnerable segment of the population among frequent movers and nondrivers, especially new registrants among students, but also the housebound elderly and the urban poor.

The real significance of the new federal identification rule, however, is not in its limited coverage or the total number of people that it compels to produce identity documents at the polls. The HAVA ID requirement is significant for other reasons. First, it is difficult to implement, especially in states that do not require voters to present any documentary identification at the polling place on election day. The identification mandate requires election officials to flag suspect individuals on lists of eligible voters used by often inadequately trained poll workers. The HAVA thus sanctions the disparate treatment of voters by requiring that only some, not all, present documentary proof of their identity at the polling place before they are allowed to exercise their right to vote.

The second reason the HAVA ID rule is significant is because it was justified by unfounded allegations of voter fraud. Moreover, by mandating voter identification, it embedded a party tactic into federal law and signaled approval for a new partisan movement in the states to encumber voters with unnecessary identification requirements.

Before the HAVA, only fourteen states required voters to produce some kind of documentary evidence at the polls of their identity or primary residential address. None of these states blocked voters who lacked the requisite identification from casting a regular polling place ballot as long as such voters' names and addresses or birth dates appeared on the registration rolls, or in some states, if voters could be vouched for by election workers or signed affidavits swearing they were who they said they were and lived where they said they lived (see table 7.2).

By 2008, thirteen more states had enacted tighter polling place voter identification laws. Nine of those states had never before required documentary proof of identity to vote, whereas two, Florida and Georgia, revised their existing voter identification laws to require that voters without identification cast only provisional ballots, eliminated certain forms of previously acceptable documents, and mandated that identification documents contain a photograph of the voter and be issued by a federal or state (or in some states, local) government (see table 7.3).[69]

The manipulation of the Florida voter identification laws by the state's Republican-dominated legislature and governor is a particularly egregious example of how party tactics get embedded in election codes. Instead of addressing the corruption and partisan saturation of election administration, the legislature created a successive string of new identification rules to guard against nonexistent voter fraud, layering in requirements that compel the unequal treatment of voters at the polls.

Citing concerns about voter fraud, between 2003 and 2007, Florida lawmakers voting along party lines, with Republicans in favor and Democrats opposed, revised voter identification requirements in every legislative session. New polling place voter identification requirements were first inserted in Florida law in response to the egregious absentee ballot fraud orchestrated by campaign workers in the 1997 Miami mayoral race.[70] In addition to requiring the secretary of state to hire only a private company to manage the state "felon exception" list, reform legislation passed in 1998 added a photo identification requirement to section 98.471 of the state election code ("Use of precinct register at the polls"). Before this, the law had given the secretary of state discretion in determining acceptable forms of identification. The old law read, "the clerk or inspector shall

TABLE 7.2
States with documentary polling place voter identification requirements before the enactment of the Help America Vote Act of 2002

	Year first adopted[a]	Statute/code source	Rule (as of 2008–2009)	Exception
Alaska	Before 1993*	Alaska Stat. § 15.15.225 (2008)	Voters "shall" show one form of identification with name and current address, including an official voter registration card, driver's license, state identification card, current and valid photo identification, birth certificate, passport, or hunting or fishing license; or an original or a copy of a current utility bill, bank statement, paycheck, government check, or other government document.	Election officials may waive the identification requirement if the they know the identity of the voter. The identification requirement may not be waived for voters who are first-time voters who initially registered by mail or by facsimile or other electronic transmission and did not provide identification. A voter who cannot exhibit a required form of identification shall be allowed to vote a "questioned" ballot.
Arkansas	1999	Ark. Code § 7–5–305 (2008)	After voter states name and address and states or confirms birth date, election official "shall" request the voter, "for purposes of identification," to provide a valid driver's license, photo identification card issued by a governmental agency, voter card, social security card, birth certificate, U.S. passport, employee identification card issued by a governmental agency containing a photograph, employee identification card issued in the normal course of business of the employer, student identification card, Arkansas hunting license, or U.S. military identification.	Voters unable to present documentation shall be permitted to vote a regular ballot; election officials shall indicate on the precinct voter registration list that the voter did not provide identification and the county board of election "may" review these lists, providing any suspicious cases to the prosecuting attorneys.

State	Year	Citation	Identification requirement	If lacking proper identification
Connecticut	1993	Conn. Gen. Stat. Ann. § 147-9-261 (2009).	After announcing his or her name and address "in a tone sufficiently loud and clear as to enable all the election officials present to hear the same, a voter must show his or her Social Security card or "any other preprinted form of identification which shows his name and either his address, signature or photograph."	A voter who lacks proper identification may sign an affidavit attesting to identity, under penalty of false statement.
Delaware	Before 1998*	Del. Code tit. 15, § 4937 (2009)	Voters state name and address, and "provide proof of identity" to the clerk.	A voter who lacks proper identification may sign an affidavit attesting to identity.
Florida	1998	Fla. Stat. § 101.043 (2008)	"The clerk or inspector shall require each elector, upon entering the polling place, to present one of the following picture identifications: Florida driver's license; Florida identification card issued . . . ; U.S. passport; debit or credit card; military identification; student identification; retirement center identification; neighborhood association identification; public assistance identification." If the identification document does not contain the voter's signature, an additional identification that provides a signature shall be required.	Voters who are unable to provide the required identification may vote a provisional ballot; the canvassing board shall determine the validity of the ballot pursuant to state law.

(continued)

(TABLE 7.2—cont.)

	Year first adopted[a]	Statute/code source	Rule (as of 2008–2009)	Exception
Georgia	1997	Ga. Code Ann. § 21-2-417 (2008)	Each elector "shall present" to a poll worker proper identification, which includes any one of the following: a Georgia driver's license, a Georgia voter identification card, or any other state or federally issued personal identification card, a U.S. passport, a government employee identification card with a photo, a valid Georgia student identification card with a photo, a U.S. military identification card, or a valid tribal identification card.	Voters without documentation shall be permitted to vote a provisional ballot by signing an identity affidavit that notes false swearing is a felony crime.
Hawaii	Before 1993*	Hawaii Rev. Stat. § 11-136 (2008)	"Every person upon applying to vote shall sign the person's name in the poll book. . . . Every person shall provide identification if so requested by a precinct official."	Discretion granted election officials to verify voter's information with the official register.
Kentucky	1988	Ky. Rev. Stat. Ann. § 117.227 (2009)	Voters are required to present an identification document, "such as a motor vehicle operator's license, Social Security card, or credit card. The election officer confirming the identity shall sign the precinct voter roster and list the method of identification." In addition to the forms of identification specifically provided for by law, any identification card that bears both the picture and signature of the voter, or any identification card that has been issued by the county, and that has been approved in writing by the State Board of Elections, shall be acceptable for confirmation of the voter's identity.	Voters are not required to present identification if an election officer can "confirm the identity of each voter by personal acquaintance. . . ."

State	Year	Statute		
Louisiana	1997	La. Rev. Stat. Ann. § 18:562 (2008)	Voter must identify himself to a commissioner, giving his name and address; the commissioner then announces the voter's name and address; the voter provides a Louisiana driver's license, a Louisiana special identification card, or "other generally recognized picture identification card that contains the name, address, and signature of the applicant. . . ."	Voters without documentation may vote after signing an affidavit, and providing further identification such as a current registration certificate, giving a birth date, or providing other information requested by the commissioners; "an applicant that is allowed to vote without the picture identification required . . . is subject to challenge."
Missouri	2002[b]	Mo. Rev. Stat. § 115.427 (2008)[c]	Before receiving a ballot, a voter shall establish his or her identity by presenting a form of personal identification; acceptable identification includes a nonexpired Missouri drivers license or state identification card, identification issued by a Missouri institution of higher education, a copy of a current utility bill, a bank statement, a paycheck, a government check or other government document that contains the name and address of the voter, or a driver's license or state identification card issued by another state.	A voter lacking proper identification may vote if two election judges, one from each party, attests to personally knowing the voter.
South Carolina	1984	S.C. Code § 7-15-220 (2008)	"When any person presents himself to vote, he shall produce his valid South Carolina driver's license or other form of identification containing a photograph issued by the Department of Motor Vehicles, if he is not licensed to drive. . . ."	—

(*continued*)

(TABLE 7.2—cont.)

	Year first adopted[a]	Statute/code source	Rule (as of 2008–2009)	Exception
Tennessee	Before 2001*	Tenn. Code Ann. § 2-7-112 (2008)	Voters at the polls sign the poll book and the registrar shall compare the voter's signature with other evidence of identification supplied by the voter; this identification shall be a valid voter's registration certificate, Tennessee driver license, Social Security card, credit card bearing the applicant's signature or other document bearing the applicant's signature.	A voter unable to provide identification shall be required to execute an affidavit of identity.
Texas	1985	Tex. Bus. & Com. Code § 63.001-.0101	Before a voter may be "accepted" for voting, he or she must present a voter registration certificate.	A voter who does not present a voter registration certificate and whose name is on the list of registered voters may vote by signing an affidavit stating the voter does not have the voter registration certificate at the time of offering to vote and by providing identification (a driver's license or personal identification card issued by the Texas Department of Public Safety or a similar document issued to the person by an agency of another state, regardless of whether the license or card has expired; a photo identification; a birth certificate; U.S. citizenship

papers or passport; official mail addressed to the person by name from a governmental entity; a copy of a current utility bill, bank statement, government check, paycheck, or other government document that show the name and address of the voter; or any other form of identification prescribed by the secretary of state). A voter who does not present a voter registration certificate and whose name is not on the list of registered voters may vote with a provisional ballot.

A voter lacking proper identification may vote if he or she signs an affidavit attesting to identity under penalty of false swearing.

| Virginia | 1996 | Va. Code Ann. § 24.2-643 (2009) | Voter must present any one of the following forms of identification: Commonwealth of Virginia voter registration card, Social Security card, valid Virginia driver's license, any other identification card issued by a government agency of the common-wealth or the United States, or any valid employee identification card containing a photograph of the voter. |

Source: Election Reform Information Project, "Election Reform Briefing: Voter Identification," April 2002; Election Reform Information Project, "Election Reform: What's Changed, What Hasn't and Why, 2000–2006," February 2006; state statutes.

a Earliest version of the current law (current version may have been amended since first passage of the law). Asterisk indicates that the precise year was not available.

b Missouri passed its first voter identification law four months before the president signed the Help America Vote Act.

c See also, Secretary of State's Office, "Acceptable IDs to Vote," available at: http://www.sos.mo.gov/elections/voterid/default.asp (accessed June 2009).

TABLE 7.3
States enacting more restrictive voter ID laws, and party control of state government, 2002–2008

	Documentary ID law before HAVA (2002)	Year of change	Party control of legislature[a]	Party control of governor	Legislation or other initiative	Act or statute
Alabama	No	2003	D	R	HB 193	2003 Ala. Acts 381
Arizona	No	2006	R	D	Proposition 200 ballot initiative (2004)	Amending Ariz. Rev. Stat. § 16–152
Colorado	No	2003	R	R	SB 102	2003 Colo. Sess. Laws, Chap. 164
Florida	Yes	2003[b]	R	R	HB 29-B (plus other laws passed in 2001 and 2005)	2003 Fla. Laws, Chap. 415
Georgia	Yes	2005[c]	R	R	HB 244 (upheld in federal court Sept. 2007)	2005 Ga. Laws, Act 53
Indiana	No	2005	R	R	SEA 483 (upheld by U.S. Supreme Court Jan. 2008)	2005 Ind. P.L. 109
Michigan	No	2007	R[d]	D	SB 513 (law first passed by Republicans in 1996 (as PA 583) and again in 2005, upheld by Michigan Supreme Court	2005 Mich. Pub. Acts 71
Montana	No	2003	R	R	HB 190	2003 Mont. Laws, Chap. 475
North Dakota	Yes[e]	2003	R	R	SB 2394	2003 N.D. Sess. Laws, Chap. 172

State	Year	Party		Bill	Party	Citation
Ohio	2006	R	No	HB 3	R	Ohio Rev. Code § 3505.18 (2006)
South Dakota	2003	R	No	HB 1176	R	2003 S.D. Laws, Chap. 82
Washington	2005	D	No	SB 5499[f]	D	Wash. Rev. Code § 29A.44.205 (2005)

Source: Council of State Governments, *The Book of the States* (Lexington, Ky.: Council of State Governments, vols. 34–40); U.S. Census Bureau, *Statistical Abstract of the United States* (Washington, D.C.: GPO, 2002–2008); National Association of Secretaries of State, "NASS Voter ID Survey of States: Fall 2003," October 2003, available at http://www.nass.org/index.php ?option=com_docman&task=doc_download&gid=80.

Notes: D, Democratic Party; HAVA, Help America Vote Act of 2002; HB, House bill; PA, Public act; R, Republican Party; SB, Senate bill; SEA, Senate enrolled act.

[a] In all cases party control was unified.

[b] Original law enacted in 1998.

[c] Original law enacted in 1997.

[d] Republicans controlled both houses of the legislature in 2005, when SB 513 reenacted a 1996 voter identification law that was blocked from implementation by a Michigan Attorney General's Opinion (No. 6930) finding it unconstitutional. Democrats took control of the lower house in 2006. In 2007, the Michigan Supreme Court overruled that opinion and upheld the 2005 law reenacting the voter identification requirement.

[e] North Dakota does not require voter registration; prior to 2003, precinct officials could request identification from voters they believed were not qualified to vote as part of the challenge process. Challenged voters were required to sign an affidavit attesting to identity.

[f] A more stringent voter identification law for those voting at the polling place passed following the 2004 election contest (see chapter 6 for details). Since most Washingtonians vote by mail, the application of the law is limited; moreover, it provides for wide range of acceptable identification documents.

require each elector, upon entering the polling place, to present one of the forms of identification which are on the list of forms approved by the Department of State pursuant to section 98.461 [which required the list to at least include a voter registration card or Florida driver's license]." The 1998 revisions curtailed the secretary's discretionary power to determine acceptable forms of voter identification and mandated instead that the clerks require each elector "to present a Florida driver's license, a Florida identification card issued under section 322.051, or another form of picture identification approved by the Department of State." Voters without identification, however, could still vote, pursuant to section 101.49, by filling out an affidavit and swearing by oath to the name and address before an inspector or clerk of the election.

In 2003, section 98.471 was renumbered section 101.043, renamed "Identification required," and amended as follows: "The clerk or inspector shall require each elector, upon entering the polling place, to present a current and valid picture identification as provided in section 97.0535(3)(a). If the picture identification does not contain the signature of the voter, an additional identification that provides the voter's signature shall be required." A voter who fails to furnish identification and is a first-time voter who registered by mail, is allowed to vote only a provisional ballot. The county canvassing board determines whether the voter is duly registered at the precinct where he or she cast the provisional ballot. If it is determined that the person voting the provisional ballot was not registered or entitled to vote at the precinct where the ballot was cast, the ballot is to be marked "Rejected as Illegal." This means that in Florida a duly registered U.S. citizen who just six years before could vote a regular ballot by swearing to his or her identity and eligibility, now risked forfeiting his or her vote by casting a ballot in the wrong precinct. Given the frequency with which precinct polling places are moved, especially in densely populated and expanding communities, it is not difficult to understand how this kind of a mistake could be made.

As the *New York Times* artfully understated the point at the time, "Florida's voter-identification law is inartfully written."[71] The 2003 revisions retained subsection 2 of 98.471, which instructed the inspectors or election clerks to allow voters unable to furnish identification to sign an affidavit swearing to their identity and still vote a regular ballot, pursuant to section 101.49. But the same new law appeared to replace section 101.49 with a new section, 101.049 (titled "Provisional ballots; special circumstances"), that does not pertain to identity affidavits or to the rules for allowing voters lacking documentary identification to vote. Did section *101.049* supersede section *101.49* or did lawmakers forget to remove section 101.49 when they inserted section 101.049? Was this a case of statutory befuddlement? It is not clear whether lawmakers intended the affidavit option to remain law or not. Nevertheless, in 2004, voting rights advocates and lawyers believed that duly registered voters lacking identification still had the right to vote a regular ballot. Florida elections officials, however, were confused. Reporting on the state's September 2004 primary elections, the *New York Times* editorial writers observed:

> elections officials at some polling places misstated the law and tried to keep eligible voters from voting. . . . In Broward and Miami-Dade Counties, poll watchers from People for the American Way saw voters being turned away after being told about half the law—the photo-identification requirement—but not the other half, the affidavit option. . . . Osceola County's sample ballot, mailed out before last week's election, said "Photo and Signature ID Required at Polls," and it did not tell voters they could in fact vote without identification. . . . [A spokeswoman for the secretary of state said] the affidavit option in the law was merely a "courtesy to the voter."[72]

Was it a courtesy or a statutory requirement? By the time Florida lawmakers revised the law again the following year, for at least the third time in almost as many years, the affidavit option was clearly out, replaced with a provisional ballot that would only count after the canvassing board made a determination that the ballot and the voter met all the legal requirements that the Florida lawmakers created for them. That is, if they could figure out what those requirements were. Because the HAVA did not stipulate the conditions under which provisional ballots must be counted, the states have taken it upon themselves to write their own rules. In Florida, as in a number of other states adopting the most stringent criteria for counting provisional ballots, the rules disqualify any provisional ballot not properly executed or cast in the wrong precinct. Casting a ballot in the wrong precinct is easy to do when a voter is new or unfamiliar with the polling place, or when the polling place has moved, the precinct has moved, or a clerk mistakenly sends the voter to the wrong precinct table in the right polling place. The 2005 revisions to section 101.043, the "identification required at the polls" law, removed all official discretion from the secretary of state to determine acceptable forms of ID. Now, only specific forms of photo identification will do: a Florida driver's license, Florida identification card issued by the Department of Highway Safety and Motor Vehicles, U.S. passport, employee badge or identification, buyer's club identification, debit or credit card, military identification, retirement center identification, neighborhood association identification, and public assistance identification. Whereas before 2005, legally registered, voting rights–bearing citizens attempting to cast legal ballots in Florida who were unable to provide the requisite documentary proof of their identity and address to a poll worker could still exercise their rights by signing an affidavit attesting to their identity (under penalty of perjury and a felony conviction for false swearing), now those same voters, if they lack any of the listed forms of identification or simply forget to bring their ID with them to the polls, can vote only a provisional ballot that is not counted unless it passes muster with a county canvassing board.

The Florida example is illustrative of a trend across the country toward the incremental adoption of provisional ballots as a catch-all solution for all kinds of different problems caused by election administration, voter error, or confusion. This is one of the more perverse outcomes of the national election reform effort that followed the Florida 2000 debacle. What voting rights advocates once envisioned as a fail-safe option to protect voters from election administration mistakes or from political manipulation exercised through election administration, the provisional ballot is becoming the sewer of the U.S. electoral system, the place to conveniently flush away unwanted ballots cast by unwanted voters.

In 2007, Florida lawmakers altered their voter identification law again. Having put the basic legal framework in place, this time all they did was home in on the enumerated forms of acceptable voter identification and begin the process of excising a few of those they had first specified two years before. From now on, no more employee badges or buyer's club identification cards are allowed.

Voter identification laws are a throwback to the post-Reconstruction era when the newly enfranchised freedmen of the South were often forced to carry their registration papers with them to the polls. Requiring voters to bring documentary evidence of their identity to the polls begs the question of what purpose preelection voter registration is supposed to serve if voters must prove their identity all over again when they vote. Earlier election administration reformers such as Joseph P. Harris ruled out identification papers as a form of voter identification. He concluded that proper registration and signature matching worked best in protecting the rights of the voter, given the historical uses of identity requirements to foil the exercise of those rights, and the realities of administering elections in modern mass societies.[73]

Moreover, the language of today's suffrage restriction movement justifying documentary voter identification requirements is also reminiscent of the post-Reconstruction era. More than a century ago, the leaders of the New South set about to reestablish uncontested white supremacy by using legal means to circumvent the Constitution. They did this with a kind of racial rhetoric about the vote that has persisted. This rhetoric emphasized the need to "purify" the ballot, purging it of the degradation and pollution associated with race-mixing in "sacred" spaces such as the polling place.[74] Today's faux democracy defenders, who rattle the cages for more onerous voter registration and voter identification procedures, also exalt the "sacredness" of the ballot and call for vigilance in protecting "our most cherished of all rights, the right to vote." Like those who labored to redeem white manhood by resurrecting apartheid in the South, today's proponents of voter ID insist their movement is just and their goals honorable. Their fight for electoral "integrity" and "ballot security," they say, is not to keep *worthy* voters out. Just the opposite. Confiscating the language and imagery of their opponents, they paradoxically claim that they are protecting voting rights by making it harder to vote, measuring the worth of any one vote by the difficulty a voter has in casting it. As with a deity, the sacred status of the vote is revealed by its inaccessibility. We have only to read through a sampling of the countless anonymous blogged responses to news reports about the new crop of restrictive voter identification laws (where the language is often less biblical and the sentiment more openly mean-spirited) to see that plenty of Americans still agree with these ideas.[75]

Partisanship, Exclusion, and the Myth of Fraud

Today, stringent voter identification laws have been championed almost exclusively by Republicans and, with two exceptions (in Alabama in 2003, and in Washington in 2005), have been enacted only when Republicans achieved unified control over state government (see table 7.3).[76] Including a more restrictive federal voter identification mandate in the HAVA was not possible due to Democratic opposition in Congress. But because the HAVA required the states to amend their election codes, the partisan strategy could be executed at the state level. And it was. One study that examined roll call votes for voter identification laws introduced in ten states during the 2005–2007 period found that, 95 percent of all Republicans and just 2 percent of all Democrats voting on those measures supported them.[77]

There were five states with unified Republican Party control in the 2002–2008 period that did not pass stricter voter identification laws (Idaho, New Hampshire, South Carolina, Texas, and Utah).[78] But their inaction can be explained by their already existing tight ballot security regimes. Two (South Carolina and Texas) already had identification requirements on the books, and two (Idaho and New Hampshire) allow election day registration that requires voters to produce documentary identification if they want to register and vote on the same day. In the remaining state, Utah, Republicans face little party competition, and there are few racial minorities; Republicans in Utah appear to have no problem with registered voters simply signing for their ballots.

State-level partisan maneuvering is most clearly evident in Indiana and Georgia, the two states that have enacted the strictest voter identification laws in the nation since the HAVA opened the door. The Indiana law passed in 2005, during a brief two-year period when Republicans enjoyed majorities in the state legislature for the first time in two decades, and George W. Bush's former budget director occupied the governor's office. That same year, Georgia also enacted a strict voter photo identification requirement after Republicans gained control of both houses of the state legislature for the first time in 133 years, sharing power with a Republican governor, another historical anomaly.

What began as a long-term, low-intensity partisan war against the NVRA and its enfranchising possibilities, finally ended as a controversy argued before a conservative, Republican-dominated Supreme Court. In *Crawford v. Marion County Election Board*, the Supreme Court has given the imprimatur of constitutionality to restrictive voter identification laws that require voters who cast a polling place ballot to present a current government-issued photo ID in order to exercise their right to vote.

The myth of voter fraud haunts the opinions of both the U.S. Court of Appeals for the Seventh Circuit and the U.S. Supreme Court in *Crawford*. The Seventh Circuit opinion written by Judge Richard A. Posner, asserts that "voting fraud" harms voters more than the Indiana photo identification requirement. Posner rejects the arguments of opponents of photo identification that liken the burden on voters to a poll tax. "The Indiana law is not like a poll tax," he instructs, "where on one side is the right to vote and on the other side the state's interest in defraying the cost of elections or in limiting the franchise to people who really care about voting or in excluding poor people or in discouraging people who are black." He agrees that the requirement might foil the efforts of some small number of eligible voters from casting a ballot, repeating the oft-heard but inaccurate claim that one needs photo identification to board an airplane: "Even though it is exceedingly difficult to maneuver in today's America without a photo ID (try flying, or even entering a tall building such as the courthouse in which we sit, without one; see *United States v. Smith*, 426 F.3d 567 (2d Cir. 2005)), and as a consequence the vast majority of adults have such identification, the Indiana law will deter some people from voting."[79]

But even here, the law may not be at fault. Posner adopts a calculus of voting to explain why. He tells us that "The benefits of voting to the individual voter are elusive (a vote in a political election rarely has any instrumental value, since elections for political office at the state or federal level are never decided by just one vote), and even very slight costs in time or bother or out-of-pocket expense deter many people from voting, or at least from voting in elections they're not much interested in." He goes on to reason that for some people, at least, disinterest in politics may explain why they lack photo identification: people "who have not bothered to obtain a photo ID will not bother to do so just to be allowed to vote." Moreover, it may be the case, that some who do have the identification but forget to bring it to the polling place "will say what the hell and not vote, rather than go home and get the ID and return to the polling place."

"The purpose of the Indiana law is to reduce voting fraud," says Posner, "and voting fraud impairs the right of legitimate voters to vote by diluting their votes—dilution being recognized to be an impairment of the right to vote."[80] Yet Posner cites no statistics, no studies, or any evidence at all on the incidence of voter fraud in contemporary U.S. elections, including in Indiana. Appellees in the case argued that the Indiana voter registration lists were widely known to be bloated with "deadwood," the alleged fodder of fraud. The problem was so bad, the state had to be sued by the federal government before it took steps to weed out the names of dead and ineligible voters. At the same time, the state argued it needed to impose a photo identification mandate on voters to prevent the fraud alleged to result from its own negligence.

Posner accepted these justifications. Moreover, he argued that voter impersonation is difficult to prevent "because busy poll workers are unlikely to scrutinize signatures carefully and argue with people who deny having forged someone else's signature." In response to opponents' claim that no one in Indiana or elsewhere was known to have been prosecuted for impersonating registered voters, Poser dismissed the value of prosecution data as a measure of voter fraud. "The absence of prosecutions," he writes, "is explained by the endemic under-enforcement of minor criminal laws (minor as they appear to the public and prosecutors, at all events) and by the extreme difficulty of apprehending a voter impersonator."

But, again, Posner's assertions about matters of fact bearing on his reasoning are poorly supported. He cites no evidence that minor criminal laws are endemically underenforced. Quite to the contrary, the stepped-up enforcement of minor criminal laws across the United States against offenses such as fare beating, littering, public drinking, and disturbing the peace is so significant that it is credited by some with lowering crime rates over the past fifteen years.[81] A prolific scholar of the law, Posner, who has written a sharp critique of the "law and literature" movement in U.S. jurisprudence,[82] violates his own warnings against the discovery of legal justification in fiction and imagines a madcap scenario to explain why voter identification laws are justified. He tells a tale of voter impersonators lurking around the polling place, scanning the voter registration rolls, and matching names to the obituaries to figure out if any of the dead are still on the rolls. The myth of voter fraud takes over from there:

[the voter impersonator] enters the polling place, gives a name that is not his own, votes, and leaves. If later it is discovered that the name he gave is that of a dead person, no one at the polling place will remember the face of the person who gave that name, and if someone did remember it, what would he do with the information? The impersonator and the person impersonated (if living) might show up at the polls at the same time and a confrontation might ensue that might lead to a citizen arrest or a call to the police who would arrive before the impersonator had fled, and arrest him. A more likely sequence would be for the impersonated person to have voted already when the impersonator arrived and tried to vote in his name. But in either case an arrest would be most unlikely (and likewise if the impersonation were discovered or suspected by comparing signatures, when that is done), as the resulting commotion would disrupt the voting. And anyway the impersonated voter is likely to be dead or in another district or precinct or to be acting in cahoots with the impersonator, rather than to be a neighbor (precincts are small, sometimes a single apartment house). One response, which has a parallel to littering, another crime the perpetrators of which are almost impossible to catch, would be to impose a very severe criminal penalty for voting fraud. Another, however, is to take preventive action, as Indiana has done by requiring a photo ID.

To summarize Judge Posner's opinion, voting is, on the one hand, of little benefit to the individual and most people who do not vote know this. In fact, it is so inconsequential an activity that committing a fraud against it is akin to littering, another minor crime that goes unprosecuted.[83] On the other hand, it is a monumental crime because committing it deprives others of their civil rights through "vote dilution," as recognized by the Supreme Court (something even the poll tax did not do because that controversy involved balancing the right to vote with a state interest in things such as "limiting the franchise to people who really care about voting or in excluding poor people or in discouraging people who are black"). Poll workers are usually too busy to scrutinize a signature but apparently not too busy to scrutinize a picture, match it to the face before them, and check for a valid address and expiration date on the ID. One source of fodder for vote fraud is the massively out-of-date voter registration rolls. But the fact that the rolls are so poorly maintained is not relevant to the proclaimed grave concern over the undetectable, unprosecuted, trivial but monumental crime of voter fraud. Obtaining a photo ID is not really so difficult if you really want to vote, although why would you? If you do not have an ID, you can get one by presenting a motor vehicles official with a birth certificate (or copy) and another official document with your name and address on it, such as a utility bill. As everyone who drives knows, this is much easier to do than sending in ID with your absentee ballot, such as a copy of the same birth certificate and document with your name and address on it that everyone else needs to produce in order to get a government-issued ID! And if people would just stay home on election day, no one would be harmed by the new ID law—except, maybe the Democratic Party, which, apparently, few want to join anyway, at least in Indiana, a conclusion we can draw from Posner's admonition that Democrats need to work much harder there to get out their vote.[84]

The plaintiffs appealed the case. But they were no more able to dislodge the myth of voter fraud from the minds of Supreme Court justices than they were with Judge Posner. The Supreme Court majority opinion was written by the 87-year-old Justice John Paul Stevens, a Chicagoan who grew up in a prominent and wealthy Republican family whose business interests would have required them to rub elbows with machine politicians.[85] Justice Stevens, writing for Justices Roberts and Kennedy, argued that the appropriate framework for judging the constitutionality of the Indiana voter identification law was a balancing test devised for judging other election laws in which the state law's burden on a political party, an individual voter, or a "discrete class of voters" must be justified by a relevant and legitimate state interest "sufficiently weighty to justify the limitation."[86] He cited three such weighty interests, the first of which was the state's interest in deterring and detecting voter fraud.

Justice Stevens acknowledged that the trial record admitted no evidence of voter impersonation, the kind of fraud that the Indiana law addresses. Siding with the petitioners, he acknowledged that the Indiana criminal code punished such conduct as a felony. He then was seduced by the myth:

> It remains true . . . that flagrant examples of such fraud in other parts of the country have been documented throughout this Nation's history by respected historians and journalists, that occasional examples have surfaced in recent years, and that Indiana's own experience with fraudulent voting in the 2003 Democratic primary for East Chicago Mayor—though perpetrated using absentee ballots and not in-person fraud—demonstrate that not only is the risk of voter fraud real but that it could affect the outcome of a close election (citations omitted).

In a footnote citing the one instance of "fraud in other parts of the country . . . documented by historians," Justice Stevens, like Judge Posner before him, falls prey to the myth. The instance Stevens relates is an 1868 New York City election, the account taken from M. R. Werner's 1932 book, *Tammany Hall*. Stevens quotes Werner citing "Big Tim" Sullivan, one of Boss Tweed's underlings who insisted that his "repeaters" have whiskers: "When you've voted 'em with their whiskers on, you take 'em to a barber and scrape off the chin fringe. Then you vote 'em again with the side lilacs and a mustache. Then to a barber again, off comes the sides and you vote 'em a third time with the mustache. If that ain't enough and the box can stand a few more ballots, clean off the mustache and vote 'em plain face. That makes every one of 'em good for four votes."[87]

The other "scattered instances" of in-person voter fraud cited by Stevens were actually only a single instance alleged to have occurred in the 2004 Washington state governor's race (discussed in chap. 6). Stevens's source for this claim is a January 7, 2005, article in the *Seattle Post-Intelligencer* that does not, as Stevens says, confirm any in-person voting fraud. The article reports on the newspaper's own review of voting records that turned up eight people who died before the November general election but were credited with voting in King County. Bill Huennekens, elections supervisor, is quoted as saying, "These are not indications of fraud. Fraud is a concerted effort to change an election." Four of the cases were attributed to administrative error. The newspaper visited the homes of some of the dead voters and found no fraud, only cases of elderly widows and widowers whose spouses had died in the months before the election but for a variety of reasons were sent absentee ballots in the mail. In a number of cases, those spouses sent in the wrong ballot or voted their recently deceased spouse's ballot to honor their wishes. "Bob Holmgren said yesterday that he voted on behalf of his late wife, Charlette Holmgren, who died Sept. 29. The West Seattle man filled out his own ballot and hers, and signed both of them. 'Her vote was important to her,' Holmgren said. 'She was very strongly against [Democratic] Governor-elect Gregoire.'"[88]

Myth versus Facts

What was injured by *Crawford*? We cannot say for sure how many individual voters are or will be injured by voter identification restrictions.[89] But this is the wrong way to frame the important constitutional questions at hand because, to provide an answer, we must meet an impossible standard of empirical precision.[90]

What is harmed by *Crawford* is not so much the individual voter, but the opportunity to expand the meaning of political equality central to democracy. *Crawford* instructs the lower courts to pursue a misguided standard,[91] to balance a showing of individual harm against an important state interest in protecting the integrity of the electoral process. But this is nothing more than a judicial conceit that creates a false opposition between access and integrity.[92] Restrictive voter identification rules that cause people to lose their votes also undermine the integrity of the electoral process. The point is there is no integrity without access. We need to simplify our electoral system, not encumber it with more tangled rules justified by myth.

Appendix 1

Allegations of Voter Fraud in the 2004 Election Cycle

by the American Center for Voting Rights Compared to Substantiated Number of Fraudulent Votes Cast

	Allegations of voter fraud in the ACVR report[1]						Facts		
ACVR ID#[2]	State	Location	Election	Description of incident(s)	Number of alleged fraudulent voter registration applications	Number of alleged fraudulent votes cast	Number of actual illegal ballots cast	Number of actual fraudulent ballots cast[3]	Disposition of incident(s)
6.1a	Ala.	Greensboro, Hale County	9/04 Mayoral runoff election	Johnnie B. Washington narrowly defeated Vanessa Hill in the August 2004 primary, forcing the two candidates into a run-off which Washington then won by 90 votes; 251 of Washington's 762 votes were cast by absentee ballot. Hill received only 51 absentee ballots among her 672 votes. Hill contested the election "on the basis of a number of suspicious absentee ballots cast in the days leading up to the election."[4]	0	0	162 illegal absentee ballots	at least 22[5]	The case was heard in Hale County Circuit Court by Montgomery Circuit Court Judge William Shashy after all three Hale County judges recused themselves. Shashy voided Washington's victory in favor of Hill, adopting the report of Special Master James Anderson, which found 148 absentee ballots had been illegally cast for Washington and 8 illegal ballots cast for Hill. There were 8 illegal ballots for which the candidate chosen could not be determined. The Alabama Supreme Court upheld Shashy in December 2006, and Hill was sworn in as mayor more than two years after the election. In August 2008, Hill lost her reelection bid to Washington by 41 votes and again contested the election.[6]

| 6.1a | Ala. | Marion, Perry County | Non-election-specific allegations | The *Tuscaloosa News* finds similar "irregularities" in a local election in Marion, including absentee ballots cast from empty homes, a "mysterious influx of voters, described as suspicious by one official," and allegations of "intimidation and bribery to secure votes and voters who may be long dead."[7] | 0 | 0 | 0 | 160 illegal absentee ballots | 0 | This case appears to refer to the 2004 Marion mayoral reelection of Anthony Long, who defeated Robert Bryant by 123 votes out of 2,156 cast. Bryant challenged the results in Perry County Circuit Court, which found a host of absentee ballot irregularities, including: (1) 17 Long voters failed to indicate a reason on their ballot applications; (2) 7 Long voters and 7 Bryant voters failed for voting absentee to indicate a reason for voting absentee on their ballot affidavits; (3) 2 voters failed to indicate reasons for voting on their absentee ballot applications and affidavits; (4) 12 Long voters and 1 Bryant voter provided inconsistent reasons for voting absentee on their applications and ballot affidavits; (5) 7 voters had not had their voting rights restored after being convicted of felonies; (6) 7 voters failed to provide proper government-issued ID; (7) 2 absentee ballots were corrected with "whiteout," switching the vote from Bryant to |

(continued)

	Allegations of voter fraud in the ACVR report[1]						Facts		
ACVR ID#[2]	State	Location	Election	Description of incident(s)	Number of alleged fraudulent voter registration applications	Number of alleged fraudulent votes cast	Number of actual illegal ballots cast	Number of actual fraudulent ballots cast[3]	Disposition of incident(s)
									Long; (8) 96 voters provided improper addresses (post office boxes) on their absentee ballot applications; (9) signatures of 2 Bryant voters were deemed inconsistent. The court also recommended that the DA investigate the movement of voters into the city just before the election; the court rejected the ballots of at least 8 people who testified that they temporarily moved into Marion, voted, and left town. After adjusting the count to reflect the deduction of illegal ballots, the court ordered a run-off. Long appealed to the Alabama Supreme Court which affirmed the lower court and a new election was held on June 10, 2008, in which Long defeated Bryant, 948 to 680.[8]

| 6.2a | Colo. | 47 of 64 counties | 11/04 general election | "122 people voted twice statewide, casting absentee ballots through the mail, then showing up in person to vote on Election Day; 120 felons cast illegal ballots statewide; In Denver 81 residents voted twice and 52 felons cast ballots; In Jefferson County, elections officials requested that prosecutors investigate 30 cases of people attempting to vote twice and 256 cases of suspicious signatures on absentee ballots; In El Paso County, officials reported 23 cases or prisoners or parolees who voted."[9] | 0 | 498 | 0[10] | 0 | According to Dana Jaclyn Williams, public information officer for Colorado Secretary of State Gigi Dennis, the Secretary of State's Office researched two-time and felon voting in the 2004 election and, as a result, turned over to the attorney general six voters who may have voted twice in two different counties and 31 felons who may have illegally cast a ballot. In 2004, a new state law for the first time required counties to report suspected voting irregularities to the secretary of state. The *Denver Post* article cited by the ACVR misstated the AP report on which it was based: 47 counties reported to the secretary, but only 12 reported problems, as corroborated by the data provided by Williams. Among these 12 counties, in addition to the cases reported by the Secretary of State's office to the attorney general, county clerks referred 48 cases of possible double-voting, and 64 cases of possible felon voting to county DA.[11] There is no evidence that any of these |

(continued)

	Allegations of voter fraud in the ACVR report[1]						Facts		
ACVR ID#[2]	State	Location	Election	Description of incident(s)	Number of alleged fraudulent voter registration applications	Number of alleged fraudulent votes cast	Number of actual illegal ballots cast	Number of actual fraudulent ballots cast[3]	Disposition of incident(s)
									potentially illegal votes was fraudulently cast with an intent to manipulate electoral outcomes.
6.2a	Colo.	Statewide	11/04 general election	News reports claim that as many as 6,000 felons ineligible to vote are on Colorado rolls; 536 felons registered to vote in 2004, "many" of them signed up by third-party groups (i.e., the Colorado Voting Project is reported to have signed up 77 voters on a single day at the Denver County jail).[12]	6,006	0	0	0	Before 2004, Colorado, like a number of states, only loosely policed its felon disfranchisement laws, which prohibit prisoners and parolees from voting. In fall 2004, Secretary of State Donetta Davidson said she was unaware that state felons were registered to vote and blamed the Department of Corrections for failing to provide a list of felony convictions. The Department of Corrections told the press that she never asked for such a list.[13]
6.2b	Colo.	Statewide	11/04 general election	Numerous canvassers have been indicted for voter registration fraud: (1) an "ACORN worker's girlfriend" was charged	<200 (est.)	0	0	0	In sum, these allegations refer to total of seven people charged with filling out and in some cases submitting false and

with felony forgery (she told a reporter she registered herself 25 times and friends 40 times); (2) an ACORN worker pleads guilty to filling out false voter registration forms; (3) an ACORN worker was charged with falsely filling out multiple voter forms; (4) a "man charged with five counts of perjury for filling out several phony registration forms for ACORN workers;" (5) two men were charged with forgery related to voter registration drives; (6) a man charged with forging 48 voter registration applications.[14]

duplicate voter registration applications for approximately 120 people during the 2004 election cycle in Colorado: (1) Kym Cason admitted to a Denver television station that she forged the signatures of 3 people on 40 voter registration forms to help her boyfriend, an ACORN canvasser, earn an extra $50;[15] (2) Monique Mora who pleaded guilty to six misdemeanor counts of procuring false registrations and was sentenced to six months probation and 100 hours of community service; (3) Pelonne Page pleaded guilty to six misdemeanor counts of procuring false registrations and was sentenced to one year of probation and 150 hours of community service; (4) Lloyd "Frosty" Herrera filled out voter registration forms using fake names to assist his friends, ACORN canvassers, Monique Mora and Pelonne Page; (5) Joseph Battles and Keith Bohannon were charged with a total of 48 counts of forgery; (5) John MaCarthy

(continued)

	Allegations of voter fraud in the ACVR report[1]							Facts	
ACVR ID#[2]	State	Location	Election	Description of incident(s)	Number of alleged fraudulent voter registration applications	Number of alleged fraudulent votes cast	Number of actual illegal ballots cast	Number of actual fraudulent ballots cast[3]	Disposition of incident(s)
									worked for the Campaign Finance Company; MaCarthy's false registrations were discovered before they were submitted to county clerks.[16]
6.2c	Colo.	Denver, Douglas, Adams, Boulder, and Lake counties	11/04 general election	Denver 9 News investigates voter registration fraud in five counties and alleges 719 "potentially" fraudulent forms turned in by third-party groups such as ACORN, New Voters Project, and Colorado Progressive Coalition. The report includes testimony from Tom Stanislawski, a Colorado resident who claimed his party registration had been changed without his knowing it. Furthermore, at least 2,000 people had at least eight or more changes to their voter registration forms. Kym Cason said she registered herself 25 times and her friends 40 times. Gerald Obi said he was pressured	2,800 (est.)[18]	0	0	0	These allegations and subsequent events overlap with those reported in 6.2b. The media tend to label duplicate forms as fraudulent, which may or may not be the case.[19] For example, as long as Kym Cason was an eligible Colorado resident, the extra 24 forms she submitted for herself to the Denver clerk and recorder were simply duplicative and a nuisance to local election officials.

No.	State	Jurisdiction	Election	Description					Notes
				to register 35 times. John Turner, alleged child molester, registered from behind bars in Douglas and Adams counties.[17]					
6.2c	Colo.	3 counties	11/04 general election	Criminal probe into alleged fraudulent voter registration forms announced; state attorney general is joined by three county prosecutors; ACORN takes responsibility for some fraudulent forms.[20]	See above.	0	0	0	See above (see also, note 9).
6.2d	Colo.	1 county	11/04 general election	John MaCarthy, a worker for Choose 2 Vote, charged with forgery and procuring false registrations for nearly 50 voters.[21]	50	0	0	0	See above.
6.3a	Fla.	Statewide	11/04 general election	Florida Department of Law Enforcement opens an investigation into voter registration fraud, targeting ACORN. Former ACORN worker, Mac Stuart, alleges that ACORN held on to voter registration forms it collected, forged registration applications, altered party choice on applications, and photocopied applications and sold them to groups like Moveon.org in violation of Florida election law.[22]	"hundreds if not thousands"	0	0	0	See chapter 6 for a discussion of this case.

(continued)

ACVR ID#[2]	State	Location	Election	Allegations of voter fraud in the ACVR report[1]			Facts		
				Description of incident(s)	Number of alleged fraudulent voter registration applications	Number of alleged fraudulent votes cast	Number of actual illegal ballots cast	Number of actual fraudulent ballots cast[3]	Disposition of incident(s)
6.3a	Fla.	Broward, Miami-Dade, Pinellas, and Hillsborough counties	11/04 general election	Florida voters were "disenfranchised" by ACORN: (1) ACORN fails to turn in forms it collected from 11 South Florida residents before voter registration deadline; 10 voters from Miami-Dade, and one from Broward County sue ACORN; (2) 2,500 Pinellas County and 1,500 Hillsborough County residents thought they were registered in time to vote in the August 31 primary, but were not—the majority of the late registrations reportedly came from ACORN.[23]	4,000	0	0	0	An investigation by the FDLE found no evidence of criminal activity committed by ACORN.[24]
6.3a	Fla.	St. Petersburg	11/04 general election	ACORN accused of altering voter registration information: (1) Charles Schuh, former mayor of St. Petersburg, claims his age and party registration were changed by an ACORN	15	0	0	0	These charges were investigated by the FDLE. In reference to Schuh's registration as well as that of 14 others turned in, State Attorney Bernie McCabe said that, "It does not

(continued)

				worker; (2) state attorney's office investigating allegations that ACORN fraudulently changed party affiliations on forms in St. Petersburg.[25]		0	0	appear right now that it can result in any impact on the election because the phony people aren't going to be voting."[26]
6.3c	Fla.	Miami-Dade County	11/04 general election	Mac Stuart, fired ACORN voter registration coordinator, claims ACORN breaks a variety of Florida election laws and fails to turn in all the voter registration applications it collects.[27]	181	0	0	See chapter 6 for a discussion of this case.
6.3d	Fla.	Duval County	11/04 general election	Duval County election officials ask prosecutors to investigate 25 possible fraudulent voter registration applications; the AP checks out the reputedly bogus addresses on the forms and finds only one that matched an occupied house.[28]	25	0	0	An FBI investigation into possible fraud or double-voting in Duval County found no voters cast more than one ballot on election day or through absentee voting. Duval elections officials had turned over 54 ballots to federal authorities, and in each case the problems were explained by clerical error.[29]
6.3e	Fla.	Duval, Broward, Palm Beach, Volusia, and Sumter counties	11/04 general election	Nearly 100 voters cast more than one vote in at least five counties (41 double votes in Duval County were allegedly counted); these cases include (1) at least 30 suspected cases of	0	74+	3	On double-voting in Duval County, see 6.3d above. There were a handful of cases in Broward County in which people voted early and tried to vote again at the polls, but these double votes

(continued)

	Allegations of voter fraud in the ACVR report[1]					Facts			
ACVR ID#[2]	State	Location	Election	Description of incident(s)	Number of alleged fraudulent voter registration applications	Number of alleged fraudulent votes cast	Number of actual illegal ballots cast	Number of actual fraudulent ballots cast[3]	Disposition of incident(s)
				people voting early and at the polls in Broward County; (2) 3 cases of people voting absentee and showing up at the polls to vote in Palm Beach County; (3) "reports" of double-voting in Volusia and Sumter counties.[30]					were likely the result of voter confusion and none were counted.[31] In March 2005, the Department of Elections sent letters to 21 Volusia County voters suspected of casting two ballots, asking them to contact the department to explain the situation. Most complied with stories of confusion; only three cases were referred to the Elections Commission or State Attorney's Office. According to the supervisor of elections, these three voters cast absentee ballots and then were able to vote at their polling places because the printed registers with the names of people who had already voted arrived late. In at least one of the three cases, the voter was confused by a mailing that seemed to indicate a problem with her absentee ballot.[32]

6.3e	Fla.	Statewide	11/04 general election	Florida had more than 64,000 dead people on its rolls.[33]	64,000	0	0	The *Chicago Tribune* produced this number by comparing Florida voter registration rolls with the Social Security Administration database of death claims. The number is not surprising if we keep in mind that 144,608 Florida residents over the age of 55 died in 2004.[34]
6.3e	Fla.	Statewide (and New York, Ohio, Georgia, and North Carolina)	Multiple elections prior to 2004, going back as far as 1988	Florida has people on its rolls who are registered to vote in other states, some of whom double-voted: (1) more than 46,000 people were illegally registered in New York and Florida, and between 400 and 1,000 of these people actually voted twice in at least one election; (2) more than 27,000 people were illegally registered to vote in Ohio and Florida, and as many as 400 voted in both states in the same election in the last four years; (3) more than 68,000 people were found registered in Florida and either Georgia or North Carolina, and 1,650 voted in Florida and another state in 2000 and 2002.[35]	141,000	2,450–3,050	6[36]	6 (all likely illegal ballots were also likely fraudulent, based on what is known about two of these alleged double-voters)	Reporters Buettner of the *Daily News*, Hiassan and Smyth of the *Cleveland Plain Dealer*, and Kassab of the *Orlando Sentinel* all performed the data matching that produced these allegations or worked with colleagues who matched the data with computerized files they obtained from state agencies. They all claimed to have matched at least voters' names and birthdates, and sometimes addresses, and to have called the handful of individuals named in their stories to verify their double-voting claims.[37]

ACVR ID#[2]	State	Location	Election	Description of incident(s)	Number of alleged fraudulent voter registration applications	Number of alleged fraudulent votes cast	Number of actual illegal ballots cast	Number of actual fraudulent ballots cast[3]	Facts	Disposition of incident(s)
6.4a	Ill.	East St. Louis, St. Clair County	11/04 general election	Nine party and precinct workers were convicted of vote buying.[38]	0	Unknown	Unknown	Unknown		The allegations are not disputed.[39]
6.5a	Ky.	Pike County	2000, 2002	Two cases of vote buying in eastern Kentucky: (1) the 2000 primary election for state senate; (2) a judicial election in Pike County in 2002. Both involved questionable campaign donations and payments to hundreds of people for "vote hauling," a practice of paying third parties to transport voters to the polls, which is legal in Kentucky.[40]	0	Unknown	Unknown	Unknown	These cases eventually involved 13 indictments of 11 people (with Ross Harris, the millionaire coal operator, and Loren Glenn Turner, his employee and "bag man" in the vote-buying schemes, charged in both cases). Harris was convicted in both cases and died in jail of cancer on July 26, 2006. Turner was convicted in one case and pleaded guilty in the other, but had the latter conviction overturned on appeal when the U.S. 6th Circuit Court of Appeals ruled the federal mail fraud law could not be used to prosecute election fraud in a local election.[41] The third person in that	

6.6a	Mich.	Wayne, Oakland, Ingham, and Eaton counties	11/04 general election	Multiple allegations that third-party groups like ACORN/Project Vote and PIRGIM were attempting to "register nonexistent people or forging applications for already-registered voters," with "names taken out of the phone book and as many as eight people registered from a single apartment address"[43]	"thousands"	0	0	0	An eight-month investigation by the Ingham County Sheriff's Office into hundreds of phony voter registration forms submitted by PRIGIM workers resulted in misdemeanor charges filed against a Lansing man, Edward Pressley. In October 2008, Ed Brayton of the *Michigan Messenger* followed up on the allegations against ACORN and found them unsubstantiated: "In response to a *Michigan Messenger* request for specific examples of voter fraud perpetrated by ACORN in the state, a Michigan GOP spokesman sent a fact sheet that made reference to a *Detroit Free Press* story from 2004 about

case was convicted. Two people in the second case were convicted of mail fraud but had their charges for conspiracy to commit voter fraud dismissed; one other pleaded guilty, one person was acquitted at trial, and four people had their cases dismissed.[42]

(*continued*)

					Allegations of voter fraud in the ACVR report[1]			Facts	
ACVR ID#[2]	State	Location	Election	Description of incident(s)	Number of alleged fraudulent voter registration applications	Number of alleged fraudulent votes cast	Number of actual illegal ballots cast	Number of actual fraudulent ballots cast[3]	Disposition of incident(s)
									campaign workers with Project Vote and PIRGIM (Public Interest Research Group in Michigan) who were under investigation for voter registration fraud in four counties. When asked if any convictions resulted from those investigations or if there were any examples of anyone connected with ACORN ever being charged with wrongdoing in Michigan, the spokesman did not respond."[44]
6.7a	Minn.	Hennepin County	11/04 general election	When police stop Joshua Reed of St. Louis Park, a registration worker fired by ACORN, for a traffic violation, they find 300 completed voter registration applications in his trunk. Most are then processed, but some were damaged by water and	18+	0	0	0	The allegations are not disputed.

illegible. Reed pleads guilty to failing to promptly turn in the forms (Minn. law requires they be turned in within 10 days), and to forging signatures on 18 other voter registration forms.[45]

	State	Location	Election	Allegation				Outcome
6.8a	Mo.	St. Louis, Kansas City	Unspecified (9/03)	ACORN is accused of filing blatantly fraudulent voter registration applications, including one for a sitting St. Louis alderman, and another for a baby. The fraud involves making up names and submitting duplicates of eligible voters. ACORN blames five or six temporary workers who it fired after discovering the fraud.[46]	1,600	0	0	At least 1,000 fraudulent cards were part of a batch of 5,379 submitted by ACORN that were collected by four workers, all of whom were fired after they admitted filling out the forms with fake names, addresses and Social Security numbers.[47]
6.8b	Mo.	St. Louis	2001 mayoral primary	Nonaresa Montgomery, the head of Operation Big Vote, is convicted of perjury before a grand jury investigating fraudulent voter registration forms turned in to the city elections board. Six Operation Big Vote volunteers pleaded	3,800	0	0	The allegations are not disputed. Montgomery testified before a grand jury that she had no way of tracking the bogus cards, but evidence was produced at trial that showed she brought photocopies of some or all of the fraudulent registrations

(continued)

ACVR ID#[2]	State	Location	Election	Description of incident(s)	Number of alleged fraudulent voter registration applications	Number of alleged fraudulent votes cast	Number of actual illegal ballots cast	Number of actual fraudulent ballots cast[3]	Disposition of incident(s)
				guilty to filling out fraudulent forms.[48]					to a campaign meeting five days after the cards had been submitted to the city board of elections.[49]
6.8c	Mo.	St. Louis City and Jackson County	Unspecified (2003–2004)	Citing a study by the CEFM, which accuses ACT and Missouri Pro-Vote of submitting "thousands of duplicative and fraudulent voter registration forms."[50]	10,000 (est.)	0	0	0	The ACVR report misstates the findings of its own source. The report by the CEFM presents no evidence of any fraudulent voter registration forms submitted by the two voter registration drives. According to the report, of 34,542 forms submitted to the St. Louis Board of Election Commissioners by the two organizations between 2003 and 2004, 244 were rejected as "ineligible," 7 were rejected due to the felon status of the applicants, 130 were labeled "questionable" or still under review by elections officials, and 40

were rejected due to lack of age qualifications. Another 383 should have been filed with county rather than city officials. Some 9,007 were duplicates. Of the 780 voter registration cards submitted by ACT in Jackson County in the three weeks before the CEFM report was drafted, 623 were still under review by elections officials; 10 were rejected for signature problems, 15 for address problems, 8 because the applicant lived out of state, and 5 for lack of age qualifications. Another 49 were sent new cards to fill out due to signature problems.[51]

6.8d	Mo.	St. Louis City	Unspecified (2004)	24,000	0	0	0	A state audit finds that "nearly 10 percent, or 24,000, of the city's registered voters are either dead, been convicted of a felony, registered in another jurisdiction or otherwise questionable."[52]

According to an internal review of operations at the St. Louis Board of Election Commissioners, gross problems with management and record-keeping were a hallmark of the board during this period.[53]

(continued)

| | | | | | Allegations of voter fraud in the ACVR report[1] | | | | Facts |
ACVR ID#[2]	State	Location	Election	Description of incident(s)	Number of alleged fraudulent voter registration applications	Number of alleged fraudulent votes cast	Number of actual illegal ballots cast	Number of actual fraudulent ballots cast[3]	Disposition of incident(s)
6.8d	Mo.	Statewide	2000, 2002 federal elections	More than 300 people may have voted twice in the same election, although the number "could be even higher."[54]	0	300+	3	3 (the 3 illegal ballots were also fraudulent)	As a result of a special initiative to combat alleged voter fraud and voter intimidation by the U.S. Justice Department, three people pleaded guilty to voting in Missouri and Kansas in the 2000 and 2002 elections.[55] See appendix 3 for more details.
6.9a	Nev.	Clark County	11/04 general election	Las Vegas-area election official comments on "obviously fraudulent" forms, including for the fictional horror movie character, Freddy Kreuger, and for illegal immigrants, and cases of party switching among registered voters.[56]	"hundreds"	0	0	0[57]	Clark County Registrar of Voters Larry Lomax subsequently said he knew of no prosecutions related to voter fraud stemming from any fraudulent voter registration forms and said he was "fairly confident" all the fraudulent forms had been turned over to investigators.[58] An investigation by the Nevada Department of Public Safety uncovered no organized effort to falsify registrations by any particular group or organization.[59]

| 6.9b | Nev. | Clark County | 11/04 general election | Sproul Associates controversy: Eric Russell, "disgruntled" former employee, alleges witnessing supervisors tearing up registration forms for people choosing registration forms for people choosing affiliation with the Democratic Party. Sproul denies the accusations. An investigation prompted by Secretary of State Dean Heller finds "no evidence of an organized or concerted effort which would influence or impact the result of the elections in Clark County based on these allegations."[60] | 0 | 0 | 0 | The outcome of any federal investigation of Sproul Associates for voter registration fraud is not known, nor is the alleged extent of the fraud, if, in fact, it occurred. No charges were ever brought. In Nevada, there were at least two lawsuits on behalf of would-be voters who said they registered with canvassers working for Voter Outreach of America, a firm operated by Sproul, but whose forms were never turned in. In one case, the voters, a married couple, produced receipts showing they had tried to register as Democrats. In a last-minute ruling just before the November election, a judge allowed them to cast ballots.[61] |
| 6.9c | Nev. | Clark County | 11/04 general election | More than 700 felons allegedly are illegally registered to vote.[62] | 719 | 0 | 0 | 0 | Implying the registered felons are evidence of fraud, the ACVR report neglects to point out that the article it cites as the source for this information also says, "Officials noted that Nevada recently loosened laws prohibiting |

(continued)

ACVR ID#[2]	State	Location	Election	Description of incident(s)	Number of alleged fraudulent voter registration applications	Number of alleged fraudulent votes cast	Number of actual illegal ballots cast	Number of actual fraudulent ballots cast[3]	Disposition of incident(s)
									some felons from voting and said some of the 719 felons identified by the *Tribune* may now be eligible under those provisions or upon request by the felon for a reinstatement of voting rights."[63] It is not clear that any of the registered felons registered to vote after they were convicted of felonies, suggesting this was a record-keeping problem on the part of state and local officials.
6.10a	N.M.	Bernalillo County	11/04 general election	Registration fraud allegations include: (1) the registration of two underage teenagers discovered when the father of one of them received voter registration cards for them in the mail—the Social Security number was wrong and the date of birth made the son appear old	2	0	0	0	Among these allegations, only the fraudulent registration of the underage teenage boys can be verified; in some cases, the other allegations do not even implicate fraud. The boys did not vote.[65]

6.10b	N.M.	Bernalillo County	11/04 general election				

enough to vote; (2) the daughter (Patricia Laven) of a man who died two and a half years before received his voter registration card in the mail; (3) cards listing false addresses and other incorrect information; (4) one voter was re-registered four times over a two month period; (5) more registration a woman registered in March 2004 with the last name of "Maestas-Perea" and in May with the name "Perea-Maestas."[64]

ACORN was linked to fraudulent forms (they fired the worker who filed the fraudulent registration of the 13-year old), including the discovery of about a dozen completed forms in the apartment of a former worker arrested on drug charges, and woman who was unable to vote because her name was not on the list of registered voters, although she claimed she registered through an ACORN drive.[66]

0

0

0

0

As the ACVR report points out, the surge in complaints about voter registration fraud led David Iglesias, U.S. attorney for New Mexico, to form a task force in September 2004. Iglesias was subsequently praised for his initiative and chosen by Justice Department colleagues to help train other U.S. attorneys in investigating voter fraud. Iglesias maintains he was fired when his investigation failed to find enough evidence of fraud to prosecute anyone, including ACORN.[67]

(continued)

Allegations of voter fraud in the ACVR report[1]

ACVR ID#[2]	State	Location	Election	Description of incident(s)	Number of alleged fraudulent voter registration applications	Number of alleged fraudulent votes cast	Number of actual illegal ballots cast	Number of actual fraudulent ballots cast[3]	Disposition of incident(s)
								Facts	
6.10c	N.M.	Albuquerque	11/04 general election	A college student claims he was fired from a group affiliated with the governor for registering too many Republicans. The group, Moving America Forward, denies the allegation[68]	0	0	0	0	Like the accusations against Sproul Associates, this allegation suggests possible illegal activity on the part of a voter registration organization that, if it occurred, was nevertheless unlikely to lead to fraudulent voting.
6.10c	N.M.	Albuquerque	11/04 general election	As estimated 100-200 mostly Republican voter registration forms are stolen from a New Voters Project office in Albuquerque.[69]	0	0	0	0	The allegations are not disputed.
6.10c	N.M.	Albuquerque	11/04 general election	A woman claims that a man "working for Governor Richardson" came to her door to collect her absentee ballot, which is illegal in N.M.[70]	0	0	0	0	The director of the governor's political organization denied that the man worked for them or that they collected absentee ballots.
6.11a	Ohio	Statewide	2004	Discussion of news reports debunking the theory that the exit polls present data supporting the claims the 2004 election was "stolen" by Republicans in Ohio.[71]	0	0	0	0	It is not clear why this issue is raised in the ACVR report; the authors appear to take the position that Bush's victory in Ohio was not due to election fraud.

| 6.11c | Ohio | Defiance, Lucas, Cuyahoga, Lake, Mahoning, Franklin, Hamilton, Summit, and Trumball counties | 2004 | A compilation of allegations concerning voter registration fraud allegedly committed by workers with the NAACP National Voter Fund, ACORN, America Coming Together, and the AFL-CIO; taken together these allegations cover the following categories of alleged registration fraud: (1) registration of fictitious people; (2) registrations for dead people; (3) registration cards with forged signatures or incorrect information for people already registered to vote, and forgeries of cards in one county for people already registered to vote in another; (4) submission of registration applications after the deadline.[72] | 2,497 | 0 | 4 | 4[73] | Chad Staton pleaded guilty to filing 124 false registration applications in Cuyahoga County;[74] in June 2004, ACORN fired two workers for filing fake registrations in Franklin County; Boards of Elections in Cuyahoga and Franklin counties asked prosecutors to investigate potentially forged signatures in applications collected in a drive in which workers were allegedly paid per application; Kevin Dooley of Columbus was indicted for false election registration and for submitting false election signatures; referrals of irregularities in registration applications and requests for absentee ballots made by the Board of Elections to the Sheriff's Office in Lake County; in Trumball County the board asked prosecutors to investigate fraud in registration applications. In September 2004, the Attorney General's Office joined a review of 803 allegedly fraudulent voter registration cards |

(continued)

	Allegations of voter fraud in the ACVR report[1]						Facts		
ACVR ID#[2]	State	Location	Election	Description of incident(s)	Number of alleged fraudulent voter registration applications	Number of alleged fraudulent votes cast	Number of actual illegal ballots cast	Number of actual fraudulent ballots cast[3]	Disposition of incident(s)
									received by local elections officials across the state. The outcome of that review is not known; in response to my February 2006 public records request for records related to voter and voter registration fraud in Ohio after 2000, the office replied that it "[did] not have any compilations of public records responsive to [my] request."[75]
6.12a	Pa.	Statewide	11/04 general election	Voter rolls surge to "almost inexplicable dimensions," nearly matching census estimates for the population in Philadelphia.[76]	0	0	0	0	According to press reports, at 260,000 new registrants since the April primary, the Democratic surge was larger than the Republican surge, which added 156,000 new party registrants to the rolls statewide.[77] When asked about Philadelphia's numbers, Bob Lee, the long-time city voter registration administrator,

					10,000	0	0	0

ACVR reports on a Republican Party mailing to 130,000 newly registered voters in Philadelphia, urging them to vote Republican; 10,000 came back as returned mail for bad addresses or addressee unknown. The party investigated and found that some of these addresses were for vacant lots and boarded-up buildings. One sample of 100 registrants turned up 15 dead people.[79]

6.12b Pa. Philadelphia 11/04 general election

was adamant that journalists like those whose stories are cited in the ACVR report do not understand how voter registration rolls are maintained, do not understand the difference between active and inactive voters, and typically ignore the role of state and federal law in governing list maintenance. Lee did not find the surge in registration in the city unreasonable or unexpected given his sense of the public's interest in the election.[78]

The methodology of using return mail to identify fraudulently registered or ineligible voters is notoriously unreliable. Given this fact, and the availability of plausible alternative explanations for the return mail, the burden of proof that registrations so identified are fraudulent and productive of fraudulent ballots is on those employing the methodology.

(continued)

				Allegations of voter fraud in the ACVR report[1]				Facts	
ACVR ID#[2]	State	Location	Election	Description of incident(s)	Number of alleged fraudulent voter registration applications	Number of alleged fraudulent votes cast	Number of actual illegal ballots cast	Number of actual fraudulent ballots cast[3]	Disposition of incident(s)
6.12b	Pa.	Philadelphia	11/04 general election	ACVR raises an issue with locating polling places in private buildings (news reports estimate that more than half, about 900 of Philadelphia's 1,681 polling places, are in private buildings).[80]	0	0	0	0	The ACVR report makes no specific allegation of fraudulent voting, however worthy of concern this issue may be.
6.12c	Pa.	Philadelphia	11/04 general election	Rep. Curt Weldon (R) reported to CBS 3 that he confronted college students walking out of the Curran-Fromhold Prison in northeast Philadelphia with absentee ballots collected from inmates; it is illegal in Pa. for third parties to collect absentee ballots.[81]	0	Unknown number of absentee ballots	0	0	Pretrial detainees and confined misdemeanants are permitted to vote absentee under Pa. laws. There is no evidence of illegal or fraudulent ballots cast by ineligible felon voters in this election.[82]
6.12d	Pa.	Philadelphia	5/05 primary election	A deputy city commissioner requests that the city DA investigate allegations that Gerri Robinson, Hill Creek tenant council president, promised cottage cheese in exchange for voting for certain candidates in a May primary.[83]	0	Unknown	Unknown	Unknown	Labeled a case of "Vote-buying in Philadelphia" in the ACVR report, this allegation is hardly that. The tenant council president, who allegedly unloaded two cartons of cottage cheese by the end of the day, did not think she

(continued)

								was doing anything wrong. Apparently, neither did the DA, as no investigation ensued.
6.14a	Wash.	King and Pierce counties, and statewide	11/04 general election	Reports on the gubernatorial contest between Republican Dino Rossi and Democrat Christine Gregoire, which after a hand recount by 129 votes (later adjusted by a court to 133) out of 2.8 million cast. The ACVR says the ensuing litigation established that there was "clear evidence of vote fraud and irregularities that cast serious doubt upon the validity of a number of votes far exceeding Gregoire's margin of victory." The judge refused to order a new election because, given the secret ballot, the court could not determine how to allocate the illegal votes.[84]	0	1,678[85]	1,678	8[86]	See chapter 6 for a discussion of this case.
6.15a	W.Va.	Lincoln County	Local and federal elections going back to 1990	Allegations refer to *U.S. v. Adkins, et al.*, set to go to trial in August 2005. The federal indictment alleges that the defendants participated in a conspiracy to buy votes, paying voters in liquor, laying	0	Unknown	Unknown	Unknown	The allegations are not in dispute. Seven people were eventually indicted. Six pleaded guilty to various charges related to conspiracies to buy votes in Lincoln County; one case was dismissed.[88]

ACVR ID#[2]	State	Location	Election	Description of incident(s)	Number of alleged fraudulent voter registration applications	Number of alleged fraudulent votes cast	Facts Number of actual illegal ballots cast	Number of actual fraudulent ballots cast[3]	Disposition of incident(s)
				gravel, and fixing traffic tickets (one of the defendants, Greg Stowers, is Lincoln County circuit clerk).[87]					
6.15a	W.Va.	Logan County	5/04 primary election	Cite case of Logan County officials and one other person for lying to a grand jury, pleading guilty to vote buying.[89]	0	Unknown	Unknown	Unknown	The allegations are not in dispute. Eventually, five people, including four Logan County officials (the sheriff, police chief, county attorney and a former mayor), and the president of the local VFW post pleaded guilty to various charges related to vote buying.[90]
6.16a	Wisc.	Statewide	11/04 general election	Reports on the unfolding investigation by the *Milwaukee Journal Sentinel* of election day irregularities, including: (1) at least 278 felons illegally voted; (2) about 7,000 more ballots cast than people recorded as voting; (3) about 1,200 ballots cast by people with invalid addresses, about three-quarters of whom	1,300	9,800 (est.)	224[92]	5[93]	Serious administrative problems in the 2004 election plagued the City of Milwaukee Election Commission and are documented in a number of postelection audits and reports.[94] See chapter 6 for a discussion of these issues.

				registered on election day; (4) 1,300 same-day registration cards could not be processed due to bad address data.[91]					
6.16a	Wisc.	Statewide	11/04 general election	Reports on the preliminary findings of a joint (federal and state) task force investigation of election irregularities in Wisconsin in the 2004 election. Among them, more than 100 instances of illegal voting (including double-voting, voting under fictitious names and addresses, voting using the names of dead people); more than 200 felons illegally cast ballots; approximately 65 fake voter registrations; an acknowledgement that the number of votes cast "far exceeds the total number of recorded voters" (that number was put at 4,609).[95]	65	5,000 (est.)	224	5	These reports are duplicative of those above.
6.16b	Wisc.	Milwaukee, Racine, and Kenosha	11/04 general election	Four ACORN workers, Urelene Lilly, Marcus L. Lewis, Damien Jones, and Robert Marquise Blakely, are charged with submitting multiple voter registration applications for fictitious people or with falsifying information on voter registration forms.[96]	100 (est.)	0	0	0	Urelene Lilly was convicted, Marcus Lewis and Marquise Blakely pleaded guilty, and Damien Jones's conviction was later reversed on appeal.[97]

(continued)

| | | | Allegations of voter fraud in the ACVR report[1] | | | | | Facts | |
ACVR ID#[2]	State	Location	Election	Description of incident(s)	Number of alleged fraudulent voter registration applications	Number of alleged fraudulent votes cast	Number of actual illegal ballots cast	Number of actual fraudulent ballots cast[3]	Disposition of incident(s)
6.16c	Wisc.	Milwaukee	11/04 general election	Milo Ocasio, a parolee, and Kimberly E. Prude, on probation (both had felony convictions), are charged with illegal voting.[98]	0	2	2	0	Ocasio pleaded guilty; Prude was convicted at trial.[99]
6.16c	Wisc.	Milwaukee	11/04 general election	Enrique Sanders, Theresa Byas, and Brian L. Davis are charged with double-voting.[100]	0	0	0	0	All three had their cases dismissed.
6.16d	Wisc.	Milwaukee	11/00 general election	The story of Connie Milstein, a Gore volunteer and New York resident who was videotaped offering homeless men cigarettes to vote, is repeated here. Milstein did not contest a civil complaint against her and paid a $5,000 fine.[101]	0	25[102]	0	0	The allegations in this case are not disputed. One voter interviewed for the WISN-TV (an NBC affiliate) story said he was given a single pack of cigarettes after he accepted a ride to the polls. Both he and another man interviewed said they were planning on voting before the Gore campaign workers visited their homeless shelter. Milstein did not contest a civil fine levied against her.[103]

| 6.16d | Wisc. | Kenosha | 2002 | Gov. Doyle's campaign held a "bingo and kringle" party at a home for the mentally ill and reportedly used quarters as bingo prizes to "induce" the residents to cast absentee ballots. No charges were ever filed, but it is illegal in Wisconsin to use anything worth more than $1 to lure someone to vote. At least two votes were cast at the bingo party.[104] | 0 | 2 | 0 | 0 | This incident is disputed. The two alleged Doyle campaign staffers did not work for Doyle; one worked for the Democratic Party and the other was a volunteer. The Doyle campaign knew nothing of the bingo game; bingo games like the one at the Dayton Residential Care facility in Kenosha, where this incident allegedly took place, are routinely sponsored by area churches and other organizations. A staffer had earlier picked up absentee ballots for residents who had requested them; Dayton's owner and administrator, a Republican, said two residents told him they voted on the day of the bingo game but he does not know whether they filled out their ballots before or after the game; he also told the *Milwaukee Journal Sentinel* that |

(continued)

Allegations of voter fraud in the ACVR report[1]

ACVR ID#[2]	State	Location	Election	Description of incident(s)	Number of alleged fraudulent voter registration applications	Number of alleged fraudulent votes cast	Facts		Disposition of incident(s)
							Number of actual illegal ballots cast	Number of actual fraudulent ballots cast[3]	
									neither the Democratic Party worker nor the volunteer encouraged residents to vote for Doyle. Perhaps this is why no charges were filed.[105]

Notes: ACORN, Association of Community Organizations for Reform Now; ACT, America Coming Together; AFL-CIO, American Federation of Labor and Congress of Industrial Organizations; AP, Associated Press; AVCR, American Center for Voting Rights; CEFM, Center for Ethics and the Free Market; DA, district attorney; FBI, Federal Bureau of Investigation; FDLE, Florida Department of Law Enforcement; GOP, Republican Party; NAACP, National Association for the Advancement of Colored People; PIRGIM, Public Interest Research Group in Michigan; VFW, Veterans of Foreign Wars.

[1] American Center for Voting Rights, Legislative Fund (ACVR), "Vote Fraud, Intimidation & Suppression in the 2004 Presidential Election" (Washington, D.C., August 2005); available at http://www.docstoc.com/docs/6054957/VOTE-FRAUD-INTIMIDATION-SUPPRESSION-IN-THE-PRESIDENTIAL-ELECTION-Legislative. Note, only allegations of voter fraud, the majority of all allegations made in this report, are analyzed here.

[2] ACVR *ID#* refers to the chapter in the ACVR report in which the incident is reported.

[3] All ballots deemed fraudulent by a reliable source are also considered illegal ballots, but not all illegal ballots are necessarily fraudulent. Thus, the number of fraudulent ballots is a subset of the number of illegal ballots.

[4] Johnny Kampis, "Judge Won't Rule Yet in Greensboro Mayor Case," *Tuscaloosa News,* March 9, 2005; see also Johnny Kampis, "Absentee Ballots Raise Questions in Greensboro," *Tuscaloosa News,* September 5, 2004; Johnny Kampis, "Fraud Grips Black Belt," *Tuscaloosa News,* September 12, 2004; Johnny Kampis, "AG's Office Investigates Black Belt Ballot Issue," *Tuscaloosa News,* January 29, 2005.

[5] The Special Master's report lists the names, ballot numbers, and for all but six of the 162 illegal ballots, the reasons for why each was cancelled. At least twenty-two were voided because according to direct testimony and other evidence obtained by the Special Master, the signatures of the voter or the witness were forged. The remaining 140 illegal ballots were voided because they did not meet the qualifications required of absentee ballots under Alabama law (§ 17-10-23 (envelopes not postmarked as of the date prior to the day of election) and § 17-11a-1(c) (related to improper voter identification)). *In Re: The Matter of Vanessa Hill v. J.B. (Johnny) Washington,* Order, Case No. CV-04-121, Circuit Court of Hale County, Ala., January 23, 2006; and telephone interview with Special Master James Anderson, June 11, 2009.

[6] Tom Gordon, "Washington Takes Office in Greensboro; Absentee Ballots under Dispute in Close Mayoral Race," *Birmingham News,* October 14, 2004; *In Re: The Matter of Vanessa Hill v. J.B. (Johnny) Washington; J.B. (Johnny) Washington v. Vanessa Hill,* Appeal from Hale Circuit Court, Case No. CV-04-121 (Alabama Supreme Court, December 15, 2006); Robert DeWitt, "Hill Named Mayor of Greensboro," *Tuscaloosa News,* December 16, 2006; Drew Jubera, "Mayor's Return to Alabama a Strike against Voter Fraud," *Atlanta Journal-Constitution,* January 29, 2007; Jason Morton, "Mayor Contests Election Results," *Tuscaloosa News,* September 4, 2008.

7 Kampis, "Fraud Grips Black Belt"; see also Kampis, "Absentee Ballots Raise Questions in Greensboro"; Kampis, "AG's Office Investigates"; Kampis, "Judge Won't Rule."

8 Tom Gordon, "Absentee Votes Could Again Determine Outcomes in Two Black Belt Town Mayoral Elections," *Birmingham News*, August 26, 2008; *Anthony Long v. Robert Bryant*, Appeal from Perry Circuit Court, Case No. CV-04-94 (Alabama Supreme Court, January 18, 2008).

9 ACVR, "Vote Fraud," 37, citing, Susan Greene and Karen E. Crummy, "Voter Fraud Probed in State," *Denver Post*, March 24, 2005.

10 A twenty-two-year-old woman, Katherine Anne Blair, pleaded guilty to a misdemeanor charge for voting in El Paso County, Colorado, and also attempting to vote in Collier County, Florida. Only her El Paso absentee ballot was counted. See Perry Swanson, "Woman Guilty of Trying to Vote Twice," (*Colorado Springs) Gazette*, July 30, 2005. The Colorado attorney general did not respond to my certified letter making a public records request for copies of records related to cases or complaints of voter fraud.

11 Letter from Dana Jaclyn Williams to author, October 6, 2006; see also Associated Press State & Local Wire, "Hundreds in Colorado Investigated for Voter Fraud," March 24, 2005.

12 Susan Greene and Jeffrey A. Roberts, "6,000 Felons on Voter Lists," *Denver Post*, October 10, 2004.

13 Susan Greene and Karen E. Crummy, "Voter Fraud Probed in State," *Denver Post*, March 24, 2005. See also testimony by Carol Peeples of Colorado Voting Project before the third meeting of the Blue Ribbon Election Panel convened by Secretary of State Donetta Davidson following the 2004 election to review election processes in Colorado; at the meeting in Denver on January 14, 2005, Peeples reported on a survey of Colorado's sixty-four clerk and recorder offices conducted by the Right to Vote Campaign, which found that the clerks expected the secretary of state to provide current lists of prisoners and parolees (January 14, 2005 testimony on file with author, and discussed in telephone conversation with Carol Peeples on June 12, 2009). "Many clerks commented that it had been a long time since they had received a list from the secretary of state's office," said Peeples, who also followed up with *Denver Post* reporters Greene and Crummy on the newspaper's method for identifying registered felons. Greene and Crummy compared Colorado's voter registration list with a recent roster from the Department of Correction to match first and last names and dates of birth, an unreliable method likely to produce "false positives," or invalid matches; see Michael McDonald and Justin Levitt, "Seeing Double Voting: An Extension of the Birthday Problem," *Election Law Journal* 7, no. 2: 588–602. The reporters could not say whether the names on their list had already been flagged as ineligible by a clerk, or whether the alleged registered felons had experienced felons had been essentially boils down to overdue bookkeeping on the part of the secretary of state."

14 "Briefing," *Rocky Mountain News*, November 10, 2004; Gary Gerhardt, "2 Charged in Vote Fraud," *Rocky Mountain News*, October 28, 2004; Sue Lindsay, "Prosecutors Charge Another Man in Registration Fraud," *Rocky Mountain News*, November 2, 2004; Greene and Crummy, "Voter Fraud Probed in State," March 24, 2005; Peggy Lowe, "Partisan Fingers Point on Voter-Fraud Issue," *Rocky Mountain News*, October 14, 2004.

15 "I was just helping out downtown," she said. "Everybody needs an extra dollar here now and then to make their quota for the day." See Associated Press State & Local Wire, "Investigation Reveals Potentially Fraudulent Voter Forms," October 12, 2004.

16 "State Files Criminal Charges against Former Aurora Man in Connection with Alleged Voter Registration Fraud," press release, Colorado Department of Law, August 20, 2004; Jon Sarche, "Election Concerns Not Expected to Threaten Overall Results," Associated Press, October 12, 2004; Associated Press, "Investigation Reveals Potentially Fraudulent Voter Forms," October 12, 2004; "Charges Filed over Phony Voter Registrations," press release, Denver District Attorney, October 27, 2004; "Man Charged with Perjury for Phony Voter Registration Signatures," press release, Denver District Attorney, November 1, 2004; Sue Lindsay, "Prosecutors Charge Another Man in Registration Fraud," *Rocky Mountain News*, November 2, 2004; Greene and Crummy, "Voter Fraud Probed in State," March 24, 2005; "Woman Gets Probation in Voter Registration Fraud Case," KUSA-TV 9 News website, http://www.9news.com (accessed October 5, 2005).

17 Associated Press, "Investigation Reveals Potentially Fraudulent Voter Forms," October 12, 2004; "I-Team Investigation Uncovers Voter Registration Fraud," KUSA-TV 9 News website, http://www.9news.com (accessed May 26, 2005); "Briefing," *Rocky Mountain News*, November 10, 2004.

18 The compilation of fraud allegations in the ACVR report contains multiple citations to the same cases. Because the report's persuasiveness is in its heft alone, I include duplicate counts of alleged fraudulent voter registration forms in this column.

19 According to Carole Snyder, Adams County, Colorado clerk and recorder, who said she received forty-two applications for the same would-be voter, "Those are not really what I call fraudulent, but are really just a pain in the neck." Quoted in Valerie Richardson, "Colorado Combats Voter Fraud," *Washington Times*, October 18, 2004, A6.

20 John Sanko, "3 Prosecutors Join Vote Fraud Probe," *Rocky Mountain News*, August 7, 2004; Gabrielle Crist, "Faulty Voter Applications Are Blamed on Workers," *Rocky Mountain News*, October 15, 2004; Valerie Richardson, "Colorado to Tackle Voter-Fraud Fears," *Washington Times*, October 14, 2004.

21 "I-Team Uncovers Partisan Tactics in Colorado Voter Registration Drives," KUSA-TV 9 News website, http://www.9news.com (accessed May 26, 2005).

22 Jeremy Milarsky, "Ex-Worker Sues Activist Group," *(South Florida) Sun-Sentinel*, October 30, 2004; Brittany Wallman and Alva James-Johnson, "Filled-in Voter Forms Surface," *(South Florida) Sun-Sentinel*, October 27, 2004; see also, Exhibits Q, Q1, Q2, and R in ACVR, "Vote Fraud."

23 Brittany Wallman, "Voter Registration Drive a Subterfuge, Lawsuit Claims," *(South Florida) Sun-Sentinel*, October 30, 2004; Tom Zucco, "Signup Mistakes Blamed on Group," *St. Petersburg Times*, October 4, 2004; Tom Zucco, "Activist Group Blamed for Voter Roll Goofs," *St. Petersburg Times*, October 4, 2004.

24 "Voter Fraud Charges Collapse," *St. Petersburg Times*, December 15, 2005.

25 Zucco, "Signup Mistakes Blamed on Group"; Dara Kam, "Voter Registration Process Causes Concern," *Palm Beach Post*, October 7, 2004. See also Lucy Morgan, "Group Faces Accusations of Broken Voting Laws," *St. Petersburg Times*, October 22, 2004.

26 Associated Press State & Local Wire, "FDLE Investigating Suspicious Leon County Voter Applications," October 5, 2004.

27 Depositions of ACORN-Associated Individuals in Mac Stuart Case (see Exhibits Q, Q1, and Q2 in ACVR, "Vote Fraud").

28 Brendan Farrington, "Fla. Officials Asked to Probe Vote Fraud," Associated Press, October 7, 2004.

29 Joe Black, "FBI Finds No Double Voting at Duval Polls or in Absentee," *Florida Times-Union*, July 30, 2005.

30 David DeCamp, "Double Voting Being Investigated," *Florida Times-Union*, January 25, 2005; Amy Sherman, "Double-Voters' Names Going to Prosecutors," *Miami Herald*, November 14, 2004; Erika Bolstad, "Absentee-Ballot Glitches Prompt Request for Inquiry," *Miami Herald*, November 17, 2004; George Bennett, "Possible Attempts to Double Vote Eyed," *Palm Beach Post*, November 5, 2004; Ludmilla Lelis and Jeff Libby, "Volusia Canvassers Examine 3 in Vote Fraud," *Orlando Sentinel*, November 4, 2004; Lindsay Jones and John Pacenti, "Area Voters Encounter Few Snags," *Palm Beach Post*, November 3, 2004.

31 Andrew A. Green and Stephanie Desmon, "Ehrlich on Offensive Against Early Voting, Knight Ridder Tribune Business News, May 18, 2006.

32 James Miller, "Recounters Wary of Fraud; Officials Report Possible Double Voting," *Daytona Beach News-Journal*, November 5, 2004; "In Brief: Double Vote Cases Get Attention," *Daytona Beach News-Journal*, May 18, 2005; James Miller, "Area Woman Faces Fine for Voting Twice," *Daytona Beach News-Journal*, September 6, 2005.

33 Geoff Dougherty, "Dead Voters on Rolls, Other Glitches Found in 6 Key States," *Chicago Tribune*, December 4, 2004.

34 See Centers for Disease Control, National Center for Health Statistics, National Vital Statistics System (Mortality), Worktable 23F, "Deaths by 10-year Age Groups: United States and Each State, 2004," available at: http://www.cdc.gov/nchs/data/statab/mortfinal2004_worktable23f.pdf.

35 Russ Buettner, "Exposed: Scandal of Double Voters," *(New York) Daily News*, August 22, 2004; Scott Hiaasen, Dave Davis, and Julie Carr Smyth, "Voters Double-Dip in Ohio, Fla.," *(Cleveland) Plain Dealer*, October 31, 2004; Roger Roy and Beth Kassab, "Double Votes Taint Florida, Records Show," *Orlando Sentinel*, October 23, 2004.

36 In the three articles used as sources for these allegations, only two voters are reliably identified as having cast two votes in the same election. One is Randall Funderburke, age 44, who Roy and Kassab report cast an absentee ballot in Thomas County, Georgia, and then four days later voted at the polls in Tallahassee, Florida. Funderburke was charged in Tallahassee with false submission of voter registration information, a felony, and sentenced to eighteen months probation. The other is Normal Siegel, age 84, a registered Republican in Pinellas Park, Florida, and Queens, New York, whom Buettner claims voted twice in seven elections, including presidential elections between 1988 and 2000. A follow-up article on Buettner's claims that appeared two days later in the *Daily News* stated that the director of the New York City Board of Elections planned to present the names of five double-voters used as examples in Buettner's story; Russ Buettner, "City Mulls Action Against Two-Timing Voters," *(New York) Daily News*, August 24, 2004. For this reason, I have added four likely double-voters to the two actually mentioned, Funderburke and Siegel, to arrive at a total of six double-voters identified in these news stories (the article by Hiaasen, Davis, and Smyth did not identify any double-voters with any certainty).

37 See Russ Buettner, "Snowbirds' Double Voting Demonstrates Vulnerability of Voting's Honor System," *IRE Journal* (January–February 2005). When asked by authorities in both states who wanted to follow up on Buettner's claim that 400–1,000 people had double-voted in New York City and Florida over the past several years, Buettner refused to share his data. He says, "We politely suggested they do their own work." See also Steven Isbitts, "Double-Dipping Voters Get Federal Attention," *Tampa Tribune*, October 5, 2004. In summer 2007, Christopher Ro, my research assistant, contacted reporters Hiaasen, Smyth, and Kassab by e-mail to inquire about their data-matching methods (e-mail from Christopher Ro to author, July 5, 2007). Hiaasen replied: "If memory serves, we simply obtained the most recent statewide voter registration files and compared, though I don't remember how many fields we used to confirm a match. Our next step, I believe, was to obtain the voter file from the most populous counties in both Florida and Ohio, to get the most current records showing whether these folks actually voted or not (state lists often have registrations but don't record voter history, or they didn't in 2004). For those people we suspected of voting twice—a modest number, as I recall—we confirmed the voters using property records and other available data. 27,000 is an artificially high number. As I believe the story explained, this is more a consequence of the states' inability to keep up with voters who have moved." Kassab said, "I remember off the top of my head that we basically cross-referenced vote rolls from both states (matching name and date of birth) and then called many of the matches to verify our results."

38 Associated Press, "Federal Jury Convicts Five People in Federal Vote Fraud Trial," June 29, 2005; Beth Hunddsdorfer, "Four Plead Guilty to Vote-Buying," *Belleville News-Democrat*, March 23, 2005; Mike Fitzgerald and Beth Hundsdorfer, "ESL Party Chairman is Indicted," *Belleville News-Democrat*, March 24, 2005; Michael Shaw and Doug Moore, "Five Are Charged with Election Fraud," *St. Louis Post-Dispatch*, March 24, 2005; Mike Fitzgerald, "Powell Loses Race for Council," *Belleville News-Democrat*, April 6, 2005; Michael Shaw and Douglas Moore, "Murder Plot Charge Stems from Voting Probe, *St. Louis Post-Dispatch*, January 22, 2005.

[39] *U.S. v. Scott*, Case No. 05-CR-30040 (S.D. Ill. 2005); *U.S. v. Nichols*, Case No. 05-CR-30041 (S.D. Ill. 2005); *U.S. v. Terrance Stith*, Case No. 05-CR-30042 (S.D. Ill. 2005); *U.S. Sandra Stith*, Case No. 05-CR-30043 (S.D. Ill. 2005); *U.S. v. Powell, et al*, Case No. 05-CR-30044 (S.D. Ill. 2005). See also, Jim Suhr, "Feds Hope Convictions Curb Vote-Buying," AP Online, July 1, 2005, available at: http://www.ewoss.com/articles/D8B2P36O0.aspx.

[40] Elizabeth J. Beardsley, "Senator, 2 Other Men Are Indicted," *(Louisville) Courier-Journal*, May 6, 2005; Lee Mueller, "Federal Vote-Fraud Trials to Be Separate," *Lexington Herald Leader*, May 18, 2005.

[41] *U.S. v. Turner*, 459 F.3d 775 (6th Cir. 2006).

[42] *U.S. v. Turner, et al*, Case No. 05-CR-00002 (E.D. Ky. 2005); *U.S. v. Hays, et al.*, Case No. 05-CR-00011 (E.D. Ky. 2005); see also, James Dao, "Where Prosecutors Say Votes Are Sold," *New York Times*, August 29, 2004, A12; John Cheves and Beth Musgrave, "Vote-Buying Case Appears to Continue: Federal Grand Jury Hears Witnesses in Lexington," *Lexington Herald-Leader*, December 2, 2005, B1; Lee Mueller, "Ross Harris, Key Figure in Inquiry, Dies," *Lexington-Herald Leader*, June 27, 2006; Lee Mueller and John Stamper, "Pikeville Man Sentenced to Six Months for Vote Fraud: Prosecutors Said He Was Bag Man For Ross Harris," *Lexington Herald-Leader*, February 16, 2007, C3.

[43] Dawson Bell, "Campaign Workers Suspected of Fraud," *Detroit Free Press*, September 23, 2004.

[44] Ed Brayton, "GOP Sound and Fury about ACORN Is a Little Bit Nutty," *Michigan Messenger*, October 1, 2008, available at: http://michiganmessenger.com/5366/gop-sound-and-fury -about-acorn-is-a-little-bit-nutty. In October 2006, I sent public records requests to the Michigan secretary of state and attorney general for copies of records related to voter fraud cases or complaints, including voter registration fraud, since 2000. The secretary of state had no records of referrals of such cases to U.S. attorneys or local prosecutors, but did supply several e-mails and court documents related to cases of absentee ballot fraud in two local elections. The first was a River Rouge School District special election in April 2002, in which Allen Randy Durham, a school system employee, pleaded guilty to one count of improper possession of absentee ballots and two counts of absentee ballot tampering. The second involved absentee ballot tampering in a January 2001, Ecorse (Wayne County) special election to replace four city council members following a successful recall election the previous fall. Two city council members were eventually convicted of single counts of improper possession of an absentee ballot and vote tampering. The Attorney General's Office responded to my request for copies (electronic format preferred) of indictments for voter (and registration) fraud and records of settlements in voter fraud cases brought by the attorney general, nonexempt records of referrals of fraud cases from the Michigan Department of State or county prosecuting attorneys, and records of investigations of those cases, so referred, by informing me that it would cost $1,441.01 (letter to author from Christine S. Dingee, dated March 7, 2006). Unable to fund this request, I was unable to obtain any records of voter fraud cases handled by the Michigan Attorney General's office from 2000 to 2006.

[45] Patrick Sweeney, "Stash of Voter Cards Probed," *St. Paul Pioneer Press*, October 8, 2004; Associated Press, "Man Pleads Guilty in Voter Registration Scam," December 7, 2004.

[46] Jo Mannies, "Voter Registration Fraud Dogs City; The Latest Case is Traced to Workers Whom Activist Group Fired," *St. Louis Post-Dispatch*, September 19, 2003, B1; David A. Lieg, "Political Groups Using Incentives to Encourage Voter Registration," Associated Press, June 27, 2004.

[47] Mannies, "Voter Registration Fraud Dogs City," September 19, 2003; Jo Mannies, "Election Board Will Investigate Carter's Role in Vote Case; Prosecutor Has Called Her A Key Witness," *St. Louis Post-Dispatch*, November 19, 2003, C1.

[48] Robert Patrick, "Jury Finds Montgomery Guilty in Vote Fraud Case," *St. Louis Post-Dispatch*, February 11, 2005; Robert Patrick, "Darlene Green Testifies in City Vote Fraud Trial," *St. Louis Post-Dispatch*, February 10, 2005; Associated Press, "Head of 2001 Voter-Registration Drive Convicted of Perjury," February 10, 2005. A seventh volunteer, Michelle Robinson, pleaded guilty to falsifying thirteen registration cards, one in the name of the mother of St. Louis circuit attorney Jennifer Joyce, another in the name of a well-known alderman who had died in 1990. Associated Press, "St. Louis Vote Fraud Sentence Includes Meditation," April 1, 2006.

[49] Robert Patrick, "6 Plead Guilty in Vote Fraud Case," *St. Louis Post-Dispatch*, December 17, 2004, B1; Associated Press State & Local Wire, "Head of 2001 Voter-Registration Drive Convicted of Perjury," February 10, 2005; Robert Patrick, "Jury Finds Montgomery Guilty in Vote Fraud Case," *St. Louis Post-Dispatch*, February 11, 2005, B1.

[50] Center for Ethics and the Free Market, "Laying the Groundwork: A Study of Voter Registration in Missouri," June 2004 (Exhibit S in ACVR, "Vote Fraud").

[51] Ibid., 8–9.

[52] Associated Press, "Audit Critical of City Election Board," May 26, 2004.

53 To perform the audit, the State Auditor's Office obtained and matched the following data: voter registration records and reports of federal felony convictions from the Missouri Secretary of State's Office; voter registration data from St. Louis County Board of Election Commissioners, and from Madison and St. Clair counties in Illinois; Department of Health and Social Services (DHSS) Vital Statistics records of deceased persons; Missouri felony convictions from the Missouri Department of Corrections offender database; a listing of vacant lots maintained by the St. Louis City assessor; and the results of a March 2003 match between St. Louis Board of Election Commissioners voter registration data and the DHSS Vital Statistics unit's deceased persons data. Records were matched on names, dates of birth, and, when available, full or partial Social Security numbers. Street addresses were matched against the vacant lot listing. The report identifies 935 instances of possible voting felonies committed by individuals in the match results. It does not, however, indicate the elections in which these possibly ineligible voters may have voted. "It should be noted," write the authors of the report, "that the results of data matches such as those we performed indicate a high likelihood that an individual may be inappropriately registered or inappropriately voted in a particular election. Each instance must be investigated thoroughly before a voter is removed from the voter registration records or referred to law enforcement for possible legal action." Of the 935 possible voting felonies, 907 were individuals with felony convictions. The state auditor's findings of possible voting felonies must be seen in the context of the massive administrative problems suffered by the St. Louis Board of Elections Commissioners, which caused hundreds of voters to be turned away from the polls during the 2000 election. The Justice Department sued the Board to force it to address these problems and comply with federal voting laws (see chap. 6 for details). See also Robbyn Wahby and Shonagh Clements, "Consultants' Report" Report to the Board of Election Commissioners of the City of St. Louis (in preparation for the November 2002 general election), November 5, 2002 [on file with author]. This report, commissioned by the board and prepared by two consultants, one appointed by the mayor of St. Louis and the other by the governor, found that "The basic culture of the organization lends itself to chaos, crisis creation, and short-term fixes to broad, complex, long-term challenges. Neither the St. Louis community nor the individuals within the Election Board trust that the Election Board can accomplish beyond mediocrity," (p. 1).

54 Greg Reeves, "One Person, One Vote? Not Always," *Kansas City Star*, September 5, 2004.

55 *U.S. v. McIntosh*, Case No. 04-20142 (D. Kan., 2004); *U.S. v. Scherzer*, Case No. 04-CR-00401 (W.D. Mo., 2004); *U.S. v. Goodrich*, Case No. 04-CR-00402 (W.D. Mo., 2004).

56 Adrienne Packer and J. M. Kalil, "Vote Fraud Allegations: Judge Denies Request," *Las Vegas Review-Journal*, October 16, 2004; Erin Neff and Brian Haynes, "Fake Voter Sign-Ups Increasing," *Las Vegas Review-Journal*, July 9, 2004; Adrienne Packer, "County Battling Vote Fraud," *Las Vegas Review-Journal*, July 17, 2004.

57 Neither the Nevada secretary of state nor the attorney general responded to my certified letters of October 2006, making public records requests for copies of records related to voter fraud in Nevada between 2000 and 2006. There is no other available evidence suggesting any fraudulent voter registration was used to cast an illegal ballot or that any ineligible voter, including any of the felons on the rolls as identified by the *Chicago Tribune* or Catherine Smith, Clark County elections investigator, cast an illegal ballot in the 2004 election. When he called the Clark County Registrar of Voters in summer 2007 to follow up on the disposition of the voter registration fraud allegations appearing in the newspapers, Christopher Ro, my research assistant, was told that the FBI was investigating the fraudulent forms and had told the Clark County office not to comment on the matter.

58 Erin Neff, "Clark County May Lead Nation in Voter Sign-Ups," *Las Vegas Review-Journal*, October 2, 2004.

59 Sean Whaley, "No Evidence of Organized Fraud," *Las Vegas Review-Journal*, October 29, 2004. The report found that paid voter registration canvassers had engaged in fraud for financial gain. "At this time," it concluded, "it appears that many of these organizations have become victims of their own employees obtaining money under false pretense."

60 Adam Goldman, "Executive Denies Voter Registration Forms Destroyed in Nevada," Associated Press, October 31, 2004; Jo Becker and Thomas B. Edsall, "Registering Voters: Add One, Take Away Two," *Washington Post*, October 14, 2004; Adrienne Packer and J. M. Kalil, "Vote Fraud Allegations: Judge Denies Request," *Las Vegas Review-Journal*, October 16, 2004; Kirsten Searer, "Extent of Vote Fraud in County Unknown," *Las Vegas Sun*, July 21, 2004; Ken Ritter, "Nevada Judge Declines to Reopen Voter Registration in Vegas Area," Associated Press, October 15, 2004; Nevada Secretary of State, "Alleged Vote Fraud Investigations Ongoing," press release, October 28, 2004.

61 Associated Press State & Local Wire, "Reno Judge OKs Vote by Sparks Couple," November 2, 2004.

62 Michael Martinez and Geoff Dougherty, "Felons Slip through the Net of Voter Registration Rules," *Chicago Tribune*, October 31, 2004.

63 In 2003, the Nevada legislature adopted Assembly Bill 55, revising the state felon disfranchisement laws to require the automatic restoration of voting rights for first-time, nonviolent offenders on completion of their sentence. The new law had an immediate effect on an estimated 40,000 people in the run up to the 2004 general election. See "Re-enfranchising Ex-Felons, Assembly Bill 55, State of Nevada, 2003," Applied Research Center, available at http://www.arc.org/pdf/168pdf.pdf. Violent and second-time offenders must apply to the court in which they were convicted to restore their voting rights. Nevada Revised Statutes, §§ 213.090, 213.155, and 213.155.

64 Dan McKay, "Too Young to Vote," *Albuquerque Journal*, August 20, 2004; "Dead Man Registered to Vote Again," KRQE News 13 Report, August 16, 2004; Dan McKay, "Clerk Seeks Vote-Fraud Review," *Albuquerque Journal*, October 29, 2004; "Probe Irregularities in Voter Registration" *Albuquerque Journal*, August 9, 2004.

65 In response to a reporter's question about how most actual fraudulent votes were recorded in recent New Mexico elections, the state chief elections officer, Secretary of State Mary Herrera (who was Bernalillo County clerk when the two underage boys were fraudulently registered) said, "I don't know of any." Quoted in Michael Coleman, "Seeds of Doubt; If ACORN Fraud Is Rampant, Show Us the Ballots," *Albuquerque Journal*, October 26, 2008, B3. My October 2006 public records request to the Secretary of State's Office for copies of records related to voter fraud cases since 2000 went unanswered.

66 McKay, "Too Young to Vote;" Shea Andersen, "More Glare on Voter Sign-Ups," *Albuquerque Tribune*, August 25, 2004; Associated Press, "Albuquerque Police Find Voter Registration Forms at Albuquerque Apartment," October 16, 2004; Dan McKay and Andy Lenderman, "County's Early-Polling Places 'Slammed' With Voters, Calls," *Albuquerque Journal*, October 19, 2004; Andy Lenderman, "Fight over Voter ID Heats Up," *Albuquerque Journal*, September 19, 2004.

67 See David Iglesias, *In Justice: Inside the Scandal That Rocked the Bush Administration* (Hoboken: John Wiley & Sons, 2008). An investigation by the Justice Department inspector general into the firing of the U.S. attorneys concluded that Iglesias was terminated because of complaints by Republican operatives in New Mexico over his handling of voter fraud and public corruption matters. See, U.S. Department of Justice, Office of the Inspector General and Office of Professional Responsibility, "An Investigation into the Removal of Nine U.S. Attorneys in 2006," Washington, D.C., September 2008, 149–200.

68 Lenderman, "Fight over Voter ID Heats Up."

69 Associated Press, "Activist Reports Theft of Voter Forms," September 23, 2004.

70 Andy Lenderman, "Woman Reports Ballot Ruse," *Albuquerque Journal*, October 23, 2004.

71 Larry Eichel, "Election Numbers Still Leave Questions for Some," *Philadelphia Inquirer*, November 23, 2004; Stephanie Zimmermann, "Jackson Rallies for Ohio Vote Probe," *Chicago Sun-Times*, November 28, 2004; "Preserving Democracy: What Went Wrong in Ohio," Report of the House Judiciary Committee Democratic Staff, Washington, D.C., January 5, 2005; U.S. Count Votes, "Analysis of the 2004 Presidential Election Exit Poll Discrepancies," National Election Data Archive Project, April 12, 2005, Park City, Utah, available at: http://www.election mathematics.org/em-exitpolls/Exit_Polls_2004_Edison-Mitofsky.pdf; Terry M. Neal, "Vote Fraud Theorists Battle over Plausibility," *Washington Post*, April 24, 2005; "Evaluation of Edison/ Mitofsky Election System 2004, Edison Media Research and Mitofsky International, January 19, 2005; Election Science Institute, "Ohio Exit Polls 'Not a Smoking Gun' for Fraud, Study Says," press release, May 14, 2005; Farhad Manjoo, "No Exit," Salon.com, June 15, 2005, available at: http://www.salon.com/news/feature/2005/06/15/exit_polls/index.html; "Democracy at Risk: The 2004 Election in Ohio," Report of the Democratic National Committee's Voting Rights Institute, June 22, 2005, available at: http://a9.g.akamai.net/7/9/8082/v001/www.democrats .org/pdfs/ohvrireport/fullreport.pdf.

72 See *State of Ohio v. Chad Staton*, Case No. 04-CR-09070, Defiance Municipal Court, Defiance County, Ohio, October 26, 2004 (Exhibit T in ACVR, "Vote Fraud"); "Man Arrested after Voter Forms Turned in for Mary Poppins, Michael Jordan, Ohio Officials Say," Associated Press, October 19, 2004; Lisa A. Abraham, "Suspicious Voter Cards Are Piling Up," *Akron Beacon Journal*, September 29, 2004; Mark Naymik, "Voter Registration Drive Raises Some Questions," *(Cleveland) Plain Dealer*, March 18, 2004; Robert Vitale, "Made-Up People," *Columbus Dispatch*, June 2, 2004; Robert Vitale, "Two Fired over Bogus Voter Registration Forms," *Columbus Dispatch*, June 3, 2004; Cindi Andrews, "Alleged Fraudulent Voter Cards Scrutinized," *Cincinnati Enquirer*, October 8, 2004; Mark Hansel, "Voting Organizer Discusses Fraud," *Cincinnati Post*, October 16, 2004; "Voter Aide Indicted in Fake Registration," *Toledo Blade*, January 6, 2005; Steve Luttner and Michael Scott, "1,000 Cases of Suspicious Voter Registrations," *(Cleveland) Plain Dealer*, September 24, 2004; John Arthur Hutchinson, "Possible Election Fraud Is Probed," *Lake County New Herald*, September 22, 2004; Scott Hiaasen, "Fowl Play," *(Cleveland) Plain Dealer*, October 22, 2004; Lisa A. Abraham, "Elections Chief Fears Scheme," *Akron Beacon Journal*, August 19, 2004; Lisa A. Abraham, "Prosecutor to Probe Vote Fraud," *Akron Beacon Journal*, August 25, 2004.

73 A survey of the director or deputy director of each of Ohio's eighty-eight county boards of elections by researchers working with the Coalition on Homelessness and Housing in Ohio and the League of Women Voters of Ohio during the first week of June 2005, found just four instances of fraudulent votes cast over two federal election cycles, 2002 and 2004. The report does not indicate in which election the four votes were cast; thus, I may be overreporting the number of fraudulent votes for 2004. Coalition on Homelessness and Housing in Ohio (COHHIO) and the League of Women Voters of Ohio, "Let the People Vote," Joint Report on Election Reform Activities in Ohio, June 14, 2005, Columbus, Ohio, available at: http://www.cohhio.org/ alerts/Election%20Reform%20Report.pdf.

74 Joe Mahr, "Voter Fraud Case Traced to Defiance County Registrations Volunteer," *Toledo Blade*, October 19, 2004.

75 See letter from Martin D. Susec to author, dated March 9, 2006. A search of the Ohio attorney general's website on June 15, 2009, found no documents or press releases concerning this matter.

76 Mary Claire Dale, "Election-Eve Song: Republicans Charge Fraud, Democrats Intimidation," Associated Press, October 26, 2004.

77 Kate Zernike, "The 2004 Campaign: Battlegrounds—Pennsylvania," *New York Times*, October 31, 2004.

78 E-mail communication from Christopher Ro to author, July 16, 2007, reporting on his extensive telephone conversation with Bob Lee.

79 Tom Infield, "Both Parties Complain of Vote Fraud," *Philadelphia Inquirer*, October 25, 2004.

80 Chris Brennan, "GOP Fails in Effort to Move Polls," *(Philadelphia) Daily News*, October 18, 2004; Mary Claire Dale, "Americans Vote among Kegs, Caskets, Home-Cooking," *Philadelphia Inquirer*, December 4, 2003; Michael Currie Schaffer, "GOP Bid for Poll Shifts Rejected," *Philadelphia Inquirer*, October 21, 2004.

81 "Lawmaker Threatens Political Lawsuit," KYW CBS 3, October 29, 2004, available at: http://kyw.com; "Whose Vote Fraud?" *New York Post*, February 27, 2005.

82 After first denying my February 2006 public records request for copies of records related to voter fraud prosecutions in Pennsylvania since 2000 on the grounds that I was not a Pennsylvania resident and, therefore, had no right of access to any public records, the director of the office's Criminal Law Division, in response to my appeal, informed me that a review of the files indicated the Office of the Attorney General had undertaken no voter fraud prosecutions during the previous five years. Letter from Sheri L. Phillips to author, dated February 17, 2006; letter from Richard A. Sheetz Jr. to author, dated April 13, 2006.

83 Eamon Javers, "Cheesy Way to Lure Voters," *Business Week*, August 1, 2005.

84 David Ammons, "Washington Governor's Election Certified, Showing Democrat Win," Associated Press, December 30, 2005; Keith Ervin, "Higher-Up Linked to Flawed Report," *Seattle Times*, May 21, 2005; Keith Ervin, "Prosecutors to Challenge 110 Voters," *Seattle Times*, April 29, 2005; Rebecca Cook, "King County Election Director Answers Questions under Oath," Associated Press, April 25, 2005; David Postman, "Dems Flag 743 Votes They Say Felons Cast," *Seattle Times*, May 7, 2005.

85 The ACVR report does not distinguish between illegal and fraudulent votes, labeling "illegal and fraudulent" the number of ballots recognized by Chelan County Superior Court Judge John Bridges as only illegal. In his order dismissing the election contest brought by Dino Rossi, the Republican gubernatorial candidate, Judge Bridges said, "The Court concludes that, having neither pled nor disclosed . . . fraud [it] cannot now be claimed and that to the extent that it was claimed, neither the act of fraud nor the causation arising therefrom were proved by the higher burden of proof of clear, cogent and convincing." *Timothy Borders et al. v. King County et al.*, No. 05-200027-3, Chelan County Superior Court, State of Washington (June 6, 2005), 24.

86 In 2005, eight people were prosecuted for criminal voter fraud in the 2004 election. See chapter 6, note 150 for details.

87 Jennifer Bundy, "Lincoln Circuit Clerk Accused of Vote Buying," Associated Press, May 5, 2005; Lawrence Messina, "Election Fraud Charges Seem Like Old News in Lincoln County," Associated Press, May 10, 2005; Lawrence Messina, "In W.Va. County, Vote-Buying Indictments Turn Few Heads," Associated Press, June 20, 2005; Tom Searls, "Motions Shed Light on Vote Fraud Probe," *Charleston Gazette*, June 24, 2005.

88 *U.S. v. Adkins, et al.*, Case No. 04-CR-00162 (S.D.W. Va., 2004).

89 Lawrence Messina, "Agents Secretly Filmed, Recorded Election Activities," Associated Press, June 1, 2005; Messina, "Election Fraud Probe Fuels Partisan Rancor," Associated Press, May 15, 2005; Jennifer Bundy, "Logan Lawyer Pleads Guilty to Mail Fraud Charge," Associated Press, January 7, 2005; Toby Coleman, "Ex-Police Chief Gets Lesson in Civics," *Charleston Gazette*, February 16, 2005; Allison Barker, "Ex-Sheriff Given Home Confinement, Probation for Vote Buying," Associated Press, January 21, 2005; Toby Colman, "Logan Lawyer Gets Year in Prison," *Charleston Gazette*, April 5, 2005; Jennifer Bundy, "Former VFW Post Leader Sentenced to Home Confinement," Associated Press, January 14, 2005; Associated Press, "Woman Gets One-Year Sentence in Vote Fraud Investigation," January 27, 2005.

90 *U.S. v. Mendez*, Case No. 05-CR-00101 (S.D.W. Va., 2005); *U.S. v. Porter*, Case No. 05-CR-00145 (S.D.W. Va., 2005); *U.S. v. Hrutkay*, Case No. 05-CR-00149 (S.D.W. Va., 2005); *U.S. v. Stapleton*, Case No. 00173 (S.D.W. Va., 2005); *U.S. v. Esposito*, Case No. 05-CR-00002, 2005).

91 Greg J. Borowski and Mark Maley, "Review Indicates 278 Felons Cast Ballots Illegally in State," *Milwaukee Journal Sentinel*, April 1, 2005; Greg J. Borowski, "Some Sites Show Huge Vote Gaps," *Milwaukee Journal Sentinel*, February 2, 2005.

92 As part of a broad investigation of alleged illegal voting in Milwaukee in the 2004 election, the Milwaukee Police Department participated in a joint federal criminal Voter Fraud Task Force, focusing on reports of 1,300 "un-enterable" on-site voter registration cards, 2,400 "undeliverable" verification cards, and absentee ballots. Its Special Investigations Unit released a report in February 2008 concluding that 224 ineligible felons had cast ballots in Milwaukee County in 2004. A thorough reading the sixty-seven-page report drives home the Special Investigations Unit's conclusion—systemic problems in the administration of the election were almost completely responsible for the irregularities discovered and reported by the newspaper, not fraud. Over and over again, the investigators found that data-entry errors, typographical errors, procedural missteps, misapplication of the rules, and the like accounted for almost all the problems observed by the media and the Republican Party. For example, in investigating the August 4, 2005, formal complaint of the Republican Party of Wisconsin that sixty individuals had voted more than once in the November general election, the report found that only twenty-one people were listed twice in the electors' database due to "data entry errors by employees of the Milwaukee Election Commission"; moreover, "none of these people voted twice." Milwaukee Police Department, Special Investigations Unit, "Report of the Investigation into the November 2, 2004 General Election in the City of Milwaukee," n.d., 35, available at: http://graphics2.jsonline.com/graphics/news/MPD_2004voterfraudprobe_22608.pdf. In investigating another complaint by the Republican Party of Wisconsin that nine more people had voted twice, the report found more mistakes ("this appears to be a mistaken entry by the Election Commission employees. . . . This appears to be a mistaken entry by the Election Commission employees. . . . It appears that these voters are a father and son. . . . it appears that there was an error by a Poll Inspector on Election Day. . . . again, this appears to be an error at the poll site. . . . these are not the same person. It appears that they are father and son. . . . These are not the same person and it appears that the two maybe [sic] father and son. . . . this appears to be another mistaken entry at the poll site. . . . the remaining three persons have closely matching names but are not the same person" (33–34). The release of the report was not authorized by the Milwaukee Police Department. It appears to have been leaked to the press by investigators and to (Republican) Attorney General J.B. Van Hollen; see "Attorney General Van Hollen's Statement on Milwaukee Police Department's Report on 2004 Election," press release, Wisconsin Department of Justice, February 26, 2008; see also, Greg J. Borowski, "Tighter Voting Laws Urged; Milwaukee Police Report Findings from Probe into 2004 Polling," *Milwaukee Sentinel,* February 27, 2008, available at http://www.jsonline.com/news/statepolitics/29543514.html; John Fund, "Milwaukee Puts a Vote-Fraud Cop Out of Business," *Wall Street Journal,* November 4, 2008, A17; John Diedrich, "Chief Flynn Says NPD Vote Fraud Unit on the Job," *Milwaukee Journal Sentinel,* November 4, 2008, available at http://www.jsonline.com/news/milwaukee/33825499.html.

93 This number refers to the five convictions and guilty pleas obtained by U.S. Attorney Steven Biskupic under the U.S. Department of Justice BAVII. See chapter 6 for details.

94 See, for example, Jeff Ripp, Cherry Hill, and Ben Monry, "An Evaluation: Voter Registration," Wisconsin State Legislative Audit Bureau, Report 05-12, September 2005; City of Milwaukee Election Task Force, "Official Report," June 27, 2005; Milwaukee Police Department, "Report."

95 ACVR, "Vote Fraud," 68–69, citing, "Preliminary Findings of Joint Task Force Investigating Possible Election Fraud," May 10, 2005, available at: http://www.wispolitics.com/1006/electionfraud.pdf. This report, like the February 2008 report of the Milwaukee Police Department, a member agency of the Joint Task Force on the 2004 election, may have been an unauthorized leak to the media. As of August 2007, no final report of the task force had been prepared. See email communications between blogger John Washburn and Milwaukee County deputy district attorney James L. Martin, August 24 and 27, 2007. Washburn requested a copy of the final report under Wisconsin's open records laws; Martin informed him that the final report did not exist; Washburn posted the email exchange on his blog, Washburn's World, on September 7, 2007: http://washburnsworld.blogspot.com/2007_09_01_archive.html.

96 Greg J. Borowski, "A New Push to Repair Election," *Milwaukee Journal Sentinel,* May 15, 2005; Derrick Nunnally and Greg J. Borowski: "Arrest Warrants Issued in Alleged Vote Fraud Case, *Milwaukee Journal Sentinel,* May 12, 2005; Tom Kertscher, "Racine, Kenosha Voter Application Fraud Alleged," *Milwaukee Journal Sentinel,* October 29, 2004.

97 Urelene Lilly was accused of submitting about seventy-five fraudulent forms; Jones supervised a voter registration drive in Racine and allegedly pressured workers who had been deputized as registrars to witness and sign registration applications collected by canvassers who were not deputy registrars, in violation of election laws. Marcus Lewis was accused of submitting a voter registration card for a dead person, and submitted multiple forms for some family members. See Associated Press, "Milwaukee Election Fraud Alleged in Charges against Two," May 12, 2005. Marquis Blakely worked for Damien Jones and admitted to falsifying "several" forms by copying names out of the telephone book. See Amended Criminal Complaint, *State of Wisconsin v. Damien Donnelle Jones and Robert M. Blakely,* Racine County Circuit Court, No. 04-CF-1336 (October 28, 2004). Jones was convicted of failing to stop others from submitting false registration cards, but his conviction was later overturned on appeal, with the court finding him a victim of a "miscarriage of justice" and guilty more of bad supervision, a "nonexistent crime," than of fraud. Derrick Nunnally and Greg J. Borowski, "Arrests Sought in Election Fraud; 2 Accused of Falsifying Voter Registration Cards," *Milwaukee Journal Sentinel,* May 11, 2005; Ryan J. Foley, "Wis. Court: Voter Registration Official Did Not Commit a Crime," Associated Press State & Local Wire, April 25, 2007; Ryan J. Foley, "Prosecutor to Press Election Fraud Charges Despite Court Ruling," Associated Press State & Local Wire, April 25, 2007.

98 Derrick Nunnally, "Federal Charges Filed against Three Voters," *Milwaukee Journal Sentinel,* June 23, 2005.

[99] *U.S. v. Ocasio*, Case No. 05-CR-00161 (E.D. Wis., 2005); *U.S. v. Prude*, Case No. 05-CR-0162 (E.D. Wis., 2005). The Prude case is particularly troubling because Prude, a forty-three-year-old grandmother who had never voted before, spent nearly two years in jail for casting a ballot while she was on probation for trying to cash a counterfeit county government check. According to one of her lawyers, Donna Kuchler, Prude was not a political person, but on October 22, 2004, she went to a rally in Milwaukee for John Kerry featuring the Rev. Al Sharpton. At the rally, Kerry campaign workers asked Prude if she was interested in working on the campaign. The job would pay her and Prude needed the money, so she agreed to help the campaign's get-out-the-vote effort on election day. After the rally, Rev. Sharpton led a march to city hall where prospective voters were able to register and vote early. Prude registered and cast an absentee ballot and was hired as an election inspector to work at the polls on election day. According to U.S. Attorney Biskupic, Prude's employment as a poll worker made her a target for prosecution because she was put in a position that allowed her to handle official voting materials, despite being ineligible to do so because of her felon status. Prude claimed she did not know she was ineligible to vote; she had received no jail time for her conviction. She testified that as soon as she realized she was ineligible to vote, she called the Milwaukee Board of Elections and asked them to void her ballot. She says she was told not to worry about it. Telephone interview with Tony Cotton (Kuchler's associate), April 4, 2007; Interview with Donna Kuchler, Wautasaw, Wis., June 19, 2007; Interview with Steven Biskupic, Milwaukee, Wis., June 22, 2007. At her trial, Prude said, "I made a big mistake, like I said, and I truly apologize for it." (See Eric Lipton and Ian Urbina, "In 5-Year Effort, Scant Evidence of Voter Fraud," *New York Times*, April 12, 2007, A3.) She was convicted of casting an illegal vote, and sent to jail for nearly two years for violating the terms of her probation. Prude's appeal was denied. At a hearing, Judge Diane P. Wood of the Seventh Circuit Court of Appeals expressed puzzlement: "I find this whole prosecution mysterious. I don't know whether the Eastern District of Wisconsin goes after every felon who accidentally votes. It is not like she voted five times. She cast one vote." Bruce Murphy, "The Witch Hunt Against Felons Who Vote," *Milwaukee Magazine*, June 5, 2007, available at http://www.milwaukeemagazine.com/murphyslaw/default.asp?NewMessageID=14698. See also Neil E. Saxton, "Affidavit in Support of Criminal Complaint and Arrest Warrant," *U.S. v. Prude*, Case No. 05-CR-0162 (E.D. Wis., 2005); Bill Glauber, "Her First Vote Put Her in Prison," *Milwaukee Journal Sentinel*, May 21, 2007; *U.S. v. Prude*, 489 F.3d 873 (7th Cir. 2007); Bill Glauber, "Voter Fraud Conviction Upheld," *Milwaukee Journal Sentinel*, June 15, 2007.

[100] Nunnally, "Federal Charges Filed;" Derrick Nunnally, "2 More Charged with Voting Twice," *Milwaukee Journal Sentinel*, June 24, 2005; Telephone interview with William U. "Chip" Burke (lawyer for Theresa Byas), April 4, 2007.

[101] David Doege, "$5,000 Settles Election Case," *Milwaukee Journal Sentinel*, May 3, 2001.

[102] At most, twenty-five people may have cast ballots in exchange for cigarettes, according to the Milwaukee County district attorney. Thomas Hruz, "A Vote against Fraud: Defending Reasonable Measures to Protect the Voting Process in Wisconsin," *Wisconsin Interest*, spring 2001, 28.

[103] "Cigarettes Distributed for Gore Vote," WISN-12 News, November 5, 2000, available at: http://html.wisn.com/mil/election2000/itsyourvote/stories/-20001105-134550.html (accessed October 31, 2009).

[104] Steve Schultze and Hahal Toosi, "Bingo Game Spurs Probe of Doyle's Campaign," *Milwaukee Journal Sentinel*, October 24, 2002; Steve Schultze, "No Charges to Be Filed over Bingo Party," *Milwaukee Journal Sentinel*, November 2, 2002; "At Least 2 Votes Cast at Bingo Event in Kenosha, TV Station Says," *Milwaukee Journal Sentinel*, October 29, 2002.

[105] See "George Will Cited Dubious John Fund Anecdote to Support Column on Voter Fraud," Media Matters for America, October 25, 2004, available at: http://mediamatters.org/research/200410230004; Julia Westhoff, "District Attorney Investigates Doyle Bribe Accusations," *Badger Herald*, October 24, 2002; Jenny Price, "Vote Bribe Probe Targets Doyle; Democrats Toss Accusations at Gov. McCallum," *Wisconsin State Journal*, October 24, 2002; Steve Schultze and Nahal Toosi, "Bingo Game Spurs Probe of Doyle's Campaign; Republicans Say Event Was Used to 'Buy' Votes," *Milwaukee Journal Sentinel*, October 24, 2002; Steve Schultze, "Accusations Ring Hollow; Rivals Offer Little Proof of Other's Misdeeds," *Milwaukee Journal Sentinel*, October 30, 2002.

Appendix 2

Selected State Election Codes and Case Law Criminalizing Election Fraud in Twelve States

The following is a summary of selected state election codes and case law criminalizing election fraud in twelve states: Alabama, California, Florida, Georgia, Illinois, Minnesota, Mississippi, New York, Oregon, Pennsylvania, Texas, and Wisconsin.[1]

Alabama
STATUTORY

Article VIII, § 178 states that all citizens over the age of 18 who have resided in Alabama for at least two years are eligible to vote. § 182 of the Alabama Constitution states the grounds for which a person can be disqualified from voting:

> All idiots and insane persons; those who shall by reason of conviction of crime be disqualified from voting at the time of the ratification of this Constitution; those who shall be convicted of treason, murder, arson, embezzlement, malfeasance in office, larceny, receiving stolen property, obtaining property or money under false pretenses, perjury, subornation of perjury, robbery, assault with intent to rob, burglary, forgery, bribery, assault and battery on the wife, bigamy, living in adultery, sodomy, incest, rape, miscegenation, crime against nature, or any crime punishable by imprisonment in the penitentiary, or of any infamous crime or crime involving moral turpitude; also, any person who shall be convicted as a vagrant or tramp, or of selling or offering to sell his vote or the vote of another, or of buying or offering to buy the vote of another, or of making or offering to make a false return in any election by the people or in any primary election to procure the nomination or election of any person to any office, or of suborning any witness or registrar to secure the registration of any person as an elector.

Any qualified voter can challenge whether another person is qualified to vote. This challenge must be communicated to the elections inspectors prior to the person actually casting their vote.[2] At every polling place, there is one person who is designated a "challenger." His or her sole responsibility is to ensure that every person voting is a validly registered voter.[3] When people are challenged, they will be permitted to vote if they take an oath in which they affirm that they are validly registered.[4]

§ 17-12-7 makes it a criminal act (punishable up to six months "hard labor") for an elections inspector to knowingly prevent a validly registered voter from voting. § 17-12-8 imposes the same penalty if an inspector knowingly permits an unregistered voter from voting. § 17-23-1 makes voting twice in the same election, voting when not legally registered or qualified to vote or any other kind of "illegal or fraudulent voting" punishable by imprisonment from two to five years. § 17-23-2 makes it illegal to impersonate someone in an attempt to vote, punishable from one to two years. § 17-23-3 imposes a fine of up to $500 for attempting to bribe someone to vote or not vote for a certain candidate. § 17-23-4 prohibits purchasing someone's vote with cash, "intoxicating liquors, or other valuable things," imposing up to a $100 fine for violations.

Postelection challenges are governed by § 17–15 of the Alabama Elections Code. § 17-15-1 states that any registered voter can challenge the validity of an election on the grounds that there was fraud, corruption, illegal votes, the rejection of legal votes, bribes, coercion, or other activities that would prevent fair and free elections. But § 17-15-2 states that "[n]o election shall be annulled or set aside because of the rejection of legal votes unless it appears that such legal votes, if given to the person intended, would increase the number of his legal votes to or above the number of legal votes received by any other person for the same office."

CASE LAW

Alabama has seen several prosecutions under these various criminal statutes. Many deal with attempts to submit large numbers of absentee ballots. See, for example, *Evans v. State*, 794 So. 2d 415 (2000). See also *Gandy v. State*, 82 Ala. 61, 2 So. 465 (1887); *Wilder v. State*, 401 So. 2d 151 (1981); *Wilson v. State*, 52 Ala. 299 (1875); and *Bozeman v. State*, 401 So. 2d 167 (1981). The number of criminal prosecutions is difficult to ascertain because only the ones in which an appeal was granted are reported on Lexis or Westlaw, but there appear to be more prosecutions than in other states.

Alabama courts, as in most states, are hesitant to set aside elections. Because the contestant has the burden of proof, it is often difficult to establish not only that there were fraudulent votes but also for whom the fraudulent votes were cast. The Alabama courts have adopted the same test as established in the Florida case, *Boardman v. Esteva*, 323 So. 2d 259 (1975) (known as the "Boardman Factors," see below). In *Wells v. Ellis*, 551 So. 2d 382 (1989), the Supreme Court of Alabama, in overturning a lower court ruling to invalidate an election, officially adopted the Boardman Factors by stating:

> The Boardman factors to be considered in determining whether an election should be set aside [are]: (a) the presence or absence of fraud, gross negligence, or intentional wrongdoing; (b) whether there has been substantial compliance with the essential requirements of the absentee voting law; and (c) whether the irregularities complained of adversely affect the sanctity of the ballot and the integrity of the election. . . . We find the *Boardman* rationale to be the correct one for resolving absentee voting statute disputes and, therefore, we adopt the law set out in that decision as it relates to the construction of Ala. Code 1975, § 17-10-1 et seq.

For other examples of decisions on the issue, see *Garrett v. Cuninghame*, 211 Ala. 430, 438 (1924); *Campbell v. Jefferson County*, 216 Ala. 251, 251 (1927); *Woodall v. City of Gadsden*, 278 Ala. 634 (1965); and *Williams v. Lide*, 628 So. 2d 531 (1993).

California
STATUTORY

California's Elections Code is one of the more detailed codes of all of the states, with dozens of provisions that prohibit illegal activity associated with elections. The majority of statutes make the illegal behavior a felony, punishable by up to three years in prison, although some provide for slightly more or fewer penalties. The following is a sampling of the provisions that are most relevant to prohibiting voter fraud.

§§ 18100–18110 prohibit fraudulent registration, including registering under a false name, registering under a false address, and registering a non-existent person. § 18500 is a general "catch-all" provision of the code that prohibits any person from committing fraud, aiding or abetting fraud "in connection with any vote cast, to be cast, or attempted to be cast. . . ." § 18560 makes it a felony to vote in an election that he or she is not entitled to vote in, vote more than once, or impersonate another voter. § 18502 prohibits interfering with someone's right to vote, which is intended to prevent voter intimidation or coercion. § 18520 makes it a felony to "give, offer, or promise any office, place, or employment, or promise to procure or endeavor to procure any office, place, or employment to or for any voter, or to or for any other person, in order to induce that voter at any election to" vote or not vote for a certain candidate. § 18522 makes it illegal to pay money in exchange for voting or not voting for a certain candidate. § 18524 makes it illegal to falsify or assist someone in falsifying residence in order to vote in a certain ward or precinct. § 18543 prohibits challenging someone's right to vote without probable cause to believe that the person is ineligible to vote.

§ 10 of the code makes the secretary of state the chief elections officer with the duty of monitoring and certifying all elections. The code also creates inferior offices such as precinct board members who are to administer elections and count ballots.

Division 16 of the Elections Code outlines election contests. A contest may be brought on the grounds that, among other things, there was fraud on the part of the precinct board or illegal votes were cast.[5] § 16203 states that the effect of illegal voting will not result in voiding the election "unless it appears that a number of illegal votes has been given to the person whose right to the office is contested . . . which, if taken from him, would reduce the number of his legal votes below the number of votes given to some other person for the same office, after deducting therefrom the illegal votes which may be shown to have been given to that other person."

CASE LAW

The courts have strictly interpreted California's election contest laws. The contestant has the burden of proof to show that not only were illegal votes casts but also that they were cast for the contestee.[6] The court in *Wilks v. Mouton*, 42 Cal. 3d 400 (1986), declared that "[s]trict rules embodied in the Elections Code govern a court's review of a properly contested election. It is a primary principle of law as applied to election contests that it is the duty of the court to validate the election if possible. That is to say, the election must be held valid unless plainly illegal." See also *Friends of Sierra Madre v. City of Sierra Madre*, 25 Cal. 4th 165 (2001).

There are very few cases in California in which an election was overturned. In most, the courts have dismissed the challenge because the contestant failed to meet their burden showing that illegal votes were cast. Even when they do show that illegal voting occurred, courts often dismiss because the contestant failed to show for whom they were cast or that the number of votes was sufficient to change the outcome.[7]

One of the few cases in which an election was overturned was *Gooch v. Hendrix*, 5 Cal 4th 266 (1993). In that case, the court held that "widespread illegal absentee ballot voting practices that permeated a consolidated school board election furnished sufficient, essentially uncontroverted circumstantial evidence that it appeared the illegal votes affected the outcomes of the consolidated elections, warranting setting them aside . . . even though it could not be determined on a vote-by-vote basis for whom the illegal votes had been cast."

Florida
STATUTORY

Title IX of the Florida Code governs elections. Fla. Stat. § 102.168 (2001) permits an unsuccessful candidate or Florida taxpayer to challenge any election in Circuit Court. Subpart 3 of that statute lays out the grounds for challenging an election, including fraud, bribery, or illegal/unregistered voting at a level that would place "doubt" in the result of the election. Fla. Stat. § 102.1682 states that, if a challenge to an election is successful under § 102.168 and it is determined that the winner of an election was actually the loser, then the judge shall issue a "judgment of ouster." This would have the effect of placing the "true" winner in office. But courts avoid doing this and resort to other remedies (discussed below). For example, a Florida Appeals Court in *McPherson v. Flynn*, 397 So. 2d 665 (1981) declared that this statute could not be used to overturn elections for the legislative branch because it violated the separation of powers.

Fla. Stat. § 104.041 (2009) makes committing fraud in connection with an election a third-degree felony. § 102.012 (2009) states that the supervisor of elections from each county shall appoint two election boards for each precinct who will have the charge of administering the voting process and monitoring for fraud. § 102.166 (2009) requires there to be an automatic manual recount if the unofficial returns from the first count indicate that the margin between the candidates is less then one-quarter of 1 percent.

CASE LAW

Florida has an extensive history of elections winding up in court. There are countless cases in which election fraud was alleged (and a surprising number in which the allegations were sustained in court). Probably the most significant recent case involving voter fraud in Florida was *In re The Matter Of The Protest Of Election Returns And Absentee Ballots In The November 4, 1997 Election For The City Of Miami, Florida*, 707 So. 2d 1170 (1998). In that case, the court heard a challenge to the mayoral election for Miami brought under the various statutes already listed. The court determined that widespread fraud did occur through the use of absentee ballots. The court noted, however, that there was no history in Florida of ever ordering a new election. Instead, the court concluded that the proper remedy for voter fraud was to throw out the votes associated with the fraud. In this case, the court threw out every single absentee ballot (whether it was proven to be fraudulent or not) and counted only in-person votes to determine the winner.[8] There are numerous other examples of Florida courts throwing out all absentee ballots because of fraud. See *State ex rel. Whitley v. Rinehart*, 140 Fla. 645 (1939); *Griffin v. Knoth*, 67 So. 2d 431 (Fla. 1953); and *Wood v. Diefenbach*, 81 So. 2d 777 (Fla. 1955).

In *Boardman v. Esteva*, 323 So. 2d 259 (1975), the court stated:

> In determining the effect of irregularities on the validity of absentee ballots cast, the following factors shall be considered: (a) the presence or absence of fraud, gross negligence, or intentional wrongdoing; (b) whether there has been substantial compliance with the essential requirements of the absentee voting law; and (c) whether the irregularities complained of adversely affect the sanctity of the ballot and the integrity of the election.

The history of Florida case law appears to be teeming with cases of alleged election fraud.[9]

Georgia
STATUTORY

Article II of the Georgia Election Law establishes the State Election Board led by the secretary of state. The State Election Board has the responsibility, among other things, for investigating "when necessary or advisable the administration of primary and election laws and frauds and irregularities in primaries and elections and to report violations of the primary and election laws either to the Attorney General or the appropriate district attorney who shall be responsible for further investigation and prosecution."[10]

The Georgia law has over forty possible criminal offenses directly associated with election fraud (§§ 21-2-560 to 21-2-602). Some, but not, all the felonies punishable by one to ten years and up to a $10,000 fine are falsely registering oneself or another, or registering under a false name;[11] bribing, accepting a bribe, or participating in a conspiracy to bribe someone in return for voting for a certain candidate;[12] voting more than once in an election;[13] counterfeiting ballot cards;[14] and various "frauds" by poll officers (such as intentionally miscounting votes and tampering with voting machines).[15]

Any registered voter in the state may challenge, prior to an election and in writing, the registration of another voter. On receiving written notice, the Board of Registrars (a subdivision of the State Election Board) must hold a hearing on the matter. The burden of proof is on the person making the challenge who must show "that the person being challenged is not qualified to remain on the list of electors."[16] The board has authority to subpoena and examine witnesses and evidence, as well as reach a final decision (although the decision can be appealed to state court).[17]

Article 13 of the code governs postelection contests. § 21-2-522.1 states that there is a rebuttable presumption that any vote cast in an election is a valid vote. This places the burden on the challenger to rebut the presumption (i.e., prove that it was an invalid or illegal vote). All issues are to be decided by a judge, unless the contestant specifically requests a jury trial. The court has great discretion on what remedy to use. It can declare the true winner based solely on the legal votes, it can discard entire precincts (in the case of misconduct by poll officers), or if "the election . . . is so defective as to the nomination, office, or eligibility in contest as to place in doubt the result of the entire election . . . [the] court shall declare the primary, election, or runoff to be invalid."[18]

CASE LAW

A Georgia Appellate Court stated in *Nichols v. Acree*, 112 Ga. App. 287 (1965), that a new election should be held "[i]f the contestant can sustain his charges, or enough of them to cast doubt upon whether the election was fairly and lawfully conducted. . . . If he cannot, the election should stand." Recently, the Georgia Supreme Court overturned a lower court decision to invalidate an election in *Middleton v. Smith*, 273 Ga. 202 (2000). In that case, the court stated that to carry the burden necessary to overturn an election, the challenger must show "a specific number of illegal or irregular ballots— and that number must be sufficient to cast doubt on the result of the election. It is not sufficient to show irregularities which simply erode confidence in the outcome of the election. Elections cannot be overturned on the basis of mere speculation, or an appearance of impropriety in the election procedures." Nonetheless, Georgia seems to have a history of overturning more elections than most states, probably as a result of the great discretion that the statutes give the courts.[19]

Illinois
STATUTORY

Article 1A of the Illinois Election Code establishes a State Board of Elections, with the secretary of state at the helm, to, among other things, "[r]eview and inspect procedures and records relating to conduct of elections and registration as may be deemed necessary, and to report violations of election laws to the appropriate State's Attorney."[20]

§ 10 ILCS 5/3-1 states that all U.S. citizens eighteen years of age or older who have resided in the state for at least thirty days prior to an election are eligible to vote. But § 10 ILCS 5/3-5 specifically excludes from eligibility those residents who, at the time of the election, are incarcerated as a consequence of a felony conviction.

Article 29 of the Illinois Election Code criminalizes various acts associated with election fraud. Included in the prohibitions are buying or selling votes, voting more than once, voting when not a validly registered voter, registering under false information (name, address, or age), "ballot box stuffing," participating in a conspiracy to commit fraud, or preventing a validly registered voter from voting. The majority of crimes under these statutes are felonies.

§ 10 ILCS 5/23-2 gives the legislature jurisdiction to hear election contests for its own seats. For all other elections, the state courts have jurisdiction. Under § 10 ILCS 5/23-1.2a, an election may be contested:

(1) by any candidate whose name was on the ballot for that office, (2) by any person who filed a declaration of intent to be a write-in candidate for that office, or (3) by any person who voted in that election, provided that such person's challenge is supported by a verified petition signed by persons who voted in the election in a number no less than the largest number of signatures required to nominate a person to be a candidate of any political party which nominated a candidate for the office being contested.

The courts have authority, if they so choose, to defer the investigation and recounting of votes to the State Board of Elections.[21] The courts, however, would have the final determination on the outcome of the contest. "The judgment of the court in cases of contested election, shall confirm or annul the election according to the right of the matter; or, in case the contest is in relation to the election of some person to an office, shall declare as elected the person who shall appear to be duly elected."[22]

Case Law

There appear to be a large number of contested elections in Illinois. Probably the most often quoted rule established by the Illinois Supreme Court is that "there should be no reason for a recount of the votes unless there is a positive and clear assertion, allegation or claim that such a recount will change the result of the election."[23] This language has been used to dismiss many requests for a recount/election challenge because of insufficient evidence presented by the challenger in the initial pleadings.[24]

Nonetheless, there have been several instances in which the Illinois courts have ordered a recount and overturned an election in which they declared the loser to be the true winner. See, for example, *Burton v. Powell*, 26 Ill. App. 3d 563 (1975). For examples in which fraud was alleged (and proved), resulting in reapportioning or recounting of only the "valid" ballots, see *Gribble v. Willeford*, 190 Ill. App. 3d 610; *Tuthill v. Rendleman*, 387 Ill. 321 (1944); *Leach v. Johnson*, 20 Ill. App. 3d 713 (1974); and *Choisser v. York*, 211 Ill. 56, 60–61 (1904). For an interesting and thorough discussion of fraud/illegal voting cases in Illinois and how the courts handle it, see *Leach v. Johnson*, 20 Ill. App. 3d 713 (1974).

Minnesota
Statutory

§ 201.014 outlines who can be a registered voter. All those over the age of eighteen who have lived in Minnesota for at least twenty days, have not been adjudicated mentally incompetent, or are not serving any portion of a sentence (including probation) from a felony conviction are eligible to vote. "[A]ny voter registered within a county may challenge the eligibility or residence of any other voter registered within that county."[25] A county auditor then hears the challenge. The decision of the county auditor is appealable to the secretary of state, who has final authority to issue a determination.

Any person who is not eligible to vote and who attempts to or does vote is guilty of a felony.[26] Under § 201.27, if an elections officer permits or assists an unregistered voter in voting, he or she too is guilty of a felony. The same is true for any person who submits more than one absentee ballot, assists someone in submitting more than one absentee ballot, or alters another's absentee ballot.[27] § 201.275 places authority to investigate criminal activity related to voter fraud in the hands of the local county attorney.

§ 209.02 states the grounds for postelection contests: "The contest may be brought over an irregularity in the conduct of an election or canvass of votes, over the question of who received the largest number of votes legally cast, over the number of votes legally cast in favor of or against a question, or on the grounds of deliberate, serious, and material violations of the Minnesota Election Law." If there is a contest, the state court judges (not a jury trial) have the power to decide which candidate was the actual nominee or winner.[28] "If the contestant succeeds in the contest, the court may invalidate and revoke any election certificate which has been issued to the contestee."[29] The state court also has authority to hear contests for federal congressional seats. "[T]he only question to be decided by the court is which party to the contest received the highest number of votes legally cast at the election and is therefore entitled to receive the certificate of election. The judge trying the proceedings shall make findings of fact and conclusions of law upon that question."[30]

Under § 209.10, contests regarding a state legislator's seat are to be decided by the State Legislature.

CASE LAW

One of the more recent decisions regarding a contested election in which fraud was alleged was in *Derus v. Higgins*, 555 N.W.2d 515 (1996). In that case, the loser of an election alleged fraud, not on the part of a voter but on the part of a newspaper, which he believed printed false stories to sabotage his election (the court dismissed his challenge).

Mississippi
STATUTORY

The Mississippi Election Code (Title 23, Chapter 15 of the Mississippi Code of 1972) governs all aspects of elections in Mississippi. § 23-15-211 establishes a board of election commissioners and a voter registrar's office, which have the joint responsibility of monitoring and administering all elections. § 23-15-211.1 makes the secretary of state the chief elections officer of the state.

§ 23-15-17 punishes committing registration fraud (registering when not eligible to register) by up to five years in prison and a $5,000 fine. Subpart

(b) states that any person with knowledge of another person who is committing registration fraud *may* (not must) report that person to the local authorities. The local authorities are then required to report the allegation to the voter registrar's office and district attorney's office. The registrar's office would then have authority to reject or deny the person's registration, and the district attorney's office, in conjunction with the local police, would then have authority to conduct a criminal investigation.

§ 23-15-571 establishes the procedures for challenging a person's registration on the day of the election. Any person registered to vote is permitted to challenge another person. A challenge of a person may be made on the grounds: "(a) That he is not a registered voter in the precinct; (b) That he is not the registered voter under whose name he has applied to vote; (c) That he has already voted in the election; (d) That he is not a resident in the precinct where he is registered; (e) That he has illegally registered to vote; (f) That he has removed his ballot from the polling place; or (g) That he is otherwise disqualified by law." If a voter's registration is challenged, he or she must be permitted to vote; however, the ballot must be stamped "challenged" and placed in a separate ballot box. The ballots are counted like any other vote, but are to be made available for future inspection in case of subsequent litigation resulting from a contested election.

§ 23-15-913 requires all Mississippi state judges to be available on election days to resolve disputes. This statute also authorizes the Supreme Court to dispatch judges to resolve disputes "at the site of the dispute."

The procedure for postelection challenges depends on the type of election. For local primary contests, the County Executive Committee has jurisdiction to investigate any complaints.[31] For state, congressional, and judicial primaries, the State Executive Committee has jurisdiction. In both instances, the committees, by majority vote, are to "declare the true results" of the election. Because these committees are not official courts, their decisions are not reported to legal databases. Therefore, it is impossible to ascertain how often there were challenges to primary elections.

For contests of regular elections, the state circuit court is given jurisdiction under § 23-15-951.

New York

New York's law with regard to preventing voter fraud is a combination of statutory and common law.

STATUTORY

The New York Election Law governs all state and local elections. This law is extremely detailed, running to over five hundred pages long. Among other things, it establishes a Board of Elections with the responsibility of administering and monitoring elections.

Only registered voters may vote in New York state elections, and only residents of New York state may register. Election Law § 5-106 states grounds for disqualification of voters. Such grounds include offering or accepting money in return for giving or withholding a vote, § 5-106(1); being convicted of a felony in New York State court, § 5-106(2); being convicted of a crime in another state that would constitute a felony in New York, § 5-106(3); or being adjudicated incompetent (insane) in a New York State court. Most of the litigation arising under this statute comes from people claiming that they were denied the right to vote because they were improperly removed from the registration list.[32]

Election Law §§ 5-218, 5-220 provides a mechanism for challenging a voter's registration. If a citizen believes that a person is unlawfully registered, he or she may submit an affidavit to the Board of Elections. § 5-702 provides that if there is a challenge to a voter's registration, the Board of Elections must turn the voter's check card over to the local authorities. The local authorities would then have the responsibility for investigating whether a disqualified or otherwise invalid voter was registered to vote. This method for challenging a voter's registration has not brought much litigation.[33] The court in *Vacco v. Spitzer*, 179 Misc. 2d 584 (1998), ruled that this mechanism for challenging a voter's registration is to be used only prior to the election or on election day. To bring a postelection challenge, the citizen must rely on the common law.

Common law

If, following an election, there are allegations of voter fraud, the person bringing the claim must establish the following: "[F]irst, that there is a reasonable basis for the inquiry as to each vote challenged; second, that the alleged irregularities are not susceptible of inferences other than fraud; third, that specific acts of fraud, misconduct and/or irregularity occurred; and finally, that the fraud or other unlawful behavior changed the outcome of the election."[34] The plaintiff would have to prove all the elements by clear and convincing evidence.[35] If the claim is successful, the election is voided, and a new one must be held. There have been many attempts to bring claims of fraud under this common law, but almost none has succeeded.[36]

Oregon
Statutory

Title 23 of the Oregon Code governs elections. § 260.345 places the secretary of state in charge of monitoring and enforcing the election laws. However, the attorney general is in charge of monitoring and enforcing the election of secretary of state. Any voter may file a written complaint with the secretary of state alleging a violation of any election law (anonymous complaints cannot be accepted). The secretary of state is then required to conduct an investigation.

If he or she determines that a criminal act has occurred, he or she must turn the case over to the attorney general for prosecution.

§ 260.695 makes it a misdemeanor to, among other things, vote as an unregistered voter. § 260.715 makes it a felony to vote more than once in the same election; sell, offer to sell, purchase, or offer to purchase one's vote; lie in the registration process; attempt to vote in any other person's name, cast a "fraudulent ballot," steal ballots, manufacture counterfeit ballots, illegally destroy ballots, or forge an election board member's handwriting.

Chapter 258 of the Oregon Elections Code governs election contests. The circuit courts have jurisdiction to hear all election contests except for elections to the state legislature, which, because of separation of powers, has the authority to hear election contests for their own seats.[37]

Any voter or candidate is entitled to contest an election, and may do so on the following grounds: "(1) Deliberate and material violation of any provision of the election laws in connection with the nomination, election, approval or rejection; (2) ineligibility of the person elected to the office to hold the office at the time of the election; (3) illegal votes; (4) mistake or fraud in the canvass [*sic*] of votes; (5) fraud in the count of votes. . . ." Even if the contesting party proves one of these grounds, the election is not to be set aside unless the winning party knew of or participated in the fraud/illegality or the "number of votes taken from the person nominated or elected by reason of the cause of the contest would reduce the legal votes of the person below the number of legal votes given to another person for the same nomination or office."[38] The effect of setting aside an election is that the office would be deemed "vacant" and a new election would be held.[39]

CASE LAW

There are *very* few election contests that made it to the appellate level in Oregon. Not a single one out of the few reported cases resulted in an election being nullified (however, neither the lower courts nor legislature seat contests are reported). The rule most relevant to the issue of voter fraud appears to one requiring that the contestant establish that a violation of the elections law occurred by clear and convincing evidence.[40]

For an example of a criminal prosecution for various acts of voter fraud, see *State v. Huntley*, 82 Or App 350 (1986).

Pennsylvania
STATUTORY

Article III of the Pennsylvania Election Code creates county boards of elections, that, among other things administer and monitor all elections in the state.[41] Each County Board must report on a regular basis to the secretary of the commonwealth, who is the chief elections officer in the state.[42] § 2650 of the code permits any candidate to appoint "watchers," who can observe polling places or any Board of Elections meeting.

§ 3523 makes it illegal for an elections officer to permit an unregistered person to vote, punishable by up to seven years and $15,000. § 3524 makes it illegal for an elections officer to refuse to permit a validly registered person to vote. § 3525 makes it illegal for an elections officer to defraud the election system by falsifying the count, casting falsified votes, and various other listed offenses.

Pennsylvania has a substantial number of other penalties related to fraudulent behavior. § 3539 imposes a punishment of up to seven years and $15,000 for giving or receiving money in exchange for voting a certain way in an election. § 3502 punishes anyone committing perjury "regarding any material matter or thing relating to any subject being investigated, heard, determined or acted upon by any county board of elections, or member thereof, or by any court or judge thereof, judge of election, inspector of election, or overseer" up to five years in prison and a $10,000 fine. Any person voting when he or she is not registered to vote or voting more than once can be punished the same.[43] Several offenses are punishable by up to two years and a $5,000 fine. § 3516 prohibits the unlawful possession or counterfeiting of ballots, § 3517 prohibits illegally destroying or falsifying a ballot, and § 3518 prohibits tampering with voting machines. § 3547 prohibits threatening or coercing someone in hopes of affecting his or her vote (including by employers with offers of raises/ bonuses, or threats of salary reduction or termination).

Article XVII governs recounts and contests. § 3261 requires any or all ballot boxes to be opened and recounted by the Court of Common Pleas (a lower state court) upon the filing of a challenge alleging fraud by at least three voters. All candidates are permitted to observe the opening and recounting of the votes. If fraud is evident, § 3263 permits the court to recount the ballots less the fraudulent votes and state the true winner. But the decision of the court is not final or binding if a further contest is made (see discussion). The court is then to preserve all evidence of the fraud and report it to the appropriate law enforcement agencies (presumably the District Attorney's Office and local police).

If, after the recount, a further contest is made, the jurisdiction to hear the challenge depends on the type of election.

Contested nominations and elections of governor and lieutenant governor shall be tried and determined by a committee to be selected from both houses of the General Assembly.[44] The committee has the power to subpoena and examine witnesses and evidence. In addition, the committee can decide not only on the validity of such contested election but also on which of the candidates had the greatest number of legal votes. If the committee determines that the entire election was invalid, it does have the authority to order a new election.

Contested elections for president and vice-president of the United States, state judges and all other elected positions are to be tried by the Court of Common Pleas. The court has power to "decide which of the candidates voted for received the greatest number of legal votes, and is entitled to the nomination or office."[45]

Contested elections for a seat in the state House or Senate shall be tried by the Court of Common Pleas, which has the power to "decide which of the candidates voted for received the greatest number of legal votes and is entitled to the nomination or election."[46] The House or Senate would then be permitted to hear objections from any party who felt "aggrieved" by the court's decision, and then the legislature would have the power to issue a final determination on the election.[47]

Case law

Probably the most prevalent rule out of the courts regarding election fraud is that "the Election Code is to be liberally construed so that candidates running for office are not deprived of that right, nor are voters deprived of the right to elect the candidate of their choice."[48] This rule has been used to avoid voiding an election at all costs. A search produced no reported case in which a new election was ordered, but because many of the challenges are heard by committees and not courts, this does not necessarily mean none has ever occurred. Generally, courts seem to throw out the fraudulent votes and recount only the valid/legal votes.[49]

For examples of prosecutions under the various criminal statutes (or their predecessors), see *Commonwealth v. Albert*, 151 Pa. Super. 184 (1942); *Commonwealth v. Padden*, 160 Pa. Super. 269 (1947); and *Commonwealth v. Bidner*, 282 Pa. Super. 100 (1980).

Texas

Texas election law, both statutory and judicial, is complex, convoluted, and follows no clear precedent. It has also been highly criticized by legal scholars. Because many challenges must be brought before the legislature (see discussion), the records of these challenges are difficult to find.[50]

Statutory

The Texas Election Code governs all aspects of state and local elections in Texas. Tex. Elec. Code § 11.002 states that a resident of Texas cannot vote if he or she is convicted of a felony and has not completed any part of his or her sentence (including probation) or has been deemed mentally incompetent by a Texas court.

§ 63.012 makes it a third-degree felony if a person "(1) votes or attempts to vote in an election in which the person knows the person is not eligible to vote; (2) knowingly votes or attempts to vote more than once in an election; or (3) knowingly impersonates another person and votes or attempts to vote as the impersonated person."

Chapter 63 of the Texas Election Code contains detailed procedures for challenging voters at a polling place. The eligibility of a person to vote may be challenged by anyone "lawfully at the polling place."[51] But the voter must be permitted to vote if, following a challenge, he or she signs an affidavit stating the facts necessary to make him or her an eligible voter.

Tex. Elec. Code § 221.003 establishes the grounds for challenging an election. An election can be challenged on the grounds that an unregistered or otherwise "illegal" voter voted or that some other fraud occurred.[52]

Tex. Elec. Code § 221.002 establishes the various places to bring a challenge to an election. The state Senate and the House of Representatives, in joint session, have exclusive jurisdiction over a contest of a general election for governor, lieutenant governor, comptroller of public accounts, commissioner of the general land office, or attorney general. The Senate has exclusive jurisdiction for a contest of an election for state senator; the House of Representatives has exclusive jurisdiction for a contest of an election for state representative. District Courts have jurisdiction for all other election contests.

§ 221.011 gives the tribunal authority to discard any votes determined to be illegal. If the tribunal can determine the outcome of the election, § 221.012(1) permits the tribunal to declare the winner. If the fraud was so prevalent that it is impossible to determine the true outcome, § 221.012(2) requires the tribunal to nullify the election, which would thus require a new election.

CASE LAW

In *Alvarez v. Espinoza*, 844 S.W.2d 238, 242 (1992), a Texas Court explains the functioning of § 221.012(2).

> To overturn an election, the contestant must show that the outcome, as shown by the final canvass, is not the true outcome either because illegal votes were counted, or because an election official prevented eligible voters from voting, failed to count legal votes, or engaged in other fraud or illegal conduct or made a mistake. . . . The contestant has the burden to make this showing by clear and convincing evidence.

In spite of this declaration, there is much confusion over the relationship between § 221.012 and § 221.011. However, the courts have been willing to exercise their authority nonetheless. In *Green v. Reyes*, 836 S.W.2d 203 (1992), a Texas court invalidated a primary election for a state House of Representatives seat and ordered a new election because the margin of victory was 186 votes, yet it was proved that at least 220 people voted illegally because they voted in both primaries. In *Medrano v. Gleinser*, 769 S.W.2d 687 (1989), a Texas court voided an election based on the testimony of five voters that cast significant doubt on the validity of the election.

Because § 221.002 gives the Texas legislature jurisdiction to try election challenges from its own elections, it is difficult to ascertain the extent and success of election challenges. It does appear, however, that Texas is more willing to scrutinize and even overturn its elections than other states. It is difficult to know whether that means that fraud is more prevalent, the courts and legislature are more receptive, or the political forces are stronger.

Wisconsin
STATUTORY

Chapter 7 of the Wisconsin Elections Law establishes boards of canvassers and various other election officials with the responsibility of administering and monitoring elections.

§ 6.03 of the Wisconsin Elections Law bars from eligibility the mentally incompetent, those convicted of a felony, bribery or treason, and those who have wagered on the outcome of the election. §6.925 permits any qualified voter to challenge "for cause" whether any other voter is legitimately qualified to vote. If a person is challenged, he or she can take an oath or affirmation at the polling place affirming that he or she is a validly registered voter. If the person challenged does take this oath, the elections inspector must permit him or her to vote. Challenged ballots, however, are to be counted separately. In addition, the chairperson of the Board of Canvassers has the authority to review all challenged ballots to ensure legitimacy.[53]

§ 12.13 prohibits various acts all under the rubric of "election fraud." This statute makes it a felony to vote in an election in which a person is not a validly registered voter, to falsely procure registration, to register or vote more than once in the same election, to impersonate another person in registration or voting, to falsify a ballot, or for election officials to participate or assist in any of these offenses. § 12.11 prohibits offering, soliciting, or receiving "anything of value" in return for voting or refraining from voting in an election. § 12.09 makes it illegal to threaten or use force or violence to prevent a party from exercising his or her right to vote. A violation of any of these statutes is punishable by up to four years, six months in prison, and $10,000.[54] All investigations and prosecutions of criminal acts related to elections are to be carried out by the county district attorney in the county where the alleged violations occurred.[55]

§ 9.01 (known as the "Recount Statute") exclusively governs postelection challenges. Unlike other states, only the candidates in the election in question have standing to make a challenge. In order to challenge an election, the candidate must file a petition with the Board of Canvassers. The statute specifies various steps and procedures for conducting the recount. In addition, the board has the authority to receive and examine evidence, as well as subpoena and question witnesses to ascertain the validity of votes. On completing the investigation and recount, the board issues its findings, which are appealable to the courts.

CASE LAW

There appears to be a substantial number of elections that go through the recount process and end up in the Wisconsin courts. Recently, an appellate court handed down a decision in a contested election for county board of supervisors in *Carlson v. Oconto County Bd. of Canvassers,* 240 Wis. 2d 438 (2000). One of the primary legal issues in that case was what standard a challenger must meet to overturn an election. After discussing the various possible applications, the court stated that the general rule is that the challenger must establish, by clear and convincing evidence, that the outcome would have been different had the illegal/fraudulent votes not been cast. However, the court noted that "But in a case where deprivations of the right to vote are so significant in number or so egregious in character as to seriously undermine the appearance of fairness, we hold such an election must be set aside, even where the outcome of the election might not be changed."[56]

Significantly, in *McNally v. Tollander,* 100 Wis. 2d 490 (1981), the Wisconsin Supreme Court invalidated a referendum vote in which it was shown that approximately 40 percent of the electorate was denied the right to vote, even though it was not shown that the result would have been different had these people voted.[57]

Appendix 3

The Quest for Federal Data
on Voter Fraud

During the course of researching this book, I received little cooperation from the U.S. Justice Department in response to my requests for records and statistics on recent cases of voter fraud investigated and/or prosecuted by U.S. attorneys. I hoped to become better informed about the Justice Department record of investigating and prosecuting voter fraud. The long-time director of the Elections Crimes branch of the Criminal Division's Public Integrity Section can write in 2007 that "the investigation and prosecution of election crimes . . . was outranked [in official prioritizing] only by crimes involving terrorism and espionage."[1] Yet, when presented with a Freedom of Information Act (FOIA) request for data on this top government priority, the Justice Department, including the Office of the Attorney General, the Civil Division, the Criminal Division (and the Election Crimes Branch of the Public Integrity Section) and the Executive Office for U.S. Attorneys stonewalled for over two years.[2] Materials were released to me only after I appealed for help from U.S. Senator Charles Schumer.

I initiated my request in summer 2005. Unknown to me at the time, the Justice Department was already engaged in litigation with the Leadership Conference on Civil Rights (LCCR) over the disclosure of related records concerning Justice Department election-monitoring activities. As early as October 2002, the venerable civil rights coalition read the partisan smoke signals about "ballot security" coming from the Justice Department and raised big red flags. The LCCR, along with about two dozen other civil rights and public interest groups sent a letter to Attorney General John Ashcroft within days of his announcement of the department's new "voting integrity" initiative (the Ballot Access and Voting Integrity Initiative, BAVII) outlining their concerns "about the manner in which the so-called 'integrity' component of the Initiative may be implemented as well as its timing."[3] They assured Ashcroft that they shared the Justice Department commitment to free and fair elections, but reminded the attorney general of the "long experience of the civil rights community that overly aggressive 'voting integrity' efforts, instead of reducing fraud, tend to intimidate lawful voters and ultimately suppress voter turnout."[4]

In May 2004, the LCCR filed a FOIA request for records of communications relating to the monitoring of federal elections in any jurisdiction from 1988 to the present. Their interest was primarily in incidents of voter intimidation reported to the Justice Department and the department activities and programs to address these problems. But they also requested the disclosure of records referring to alleged or actual ballot security programs, "including all procedures or programs intended to discover, deter, prevent or remedy voter fraud."

The important administrative enforcement authority assigned to the Justice Department by the Voting Rights Act has meant a larger role for the Civil Rights Division in defending minority voting rights. But there is another smaller and lesser-known branch of the bureaucracy responsible for enforcement of criminal voting laws, a somewhat secretive and tightly controlled office nestled inside the Criminal Division's Public Integrity Section—the Election Crimes Branch.[5]

Four months after the LCCR made its public records request at the Criminal Division, and for the first time in the history of the fifty-four-year-old civil rights organization, the LCCR filed a FOIA lawsuit against the Justice Department because of its concern that "the Attorney General may be impeding rather than leading the effort to protect the right to vote."[6] The advocates had waited patiently throughout the summer months leading up to the 2004 presidential election for the Justice Department to produce the documents it had requested. None was forthcoming. In fact, although the FOIA law clearly requires covered agencies to determine whether to comply with a records request within twenty working days, by September 2004, the Justice Department had made no substantive response to the May FOIA letters of the LCCR at all.[7]

Meanwhile, the Justice Department publicized plans for its third annual "voting integrity" training symposium, the internal annual training conference for U.S. attorneys and agency personnel begun under Ashcroft. These meetings are closed to the public and to the media, begging the question of why the department sends out press releases announcing them. That third symposium was held in July, and afterward, news reports began to appear of meetings between Republican federal prosecutors and state and local elections officials to carry out the Justice Department directive putting in place procedures and operations to "combat voter fraud." In New Mexico, a battleground state that the Republicans lost in 2000 by a margin slimmer than the one that gave them a disputed victory in Florida, the media reported that the U.S. attorney had formed a statewide criminal task force to investigate (presumably) the volume of allegations of electoral fraud beginning to pour in.[8] The *Washington Post* reported that the New Mexico high-profile effort to stem voter fraud "is one of several criminal inquiries into alleged voter fraud launched in recent weeks in key presidential battlegrounds, including Ohio and West Virginia, as part of a broader initiative by U.S. Attorney General John D. Ashcroft."[9] The paper reported that "[t]he Justice Department has asked U.S. Attorneys across the country to meet with local election officials and launch publicity campaigns aimed at getting people to report irregularities."[10]

The LCCR litigation dragged on for more than a year. The Justice Department, whose secrecy on this civil rights matter is perplexing, released documents in drips and drabs, despite the cooperation of the LCCR in curtailing the expedited portion of its request to materials used in the BAVII training symposia held in 2002, 2003, and 2004.[11] Training materials reflect final agency policy decisions, and baring exemptions protecting certain kinds of law enforcement records from disclosure, are not exempt under FOIA. In December 2005, a federal judge ordered the department to substantially comply with the original records request. At the heart of the matter was the stalwart refusal of the Justice Department to release two key records: a new draft version of the Election Crimes Branch's long-standing training manual (7th ed.) and field communications between district election officers (DEOs) and the Election Crimes Branch. Election Crimes Branch Director Craig Donsanto's revised manual had already been distributed in draft form to attendees of the 2004 symposia. That year, these attendees included invited nonagency guests, such as a handful of Mexican visitors and state government officials from Kentucky. Distributing the election crimes manual draft to these people effectively put it in the public domain; giving it to the U.S. attorneys meant it was policy, making a mockery of Justice Department claim that the manual was a "pre-decisional" or "deliberative" document and therefore subject to one of the FOIA's many exemptions.

The field communications from DEOs could provide a good record of what federal officials observed and what the public brought to them in the way of complaints of voter intimidation or concerns over election irregularities. An analysis of these communications would help the public understand more about what some citizens face when they attempt to vote. Moreover, field records in the form of final reports from U.S. attorneys are primary evidence valuable to any program evaluation effort. If, in fact, there are public complaints about suspicious electoral activity, fraudulent behavior, or harassment, it is in the public interest to know. But the department vigorously fought to withhold these records under FOIA Exemptions 6 and 7(C), which protect government employees against an unwarranted invasion of privacy that might expose them to discrimination or threats of harm. In this case, the Justice Department was not acting as it routinely does to protect the identities of FBI agents involved in murder cases or drug stings, nor was it exerting itself to shield officials from disclosure of sensitive medical records or their Social Security numbers. Instead, the Justice Department argued to the court that DEO field records could not be released because the email communications instructing DEOs on how to file election day operations reports included the names and office extensions of Public Integrity Section paralegals. The department claimed that the paralegals could be subject to harassment if their names and office phone numbers were released. The court, noting that this information was already publicly available from the Office of Personnel Management, was not persuaded. It ordered the Justice Department to comply within a reasonable period of time,[12] but not before lawyers in the FOIA/PA office filed more motions to delay disclosure.

We now know more about the struggle inside the Justice Department to resist the overt politicization of voting rights law enforcement promoted by Bush political appointees.[13] And we see similar patterns across many executive branch agencies of the Bush administration's resistance to the disclosure of even the most basic information that the public has a right to know.[14] In this case, which involved no matters of life or death, no criminal syndicates or undercover operations, no national security issues, no trade secrets, and no allegations of public corruption or undue private influence in the affairs of government, the Justice Department stratagem to avoid disclosure would be laughable had it not consumed the time and resources of the federal courts, federal employees, and civil rights advocates for almost three years. Three federal elections and two federal court orders after the LCCR first raised reasonable concerns about the Justice Department's misguided voting integrity initiative, the two parties to the lawsuit negotiated a settlement. As the litigation wore on, the piecemeal disclosure strategy of the Justice Department (which mostly followed court orders) did produce some records, but by the summer 2007, the LCCR, exasperated, was ready to settle. It stated its satisfaction with what it had been able to pry out of the secretive Election Crimes Branch. For its part, the Justice Department agreed to pay the LCCR $115,000 in lawyers' fees.[15]

Meanwhile, and independent of the LCCR request, another civil liberties organization, the Electronic Privacy Information Center (EPIC) also sought Justice Department records related to the new voting integrity initiative. In July 2004, two months after the LCCR sent its FOIA letters, Lillie Coney, the EPIC associate director, who came to the organization with a background in voting rights, asked the Justice Department Civil Rights Division for "all information in the form of e-mails, hosted events, briefings, meeting records, letters, and other documentation on all work performed by agency personnel or contractors related to activity in preparation for and carrying out the mission of the Voting Access and Integrity Initiative for the November 2, 2004 General Election."[16] In August 2004, Coney amended her request, adding:

> all communications, policy memorandum, letters, contracts, e-mails, reports or statements, investigations, corrective or disciplinary actions based on complaints as well as the action(s) taken by the Department of Justice to investigate and address . . . false perceptions of "massive" voter fraud . . . purging of voter registration rolls . . . investigations of other crimes that resulted in processes or procedures to ascertain or gather information related to investigation of voting fraud and the disposition of these investigations or prosecutions . . . any comparative analysis of the incidence of voter fraud verses [sic] voters being denied access to vote in public elections. . . . [17]

After several months during which her letter was internally routed to the wrong office and Justice Department clerks haggled with her over copying fees, Coney received some 1,790 pages from the Civil Rights Division. Most of the material, however, consisted of published court documents, copies of indictments and government exhibits drawn from past successful election fraud litigation, and screen shots from Justice Department web pages used in the department annual BAVII training seminars. Most of Coney's queries, especially her request for an accurate accounting of the number of investigations and prosecutions and the deployment of personnel and resources to the two parts of the initiative—voter fraud detection and the protection of voter access—went unanswered.

If election crime was so high on the agenda of the Bush Justice Department why was it so resistant to reporting on the fruits of its labor to stamp it out? Independent of the advocacy groups, whose efforts to obtain documents on the BAVII were unknown to me at the time, I made a FOIA request after the LCCR commenced litigation against the Criminal Division and after EPIC received documents from the Civil Rights Division. My own two-year saga of dealing with Justice Department FOIA officials is too tedious to repeat in much detail. It involved four separate Justice Department offices breaking up my request into multiple discrete parts, which were then numbered and renumbered to the point where I could not figure out which part of my original request or my later appeals corresponded to their form letters denying me access. Then there was the ever-changing roster of clerks disappearing from employment, one after the other; the unreturned phone calls; unacknowledged emails; circular phone trees; and transferred calls, which stopped bouncing from one office to the other only when I was deposited safely into a voicemail black hole. People who work in FOIA units at the Justice Department never seem to return from lunch, or they are like the woman who was probably just doing her job when she told me in July 2006 that "someone is working on it as we speak, it shouldn't be too long. . . . it's a matter of getting the wording in the letter right. . . . they are dotting the i's and crossing the t's." I did receive 328 pages from the Civil Rights Division a couple of weeks later, fully one-third of which were photocopies of federal voting laws. Despite the academic and public (rather than commercial) uses to which I planned to put this material, the Justice Department denied my request, available under the law, for a photocopying-fee waiver. I appealed—on principle, what was this stuff? I could afford the $32.80.

The bureaucratic shenanigans finally ended five months later with a bizarre letter denying my appeal of the $32.80 fee waiver on the inexplicable grounds that the material they released to me had already been released to the Electronic Privacy Information Center—nine months before I made my request! Of course, if they had told me that in the first place, I probably would have amended or withdrawn my FOIA request.[18] As for my appeal to the Criminal Division, in October 2007, more than three months after the LCCR settled its lawsuit and a year and three months after my initial FOIA request to the division (which itself was made more than nine months after the LCCR commenced its litigation), the Criminal Division informed me that the delay was due to the LCCR litigation. They would now send me 4,305 pages already disclosed to the LCCR, again denying my own request for a fee waiver that is available to those using the materials for noncommercial, educational purposes. As I explained to the Justice Department FOIA officials, then, I do not now and did not then expect this book to be a runaway best-seller; most academic books do not fall into this category. But the FOIA officers were not persuaded.

I received the LLCR documents at the end of December 2007.[19] Despite the thousands of pages, much of it material from an array of different Justice Department officials that was endlessly duplicative, the data dump was not fully responsive to either my request or to the earlier efforts of the LCCR. There is little in the disclosure that satisfies anyone's efforts to obtain records pertaining to final policy decisions that are relevant to the investigation and prosecution of voter fraud by federal officials.[20] Moreover, none of the documents disclosed provides a means for fully evaluating the necessity, operation, or value of the BAVII program. And none provides information that would allow us to compile simple statistics on program outcomes. For example, none of the documents released to EPIC, the LCCR, or to me contains information about the workings of the DEO field operations or their final election day reports, which we might assume would include records of public reports of voting problems.

It is not that the Justice Department was not analyzing its data on voter fraud cases while it was withholding them from one of the nation's oldest civil rights groups. Indeed, while researchers were asking for public records on the alleged exploding incidence of voter fraud, the Justice Department was compiling its own misleading numbers. Press releases dated August 2,

2005; November 7, 2005; and July 26, 2006 announced an alarming number of ongoing investigations, criminal prosecutions, and convictions for "fraud." Some time after October 2005, while my FOIA request remained in limbo, someone at the Justice Department prepared a case list of BAVII-related indictments and convictions.[21] The list contained case numbers, defendant names, and descriptions of the crimes or alleged crimes, critical information without which neither I nor anyone else could proceed with an empirical analysis of the department's activities. It also appears that as the Justice Department was withholding information from civil rights advocates, it was sharing it with Republican members of Congress and their allies. In June 2006, the BAVII case list was entered into the official record of a House Administration Committee hearing on noncitizen voting by the committee chairman, Vernon Ehlers (R-Mich.).[22] Representative Bob Ney (R-Ohio) called the list a Justice Department "release," but I stumbled upon it only after seeing it cited in congressional testimony by Linda Chavez urging against the renewal of the Voting Rights Act's bilingual ballot requirements. And the case list does not appear to be a public document because it has never appeared on the Justice Department website.[23] I Googled the document title and located it on the committee hearing's website (it is no longer there). The importance of the case list in light of the Justice Department secrecy about its voter fraud program is discussed in more detail later in the appendix.

Federal prosecution records present only one measure of the incidence of fraud in federal elections. In the absence of official records, previous research has relied on the next-best thing—searches of Lexis-Nexis federal election fraud criminal case databases for estimates of the scale and incidence of fraud.[24] There are many limitations to this methodology. The first is the unknown scope of the Lexis-Nexis collections. Lexis-Nexis, a private database and information company, compiles case law from a variety of federal courts, including all ninety-four of the U.S. district courts, the courts of appeal, and the U.S. Supreme Court. Federal criminal cases in which there is no published opinion are not included among this material, and coverage can be uneven because it is dependent on what the individual courts submit to the vendor. The second problem is that the Lexis-Nexis case law material is not classified or coded to facilitate the retrieval of criminal cases by type of crime. Researchers must construct their own search strings for full-text searches, leaving much to the discretion, individual creativity, and industry of analysts to ferret out an appropriate universe of cases. As a result, the method is inefficient and sensitive to idiosyncratic research designs. The Lexis-Nexis flexible search language means there are many ways that analysts can scan for information.[25] For example, David Callahan and I relied on a simple search string ("vote OR voter OR election PRE/2 fraud"). Tova Wang and Job Serebrov, the researchers commissioned by the U.S. Election Assistance Commission to write the agency elections crime report, used an opposite approach when they pumped more than two dozen discrete word combinations into the Lexis-Nexis search engine (i.e., "election AND fraud," "voter AND fraud," "double voting," etc.). And Delia Bailey relied on a more complex Boolean search technique (i.e., "(absentee OR registration) AND fraud," "(offense* OR fraud* OR tamper* OR stuff* OR handl* OR print* OR secrecy OR secret) AND ballot," etc.). All these strategies produced hundreds if not thousands of nonproductive "hits" and irrelevant cases. For example, Wang and Serebrov report their search produced some 40,000 cases (since 2000), of which less than one-half of 1 percent were relevant to their research, most only marginally so.[26] Bailey's search of 2000–2005 boiled down to nine cases (some involving multiple defendants) of a variety election-related irregularities including campaign finance violations, whereas Minnite and Callahan's search covering twelve states in 1992–2002 identified sixty-eight cases, most of which did not deal with the kind of voter fraud that is the subject of the present study.

There is a better source of data on federal criminal election fraud cases, one known to empirical legal studies scholars and criminologists but rarely exploited by political scientists.[27] The Federal Court Cases Integrated Database (FCCID) provides an "official public record of the business of the federal courts," combining data from several federal criminal justice agencies, and ninety-four district and twelve appellate court offices throughout the United States. The database is a project of the Federal Judicial Center and the National Archive of Criminal Justice Data maintained by the Inter-University Consortium for Political and Social Research at the University of Michigan. It purports to cover every case filed in the federal courts. At two points in the life of a case, case filing and termination, records for every defendant coming through the federal criminal justice pipeline are collected across multiple federal criminal justice agencies and integrated into single defendant records.[28]

This database is a better source for measuring the incidence of federal voter fraud cases than the Lexis-Nexis federal court databases. But, in the absence of disclosure by the Justice Department, the problem of correctly identifying voter fraud cases is almost no easier. Criminal justice records are complex because crime and the legal and criminal justice systems that deal with it are complex. Despite the volumes of data collected by law enforcement agencies and courts on crime and criminals, the decentralization and fragmentation of U.S. law enforcement agencies, as well as the complexity of legal procedure, all but guarantee difficulties for the analyst. Defendants can be charged with multiple offenses and multiple counts of single violations. They can be charged individually or together in a single case with other defendants; they can be charged multiple times in the same case with superseding indictments, and mistrials resulting in second or third trials also produce multiple records for the same defendant and case. These possibilities embed individual defendant records in a web of different classificatory schemes and numbering systems that can bury the nature of the crime from view.

Each single defendant record in the FCCID includes variables for the top five filing offenses as judged by severity of penalty for each defendant. But statutory violations on their own do not always tell us what we need to know about the crime alleged. For example, if we know that an individual has been charged with violating Title 18, Section 371, all we know is that the person has been charged with participating in a conspiracy. But what kind of conspiracy? To murder the president? Rob a bank? Or vote other people's absentee ballots? To address the inherent ambiguity of the charge data, the FCCID also includes an official federal criminal citation code associated with the charge in any given case. The code is drawn from the Criminal Citation Manual developed by the Administrative Office of the U.S. Courts (AO), a federal agency that collects and standardizes case processing data from U.S. magistrates, clerks of the court, federal probation offices, and pretrial service offices. Once all of the records for a single defendant are merged together, AO agency analysts convert each individual offense into a four-digit offense code used to prepare statistical tables for publication in AO reports. In addition to representing the total universe of criminal cases flowing through the federal courts, the FCCID is an improvement over full-text searching of case law records because it integrates AO files with records drawn from other criminal justice agencies to provide a more reliable means for isolating and sorting election crime records.

For the purposes of this study, however, the FCCID data were not quite good enough. The AO Criminal Citation Manual includes one code for "Election Laws Violations," which it defines broadly to include violations of voting and civil rights laws pertaining to elections, as well as violations of the complex U.S. campaign finance laws. Any corruption of the electoral process by any actor (election officials, politicians, candidates, campaigns, voters, or others) prosecuted for criminal violations of any of these laws should be captured and coded in the FCCID, the usual caveats for human error in data processing notwithstanding—with perhaps one exception. The AO standardizes statutes, in some cases folding statute subsections into their section heads. For example, violations of all subsections of Title 42, Section 1973i, are coded as "Civil Rights Violations," even though some subsections clearly apply only to electoral malfeasance and not to other civil rights areas. Finally, the FCCID includes as general election law violations state laws that may be tried in U.S. district courts when the offense occurs on a federal reservation or military base, and statutes involving the District of Columbia, territorial laws, or federal regulations promulgated pursuant to federal statutes.[29]

Appendix 4 includes a full description of how I compiled the records of election fraud cases from the FCCID that are presented here. But I want to return—for just a moment—to that Justice Department BAVII case list mentioned previously. I said it was invaluable to this project, and here is why. First, because it represents what the Justice Department defines as election fraud, it provides an independent check on coverage and on how well the Justice Department classification scheme is represented in the FCCID. Moreover, the factual context of each case provided in the case list summaries, however brief, itself provides a check on the Justice Department classification

TABLE A3.1
Federal election crime defendants and case outcomes by type of election crime and type of defendant, FY2002–FY2005

		Convicted or pled guilty				Acquitted or case dismissed	Total
		Government officials, party, campaign or election workers					
Type of election crime	Voters	Government officials	Party or campaign workers	Election workers	Total		
Registration fraud	1	1	1	0	3	0	3
Voting by ineligibles	20	0	0	0	20	10	30
Multiple voting	5	0	0	0	5	4	9
Vote buying	0	8	27	2	37	10	47
Ballot forgery	0	0	0	1	1	0	1
Civil rights violations	0	0	2	0	2	1	3
Voter intimidation	0	2	0	0	2	0	2
Total	26	11	30	3	70	25	95

Source: U.S. Department of Justice, Criminal Division, Public Integrity Section, "Election Fraud Prosecutions & Convictions, Ballot Access & Voting Integrity Initiative, October 2002–September 2005," n.d.; author.

system and its claims regarding the number of election fraud cases it has prosecuted appearing (without the detail) in official reports. Using the data gleaned from the case list and information gathered over the Internet via the federal judiciary Public Access to Court Electronic Records project (PACER),[30] a separate review of the breakdown of court documents for each case of the ninety-five indictments summarized on the Justice Department BAVII case list is shown in table A3.1

As this table shows, only 26 voters were convicted or pleaded guilty to registration fraud or illegal voting. Fourteen of the 25 people who were acquitted or had their cases dismissed were voters, for a total of 40 voters altogether among the 95 people indicted. The other 55 people were indicted campaign and party workers, elected officials, and others whose proximity to the electoral process, compared to that of the average voter, made it easier for them to corrupt it. That is forty voters over three years, which is not what the Justice Department implies when in press releases it repeatedly cites bigger numbers that actually include a variety of "election offenses." For example, in August 2005, the Justice Department announced that 89 individuals had been charged with election fraud offenses since October 2002. In November 2005, it claimed 95 people had been charged with election fraud offenses (same as the number summarized on its case list), and in July 2006, the number had grown to 119 individuals "charged with ballot fraud offenses."[31]

Without reviewing the court documents of every individual case identified as an "election law violation" in the FCCID, a time-consuming and near-impossible feat for cases settled before the recent computerization and development of online access to federal court documents, we would not be able to distinguish those forty voters from the elected officials included among the Justice Department's ninety-five indictments, nor do we have any means of identifying them as voters in the FCCID.

Steps in Extracting Voter Fraud Records from the Federal Court Cases Integrated Database

1. I extracted records from each of the annual data sets (years 1996–2000 are contained in one file, supplemented by annual files to 2005) for which any one of the five offense variables was classified by the Administrative Office of the U.S. Courts (AO) as an "Election Law Violation" (AO code = 9902). Table A4.1 summarizes the total number of records extracted (see column 3). Because violations of several relevant sections of the Voting Rights Act are coded by the AO as "Civil Rights Violations" (AO code = 9901) rather than "Election Law Violations" (see app. 5), I also extracted all records for which any one of the five offense variables was classified as a "Civil Rights Violation," (N=2,576) and then pulled from these all records for which any one of the five offenses was Title 42, Section 1973A, 1973B, 1973C, 1973D, 1973E, 1973H, 1973I, or 1973J (N=88). Of the resulting 88 records, 6 were cases in which at least one offense was also coded an "Election Law Violation." These were dropped as duplicates (see column 4).
2. To create the combined-year file, I added the records from columns 3 and 4 (N=330), and deleted 120 duplicate records for defendants whose cases appeared in more than one fiscal year database file (93 of these records were drawn from those coded "Election Law Violations" and 27 were from those coded "Civil Rights Violations"). The resulting data set consists of 210 unique individual defendant records.
3. To these I added 32 additional defendants for cases identified by the U.S. Justice Department Ballot Access and Voting Integrity Initiative (BAVII) case list of "Election Fraud Prosecutions and Convictions" for fiscal years 2002–2005. None of the offenses for these defendants was coded "Election Law Violations" in the FCCID, nor was any of these defendants charged with violations of 42:1973(x). Finally, I located three additional

TABLE A4.1
Federal court cases integrated database, FY1996-FY2005

1	2	3	4
			All other records: At least one offense coded "Civil Rights Violation" and at least
Fiscal year	Total records	At least one offense coded "Election Law Violation"	one offense was 42:1973(x)
1996	112,346	9	0
1997	120,299	11	24
1998	135,374	29	9
1999	140,218	27	7
2000	146,471	38	3
2001	151,162	16	2
2002	158,830	13	0
2003	169,687	13	13
2004	173,113	36	10
2005	183,284	56	14
Total	1,490,784	248	82

records from this group that had been initially excluded because of what appear to be key-punch errors in the FCCID "Defendant Number" variable. In other words, they were picked up in the initial search using AO codes and charge data, but misidentified in the FCCID by defendant number.[1] Once these 35 additional records were included, the total number of election fraud defendants increased to 245.

4. Next, I excluded all defendants charged with campaign finance violations (as determined by the charge variables). This reduced the database from 245 defendants to 167 individual voters; candidates; and party, campaign, or election workers charged with some kind of illegal voting, voter intimidation, or vote buying. These data are presented in figure 3.1.

Note: if we exclude all cases of vote buying, voter intimidation, corruption by elected and election officials, and other authorities, the database is further reduced to just 48 voter defendants charged with violating election laws over a recent ten-year period.

What Do We Learn about "Election Law Violations" and the Federal Court Cases Integrated Database?

What do we learn about the FCCID from this exercise? First, because the data are produced on an annual basis and court cases often stretch across fiscal years, duplicate defendant records must be eliminated from any combined-year data sets that are constructed to compute the total number of defendants over any multiyear period and trends. In our case, over one-third of all records (36.4 percent, or 120 of 330) selected from the ten annual files were duplicate defendant records.

We also learn that the AO coding scheme for tracking "Election Law Violations" is not perfect. Some number of defendants charged with election law violations are not coded as such by court clerks who process the data.[2] How big is the problem? Another one-third (32.9 percent, or 55 of 167) of the final defendants file came from records that were not coded "Election Law Violations." Violations of Title 42, Section 1973, and its subsections are coded in the AO Criminal Citation Manual as civil rights not election law cases. Researchers interested in tracking election law cases should be mindful of this and should search for cases coded "Civil Rights Violations" in which at least one of the five charges is 42:1973 (and any of its subsections). Moreover, according to Bureau of Justice Statistics (BJS) officials, the AO coding scheme is not reliable at the subsection level; they recommend caution when searching for violations of subsections of federal statutes.[3] This bears on violations of election law, as well. By checking the FCCID data against docket sheets available through PACER, I was able to determine that violations of 42:1973gg-1 are usually coded by the AO as 42:1973A. Researchers should include all offenses coded Title 42, Section 1973A, 1973B, 1973C, 1973D, 1973E, 1973H, 1973I, or 1973J, and should check the docket sheets for accuracy against the resulting file when scanning for court records and violations of this important statute (it codifies sections of the National Voter Registration Act of 1993).

Finally, we know from the Justice Department BAVII case list, which represents the department's classification of election fraud cases and covers all indictments brought during the last three fiscal years (2003–2005) of our ten-year study period, that there were 32 defendants charged with election law violations whose case records were not coded "Election Law Violation" and who had not been charged with violations of 42:1973(x). Our search criteria missed these cases, and it is difficult to see how we might have found them without the BAVII case list. Most of these defendants were charged in vote-buying schemes and were charged simply with conspiracy (a violation of Title 18, Section 371). We would have had to review all cases in which at least one of the top five filing charges was 18:371 in the FCCID.

In addition, there appear to be some small number of data-entry errors in the FCCID. The "Defendant Number" variable for three defendants on the Justice Department case list appears to be miscoded. These are three people who were charged in vote-buying conspiracies; their docket numbers are correct, and their charges as coded in the FCCID match those appearing on their docket sheets, but the FCCID "Defendant Number" appears to be incorrect. All three records belong to the same vote-buying conspiracy, in which seven defendants were charged together and therefore share the same docket number. These defendants are coded as defendants 8, 10, and 11; as it turns out, defendants 3, 4, and 7 are missing from FCCID. I am assuming that, because the case involved only seven defendants, the records for numbers 8, 10, and 11 are miscoded and represent actual defendants 3, 4, and 7. This is confirmed by a match between the charges appearing on the docket sheet for defendants 3, 4, and 7, and the charges in the FCCID.[4]

Table A4.2 summarizes the number of cases missed for each source of error or misclassification of the data by either the Justice Department or the FCCID.

To summarize, voting law charge data and election law violations are not reliably coded by the AO as these records appear in the FCCID.[5] Although the FCCID as a source of information on the number of election fraud cases is an improvement over the results of text searches in the case law records compiled by Lexis-Nexis, additional information, such as that provided by the Justice Department case list, is required for compiling accurate statistics on the incidence of federal prosecutions. Relying only on the AO coding scheme to identify election fraud cases misses approximately one-third of all cases that should be included. Refining the search to include cases (not coded as "Election Law Violations") coded as "Civil Rights Violations" in which defendants have been charged with a violation of federal voting rights laws still misses approximately one-third of all cases. On the other hand, data-entry errors in the FCCID appear to be negligible (3 of every 100 defendants may have miscoded defendant numbers but not docket numbers).

TABLE A4.2
Cases initially missed or misclassified: Election Fraud Defendants Database

	Source of error	Number of cases	Percentage of Final Election Fraud Defendants Database[a]
1	FCCID election fraud defendant charge records coded "civil rights violation" not "election law violation" by AO	55	32.9
2	DOJ BAVII case-list defendants whose charge records were not coded by AO as "election law violation" or included a 42:1973(x) voting statute violation	32	33.0
3	DOJ BAVII case-list defendants records with miscoded FCCID defendant numbers	3	3.1
4	Errors on DOJ case list; defendants included in FCCID records for a case included on DOJ BAVII case list	2	2.1

Notes: AO, Administrative Office of the U.S. Courts; BAVIII, Ballot Access and Voting Integrity Initiative; DOJ, U.S. Department of Justice; FCCID, Federal Court Cases Integrated Database; PACER, Public Access to Court Electronic Records project.

[a] The denominator for row 1 is 167, the total number of defendant records included in the final Election Fraud Defendant database. The denominator for rows 2–4 is 97 (not 167), the total number of defendants charged during the period covered by the Justice Department BAVII case list (FY2002-2005). The ninety-seven defendants charged consist of the total number of people appearing on the BAVII case list (N = 95) plus two additional defendants who should have been included in that list but were not. These two defendants were included in the FCCID database. I examined their records in PACER to confirm that they should have been included on the original Justice Department case list.

If these calculations are accurate, then it is possible that, even with a refined search criteria that combines the AO citation code with charge data, when it comes to election law cases the FCCID data are underinclusive.[6]

Yet, in the end, this is not a serious problem for the analysis of voter fraud offered in this book. We are interested in cases of illegal voting by voters—a subcategory (election crime by voters) of a subcategory (noncampaign finance violations among all election law violations). We have access to some additional information gleaned from the Justice Department BAVII case list, but because the Justice Department does not break down its data by type of defendant, we should not rely solely on its numbers in identifying voter fraud cases, either.

Further archival research is required. Examining the actual docket sheets and court documents for all defendants on the Justice Department BAVII case list reveals that only 7 of the 35 (or 1 in 5) of the Justice Department BAVII cases that were not identified using the refined FCCID search strategy involved illegal voting by a voter. The rest were mostly cases of vote buying, voter intimidation, and absentee ballot scams perpetrated by the organizers of political conspiracies. In other words, we missed only seven cases of voter fraud over three years, a number far smaller than missing one-third of all election fraud or election law cases. Thus, we can estimate an error or "missed cases" rate of 2.3 *voter fraud* defendants charged with illegal voting per year, or 20.3 missed defendants over the full ten-year study period in the FCCID data. Using the most generous estimate possible to account for these possibly 20 missed defendants increases the total number of voter fraud cases filed in federal court from the 48 we do find to an estimated 68 people, or about 7 people per year.

Appendix 5

Reconciling Differences in Agency Coding of Federal Election Law Violations

To better understand how the Administrative Office of the U.S. Courts (AO) categorizes election law violations, I located two different editions of the AO Criminal Offense Citation Manual, one from 1988 and the other from 2007. Table A5.1 presents a list of statutes by title and section that may be violated in the commission of election fraud crimes (see columns 1–5). Column 6 compares the coding of these laws in the different editions of the Criminal Offense Citation manuals. Unless otherwise noted, an "X" indicates that the filing offense code for a violation of that statute is 9902 or "Election Law Violation" in the Federal Court Cases Integrated Database (FCCID). See Note *a* at the bottom of the table for the filing offense code definitions used for those statutes not coded 9902.

Most campaign finance laws coded by the AO as "Election Law Violations" have been dropped from the table and statutes used in cases involving illegal registration or voting, vote buying, noncitizen voting, and the use of the mails for purposes of defrauding the residents of a state of a fair election (i.e., absentee ballot fraud) have been added. The latter come from the U.S. Justice Department official election crimes training manual for U.S. attorneys, which breaks down "election crimes" into four major categories; three, election fraud, patronage crimes, and voter intimidation statutes, are included in the table, but what are described in the Justice Department manual as "campaign financing" crimes or the use of coercion to solicit contributions or influence voting are not.

Last, column 8 lists statutes charged against defendants in cases appearing on the U.S. Justice Department Ballot Access and Voting Integrity Initiative (BAVII) case list.

TABLE A5.1
Federal statutes charged in criminal election fraud cases: Administrative Office of the U.S. Courts versus the U.S. Justice Department

1	2	3	4	5	6		7		8
					Coded "Election Law Violation" by AO[a]		2007 DOJ Election Crimes Manual[b]		Statute used in BAVII prosecutions, FY2003–2005
Title	Section	Subsections	U.S. Code section description	U.S. Code subsection description	1988 manual	2007 manual	Applicable to federal elections	Applicable to nonfederal elections	
18	2		Crimes: Principals		X				X
	4		Misprison of felony			7990			X
	241		Civil rights: Conspiracy against rights		9901	9901	X	X	X
	242		Civil rights: Deprivation of rights under color of law		9901	9901	X	X	X
	245 b	1 a	Civil rights: Federally protected activities	Voter intimidation	9901	9901	X	X	
	371		Conspiracy to commit offense or to defraud United States		X	4492			X
	592		Troops at the polls		X	X	X	X	
	593		Interference by armed forces		X	X			
	594		Intimidation of voters		X	X	X		
	595		Interference by administrative employees of federal, state, or territorial governments		X	X			
	596		Polling armed forces		X	X			
	597		Expenditures to influence voting		X	X	X		X

(continued)

(TABLE A5.1—cont.)

					Coded "Election Law Violation" by AO[a]		2007 DOJ Election Crimes Manual[b]		
1	2	3	4	5	6		7		8
Title	Section	Subsections	U.S. Code section description	U.S. Code subsection description	1988 manual	2007 manual	Applicable to federal elections	Applicable to nonfederal elections	Statute used in BAVII prosecutions, FY2003-2005
	598		Coercion by means of relief appropriations		X	X			
	599		Promise of appointment by candidate		X	X			
	600		Promise of employment or other benefit for political activity		X	X			
	601		Deprivation of employment or other benefit for political contribution		X	X			
	602		Solicitation of political contributions		X	X			
	603		Making political contributions		X	X			
	604		Solicitation from persons on relief		X	X			
	605		Disclosure of names of persons on relief		X	X			
	606		Intimidation to secure political contributions		X	X			
	607		Place of solicitation		X	X			
	608		Absent uniformed services voters and overseas voters		X		X		

Title	Code	Description					
	609	Coercion of voting among the military		X	X		
	610	Coercion of federal employees for political activity	X	X	X		X
	611	Voting by aliens	X	X	X	X	X
	911	False impersonation: Citizen of the United States		X	X	4970	X
	1001	Fraud and false statements	X				X
	1015 f	Naturalization, citizenship or alien registry — False claim of citizenship to vote	X	X	X		X
	1341	Mail fraud: Frauds and swindles	X	X	X		X
	1346	Mail fraud: Definition of scheme or artifice to defraud		X	X		X
	1623	False declaration before a grand jury	X				X
	1952	Interstate and foreign travel or transportation in aid of racketeering enterprises; schemes to use the mails in furtherance of vote buying		X	X		
42	408	Social Security fraud					X
	1973	Denial or abridgement of right to vote on account of race or color through voting qualifications or prerequisites; establishment of violation	X				X

(continued)

(TABLE A5.1—cont.)

Title	Section	Subsections	U.S. Code section description	U.S. Code subsection description	Coded "Election Law Violation" by AO[a]		2007 DOJ Election Crimes Manual[b]		Statute used in BAVII prosecutions, FY2003-2005
					1988 manual	2007 manual	Applicable to federal elections	Applicable to nonfederal elections	
	1973a		Proceeding to enforce right to vote		X	X			
	1973b		Suspension of the use of tests or devices in determining eligibility to vote		X	X			
	1973c		Alteration of voting qualifications and procedures; action by state or political subdivision for declaratory judgment of no denial or abridgement of voting rights; three-judge district court; appeal to Supreme Court		X	X			
	1973d		Federal voting examiners			X			
	1973e		Examination of applicants for registration		X	X			
	1973h		Poll taxes		X				
	1973i		Prohibited acts		X	X			
		a		Failure or refusal to permit casting or tabulation of vote					
		b		Intimidation, threats, or coercion	9901	9901			
		c		False information in registering or voting; penalties	9901	9901	X	X	X

Section		Description			
	d	Falsification or concealment of material facts or giving of false statements in matters within jurisdiction of examiners or hearing officers; penalties	9901	9901	X
1973j	e	Voting more than once	X	X	
	a	Depriving or attempting to deprive persons of secured rights	9901	9901	
	b	Destroying, defacing, mutilating, or altering ballots or official voting records	X	X	
	c	False information in registering or voting; penalties	9901	9901	
1973aa		Application of prohibition to other States; *test or device* defined	X		
1973aa-1		Residence requirements for voting	9901		
1973aa-3		Penalty	9901		
1973bb-1		Twenty-sixth Amendment enforced	X		
1973gg-10	1	NVRA criminal penalties for: Intimidation in voting and registering to vote		X	
	2 A	Procurement of registration applications known to be materially false		X	X

(*continued*)

(TABLE A5.1—cont.)

1	2	3	4	5	6 Coded "Election Law Violation" by AO[a]		7 2007 DOJ Election Crimes Manual[b]		8
Title	Section	Subsections	U.S. Code section description	U.S. Code subsection description	1988 manual	2007 manual	Applicable to federal elections	Applicable to nonfederal elections	Statute used in BAVII prosecutions, FY2003-2005
		B		Procurement of ballots known to be materially false			X		X
	1974		Retention and preservation of records and papers by officers of elections; deposit with custodian; penalty for violation		X	X	X	X	
43	1605	b	Alaska Native Fund	Prohibition of expenditure for propaganda	X	X			

Sources: U.S. Code Collection, Cornell University Law School, Legal Information Institute, available at: http://www4.law.cornell.edu/uscode/ (accessed January 3, 2007); Craig C. Donsanto, "Corruption of the Election Process under U.S. Federal Law," In *Election Fraud: Detecting and Deterring Electoral Manipulation*, edited by R. Michael Alvarez, Thad E. Hall, and Susan D. Hyde, (Washington, D.C.: Brookings Institution, 2008); Craig C. Donsanto and Nancy L. Simmons, *Federal Prosecution of Election Offenses*, 7th ed. U.S. Department of Justice, Criminal Division, Public Integrity Section (Washington, D.C.: Government Printing Office, 2007); U.S. Department of Justice, Criminal Division, Public Integrity Section, "Election Fraud Prosecutions & Convictions, Ballot Access & Voting Integrity Initiative, October 2002-September 2005," Washington, D.C., n.d.

Notes: The table excludes one statute from the list of statutes used in one case appearing on the BAVII case list—Title 47, Section 223 (telephone harassment). The AO codes violations of Title 42, Section 1973gg-10(2)(B) as Title 42, Section 1973A. AO, Administrative Office of the U.S. Courts; DOJ, U.S. Department of Justice; BAVII, Ballot Access and Voting Integrity Initiative; NVRA, National Voter Registration Act of 1993.

[a]Unless otherwise noted, an X in column 6 indicates that the statute is coded as an "Election Law Violation" by the AO; other codes are 4492 = "Conspiracy to Defraud U.S."; 4970 = "Impersonating U.S. Citizen"; 7990 = "Crime: Principals"; 9901 = "Civil Rights Violation."

[b]Craig C. Donsanto and Nancy L. Simmons, *Federal Prosecution of Election Offenses*, 7th ed., U.S. Department of Justice, Criminal Division, Public Integrity Section (Washington, D.C.: Government Printing Office, 2007).

Appendix 6

Oregon Election
Law Complaints

TABLE A6.1
Total convictions or guilty pleas in criminal voter fraud cases prosecuted by attorney general, 1991–2006

Type of voter fraud charge	Case	Year prosecuted	Description of violation	Outcome
Registration[a]	Josephine County v. Jorge Jesus Hosier	2005	County received information from jury clerk that Salvador Oros, with birth date of Sept. 5, 1986, was not an eligible voter. Jury clerk was informed by a relative that Salvador A. Oros was actually a fourteen-year-old and that his older brother was using Salvador's identification except for his birth date. In addition, Hosier's real last name is DeOros. Also, "Salvador A. Oros" voted in the November 2004 general election.	Grand jury convened; pleaded guilty to filing a voter registration card using his younger brother's name, misspelling it as "Oros." Found guilty of three counts of false statements and forgery in the first degree; supervised probation for three years, 180 sanction units and 90 jail units, must refrain from certain actions and pay court fines and restitution of $1,854.00.
Registration	Secretary of State v. Terence John Finch	2003	Complaint alleges he is illegally voting in Oregon, and he has admitted to many people that he is not a U.S. citizen. Claims he sat on at least one jury trial in Linn County while living in Lebanon and has been voting by mail from Monmouth for several years.	Guilty plea, one count of making false information, Class C; one count of voting when not qualified, Class A misdemeanor; probation, $1,000 fine, 80 hours of community service.
Registration	Hezekiah Riesterer	1999	Possible false information on voter registration cards filed in batches.	Guilty, three years probation.
Registration	Columbia County v. Ross Evan Pedersen	1993	Knowingly registered at an address he never lived at; he had moved to Washington state and wanted to vote on Measure 9 and other issues; he worked in Oregon and used his boss's address to register here. He voted by challenge ballot (clerk challenged his vote).	Guilty of false voter registration and false swearing misdemeanors; fine of $250 for each offense, 18 months probation.
Ballot signature violation/illegal voting[b]	Clackamas County v. David P. Holmes	2005	Voted ballot of Michelle Lynn Holmes without her knowledge or permission.	Guilty plea, one count of making false statement, Class A misdemeanor; under diversion agreement, $750 fine, $67 unitary assessment, 40 hours of community service.

Type	Case	Year	Description	Outcome
Ballot signature violation/illegal voting	Multnomah County v. Ronald Wayne Fischer	2004	Voted ballots of three family members.	Guilty plea, one count of making false statement, and one count of forgery in the first degree; sentenced to serve five days in jail, 18 months probation, $279.59 in restitution, and $450 fine.
Ballot signature violation/illegal voting	Teri Louise Kobialka	2002	Signature verification problem; Phillip D. Larsen told county he did not live at address anymore, yet someone else signed the ballot addressed to him at old address.	Guilty of making a false statement, misdemeanor; 120 hours community service, $500 fine, two years informal probation.
Ballot signature violation/illegal voting	Donald Elgas	1997	Signature verification problem, may have signed ballots for four of his children.	Guilty plea, one count of making a false statement; $2,000 restitution fine, two years probation, 96 hours of community service.
Ballot signature violation/illegal voting	Lane County and Illona C. Whitlock v. Claudine C. Mauderli	1998	Mauderli stole, signed, and voted ballot of Whitlock.	Guilty, felony count; 18 months probation, money judgment, community service.
Ballot signature violation/illegal voting	Curry County v. Susan and David Werschkul	1991	Husband signed and voted wife's ballot.	Guilty (sentencing information not provided).
Double voting^c	Jefferson County v. Ricky Graybael	2006	Jefferson County discovered he was also registered in Wasco County and appeared to have voted in four different elections in both counties.	Pleaded guilty to one count of double voting in return for misdemeanor treatment and dismissal of two other charges.
Double voting	Marion County v. Alex Sasha Cam (actual guilty party is Marfa Scheratski)	2002	Signed brother's ballot and her own, may have also submitted ballots for two sisters (one living in Russia since 1998, the other deceased since 2000).	Guilty plea, one count of voting more than once; 24 months probation, 240 hours community service, restitution fine of $250.
Double voting	Wasco County and Hood River County v. Asa Steven Large	2001	Registered and voted twice in two counties for at least three elections.	Guilty, two counts of felony double voting; 36 months probation, 250 hours of community service, fined; must take civics class and send apology letter to editor of the *Dallas Chronicle*.

(continued)

(TABLE A6.1—cont.)

Type of voter fraud charge	Case	Year prosecuted	Description of violation	Outcome
Double voting	Marion County v. John and Joy Hall, and Jonah and Jeremiah Korkow	1999	Alleges that one of the grandparents may have signed son's ballot(s), possibly a voting twice circumstance.	Guilty, two years probation, 240 hours of community service, $1,100 fine.
Double voting	Clackamas and Washington Counties, and Secretary of State v. Theme A. Grenz	1997	Has been registered in two counties since 1994, voted twice in two elections. Also, he has publicly announced this fact.	Guilty plea, felony count of voting more than once; $3,500 fine, 18 months probation.

Source: Oregon Secretary of State's Office, Election Division, Salem, Ore.
Notes: Partial-year data (to October) for 2006.
[a] Registration fraud cases involved violations of ORS 247, and ORS 260.715(5).
[b] Ballot signature cases involved violations of ORS 260.715(1).
[c] Double-voting cases involved violations of ORS 260.715(3).

TABLE A6.2
Total complaints concerning citizenship, 1991–2006

Case	Year	Prosecuted	Description of complaint	Outcome
Josephine County v. Jorge Jesus Hosier	2005	Yes	County received information from jury clerk that Salvador Oros, with birth date of Sept. 5, 1986, was not eligible voter. Jury clerk informed by a relative that Salvador A. Oros was actually a fourteen-year-old and his older brother was using Salvador's identification except for birth date. In addition, his real last name was DeOros. Also, "Salvador A. Oros" voted in the November 2004 general election.	Grand jury convened; pleaded guilty to filing a voter registration card using his younger brother's name, misspelling it as "Oros." Found guilty of three counts of false statements and forgery in the first degree; supervised probation for three years, 180 sanction units and 90 jail units, must refrain from certain actions, pay court fines and restitution of $1,854.00.
Jackson County v. Petelo T. Faaeteete	2004	No	Mr. Faaeteete's mother brought to county's attention that he is not a U.S. citizen, voter registration received on July 15, 2004. Mr. Faaeteete was issued a ballot for November 2, 2004, general election, but his mother will be sending that ballot back to Jackson County. Response received explained he just turned 18, grew up in the United States, and has green card but is not yet a citizen, he did not understand when he signed voter registration card that he was not a U.S. citizen; mother said she contacted county and sent ballot back. So, he never voted any ballot and Jackson County advised his voter registration shall remain canceled unless he becomes qualified.	No prosecutable violation found.
Washington County v. Suong Williams	2003	No	Alleged that Williams illegally voted in Oregon; Washington County received document from U.S. Dept. of Homeland Security that she just now applied for U.S. citizenship. Williams had been registered since June 2002 and had voted at least twice. Registration inactivated as of Dec. 18, 2003.	Determined not prosecutable. Attorney general investigation found in this specific case state's ability to prove requisite culpable mental state of Ms. Williams unlikely; she had discontinued voting when she apparently became aware of her need to be naturalized in order to be a U.S. citizen, and INS has established Ms. Williams believed she was a citizen and has granted her naturalization application.

(continued)

(TABLE A6.2—cont.)

Case	Year	Prosecuted	Description of complaint	Outcome
Secretary of State v. Terence John Finch	2003	Yes	Alleges he is illegally voting in Oregon and has admitted to many people that he is not a U.S. citizen. Claims he sat on at least one jury trial in Linn County while living in Lebanon and has been voting by mail from Monmouth for several years.	Guilty plea, one count of making false information, Class C; one count of voting when not qualified, Class A misdemeanor; probation, $1,000 fine, 80 hours of community service.
Lane County v. Lela Bomar	2003	No	Voted but sent in updated registration on which she marked "no" to U.S. citizen. Ballot was not counted. She states she is a U.S. citizen and made a mistake on voter registration card; told her she must complete a correct card and file with county.	No violation.
Washington County v. Feliciano Vasquez	2003	No	He had been registered to vote and then re-registered stating he was not a U.S. citizen; so county canceled him, but he had voted.	Conty contacted him in his native language. Sent a letter admonishing him, but because the county had already handled it and not felt the case to be prosecutable, it was closed. He is cancelled until he becomes a citizen.
Brenda L. Brainard v. Cherokee Schmerber	2000	No	Complainant alleges Schmerber is not a U.S. citizen and is using an alias for other purposes. Checked with Lane County; Schmerber already found unqualified and cancelled with no voting.	No further action planned by this office.
Coos County v. Michael W. D. West	1997	No	At the time he registered to vote in 1995, it was alleged he was not a U.S. citizen. He has not voted.	Mother sent in a letter saying he is a citizen and provided his baptism certificate from California.
Louise Miille v. Mary W. Roesbury	1992	No	Was not a U.S. citizen but had voted in elections.	Investigation forwarded to attorney general. Not prosecuted based on circumstances involved.
Clackamas Co. v. Anna Chervanov	1991	No	Signed a voter registration card, seemed to be for reason of obtaining a border card; not a U.S. citizen, but is applying for citizenship.	It was explained to her that her registration was canceled until citizenship is obtained. Found no intent to violate the law.

Source: Oregon Secretary of State's Office, Election Division, Salem, Ore.
Notes: Partial-year data (to March 28) for 2006. INS, Immigration and Naturalization Service.

Notes

Chapter 1. Introduction

1. Bill Sammon, a *Washington Times* reporter writes, "Counters twisted ballots, dropped them on the floor, stepped on them, and repeatedly placed Bush votes into Gore piles. On some ballots, chads were taped over holes that had been punched by Bush voters. As the ballots were manhandled again and again, chads fell like rain on tables, floors, and judicial benches. The tiny rectangles of paper were tagged as police evidence, collected as souvenirs, stolen, fought over, and even eaten." Bill Sammon, *At Any Cost: How Al Gore Tried to Steal the Election* (Washington, D.C.: Regnery Publishing, 2002), 165; see also, Rick Bragg, "Counting the Vote: The Recount; Counting Goes On and On, with None of the Big Gains Sought by Democrats," *New York Times*, November 19, 2000; Associated Press, "Republicans Accuse a Floor Manager of Eating Chads," *Chicago Tribune*, November 18, 2000.

2. See, for example, Robert A. Cook, "Explicit Statistical Evidence of Massive Ballot Tampering in Palm Beach, FL." (*Note:* as of June 2009, the original link to this source was no longer operational; but see http://www.mail-archive.com/ctrl@listserv.aol.com/msg55032.html).

3. John B. Judis, "Soft Sell: Can the GOP Convince Blacks Not to Vote?" *New Republic*, November 11, 2002.

4. Judy Normand, "Controversy Greets Early Voting," *Pine Bluff Commercial*, Online Edition, October 22, 2002, www.pbcommercial.com/archives/index.inn?loc=detail&doc=/2002/October/22-2390-NEWS1.TXT.; Jack Whitsett, "Voting Quieter as Accusations Fly," *Pine Bluff Commercial* Online Edition, October 23, 2002, www.pbcommercial.com/archives/index.inn?loc=detail&doc=/2002/October/23-3674-NEWS1.TXT.

5. Voter registration in South Dakota increased by 5.3 percent in the five months before the November election. See "More People Now Registered to Vote in State," *Yankton Press and Dakotan,* Online Edition, October 30, 2002, www.yankton.net/stories/103002/new_20021030024.shtml; Randy Dockendorf, "State's Voters Skyrocket by 24,000," *Yankton Press and Dakotan,* Online Edition, November 5, 2002, www.yankton.net/stories/110502/com_20021105027.shtml.

6. Joe Kafka, "Indian Voters May Be Key in Close Races," *Yankton Press and Dakotan,* Online Edition, October 19, 2002, www.yankton.net/stories/101902/new_20021019020.shtml.

7. Joe Kafka, "Voter Registration Fraud Being Investigated by Authorities," *Yankton Press and Dakotan,* Online Edition, October 12, 2002, www.yankton.net/stories/101202/new_2002 1012030.shtml; Juliet Eilperin, "Voter Registrations Are Probed; In S.D., Irregularities Cloud

Democrats' Outreach to Indians," *Washington Post,* October 24, 2002, A9; "Barnett: Fraudulent Voter Applications Found," *Yankton Press and Dakotan,* Online Edition, October 26, 2002, www.yankton.net/stories/102602/new_20021026025.shtml.

8. See Michelle Malkin, "The Shambles in South Dakota," Townhall.com, October 23, 2002, http://townhall.com/columnists/MichelleMalkin/2002/10/23/the_shambles_in_south_dakota; John H. Fund, "Voter Fraud Wanders off the Reservation," *Wall Street Journal,* October 16, 2002, A20; Rush Limbaugh, "Democrats Praying for a Hail Mary Pass," Rushlimbaugh .com, October 14, 2002.

9. "Questionable Voter Registration Forms Found," *Yankton Press and Dakotan,* Online Edition, October 21, 2002, www.yankton.net/stories/102102/new_20021021032.shtml.

10. David Iglesias, the former U.S. attorney for New Mexico and one of those who got a pink slip likes to point out that the day was December 7, 2006, forty years to the day that the Japanese bombed Pearl Harbor and the United States entered the Second World War. David Iglesias, *In Justice: Inside the Scandal That Rocked the Bush Administration* (Hoboken: John Wiley & Sons, 2008), 1, 67, 129.

11. Prepared Remarks of Attorney General John Ashcroft, Voting Integrity Symposium, U.S. Department of Justice, Washington, D.C., October 8, 2002, available at www.usdoj.gov:80/ag/ speeches/2002/100802ballotintegrity.htm.

12. Ibid.

13. William Walker, "Deeply Divided America Heads to the Polls," *Toronto Star,* November 5, 2002, A1.

14. Chet Brokaw, "Voting Claims Still under Investigation," *Yankton Press and Dakotan, Online Edition,* December 7, 2002, www.yankton.net/stories/120702/new_20021207027.shtml.

15. For an in-depth look at EDR, see, R. Michael Alvarez and Stephen Ansolabehere, *California Votes: The Promise of Election Day Registration* (New York: Dēmos, 2002).

16. Kevin Fagan and Mark Simon, "Election-Day Registration Loses; Opponents Said Prop. 52 Would Have Opened Door to Fraud," *San Francisco Chronicle,* November 6, 2002, A5.

17. Kirk Mitchell, "Mail-In Balloting, Other Amendments, Two Initiatives to Ease Voting Losing Badly," *Denver Post,* November 6, 2002, E3.

18. The second edition of Fund's book, re-issued just before the November 2008 election, omits this episode.

19. John Fund, *Stealing Elections: How Voter Fraud Threatens Our Elections* (San Francisco: Encounter Books, 2004), 1.

20. Spencer Overton, "Voter Identification," *Michigan Law Review* 105, no. 4 (2006–2007), 649n. 94.

21. U.S. Congress, Senate, "Floor Statement of U.S. Senator Christopher "Kit" Bond on Election Reform," February 13, 2002.

22. Khalid al Mihdhar and Nawaf al Hazmi obtained California driver's licenses in April 2000; see Thomas R. Eldridge et al., *9/11 and Terrorist Travel,* Staff Report of the National Commission on Terrorist Attacks upon the United States (Washington, D.C.: GPO, August 21, 2004), 10. In the months preceding the 9/11 attacks, several of the hijackers obtained Florida driver's licenses, including Hazmi, and Marwan al Shehhi, Mohammed Atta, Ziad Samir Jarrah, Waleed al Shehri, Hamza al Ghamdi, Ahmed al Nami, Saeed al Ghamdi, Mohand al Shehri, Ahmad al Haznawi, and Rayez Banihammad (201–33). When Hani Hanjour was stopped for speeding by Arlington, Virginia, police he presented a Florida driver's license. See Manuel Roig-Franzia and Patricia Davis, "For Want of a Crystal Ball: Police Stopped Two Hijackers in Days before Attacks," *Washington Post,* January 9, 2002, A13.

23. Telephone interview by Elizabeth Kraushar, June 7, 2007.

24. When I contacted John Fund by e-mail in November 2007, and asked him to provide such evidence, he replied, "I know you are working on a book and interviewing people about me. Since we live in the same city, shouldn't we meet for lunch or coffee?" I explained that I was not interviewing people about him, that I was only trying to verify some of the claims in his book, and asked him again for evidence that some of the 9/11 hijackers were registered to vote. There was no reply.

25. *Abu* is a *kunya,* or honorific, commonly used in the Arabic-speaking world in place of a first name. When used with a full name, the person's first name appears after the *kunya* and the son's proper name. In this example, Mahmoud Abbas would be referred to as Abu Mazen Mahmoud. When young men who are childless use *abu*, the meaning changes from "father of" to "son of." The FBI listed as "aliases" names such as this for some of the hijackers. For example, the FBI identified several aliases for Fayez Rashid Ahmed Hassan Al Qadi Banihammad, one of the so-called muscle hijackers on United Airlines Flight 175, which crashed into the South Tower of the World Trade Center. They included Fayez Ahmad, Banihammad Fayez Abu Dhabi Banihammad, Fayez Rashid Ahmed, Banihammad Fayez, Rasid Ahmed Hassen Alqadi, Abu Dhabi Banihammad Ahmed Fayez, and Faez Ahmed. See Associated Press, "Updated List of Hijackers," September 27, 2001.

26. Five of the hijackers obtained Virginia ID cards using identity documents based on fraudulent residency information provided by one bribed Salvadoran immigrant who encountered two of the hijackers at a 7-Eleven in Falls Church, Virginia. See Eldridge et al., *9/11 and Terrorist Travel*, 29–32. Hanjour also obtained a Maryland ID card on September 5, 2001.

27. Cameron Quinn investigated the claim that some of the 9/11 hijackers were registered to vote in Virginia when she was secretary of the State Board of Elections. Quinn was unable to confirm or deny the allegation, noting difficulties in confirming the actual names of the hijackers and their Social Security and/or voter registration numbers with the FBI. See Overton, "Voter Identification," 649n. 94.

28. Evan Kolodny, director of voter registration for Broward County, Florida, reviewed statewide voter registration records going back to 1992 for matches with the hijackers' names and aliases. These records contained all information provided when voters initially registered, even if that information later changed or the voter was removed from the rolls. The review produced four possible matches of similar, but not identical, records. There were three near-matches to a name used by hijacker Mohammed Atta, Mohamed El Sayed. The name on the registration forms omitted the hyphens and did not match the address Atta provided on his driver's license application, nor did the dates on two of the registration forms match the date Atta applied for a license (the date on the third form is illegible). If Atta registered to vote while applying for a Florida license, the license application and voter registration applications would probably have had the same dates and address because the voter registration card is preprinted with information drawn from the driver's license application.

29. The Glenn Beck Show, "How Prevalent Is Voter Fraud?" November 7, 2006, transcript available, http://transcripts.cnn.com/TRANSCRIPTS/0611/07/gb.01.html.

30. See Bob Fitrakis, "Fake Voting Rights Activist and Groups Linked to White House," (Columbus) *Free Press*, December 30, 2005; see also, Bradblog, http://www.bradblog.com/?p=1282.

31. Murray Waas, "The Scales of Justice," *National Journal*, May 31, 2007.

32. St. Louis was successfully sued by the federal government for illegally purging its voter rolls in ways that contributed to the election day confusion that abrogated voters' rights. This case is discussed in more detail in chapter 6.

33. Baker served in the administration of George W. Bush's father. Friedman reported this information on his blog on March 24, 2005; see also an email from Brad Friedman to author, April 16, 2007.

34. Colleagues took photographs of the store and Box 229, which Friedman posted on his news blog, Bradblog.com. See a compendium of articles on the ACVR by Brad Friedman and his colleagues at http://www.bradblog.com/ACVR.htm.

35. See Sourcewatch's page on the American Center for Voting Rights: http://www.source watch.org/index.php?title=American_Center_for_Voting_Rights_Legislative_Fund.

36. Dimitri Vassilaros, "'Study' Is Political Fraud," *Pittsburgh Tribune-Review*, August 8, 2005, available at http://www.pittsburghlive.com/x/pittsburghtrib/s_360812.html.

37. The ACVR has never publicly disclosed the sources of its funding. When reporter Dimitri Vassilaros of the *Pittsburgh Tribune-Review*, asked Hearne to name any contributors to the nonprofit group, Hearne said he did not know and told Vassilaros to ask Brian Lunde, one of the group's directors. When asked, Lunde said he did not know and told Vassilaros to ask

Hearne. See Vassilaros, ibid. The ACVR's 501(c)3 educational nonprofit incorporated in January 2005 and a 501(c)4 legislative fund incorporated in March 2005. In federal income tax returns for 2005 for the 501(c)3 educational nonprofit, the ACVR reported $903,902 in "direct public support" and filed for extensions to avoid further disclosure until November 2007. That day never came. The ACVR folded just before its second anniversary in March 2007. In 2005, over $400,000, or nearly half of reported expenses ($853,751), was paid out to five Republican-connected law firms and consulting businesses, including Hearne's firm Lathrop & Gage in St. Louis; Dyke's consulting group, Jim Dyke & Associates; and two consulting and lobbying groups directly connected to another highly placed GOP operative, attorney Alex Vogel. Vogel is a former deputy counsel to the RNC, and former general counsel to the National Republican Senatorial Committee, and was chief counsel to former Senate Majority Leader Bill Frist (R-Tenn.). The ACVR had no paid staff, had no physical office or working telephone number, and had four uncompensated directors who collectively worked a total of 1.7 hours a week.

38. G. Bingham Powell Jr., *Elections as Instruments of Democracy: Majoritarian and Proportional Visions* (New Haven: Yale University Press, 2000), 3.

39. McCrary's treatise was written to "aid the bar and bench" by collecting the disparate ways courts were evolving election law in the United States and were building a common law tradition in this field. He sought to unify the constitutional principles that should apply in resolving election contests. The need for guidance became all the more evident the year following the publication of the treatise when the disputed presidential contest between Samuel Tilden and Rutherford B. Hayes was thrown into Congress. At the time, McCrary was a leading Republican in the House and introduced the bill that created the electoral commission to determine how the disputed Electoral College votes would be counted (he also served on the commission). His treatise was subsequently re-issued several times and served as the bible of election law during the third-party system, the high-water mark for contested congressional elections. See George W. McCrary, *A Treatise on the American Law of Elections*, 3rd ed. (Chicago: Callaghan & Co., 1887). Nearly 45 percent of all House and Senate contested election cases from the first Congress through 2002 occurred between 1861 and 1899. See Jeffrey A. Jenkins, "Partisanship and Contested Election Cases in the House of Representatives, 1789–2002," *Studies in American Political Development* 18 (fall 2004): 112–35; Jeffrey A. Jenkins, "Partisanship and Contested Election Cases in the Senate, 1789–2002," *Studies in American Political Development* 19 (spring 2005): 53–74.

40. McCrary, *Treatise*, 348.

41. Cass County Circuit Court, Illinois, May 1869. See Frederick C. Brightly, *A Collection of Leading Cases of the Law of Elections in the United States, with Notes and References to the Latest Authorities* (Philadelphia: Kay & Brother, 1871), 493–503.

42. Ibid., 366–67.

43. 50 N.H., 140 (1870).

44. The case involved a 1869 congressional election contest in the Twenty-first District of Pennsylvania between John Covode, the Republican incumbent and Henry D. Foster, his Democratic challenger. See David W. Bartlett, comp., *Digest of Election Cases: Cases of Contested Elections in the House of Representatives from 1865 to 1871, Inclusive*, 38th Cong., 2nd Sess. (1870), Mis. Doc 152, 600–631.

45. McCrary, *Treatise*, 363.

46. James Bryce, *Modern Democracies* (New York: Macmillan, 1921), 471.

47. Walter James Shepard, "The Theory of the Nature of Suffrage," *Proceedings of the American Political Science Association* 9 (1912), 106–36.

48. Howard W. Allen and Kay Warren Allen, "Vote Fraud and Data Validity," in *Analyzing Electoral History: A Guide to the Study of American Voter Behavior, ed.* Jerome M. Clubb, William H. Flanigan, and Nancy H. Zingale (Beverly Hills: Sage Publications, 1981), 156–57.

49. See Richard L. Hasen, "Vote Buying," *California Law Review* 88, no. 5 (2000): 1323–72; Pamela S. Karlan, "Not by Money but by Virtue Won?: Vote Trafficking and the Voting Rights System," *Virginia Law Review* 80, no. 7 (1994): 1455–76.

50. There are many examples of states that criminalize what we think of as voter fraud without calling it "voter fraud." Georgia, for example, has no election code offense for "voter fraud," but it does provide stiff penalties for "repeat voting" and "voting by unqualified elector"; see, for example O.C.G.A. § 21-2-560 *et seq.* In New Hampshire, the crime of voting more than once is called "wrongful voting"; see, N.H.R.S. § 63-659.34. In Alaska, voter impersonation, voting more than once, and registering to vote without being entitled to register are all simply called "voter misconduct"; See, Ala. Statutes § 15.56.040 *et seq.*

51. Chapter 4 and appendix 2 describe the codification of voter fraud in the states in more detail.

52. W. Phillips Shively, *The Craft of Political Research,* 5th ed. (Upper Saddle River, N.J.: Prentice Hall, 2002), 31.

53. Ibid., 30–38.

Chapter 2. What Is Voter Fraud?

1. Karl G. Heider, "The Rashomon Effect: When Ethnographers Disagree," *American Anthropologist* 90, no. 1 (March 1988): 73–81.

2. Robert Goldberg, "Election Fraud: An American Vice," in *Elections American Style,* ed. A. James Reichley (Washington, D.C.: Brookings Institution, 1987), 180.

3. U.S. Elections Assistance Commission, *Election Crimes: An Initial Review and Recommendations for Future Study* (Washington, D.C.: Government Printing Office, December 2006), 13.

4. R. Michael Alvarez, Thad E. Hall, and Susan D. Hyde, "Conclusion," in *Election Fraud: Detecting and Deterring Electoral Manipulation, ed.* R. Michael Alvarez, Thad E. Hall and Susan D. Hyde (Washington, D.C.: Brookings Institution, 2008), 236.

5. Fabrice Lehoucq, "Electoral Fraud: Causes, Types, and Consequences," *Annual Review of Political Science* 6 (2003), 233–56, quotations on 233, 234.

6. Ibid., 234.

7. The catchall approach is evident in Lehoucq's inclusion of two tables from his own research with I. Molina on electoral fraud in Costa Rica; see Fabrice Lehoucq and Iván Molina, *Stuffing the Ballot Box: Fraud, Electoral Reform and Democratization in Costa Rica* (New York: Cambridge University Press, 2002). The tables present lists of accusations made in party petitions to nullify election results to the Costa Rican unicameral congress between 1901 and 1948, and they include the following types of fraud: "inappropriate exclusion of voters, party observer expelled or threatened, absence of formal requisites [to vote], voter cast more than one ballot, voting booth in an inappropriate place, elections held outside of official time period, voters did not meet requirement, voters prevented from casting ballots, number of votes inflated, number of votes exceeds number of voters, elections were not held, votes not received, substitution of votes was permitted, location of polling stations changed on election day, voters were intimidated, ballots were altered, votes were annulled, number of ballots exceeds number of voters, electoral identification was rejected, electoral identification not demanded of a citizen, number of ballots does not equal number of identification cards, ballots substituted, electoral identification removed, ballots removed, ballot box altered, voting was public, vote tally conducted by unauthorized individuals, electoral documentation not surrendered for legislative elections, electoral documentation opened before election day, electoral documentation collected by unauthorized individuals, wrongfully counted absentee ballots from other provinces" (244).

8. *Laws of democracy* is borrowed from Samuel Issacharoff, Pamela S. Karlan, and Richard H. Pildes, eds., *The Law of Democracy: Legal Structure of the Political Process,* 3rd ed., University Casebook Series (Westbury, N.Y.: Foundation Press, 2007).

9. This is shorthand. As explained in what follows, generally speaking, there is no specific crime of "voter fraud," only the criminalization of behavior such as impersonating a voter that is associated with fraud.

10. And here, the EAC and I are in agreement.

11. See, *Proceedings and Debates of the Convention of the Commonwealth of Pennsylvania to Propose Amendments to the Constitution*, Vol. 3, reported by John Agg (Harrisburg, 1837), 39.

12. Porter was no partisan. He had friends on all sides because political parties in Pennsylvania during the first half of the nineteenth century, in Porter's own words, were "shreds and patches, the factions and fragments of factions." Ibid., 50. Rather, Porter was an independent-minded patrician who believed the state's constitution guaranteed the poor and rich alike an equal right of suffrage. He argued against the registry law because he believed it clearly discriminated against the poor and was therefore unconstitutional.

13. Ibid., 39–40.

14. Steven P. Erie, *Rainbow's End: Irish-Americans and the Dilemmas of Urban Machine Politics, 1840–1985* (Berkeley: University of California Press, 1988).

15. Frances Fox Piven and Richard A. Cloward, *Why Americans Don't Vote and Why Politicians Want It That Way* (New York: Beacon Press, 2000), 32–33.

16. Stephen Ansolabehere and David M. Konisky, "The Introduction of Voter Registration and Its Effect on Turnout," *Political Analysis* 14, no. 4 (2006): 83–100.

17. Richard M. Valelly, *The Two Reconstructions: The Struggle for Black Enfranchisement* (Chicago: University of Chicago Press, 2004).

18. J. Morgan Kousser, *Colorblind Injustice: Minority Voting Rights and the Undoing of the Second Reconstruction* (Chapel Hill: University of North Carolina Press, 1999), 33–34.

19. William C. Harris, *The Day of the Carpetbagger: Republican Reconstruction in Mississippi* (Baton Rouge: Louisiana State University Press, 1979), quoted in Kousser, *Colorblind Injustice*, 34.

20. Frances Fox Piven, Lorraine C. Minnite, and Margaret Groarke, *Keeping Down the Black Vote: Race and the Demobilization of American Voters* (New York: New Press, 2009).

21. Charles M. Payne, *I've Got the Light of Freedom: The Organizing Tradition and the Mississippi Freedom Struggle* (Berkeley: University of California Press, 1995); see also, Steven F. Lawson, *Black Ballots: Voting Rights in the South, 1944–1969* (New York: Columbia University Press, 1976); John Dittmer, *Local People: The Struggle for Civil Rights in Mississippi* (Chicago: University of Illinois Press, 1995); Chana Kai Lee, *For Freedom's Sake: The Life of Fannie Lou Hamer* (Chicago: University of Illinois Press, 1999).

22. See "Brief of Amici Curiae of Historians and Other Scholars in Support of Petitioners," *Crawford et al. v. Marion County Election Board*, et al., 128 S. Ct. 1610 (2008), especially, 4–13.

23. Ironically, one early study of the effects of voter registration laws concluded that they had failed miserably in their stated antifraud purpose. Instead, they provided a more efficient means for corrupt election officials to commit fraud: "[I]n some cities [the registry lists have] been made available, with the collusion of dishonest election officers, for extensive false personation, for they have been the means whereby repeaters have ascertained the names and residence of voters whom they have personated. . . ." "Crimes against the Elective Franchise," *Criminal Law Magazine* 2, no. 4 (July 1881), 454.

24. Ellen S. Podgor, "Criminal Fraud," *American University Law Review*, 48, no. 4 (April 1999), 730.

25. *Black's Law Dictionary*, 8th ed. (St. Paul: Thomson/West, 2004), 685.

26. The earliest cases dealt with the constitutionality of the Enforcement Act of 1870. See, for example, *Ex parte Siebold*, 100 U.S. 371 (1880); *Ex parte Yarbrough* 110 U.S. 651 (1884); see also, *In re Coy*, 127 U.S. 731 (1888); *U.S. v. Mosley*, 238 U.S. 383 (1915); *U.S. v. Classic*, 313 U.S. 299 (1941); *U.S. v. Saylor*, 322 U.S. 385 (1944). Those early foundations were shaky, to be sure. See Richard M. Valelly, *Two Reconstructions*, 99–120; Robert M. Goldman, *"A Free Ballot and a Fair Count": The Department of Justice and the Enforcement of Voting Rights in the South, 1877–1893* (New York: Fordham University Press, 2001); Robert M. Goldman, *Reconstruction and Black Suffrage: Losing the Vote in Reese and Cruikshank* (Lawrence: University of Kansas, 2001); Robert J. Kaczorowski, *The Politics of Judicial Interpretations: The Federal Courts, Department of Justice and Civil Rights, 1866–1876* (New York: Oceana Pub-

lications, 1985); Richard Claude, "Constitutional Voting Rights and Early Supreme Court Doctrine," *Journal of Negro History* 51, no. 2 (1966), 114–24; Homer Cummings and Carl McFarland, *Federal Justice: Chapters in the History of Justice and the Federal Executive* (New York: Macmillan, 1937), 230–49.

27. See *Anderson v. United States*, 417 U.S. 211, 227 (1974). Unlike other nonelectoral forms of fraud between private parties, in which constitutional authority for criminal prosecution derives from the Commerce Clause, or the postal and taxing powers of Congress, congressional authority to regulate the electoral process is found primarily in the Elections Clause of Article 1, Section 4 (the "Times, Place, and Manner" clause) and Article II, Section 1 of the Constitution. Library of Congress, Congressional Research Service, *Congressional Authority to Standardize national Election Procedures*, Kenneth R. Thomas, *Report for Congress*, no. RL30747 (Washington D.C.: Government Printing Office, 2003). See also, Library of Congress, Congressional Research Service, *Analysis and Interpretation of the Constitution: Annotations of Cases Decided by the Supreme Court of the United States to June 28, 2002*, edited by Johnny H. Killian, George A. Costello, and Kenneth R. Thomas, Senate Document no. 108-17 (Washington D.C.: Government Printing Office, 2004), 124–28.

28. The Illegal Immigration Reform and Immigrant Responsibility Act of 1996 (P.L. 104-208), perhaps the most radical reform of U.S. immigrations laws to date, makes it much easier than before to deport otherwise lawful noncitizens for illegal voting in federal elections (see Title II).

29. Podgor, "Criminal Fraud," 742–43.

30. Brian K. Landsberg, *Free at Last to Vote: The Alabama Origins of the 1965 Voting Rights Act* (Lawrence: University of Kansas, 2007), 173.

31. Attorneys in the Voting Section also prosecute violations of the Voting Rights Act.

32. Craig C. Donsanto and Nancy L. Simmons, *Federal Prosecution of Election Offenses*, 7th ed., U.S. Department of Justice, Criminal Division, Public Integrity Section (Washington, D.C.: Government Printing Office, 2007), 24. This definition is different from the one offered in the previous edition of the training manual, used between 1995 and 2007. In that manual, *election fraud* is defined as "conduct that corrupts the process by which ballots are obtained, marked, or tabulated; the process by which election results are canvassed and certified; or the process by which voters are registered." Craig C. Donsanto and Nancy S. Stewart, *Federal Prosecution of Election Offenses*, 6th ed., U.S. Department of Justice, Criminal Division, Public Integrity Section (Washington, D.C.: Government Printing Office, 1995), 21.

33. The expanding use of the mail fraud statute, Title 18, Section 1341, was brought to a halt in 1987 in *McNally v. United States* (483 U.S. 350) when the Supreme Court held that the statute did not apply to schemes to defraud a person of his or her "intangible rights," such as the right to good government and fair elections (also known as "honest services"). It was under this theory that the Justice Department obtained federal jurisdiction to prosecute local election fraud because all elections at some stage involve the U.S. mails. In *McNally*, the Court held that the mail fraud statute extended only to protection against schemes to deprive others of property rights. Following this decision, Congress revised Section 1341 (as Section 1346) to include protections against fraud that deprived a person of "honest services," but efforts by the Justice Department to revisit its earlier success in relying on Section 1341 to prosecute fraud in nonfederal elections have largely failed. See *U.S. v. Turner*, 459 F.3d 774 (6th Cir. 2006); Craig C. Donsanto, "Corruption of the Election Process Under U.S. Federal Law," in *Election Fraud: Detecting and Deterring Electoral Manipulation*, ed. R. Michael Alvarez, Thad E. Hall, and Susan D. Hyde (Washington, D.C.: Brookings Institution, 2008), 26; see also Donsanto and Simmons, 29n. 11, 72–74.

34. Donsanto and Simmons, *Federal Prosecution of Election Offenses*, 33. Again, this new revised policy differs significantly from the policy outlined in the previous edition of the election crimes training manual. There, a violation was described as reaching a federal crime when there is "some *substantive* irregularity in the voting act—such as bribery, intimidation, or ballot forgery—which has the potential to taint the election itself." Donsanto and Stewart, *Federal Prosecution of Election Offenses*, 22 (emphasis in original).

35. These include statutes protecting voters, candidates, poll watchers, and election officials from intimidation, the outlawing of "armed men" at the polls, laws prohibiting the coercion of voting among members of the military and other federal employees, the fraudulent assertion of U.S. citizenship, and schemes using the mails in the furtherance of vote-buying activities in states that treat vote buying as bribery. See, Donsanto and Simmons, *Federal Prosecution of Election Offenses,* 34–35.

36. Alexander Keyssar, *The Right to Vote: The Contested History of Democracy in the United States* (New York: Basic Books, 2000), 110–11.

37. To such a determination, the court uses what is known as the Screws vagueness test. In *U.S. v. Screws,* 35 U.S. 91 (1945), the Supreme Court, while finding Section 242 constitutional, limited its application to a "specific intent to deprive a person of a federal right" and found that the right must have "been made specific either by the express terms of the Constitution or laws of the United States or by decisions interpreting them." In *United States v. Price,* 383 U.S. 787 (1966), the Court held that Screws applied to Section 241, as well. See R. Paul Margie, "Comment: Protecting the Right to Vote in State and Local Elections under the Conspiracy against Rights Act," *University of Chicago Legal Forum* (1995), 483–504; Richard Craswell, "Federal Prosecution for Local Vote Fraud Under Section 241 of the Federal Criminal Code," *University of Chicago Law Review* 43, no. 3 (1976), 542–72.

38. See *United States v. Daugherty,* 952 F.2d 969, 971 (8th Cir. 1991); *United States v. Saenz,* 747 F.2d 930, 935 (5th Cir. 1984); *United States v. Canales,* 744 F.2d 413, 416 (5th Cir. 1984).

39. One critic of the NVRA has suggested in testimony before the Senate Committee on Governmental Affairs that the lack of an evidentiary record of voter fraud prosecutions should not be taken as indicative of a lack of voter fraud. See the testimony of Deborah Phillips, chair of the Voting Integrity Project, who asserts without evidence that "Prosecutors do not like election fraud cases because they take precious resources from strained budgets needed for more serious crimes." U.S. Congress, Senate Committee on Governmental Affairs, "Hearing on Election Administration Reform," 107th Cong., 2nd Sess. (May 3, 2001), S. Hrg. 107–69.

40. But "the Congress may at any time by law make or alter such regulations, except as to the places of choosing Senators." See U.S. Constitution, Article 1, Sec. 4.

41. I remind the reader that, for purposes of argument, I am applying a formal treatment to terms and that the distinctions between "eligible" and "qualified" voters are not usually respected in common parlance, state laws, or judicial commentary.

42. North Dakota repealed its voter registration law in 1951. To vote in North Dakota, eligible voters must have proper identification showing their name and current address. If they lack identification, they may still vote (1) by filing a voter's affidavit attesting to their identity and address or (2) if a poll worker knows them and can vouch for them. Poll workers use lists of previous voters to track voting on election day.

43. The courts have dealt with the question of whether voter registration is an unconstitutional burden on the vote by using a balancing test, weighing the alleged burden on rights against a state's legitimate interest in ensuring electoral integrity. State laws mandating voter registration have been upheld repeatedly by the Supreme Court as reasonable administrative burdens on the right to vote: "a person does not have a federal constitutional right to walk up to a voting place on election day and demand a ballot." *Marston v. Lewis,* 410 U.S. 679, 680 (1973).

44. Federal law does not require that individuals be U.S. citizens to vote, but all states do; it is their constitutional prerogative to set citizenship as a condition for voter eligibility and qualification.

45. Chaudhary told the *New York Times* he was living in the United States legally. See Eric Lipton and Ian Urbina, "In 5-Year Effort, Scant Evidence of Voter Fraud," *New York Times,* April 12, 2007, A1. In the charges against him, which were later dropped, the government alleged Chaudhary never completed the process of adjusting his immigration status after the expiration of his student visa in 1993. See *U.S. v. Usman Ali Chaudhary, a/k/a Usman Ali,* Superseding Indictment, Case No. 4:04-cr-59/RH (N.D. Fla., 2005).

46. *U.S. v. Chaudhary,* 5.

47. Lipton and Urbina, "In 5-Year Effort," A1.

48. 25 P.S. § 3146.2ci, and 25 P.S. § 3146.6b. See also, *Marks v. Stinson (ED PA 1994 LEXIS 5273), Civil Action no. 93-6187, 26* ("An absentee ballot cast by a voter who is in the county of residence and able to go to the polls on Election Day is void as a matter of law, and an absentee ballot voter has a duty to go to the polls and void the ballot in the event such voter is in the county and able to do so.").

49. 25 P.S. § 3146.2a.

50. Without analyzing or considering deliberately complex rules as a reason that "errors will always plague the counting of votes . . ." Edward P. Foley nevertheless confidently and uncontroversially asserts that errors in the administration of elections are inevitable. See Edward P. Foley, "The Analysis and Mitigation of Electoral Errors: Theory, Practice, Policy," *Stanford Law and Policy Review* 18 (2007): 350–81.

51. In common rather than legal parlance, *fraud* is defined as "deception deliberately practiced with a view to gaining an unlawful or unfair advantage" (emphasis added). *Webster's Revised Unabridged Dictionary* (Springfield, Mass.: C. & G. Merriam, 1913).

52. The proper venue for challenging mistakes that may have affected the outcome of an election is to follow state statutory procedures for an election challenge or contest. See Barry H. Weinberg, *The Resolution of Election Disputes: Legal Principles That Control Election Challenges* (Washington, D.C.: IFES, 2006).

Chapter 3. Are U.S. Elections Vulnerable to Voter Fraud?

1. Gustavus Myers, *The History of Tammany Hall* (New York: Burt Franklin, 1968).

2. For lively accounts of nefarious activity at the nineteenth century polling booth, see Glenn C. Altschuler and Stuart M. Blumin, *Rude Republic: Americans and Their Politics in the Nineteenth Century* (Princeton: Princeton University Press, 2000); Richard Franklin Bensel, *The American Ballot Box in the Mid-Nineteenth Century* (New York: Cambridge University Press, 2004).

3. T. Harry Williams, *Huey Long* (New York: Alfred A. Knopf, 1969).

4. Robert A. Caro, *The Path to Power: The Years of Lyndon Johnson* (New York: Knopf, 1992); Mary Kahl, *Ballot Box 13: How Lyndon Johnson Won His 1948 Senate Race by 87 Contested Votes* (Jefferson, N.C.: McFarland, 1983); Ronnie Dugger, *The Politician: The Life and Times of Lyndon Johnson* (New York: W. W. Norton & Company, 1980).

5. Edmund F. Kallina Jr., *Courthouse over White House: Chicago and the Presidential Election of 1960* (Orlando: University Presses of Florida, 1988); Seymour Hersh, *The Dark Side of Camelot* (Boston: Little, Brown, 1997).

6. Tracy Campbell, *Deliver the Vote: A History of Election Fraud, An American Political Tradition, 1742–2004* (New York: Basic Books, 2005), xviii.

7. Larry J. Sabato and Glenn R. Simpson, *Dirty Little Secrets: The Persistence of Corruption in American Politics* (New York: Times Books, Random House, 1996), 10.

8. Walter Dean Burnham, "The Changing Shape of the American Political Universe," *American Political Science Review* 59, no. 1 (1965): 7–28, quotation on 8.

9. Gerald Ginsburg and others, such as Richard Bensel, have raised questions about the accuracy of nineteenth-century electoral data that ring a cautionary note for voting studies today. See Gerald Ginsburg, "Computing Antebellum Turnout: Methods and Models," *Journal of Interdisciplinary History* 16, no. 4 (1986): 579–611. For a rejoinder to Ginsburg, see Walter Dan Burnham, "Those High Nineteenth Century American Voting Turnouts: Fact or Fiction?" *Journal of Interdisciplinary History* 16, no. 4 (Spring 1986), 613–44. Bensel analyzes nineteenth-century congressional investigations of contested elections, mining a rich vein of primary materials overlooked by scholars of elections and U.S. political development; see Bensel, *American Ballot Box.*

10. J. Morgan Kousser, *The Shaping of Southern Politics: Suffrage Restriction and the Establishment of the One-Party South* (New Haven: Yale University Press, 1974). Before some take issue with this claim of a vacuum in the academic literature, I will clarify that I am not including

here the voluminous work on the Southern disfranchisement of blacks after the Civil War. Much of the modern scholarship on this subject was spurred by the classic early work of C. Vann Woodward (see *The Origins of the New South, 1877–1913* (Baton Rouge: Louisiana State University Press, 1971 [1951]). See also, V. O. Key, Jr. *Southern Politics in State and Nation* (New York: Vintage Books, 1949).

11. Since then, numerous books dealing with the disputed 2000 and 2004 presidential elections have appeared, along with a cottage industry focused on the threat to clean elections posed by electronic voting machines. One recent edited volume takes up questions about election fraud, but addresses itself more to the technical than political dimension of the issue; see R. Michael Alvarez, Thad E. Hall, and Susan D. Hyde, eds., *Election Fraud: Detecting and Deterring Electoral Manipulation* (Washington, D.C.: Brookings Institution, 2008).

12. For example, in addition to Harris' work, see J. J. McCook, "The Alarming Proportion of Venal Voters," *Forum* 14 (September 1892), 1–13; the work of Clinton Rogers Woodruff, especially, "Election Methods and Reform in Philadelphia," *Annals of the American Academy of Political and Social Science* 17 (March 1901), 1–24; M. Ostrogorski, *Democracy and the Organization of Political Parties*, 2 vols., trans. Frederick Clarke (New York: Macmillan Co., 1902); Samuel P. Orth, *The Boss and the Machine: A Chronicle of the Politicians and Party Organization* (New Haven: Yale University Press, 1902); and Lincoln Steffans, *The Shame of the Cities* (New York: McClure, Phillips and Co., 1904). Referring to these early studies, Howard W. Allen and Kay Warren Allen write, "The evidence to demonstrate the existence of election fraud in the literature is not only anecdotal, it is unsystematic, impressionistic, and by and large inconclusive." Moreover, they continue, "Attempts to analyze fraudulent voting practices systematically and dispassionately were rare" in the studies published by political observers before 1920, and the studies that followed these mostly relied on and repeated the charges and allegations of fraud made by contemporary observers of the past. Allen and Allen argue convincingly that the literature on election fraud written between roughly 1880 and 1930 was infected by the partisanship, racial bias, and anti-immigrant and anti-urban attitudes of the upper and middle classes from whence the authors and audience for their work were drawn. Howard W. Allen and Kay Warren Allen, "Vote Fraud and Data Validity," in *Analyzing Electoral History: A Guide to the Study of American Voter Behavior*, ed. Jerome M. Clubb, William H. Flanigan, and Nancy H. Zingale (Beverly Hills: Sage Publications, 1981), 167, 171–76.

13. Philip E. Converse, "Change in the American Electorate," in *The Human Meaning of Social Change*, ed. Angus Campbell and Philip E. Converse (New York: Russell Sage Foundation, 1972), 298.

14. Joseph P. Harris, *The Registration of Voters in the U.S.* (Baltimore: Lord Baltimore Press, 1929), xi.

15. See Joseph P. Harris, "Oral History," interview by Harriet Nathan, Regional Oral History Office, Bancroft Library, University of California, Berkeley, 1980, available at http://bancroft.berkeley.edu/ROHO/Vote/.

16. Harris, *Registration of Voters*, 4.

17. Ibid., 6.

18. Charles Edward Merriam and Harold Foote Gosnell, *The American Party System: An Introduction to the Study of Political Parties in the United States* (New York: The Macmillan Company, 1929); Harris, *Registration of Voters*.

19. Harris, *Registration of Voters*, 18.

20. Ibid., 2

21. Ibid., 3.

22. Ibid.

23. Ibid., 8.

24. Joseph P. Harris, *Election Administration in the United States* (Washington D.C.: Brookings Institution, 1934), 6.

25. Burnham, "Changing Shape."

26. Ibid., 22.

27. Burnham's essay spawned a protracted debate and more research aimed at testing his several hypotheses. See Raymond Seidelman and Edward J. Harpham, *Disenchanted Realists: Political Science and the American Crisis, 1884–1984* (Albany: SUNY Press, 1985), 213–20.

28. For an original statement of this school, see Angus Campbell, Philip E. Converse, Warren Miller, and Donald Stokes, *The American Voter* (New York: John Wiley, 1960).

29. Converse, "Change in the American Electorate," 282.

30. Ibid.

31. Ibid.

32. Ibid., 298. Burnham answered his critics, conceding a role for the legal reforms in explaining turnout decline but concluding overall that the Australian ballot, the enfranchisement of women, and the advent of personal voter registration systems could account for no more than half of the "decompositional changes" (i.e., declines in turnout and party control) discussed in his 1965 article. He cited new work on the period by historians such as Richard Jensen, who, after "massive sifting of the available evidence," found that "traceable corruption, being a dangerous enterprise for its practitioners, was at most a marginal phenomenon." Walter Dean Burnham, "Theory and Voting Research: Some Reflections on Converse's 'Change in the American Electorate.'" *American Political Science Review* 68, no. 3 (1974), 1018. A further critique of Burnham was offered by Rusk, who pointed out that Burnham provided no evidence to refute the fraud claim. Rusk was less impressed with Jensen's work. He argues that his own work on the Australian ballot produced evidence supporting his claim that the open ballot system was maintained by the parties so that they could control the vote: "Bribery, intimidation, and corruption were facilitated simply because the ballot system required public voting rather than a secret vote." Jerrold G. Rusk, "Comment: The American Electoral Universe: Speculation and Evidence," *American Political Science Review* 68, no. 3 (1974): 1033; and Walter Dean Burnham, "Rejoinder to 'Comments' by Philip Converse and Jerrold Rusk," *American Political Science Review* 68, no. 3 (1974): 1050–57.

33. Mark Lawrence Kornbluh revisits the debate in *Why Americans Stopped Voting: The Decline of Participatory Democracy and the Emergence of Modern American Politics* (New York: New York University Press, 2000).

34. See, for example, J. Morgan Kousser, "Post-Reconstruction Suffrage Restrictions in Tennessee: A New Look at the V. O. Key Thesis," *Political Science Quarterly* 88, no. 4 (1973), 655–83 (see also, Gary W. Cox and J. Morgan Kousser, "Turnout and Rural Corruption: New York as a Test Case," *American Journal of Political Science* 25, no. 4 (1981), 646–63); Dale Baum, "Pinpointing Apparent Fraud in the 1861 Texas Secession Referendum," *Journal of Interdisciplinary History* 22, no. 2 (1991), 201–21; Lawrence N. Powell, "Correcting for Fraud: A Quantitative Reassessment of the Mississippi Ratification Election of 1868," *Journal of Southern History* 55, no. 4 (1989), 633–58; and Ronald F. King, "Counting the Votes: South Carolina's Stolen Election of 1876," *Journal of Interdisciplinary History* 32, no. 1 (2001), 169–91.

35. See, in particular, Allen and Allen, "Vote Fraud and Data Validity." "The unsystematic, undocumented, partisan, and emotional nature of most of the literature indicates that the charges of vote fraud were probably gross exaggerations, and it seems unlikely that a significant portion of the sharp decline in voter turnout rates after 1900 can be explained by the elimination of vote fraud" (179). In some ways, the debate over the empirical basis for election fraud claims during the Gilded Age and Progressive eras misses the point and is probably irresolvable. Newer historiography of the period emphasizing the political context in which the language of fraud and corruption are embedded shows that *fraud* meant more than a legal interpretation suggests. See Gary W. Cox and J. Morgan Kousser, "Turnout and Rural Corruption: New York as a Test Case," *American Journal of Political Science* 25, no. 4 (1981): 646–63; Peter H. Argesinger, "New Perspectives on Election Fraud in the Gilded Age," *Political Science Quarterly* 100, no. 4 (1985–1986): 669–87; John F. Reynolds, "A Symbiotic Relationship: Vote Fraud and Electoral Reform in the Gilded Age," *Social Science History* 17, no. 2 (1993): 227–51; Loomis Mayfield, "Voting Fraud in Early Twentieth-Century Pittsburgh," *Journal of Interdisciplinary History* 24, no. 1 (1993): 59–84; Mark Wahlgren Summers, "Party Games: The

Art of Stealing Elections in the Late-Nineteenth-Century United States," *Journal of American History* 88, no. 2 (2001): 424–35.

36. Allen and Allen, "Vote Fraud and Data Validity," 166.

37. Craig C. Donsanto, "Corruption of the Election Process under U.S. Federal Law," in Alvarez, Hall, and Hyde, *Election Fraud*, 34. Consistent with the overall reprioritizing of the activities of the Justice Department, in May 2002, the FBI director announced a new ranking of priorities to refocus the agency. At the top of the list were terrorism and espionage, followed by eight traditional criminal investigative functions. Among these, "combat public corruption at all levels" was second, ranked higher than the protection of civil rights, the fight against transnational and national criminal organizations, and the investigation of white-collar and violent crime. See U.S. Department of Justice, *The Internal Effects of the Federal Bureau of Investigation's Reprioritization*, Office of the Inspector General, Audit Division, Audit Report 04-39, September 2004, ii.

38. On the origins of the new initiative, see Jeffrey Toobin, "Annals of Law: Poll Positions," *New Yorker*, September 20, 2004.

39. "Newspaper: Butterfly Ballot Cost Gore White House," CNN.com Inside Politics, March 11, 2001, available at http://archives.cnn.com/2001/ALLPOLITICS/03/11/palmbeach .recount/.

40. See Allan J. Lichtman's two reports, "Report on the Racial Impact of the Rejection of Ballots Cast in the 2000 Presidential Election in the State of Florida" and "Supplemental Report on the Racial Impact of the Rejection of Ballots Cast in Florida's 2000 Presidential Election and in Response to the Statement of the Dissenting Commissioners and Report by Dr. John R. Lott," in *Voting Irregularities in Florida during the 2000 Presidential Election* (Washington, D.C.: U.S. Commission of Civil Rights, 2001), apps. 7, 10. See also Lichtman's reanalysis of the data presented to the commission confirming his original findings, "What Really Happened in Florida's 2000 Presidential Election," *Journal of Legal Studies* 32, no. 1 (2003): 221–43.

41. U.S. Department of Justice, press conference, Washington, D.C., March 7, 2001, available at http://cybersafe.gov/archive/ag/speeches/2001/0307civilrightspressconf.htm.

42. Dan Eggen and David A. Vise, "Ashcroft Takes On Voting Issues; Enforcement, Monitoring of Election Laws to Be Increased," *Washington Post*, March 8, 2001, A19. Despite the pronouncements, it is not clear that the BAVII actually was a new initiative. The name certainly was not. An identically named program was created by William French Smith, Ronald Reagan's attorney general, six weeks before the November 1984 presidential election. Like the later Ashcroft initiative, the Smith (and then Edwin Meese) initiative reflected an explicit policy change at the Justice Department that focused criminal enforcement in ways that harmed rather than protected black voting rights. See Frances Fox Piven, Lorraine C. Minnite, and Margaret Groarke, *Keeping Down the Black Vote: Race and the Demobilization of American Voters* (New York: New Press, 2009).

43. Prepared Remarks of Attorney General John Ashcroft, U.S. Department of Justice Voting Integrity Symposium, Washington D.C., October 8, 2002.

44. Craig C. Donsanto and Nancy L. Simmons, *Federal Prosecution of Election Offenses*, 7th ed. U.S. Department of Justice, Criminal Division, Public Integrity Section (Washington, D.C.: Government Printing Office, 2007), 10.

45. Federal Judicial Center, "Description," Federal Court Cases Integrated Database, 2005, conducted by the Federal Judicial Center, ICPSR04382 (Ann Arbor, Mich.: Inter-University Consortium for Political and Social Research).

46. Nor did any of these thirty-five cases involve violations of federal voting rights statutes, which would have flagged them for me in the FCCID. See appendix 4 for a fuller explanation of how I constructed the database.

47. In fiscal year 2005, there were .3 indictments for criminal election fraud per one million registered voters. In comparison, there were 41.3 criminal indictments for Social Security fraud per one million Social Security recipients, and 32.5 criminal indictments for postal, Internet, or wire fraud per one million adults in the United States. The vastly larger numbers of fraud in-

dictments for other than election fraud suggest federal law enforcement officials are capable of detecting crimes intended to be concealed.

48. Jeffrey A. Jenkins, "Partisanship and Contested Election Cases in the House of Representatives, 1789–2002," *Studies in American Political Development* 18, no. 2 (October 2004), 112–35. See also, Jenkins, "Partisanship and Contested Election Cases in the Senate, 1789–2002," *Studies in American Political Development* 19, no. 1 (April 2005), 53–74.

49. Lisa McGirr, *Suburban Warriors: The Origins of the New American Right* (Princeton: Princeton University Press, 2002).

50. Peter M. Warren, "Dornan Vows Appeal to House if Lead Is Lost," *Los Angeles Times*, Orange County Edition, November 12, 1996, A1.

51. Ibid.

52. Dexter Filkins, Peter M. Warren, and Jean O. Pasco, "Dornan, Sanchez Square Off before House Task Force," *Los Angeles Times*, Orange County Edition, April 20, 1997, A1.

53. A recount requested by Dornan reduced the final margin by five votes.

54. Nancy Cleeland, Peter M. Warren, and Esther Schrader, "Investigators Search Hermandad Offices," *Los Angeles Times*, Orange County Edition, January 15, 1997, A1.

55. See letter from Rosalyn Lever, registrar of voters, to Dornan's lawyer, William R. Hart, dated January 17, 1997, and appended to the "Minority Views" in U.S. Congress, House Committee on House Oversight, "Dismissing the Election Contest Against Loretta Sanchez: Report of the Committee on House Oversight on H.R. 355, Together with Minority Views," Task Force for the Contested Election in the 46th Congressional District of California, February 12, 1998, H. Rept. 105-416, app. A.

56. H. G. Reza, Peter Noah, and Gebe Martinez, "Many Dornan 'Suspects' Prove Legitimate Voters," *Los Angeles Times*, Orange County Edition, March 7, 1997, A1.

57. Ibid.

58. Ibid.

59. Dexter Filkins, Peter Noah, and Kimberly Sanchez, "Accusations of Double Voting Fail to Pan Out," *Los Angeles Times*, Orange County Edition, April 6, 1997, A1.

60. Ibid.

61. Privacy laws prohibit the sharing of individual data between federal agencies, except under extraordinary circumstances. In a motion by the Justice Department to quash one of Dornan's subpoenas to the INS, the department explained, "Under the Privacy Act of 1974, 5 U.S.C. 552a(b), as amended, no agency shall disclose any record which is contained in a system of records by any means of communication to any person except by the prior written consent of the individual to whom the record pertains, unless one of a series of exceptions applies. The Act applies to records maintained in a system of records by a federal agency that are retrieved by the name or other identifying information of the individual." This presented serious barriers to INS cooperation in performing the data-matching tasks requested of it by the Task Force. To get around the barriers, the Task Force subpoenaed the INS data, exercising an exemption in the Privacy Act "for either House of Congress," which allowed the Task Force to perform its own analysis of the INS data.

62. U.S. Congress, House Committee on House Oversight, "Dismissing the Election Contest."

63. Dexter Filkins, "INS Says Data Too Inaccurate for O.C. Probe," *Los Angeles Times*, Orange County Edition, May 16, 1997, A1.

64. The INS compiled the list for the Task Force under duress and expressed little confidence in the matching process. When INS Commissioner Doris Meissner conveyed the subpoenaed data to the Task Force, she wrote, "The data on these tapes do not represent the number of illegal voters or registrants in Orange County. Nor should it be inferred that any particular named individual on this tape has voted or registered to vote illegally." See Dexter Filkins, "INS Check Flags 500,000 O.C. Voters," *Los Angeles Times*, Orange County Edition, May 22, 1997, B1.

65. Peter M. Warren, "Jones: 5,087 Registrants 'Potential Noncitizens,'" *Los Angeles Times*, Orange County Edition, October 14, 1997, B1. The Task Force aided the secretary of state's investigation by signing a Memorandum of Understanding with him that permitted the INS to

verify suspect voters identified in his investigation without violating privacy restrictions. See Gebe Martinez, "Agencies Reach an Agreement on Voter Probe," *Los Angeles Times*, Orange County Edition, June 28, 1997, B1.

66. In late July 1997, Richard Gephardt, the House Minority Leader, said that the inquiry was "totally out of control. . . . It costs money to pay lawyers and defend this contested election. The ulterior motive is to keep her [Sanchez] from raising funds for her reelection campaign." He continued, "I also suspect they are trying to intimidate voting by new citizens nationwide and particularly in this district." Chairman Thomas countered that the work of the Task Force was complicated by the massive data problems and by the refusal of most of the parties subpoenaed by Dornan and the Committee to cooperate with the inquiry. Peter M. Warren, "House Inquiry Called Political Jab at Sanchez," *Los Angeles Times*, Orange County Edition, July 26, 1997, B1. Beginning in October, Gephardt introduced multiple privileged resolutions requiring the Committee to end its work. The initial resolution was defeated 222–204, and thereafter, until the Congress finally dismissed the contest in February 1998, dozens of Democrats followed with resolutions that the Republican leadership tabled. At one point, eight Democratic congresswomen pushed their way into Speaker Newt Gingrich's offices to demand an immediate halt to the fraud probe, to no avail. As the *Los Angeles Times* reported, "Behind the hoopla, the investigation churned on, with no resolution in sight." Jodi Wilgoren, "California and the West: Congresswomen Demand Speaker End Probe of Sanchez Election," *Los Angeles Times*, Home Edition, November 6, 1997, A3.

67. "Mr. Dornan's Wasteful Crusade," *New York Times*, November 16, 1997, Sec. 4, 14.

68. U.S. Congress, House Committee on House Oversight, "Dismissing the Election Contest," 38.

69. Ibid., 60.

70. California law requires that an absentee ballot be mailed back by the voter or returned to the registrar in person. If a voter cannot return his or her ballot due to illness or disability, the voter may designate a member of the immediate family (spouse, parent, sibling, children, or grandchildren) to return the ballot. Both the voter and the person designated to return the ballot must sign the outside of the absentee ballot envelope. The registrar's January 17, 1997 response to Dornan's initial allegations indicated that at that time she had uncovered only four improperly executed absentee ballots. She told the *Los Angeles Times* that another California statute permitted her to liberally construe the absentee ballot law in favor of the absentee voter and to allow her to count the sixty ballots identified by Dornan as carried in by unauthorized people. Dexter Filkins and Peter M. Warren, "News Analysis: Proof Appears Lacking; Dornan's Fervor Isn't," *Los Angeles Times*, Orange County Edition, April 18, 1997, A1.

71. Sanchez and the Minority on the Task Force argued that, because of secret balloting, House precedent requires the disputed votes to be apportioned to the contestant and contestee according to the number of legal votes cast for each candidate on a precinct-by-precinct basis. The Majority presented the argument as if all of the 748 "illegal" votes that it said it could identify were votes for Sanchez. U.S. Congress, House Committee on House Oversight, "Dismissing the Election Contest."

72. Benjamin Ginsberg and Martin Shefter, *Politics By Other Means: Politicians, Prosecutors and the Press from Watergate to Whitewater*, Rev. ed. (New York: W. W. Norton & Company, 1999), 44.

73. Cost estimates are as follows: investigation by the House Oversight Committee ($300,000), expenditures by the INS to conduct data analysis ($500,000), reimbursement to Dornan for costs associated with his contest ($320,000), and reimbursement to Sanchez for her defense ($250,000). These costs do not include the expenditures by the Orange County registrar of voters to conduct an internal review and assist the committee in its investigation, the Orange County District Attorney's Office for its criminal investigation of Hermandad Mexicana Nacionale, or the California Secretary of State's Office for its investigation of noncitizen voting in Orange County.

74. "California Won't Prosecute Noncitizen Voters," *Washington Post*, March 1, 1998, A19.

Chapter 4. Evidence from the States

1. The penal provisions of the California election code are found in Division 18, Sections 18000–18700. The EFIU does not investigate allegations of problems with local or homeowner association elections, vandalism of political signs, violations of campaign finance, or conflicts of interests on the part of public officials.

2. Telephone conversation with Paul Rutledge, California Secretary of State's Office, August 2005.

3. The California HAVA complaint form asks the complainant to provide the name of the person or organization against whom the complaint is brought, but this information was not included in the data file obtained from the EIFU.

4. The file contained a total of 2,481 records. For this analysis, I excluded 180 complaints that had not yet been resolved, resulting in a total 2,301 cases.

5. The claim that prosecutors ignore voter fraud is common. Here is a typical example from Vernon Ehlers (R-Mich.), the (former) chairman of the House Administration Committee, before a 2006 hearing on the issue of noncitizen voting: "While the successful prosecution is proof this type of election fraud is taking place, they [cases recently prosecuted by the Justice Department] represent a small fraction of a larger problem. Our criminal justice system is not well equipped to prevent election fraud. Inadequate processes make fraud difficult to detect. Even when there is evidence of a problem, the cases can be difficult to prove. Investigations are met with resistance and recalcitrant witnesses. Faced with limited resources and competing demands, prosecutors often, in fact frequently, do not pursue cases even when evidence suggests there may be a violation. Consequently, enforcement of violations after the fact is problematic and infrequent." See U.S. Congress, House, Committee on House Administration, "Hearing on 'You Don't Need Papers to Vote?': Non-Citizen Voting and ID Requirements in U.S. Elections," 109th Cong., 2nd Sess., June 22, 2006, 245–54. Of course prosecutors exercise discretion in all cases they decide to pursue. But Ehlers' assertions are not persuasive. It is reasonable to assume that most crimes are intended to be concealed, most cases brought by prosecutors are difficult to prove when the standard is a presumption of innocence; and that prosecutors always have limited resources and competing demands. These are the normal conditions faced by prosecutors and as such, fail to convince as an explanation for why there is little evidence of voter fraud in court and criminal enforcement data.

6. "Fact Sheet on the Foreign Born; Demographic and Social Characteristics: California," Migration Policy Institute, Washington, D.C., 2008; available at http://www.migrationinformation.org/datahub/state.cfm?ID=CA.

7. HAVA requires the states as a condition of receiving federal funds to establish uniform, nondiscriminatory administrative complaint procedures for any person who believes there is a violation of the HAVA election technology and administration requirements (Title III). Complaints must be in writing and notarized, and signed and sworn by the person filing the complaint.

8. A letter from Bert Black, legal adviser to the Office of the Secretary of State, explained, "Referrals by this Office would be to the county attorneys and possibly to county auditors or other election officials, who do have some investigatory duties under Minnesota voter registration law and rules. However, this office is neither the only source nor the central clearinghouse for all voter fraud issues in Minnesota. Each county auditor and each municipal clerk, may have made such referrals, and county attorneys may have preferred charges sua sponte. In order to obtain a complete picture for Minnesota, you would have to contact all possible sources." Letter from Bert Black to author, October 16, 2006.

9. The California Secretary of State's Office provides one combined election complaint form; only HAVA-related complaints must be notarized.

10. Ember Reichgott Junge, "Minnesota's New Election Complaint Procedure Takes Effect," *Minnesota Lawyer*, July 19, 2004.

11. For these five, the records released by the secretary of state consisted of copies of draft letters acknowledging their "complaint about voter fraud."

12. Amy Becker, "Strip Club Owner Jacobson Is Dancing around the Law," Associated Press State & Local Wire, January 26, 2003.

13. Steve Karnowski, "Dakota County Charges 95 People in Alleged Voter Fraud Scheme," Associated Press State & Local Wire, October 16, 2002.

14. Becker, "Strip Club Owner."

15. Jim Adams, "The Charges Laid Bare: Trying to Rig Election; 94 Accused of Helping Coates Strip Club Owner," (Minneapolis) *Star Tribune*, October 17, 2002, 1A.

16. "Nearly All of Coates Votes to Send Message to Strip Club Owner," Associated Press State & Local Wire, November 11, 2002.

17. Ibid.

18. Becker, "Strip Club Owner."

19. Jim Adams, "Array of Stories Emerging in Voter Fraud Case; Defendants Testify in a Case Connected to the Former Jake's Gentlemen's Club in Coates," (Minneapolis) *Star Tribune*, February 13, 2003, 3B.

20. Ibid. The voter registration application clearly stated that it was a felony to make a false statement on the form.

21. Ben Steverman, "Court Overturns Fine on Coates Strip Club; Jake's Has Fought Court Battles over Zoning Ordinances and Other Issues for 10 Years," (Minneapolis) *Star Tribune*, February 11, 2004, 7S.

22. Office of Dakota County Attorney James C. Backstrom, "Strip Club Owner Found Not Guilty in Voter Fraud Scheme in Dakota County," press release, March 14, 2007.

23. Bud Fitch, *Attorney General's Office Report on Investigation of Wrongful Voting at the 2004 General Election*, New Hampshire Justice Department, April 6, 2006, http://doj.nh.gov/publications/nreleases2004040606wrongful_voting.pdf.

24. Under a one-time exit clause, New Hampshire opted out of the NVRA by implementing election day registration. Free of "motor voter" rules and regulations to make voter registration more accessible by mandating state elections officials accept the use of a federal mail-in registration form or to make registration services available in state agencies, New Hampshire has some of the most restrictive voter registration rules in the country. For example, New Hampshire election law allows localities to require proof of citizenship, age, and residence for same-day registrants, and most localities do require such proof. In cases in which registrants lack proof, New Hampshire law requires them to sign affidavits attesting to their qualifications under penalty of perjury. Election officials accept mailed-in registration forms only if the prospective voter has a documented reason for why he or she cannot come to a registrar's office to fill out the form in person.

25. Fitch, *Attorney General's Office Report*, 1.

26. Ibid.

27. Ibid., 2.

28. Bill Bradbury, Oregon Secretary of State, "Testimony before the United States Senate Committee on Commerce, Science and Transportation, Hearing on Election Reform," 107th Cong., 1st Sess., March 7, 2001, 28–29.

29. Turnout increased by 160,035 votes, from 1,399,180 in 1996 to 1,559,215 in 2000. Oregon Secretary of State, "Elections History," Election Division website, http://www.sos.state.or.us/elections/other.info/stelec.htm. Berinsky, Burns, and Traugott wisely caution against the assumption that the entire increase in turnout was due to the switch to all-mail balloting, noting the greater saliency and competitiveness of the 2000 election. See Adam J. Berinsksy, Nancy Burns, and Michael W. Traugott, "Who Votes By Mail?: A Dynamic Model of the Individual-Level Consequences of Voting-by-Mail Systems," *Public Opinion Quarterly* 65, no. 2 (2001): 178–97.

30. For an empirical investigation of the initial effects of all-mail balloting on turnout in Oregon, see Priscilla L. Southwell and Justin I. Burchett, "The Effect of All-Mail Elections on Voter Turnout," *American Politics Quarterly* 28, no. 1 (2000): 72–79. Other research on the turnout question, including research on absentee balloting, which is similar to balloting in a vote-by-mail or all-mail system in the sense that some voters cast their ballots by mail, has

found mixed results. Although most studies have found a moderately positive impact of mail-voting on turnout rates, the consensus seems to be that the option to cast an early, absentee ballot (either in person or through the mail) retains habitual voters who are already a part of the electorate, rather than drawing in or adding new voters. See, for example, the work of Paul Gronke and his colleagues at the Early Voting Information Center at Reed College, including Paul Gronke, "Early Voting and American Elections," paper presented at the annual meeting of the Political Science Association, Chicago, September 2–5, 2004; Paul Gronke, "Ballot Integrity and Voting by Mail: The Oregon Experience," Report for the Commission on Federal Election Reform, Early Voting Information Center, Reed College, Portland, Ore., June 15, 2005; Paul Gronke and Peter A.M. Miller, "Voting by Mail and Turnout: A Replication and Extension," paper presented at the American Political Science Association annual meeting, Chicago, August 30, 2007.

31. Interview with John Lindback, director, Election Division, Oregon Secretary of State's Office, February 21, 2002. The earliest experiments in all-mail balloting were in referendum and initiative elections in California and Oregon localities. See David B. Magelby, "Participation in Mail Ballot Elections," *Western Political Quarterly* 40, no. 1 (1980): 79–91; Edward B. Moreton Jr., "Note: Voting By Mail," *Southern California Law Review* 58, no. 5 (1985): 1261–82; Randy H. Hamilton, "American All-Mail Balloting: A Decade's Experience," *Public Administration Review* 48, no. 5 (1988): 860–66.

32. Southwell and Burchett, "Effect of All-Mail Elections," 77n. 4. Earlier research on absentee balloting suggested it benefited Republicans for two reasons: (1) because they tend to be of higher socioeconomic status, Republican voters are more likely to possess the requisite skills needed to acquire and vote an absentee ballot, and (2) the Republican Party understands the potential bias in their favor of the absentee ballot and has been willing to mobilize their voters to use it. See J. Eric Oliver, "The Effects of Eligibility Restrictions and Party Activity on Absentee Voting and Overall Turnout," *American Journal of Political Science* 40, no. 2 (1996): 498–513.

33. Priscilla L. Southwell and Justin Burchett, "Vote By Mail in the State of Oregon," *Willamette Law Review* 34, no. 2 (1998), 346–47.

34. After ten months of deliberation, a citizens' commission unanimously recommended expanding vote-by-mail to primary elections and, by a margin of 8–2, to general elections. After a vote-by-mail bill passed the Oregon House, but failed to gain enough support in the Oregon State Senate, the League of Women Voters began the process of pressing the issue forward through a ballot initiative. Ibid., 352–53; Henry Weinstein, "Vote-by-Mail Law Upheld on Appeal," *Los Angeles Times*, July 12, 2001, A20. The text of the original initiative, Measure No. 60, can be found on the secretary of state's website, http://www.sos.state.or.us/executive/votebymail/.

35. Norman J. Ornstein, "The Dangers of Voting Outside the Booth," *New York Times*, August 3, 2001, A23. Early voters also run the risk of their votes being cast for a candidate who suddenly dies just before an election. This was the case in Minnesota in 2002, when Senator Paul Wellstone who was running for reelection was killed in a plane crash ten days before the election. The secretary of state estimated 104,000 absentee ballots had already been sent out, and after a review of the state's election laws, she concluded the counties could not mail out new ones with the name of Wellstone's replacement, former Vice President Walter Mondale, on the ballot. The Democrats filed an emergency appeal in state supreme court and got a ruling five days before the election that affected voters could request new ballots be mailed to them, but those ballots had to be returned to county officials no later than election day. There is little doubt that thousands of voters who marked their absentee ballots for Wellstone may not have had their true preferences recorded, although the actual number of votes counted for Wellstone would not have made the difference in the election. In the final count, Norm Coleman, the Republican, outpolled Mondale by 49,451 votes out of nearly 2.3 million ballots cast. Wellstone received 11,381 votes.

36. Melody Rose, "Oregon's Vote-by-Mail Fails to Fulfill Its Promise," *Oregonian*, October 20, 2002, F1; Curtis Gans, "Making It Easier Doesn't Work; No Excuse Absentee and Early

Voting Hurt Voter Turnout; Create Other Problems," press release, Center for the Study of the American Electorate, September 13, 2004; John Fortier, *Absentee and Early Voting: Trends, Promises, and Perils* (Washington, D.C.: AEI Press, 2006).

37. Deborah Phillips, "Voting by Mail Hurts Electoral Process," *Detroit News*, July 2, 1999. Phillips is the founder and president of a defunct Virginia-based organization called the Voting Integrity Project. According to Jeremy Derfner, writing for *Slate*, the Voting Integrity Project, despite its claim to nonpartisanship, was a front group for conservative Republican interests who opposed the liberalizing-voter-access features of the NVRA. See Jeremy Derfner, "The Front," *Slate*, April 4, 2000, www.slate.com/id/78548. Its lawsuit against the Oregon vote-by-mail system, *Voting Integrity Project et al. v. Keisling*, Case No. 6:98-cv-01372-AA (D. Ore., March 22, 1999) was dismissed, and later, the Ninth Circuit Court of Appeals affirmed the lower court ruling that, because Oregon did not count mail ballots before election day, the Oregon law did not violate a century-old federal statute setting election day as "the Tuesday next after the first Monday in November." See *Voting Integrity Project, et al. v. Keisling*, 259 F. 3d 1169 (9th Cir. 2001).

38. Joan L. O'Sullivan, "Voting and Nursing Home Residents: A Survey of Practices and Policies," *Journal of Health Care Law and Policy* 4, no. 2 (2002): 325–53.

39. John Fund, "Absent without Leave; Early Voting May Mean Late Election Results," *Wall Street Journal*, October 30, 2006. Fund means to impugn voters or organized groups that might intimidate voters, but does not consider the possibility that absentee ballot rules, like all balloting rules, may be manipulated by election officials and lawyers. In a provocative analysis of the overseas absentee ballots cast in the Florida 2000 election, the *New York Times* found that 680 of 2,490 ballots cast by overseas citizens unambiguously violated one or more of Florida's elections laws and should not have been counted. See David Barstow and Don Van Natta Jr., "Examining the Vote; How Bush Took Florida: Mining the Overseas Absentee Vote," *New York Times*, July 15, 2001. The *Times* obtained copies of the overseas absentee ballot envelopes, reviewed thousands of pages of documents and canvassing board meeting transcripts, and interviewed more than three hundred voters in forty-three countries. Kosuke Imai and Gary King analyzed the ballots using ecological inference and formal Bayesian model averaging techniques. They concluded that, had all the overseas ballots been treated equally and the illegal ballots discarded, Al Gore would have beaten George W. Bush by some two hundred votes. Kosuke Imai and Gary King, "Did Illegal Overseas Absentee Ballots Decide the 2000 U.S. Presidential Election?" *Perspectives on Politics* 2, no. 3 (2004), 537–49.

40. Priscilla L. Southwell, "Five Years Later: A Re-Assessment of Oregon's Vote by Mail Electoral Process," *PS* 37, no. 1 (2004), 92n. 3.

41. Don Hamilton, "How Your Vote Is Counted," *Portland Tribune*, November 2, 2004.

42. Interview with Lindback, February 21, 2002; email correspondence from Kevin Neely, public affairs and legislative assistant, Oregon Department of Justice, February 13, 2002; letter from Norma Buckno, compliance specialist, Election Division, Oregon Secretary of State's Office, October 10, 2006.

43. Letter from Buckno, October 10, 2006.

44. Oregon Secretary of State's Office, Election Division, "Ballot Signature Verification Problems—Complaints History Table," Salem, Ore., October 10, 2006; author.

45. Interview with Lindback, February 21, 2002. According to Secretary of State Bill Bradbury, Oregon is one of only two states that verifies the voter's signature. Oregon Secretary of State Bill Bradbury, speech, Public Forum on Election Integrity, Metro Council Chamber, Portland, Ore., February 18, 2005. Elections workers are not expected to be handwriting experts, but they do complete a course in signature forgery and are trained by the same organization that trains the Oregon State Police in signature recognition. Hamilton, "How Your Vote Is Counted."

46. Only two of those cases (Hosier and Finch) were found to be violations (note that both are included in the list of criminally prosecuted cases in table A6.1).

47. Interview with Lindback, February 21, 2002.

Chapter 5. Would the Rational Voter Commit Fraud?

1. Anthony Downs, *An Economic Theory of Democracy* (New York: Addison-Wesley, 1957).

2. William H. Riker and Peter C. Ordeshook, "A Theory of the Calculus of Voting," *American Political Science Review* 62, no. 1 (1970): 25–42; Richard Brody, "The Puzzle of Political Participation in America," in *The New American Political System,* ed. Anthony King, 287–324 (Washington, D.C.: American Enterprise Institute for Public Policy Research, 1978).

3. Andrew Gelman, Gary King, and W. John Boscardin, "Estimating the Probability of Events That Have Never Occurred: When Is Your Vote Decisive?" *Journal of the American Statistical Association* 93, no. 441 (1998): 1–9.

4. Because the theory expects voter abstention, the fact that many people vote requires explanation. Some people call this problem "the paradox of voting," but Rebecca B. Morton argues persuasively that it should be called the "the paradox of not voting" because it is the act of not voting that the models expect. See Rebecca B. Morton, "Groups in Rational Turnout Models," *American Journal of Political Science* 35, no. 3 (1991): 758–76; Rebecca B. Morton, *Analyzing Elections* (W. W. Norton & Company, 2006), 24–45.

5. An inexhaustive but critical selection from this literature includes John C. Harsanyi, "Rational-Choice Models of Political Behavior vs. Functionalist and Conformist Theories," *World Politics* 21, no.4 (1969): 513–29; Yoram Barzel and Eugene Silberberg, "Is the Act of Voting Rational?" *Public Choice* 16 (Fall 1973): 51–58; John A. Ferejohn and Morris P. Fiorina, "The Paradox of Not Voting: A Decision Theoretic Analysis," *American Political Science Review* 68, no. 2 (1974): 525–46; Thomas R. Palfrey and Howard Rosenthal, "Voter Participation and Strategic Uncertainty," *American Political Science Review* 79, no. 1 (1985): 62–78; Morton, "Groups in Rational Turnout Models"; John A. Aldrich, "Rational Choice and Turnout," *American Journal of Political Science* 37, no. 1 (1993): 246–78; Bernard Grofman, ed., *Information, Participation, and Choice: An Economic Theory of Democracy in Perspective* (Ann Arbor: University of Michigan Press, 1993); Donald P. Green and Ian Shapiro, *Pathologies of Rational Choice Theory: A Critique of Applications in Political Science* (New Haven: Yale University Press, 1994); Andre Blais, *To Vote or Not To Vote: The Merits and Limits of Rational Choice Theory* (Pittsburgh: University of Pittsburgh Press, 2000).

6. Riker and Ordeshook, "Theory of the Calculus of Voting."

7. Blais, *To Vote or Not To Vote,* 3–4.

8. Morton, "Groups in Rational Turnout Models;" Rebecca Morton, "A Group Majority Voting Model of Public Good Provision," *Social Choice and Welfare* 4, no. 2 (1987): 117–31; Carole J. Uhlaner, "Rational Turnout: The Neglected Role of Groups," *American Journal of Political Science* 33, no. 2 (1989): 390–422.

9. The calculation of the investment benefit could be partitioned for vote selling to reflect the various forms that the benefit takes when vote selling is involved: utility and direct monetary or material compensation (i.e., a jug of rum in George Washington's day); see Tracy Campbell, *Deliver the Vote: A History of Election Fraud, An American Political Tradition—1742-2004* (New York: Carroll & Graf Publishers, 2005), 4–5. To simplify the discussion here, I use a unified concept for the consumption benefits enjoyed by those engaging in the different forms of illegal voting.

10. For a prominent assertion of this kind see chapter 7 and the discussion of the opinion of Judge Richard Posner, writing for the majority in *Crawford v. Marion County Election Board,* 472 F.3d 436 (7th Cir. 2007).

11. U.S. Congress, Senate Republican Policy Committee, "Putting an End to Voter Fraud," February 15, 2005.

12. See IRS filing, Return of Organization Exempt From Income Tax (Form 990) for American Center for Voting Rights, 2005 [author files].

Chapter 6. The Political Work of Fraud Allegations

1. Peter H. Argesinger, *Structure, Process, and Party: Essays in American Political History* (Armonk, N.Y.: M. E. Sharpe, 1992), 105 (emphasis added).

2. See Gary W. Cox and J. Morgan Kousser, "Turnout and Rural Corruption: New York as a Test Case," *American Journal of Political Science* 25, no. 4 (1981): 646–63.

3. Frances Fox Piven, Lorraine C. Minnite, and Margaret Groarke, *Keeping Down the Black Vote: Race and the Demobilization of American Voters* (New York: New Press, 2009).

4. *Harper v. Virginia Board of Elections*, 383 U.S. 663 (1966), outlawed the poll tax in state and local elections.

5. C. Vann Woodward coined the term *Second Reconstruction* in *The Future of the Past* (New York: Oxford University Press, 1989). See also Richard M. Valelly, *The Two Reconstructions: The Struggle of Black Enfranchisement* (Chicago: University of Chicago Press, 2004; J. Morgan Kousser, *Colorblind Injustice: Minority Voting Rights and the Undoing of the Second Reconstruction* (Chapel Hill: University of North Carolina Press, 1999), esp. chap. 1.

6. Donald Green, Bradley Palmquist, and Eric Schickler, *Partisan Hearts and Minds: Political Parties and the Social Identities of Voters* (New Haven: Yale University Press, 2002), 8. In elaborating the idea that parties are images in the public or the voter's mind, this work engages, critiques, expands on, and ultimately builds on the insights of Angus Campbell, Philip E. Converse, Warren E. Miller, and Donald E. Stokes, *The American Voter* (New York: John Wiley, 1960), as well as on subsequent work on party identification in the social-psychological tradition.

7. Richard L. McCormick, "The Party Period and Public Policy: An Exploratory Hypothesis," *Journal of American History* 66, no. 2 (1979): 279–98. McCormick adopts part of Burnham's thesis explaining the precipitous decline of voter turnout at the turn of the twentieth century, and argues for the disfranchising effects of election reform on Southern blacks and poor whites and the new urban immigrants, whom he calls "discordant social groups."

8. Claude Lévi-Strauss, *Myth and Meaning: Cracking the Code of Culture* (New York: Schocken Books, 1995).

9. Wendy Doniger, "Foreword," in ibid., viii–ix.

10. Alexander Keyssar, *The Right to Vote: The Contested History of Democracy in the United States* (New York: Basic Books, 2000), xv–xvi

11. Bruce Lincoln, *Theorizing Myth: Narrative, Ideology and Scholarship* (Chicago: University of Chicago Press, 1999), 147.

12. Transcript of oral argument, *Bush v. Gore*, 531 U.S. 98 (2000), available at http://election2000.stanford.edu/949trans.pdf. See also Mark Danner, "The Road to Illegitimacy," *New York Review of Books,* February 22, 2001.

13. At the time, under Section 102.166 (the Florida law governing recounts) canvassing boards were required to determine (or as James Baker, counsel to the Bush-Cheney campaign put it "divine") the intent of the voter when the counters could not do so during their inspection of the ballots.

14. Florida law states, "No vote shall be declared invalid or void if there is a clear indication of the intent of the voter. . . ." Fla. Stat. Ann. Sec 101.5614[5]. "Florida statutory law cannot reasonably be thought to require counting of improperly marked ballots," wrote Rehnquist. See Lawrence H. Tribe, "Freeing EROG v. HSUB from It's Hall of Mirrors," in *A Badly Flawed Election: Debating Bush v. Gore, the Supreme Court and American Democracy, ed.* Ronald Dworkin (New York: New Press, 2002), 724. Tribe sees Rehnquist's commentary as a reflection of the fear on the part of elites that democracy breeds disorder (123).

15. The staff attorneys' recommendation to deny approval of the change was immediately overridden by the Bush administration attorney general.

16. "Section 5 Recommendation Memorandum: August 25, 2005." See Burmeister's subsequent disavowal of these comments, "Burmeister and Richardson Comments on AJC Voter ID Article," Theweekly.com, November 18, 2005, http://www.theweekly.com/news/2005/November/18/Burmeister_Richardson.html. See also the Justice Department statement to the *Wash-*

ington Post that the August 25, 2005, memorandum "was an early draft . . . [that] does not represent the quality of factual and legal analysis that the Justice Department expects in the final product." The Justice Department precleared HB 244 on August 26, 2005; see Dan Eggen, "Justice Plays Down Memo Critical of Ga. Voter ID Plan," *Washington Post,* November 18, 2005.

17. I am aware of only one case of voter impersonation during the period I investigated, that of Mark Lacasse in New Hampshire in 2000 (see chap. 4).

18. I leave for another day the testing for a relationship between political culture and voter fraud politics, but it is worth pointing out that each of the four states is categorized by Daniel Elazar as exhibiting different political cultures. Elazar classified all fifty states into three major political cultures: moralistic, individualistic, and traditionalistic. Moralistic political cultures are characterized by high levels of political participation, competitive party systems, strong merit-based personnel systems, and innovative administrative practices. Individualistic political cultures have strong political parties and centralized bureaucracies. Traditionalistic political cultures are conservative, low tax and spend, politically uncompetitive, and administratively handicapped compared to moralistic states. Elazar noted that all states have some combination of traits across the three ideal groups; he classified them according to which set of traits dominated the state's culture. To capture mixed qualities, he further divided the three main groups into hybrid categories. Thus, Wisconsin and Washington are both moralistic states, but Washington has a moralistic/individualistic culture. Missouri is classified as an individualistic state, whereas Florida is traditionalistic. See Daniel J. Elazar, *American Federalism: A View from the States*, 3rd ed. (New York: Harper & Row, 1984), 134–37.

19. The Missouri law was found in violation of the state constitution by the Missouri Supreme Court. See *Weinshenck v. State of Missouri*, 203 S.W.3d 201, 212 (Mo. banc 2006).

20. In highlighting an early case of what I call voter fraud politics, I do not mean to imply that ACORN itself has not made mistakes or been free of management problems; nor do I want to imply that the convictions for voter registration fraud of a handful of canvassers hired by ACORN are a trivial matter. The full story of the ACORN wars, however, has yet to be told.

21. Peter Dreier, "Community Organizing, ACORN, and Progressive Politics in America," in *The People Shall Rule: ACORN, Community Organizing, and the Struggle for Economic Justice*, ed. Robert Fisher (Nashville: Vanderbilt University Press, 2009), 12.

22. The congressional investigation into the scandal over the firing of nine U.S. Attorneys in 2006 produced an ample record showing that state GOP operatives compiled packets of news stories covering their claims that fraud was being committed which they then presented as evidence that fraud was being committed. For an analysis of the misuse of media reports as evidence of fraud see chapter 1; for an analysis of how the media set the agenda for the public debate about ACORN and voter fraud, see Peter Dreier and Christopher R. Martin, "Manipulating the Public Agenda: Why ACORN Was in the News, and What the News Got Wrong," September 2009, available at http://www.uni.edu/martinc/acornstudy.pdf.

23. "ACORN Defeats Anti-Voter Legal Attacks; Group's Voter Registration Efforts Vindicated as Baseless Lawsuits Collapse," Common Dreams Progressive Newswire, December 14, 2005; Joni James, "Voter Fraud Charges Collapse," *St. Petersburg Times*, December 15, 2005.

24. Telephone interview with Brian Mellor, General Counsel, Project Vote, April 13, 2006.

25. Quoting Mike Flynn, director of Legislative Affairs for the Employment Policies Institute; see Employment Policies Institute, "ACORN's Voter Fraud in Ohio Is Part of Larger Pattern," press release, August 11, 2006. See also Meghan Clyne, "ACORN and the Money Tree," *National Review Online*, October 31, 2004; American Center for Voting Rights, "Vote Fraud, Intimidation and Suppression in the 2004 Presidential Election," ACVR Legislative Fund Report, August 2, 2005, 41–44.

26. Nothing in the Florida election code prohibits private third-party voter registration organizations from photocopying the voter registration applications they collect before submitting them to local elections officials.

27. An investigation by the Florida Department of Law Enforcement also found no evidence of criminal activity at ACORN. James, "Voter Fraud Charges Collapse."

28. Employment Policies Institute, *Rotten ACORN: America's Bad Seed*, July 2006, 18–19; available at http://www.epionline.org/study_detail.cfm?sid=113. A *pattern and practice* of wrong-doing evokes conspiracy and as a legal term refers to the crime of racketeering.

29. Search conducted by author using Google, April 5, 2009.

30. The challenged law would have imposed a civil fine of $250 for each voter registration application submitted more than ten days after it was collected, a $500 fine for each application submitted after any voter registration deadline, and a $5,000 fine for each application that a private voter registration group failed to submit. The law also would have held the organization; the individual volunteer, member, or employee; the group's registered agent; and any person responsible for the day-to-day operation of the organization, including officers and board members, personally, jointly, and severally responsible. If the League's office was damaged by a hurricane or a flood, and just sixteen registration applications were lost, at $5,000 apiece the total fine would have wiped out the entire annual budget of $80,000. See *League of Women Voters, et al. v. Sue M. Cobb, et al.*, "Complaint for Declaratory and Injunctive Relief," U.S. District Court for the Southern District of Florida, Case No. 06-21265-civ-Jordan, May 18, 2006, 2.

31. U.S. District Court, Southern District of Florida, *League of Women Voters of Florida v. Cobb*, 447 F. Supp. 2d 1314 (S.D. Fla. 2006). After the courts voided the law, Florida lawmakers passed an amended version that made only minor changes and kept in place rules requiring private voter registration groups to deliver applications within ten days after they are collected. Failure to do so can result in fines. The state was sued again by the League of Women Voters and labor organizations (represented by the Brennan Center for Justice at New York University School of Law) after the amended law received preclearance by the U.S. Justice Department. The federal court decision in that case, *League of Women Voters of Florida v. Browning*, although dismissing plaintiff's request for a temporary restraining order, imposed tighter limits on the fines that could be levied on voter registration groups. Order, U.S., Case No. 08-21243-civ-Altonaga/ Brown (S.D. Fla. 2008). The secretary of state agreed not to enforce the law until the administrative rulemaking process was complete, and plaintiffs concluded they could continue their voter registration activities without fear of being subject to excessive penalties. See the Brennan Center website for more details and court filings, http://www.brennancenter.org/content/ resource/league_of_women_voters_of_florida_v_cobb/.

32. Matt Blunt, *Mandate For Reform: Election Turmoil in St. Louis, November 7, 2000*, Office of Missouri Secretary of State, Jefferson City, July 24, 2001, 39–46 (hereafter Blunt Report).

33. For an excellent example of how cultural myth can substitute for rational explanation, see "Politically Active after Death," in John Fund, *Stealing Elections: How Voter Fraud Threatens Our Democracy* (San Francisco: Encounter Books, 2004), chap. 4.

34. For a tale of Depression-era ballot tampering linked to public corruption and waterfront development schemes in St. Louis, see "The Real Foundations of the Gateway Arch," in Tracy Campbell, *Deliver the Vote: A History of Election Fraud, An American Political Tradition, 1742–2004* (New York: Basic Books, 2005), chap. 7. See also, Bruce Rushton, "Dead Man Voting," *Riverfront Times*, April 24, 2002. For Senator Bond's remarks, see Carolyn Tuft, "Bond Wants Federal Investigation of Problems at City Polls; He Accuses Democrats of 'Criminal Enterprise' in Keeping Polls Open Late; Democrats Criticize Election Board," *St. Louis Post-Dispatch*, November 10, 2000, A1. According to the *Riverfront Times*, "In his letters to . . . two federal agencies, Bond wrote . . . of a 'deliberate scheme' planned in advance so unregistered voters could vote illegally: 'There is reason to believe that collusion existed to commit voter fraud and voter fraud occurred on a wide scale throughout the city of St. Louis.'" See Safir Ahmed, "Slimin' the City: When It Comes to Election Day Problems in St. Louis, the Politicians' Rhetoric Doesn't Match the Reality," *Riverfront Times*, November 15, 2000.

35. *U.S. v. Board of Election Commissioners for the City of St. Louis*, Stipulation of Facts and Consent Order, Civil Action No. 4:026V001235 CEJ (E.D. Mo. 2002), 5 (hereafter St. Louis Election Board Consent Order).

36. Karen Branch-Brioso and Doug Moore, "Board Denied Voters' Rights, U.S. Says: Election Officials Here Say They've Already Taken Steps to Correct Deficiencies from 2000," *St. Louis Post-Dispatch*, May 23, 2002, C1.

37. Office of Missouri State Auditor, "Board of Election Commissioners, City of St. Louis, Missouri," Report no. 2004-40, Office of Missouri State Auditor, Jefferson City, May 26, 2004, 10 (hereafter Mo. State Auditor's Report).

38. Section 8(d)(2) of 42 U.S.C. 1973gg-6(d). St. Louis Election Board Consent Order, 3.

39. Ibid., 4.

40. In 1996, 122,003 votes were cast in the general election in the City of St. Louis. In 2002, according to records from the Federal Election Commission, both nationwide and for the state of Missouri, 12 percent of all voters on the rolls were classified as "inactive," compared to 22 percent in the City of St. Louis. Mo. State Auditor's Report, 15.

41. St. Louis Election Board Consent Order, 4.

42. David Scott, "Ashcroft, Talent Decide against Pursuing St. Louis Voter Fraud Claims," Associated Press, November 8, 2000.

43. The state auditor found that the St. Louis Election Board frequently failed to secure the minimum number of precinct-level election judges as required by state law. Section 115.081, RSMo 2000, mandates four election judges, two from each major political party, for each polling place at each primary and general election, or about 1,600 election judges per major election. The auditor found that the board has not been able to attract more than 1,200 such judges in recent elections. Mo. State Auditor's Report, 24.

44. Scott, "Ashcroft, Talent Decide"; see also, Ahmed, "Slimin' the City."

45. Blunt Report, 21–35.

46. Dirk Johnson, "The 2000 Elections: The Swing States; Judge Delays Closing of Polls in St. Louis Amid Unexpectedly Heavy Turnout," *New York Times*, November 8, 2000, B10.

47. Ibid., 36.

48. Jo Mannies and Jennifer LaFleur, "City Mislabeled Dozens as Voting from Vacant Lots; Property Records Appear to Be in Error, Survey Finds; Just 14 Ballots Are Found Suspect," *St. Louis Post-Dispatch*, November 5, 2001, A1.

49. Blunt Report, 24n. 63.

50. *U.S. v. Board of Election Commissioners for the City of St. Louis, et al.*, Civil Action No. 4:026V001235 CEJ (E.D. Mo. 2002).

51. As counsel for co-plaintiff Bush-Cheney 2000, Inc. in the appeals court litigation brought on behalf of the St. Louis Board of Election Commissioners that invalidated Judge Baker's order to keep the polls open in St. Louis on election night (see *Missouri v. Baker* 34 S.W. 3d 410; 2000 Mo. App.), Hearne should have been aware of the Justice Department's later findings of illegal purging and its consent decree with the board. For citations to Hearne's testimony, see chap. 1, n.37.

51. There is evidence suggesting restrictive photo identification requirements place a disproportionate burden on low-income people and minorities. See Brennan Center for Justice at NYU School of Law and Spencer Overton, on behalf of the National Network on State Election Reform, "Response to the Report of the 2005 Commission on Federal Election Reform," 2005, available at http://www.carterbakerdissent.com. Overton served as a commissioner on the 2005 Commission on Federal Election Reform. But for the methodological difficulties in statistical modeling of voter identification effects on turnout, see Robert S. Erikson and Lorraine C. Minnite, "Modeling Problems in the Voter ID-Voter Turnout Debate," *Election Law Journal* 8, no. 2 (2009): 85–101.

52. Tom Kertscher, "Deputy Registrar May Have Violated State Election Law; He Says He Didn't Witness Forms He Signed," *Milwaukee Journal Sentinel*, October 1, 2004, B1.

53. Jenny Price, "Voter Registration Efforts Ramped Up in Wisconsin," Associated Press State & Local Wire, October 10, 2004. Because voters can register to vote on election day, preelection voter registration drives have been less common in Wisconsin than elsewhere.

54. Price, "Voter Registration Efforts."

55. Dave Umhoefer and Greg J. Borowski, "City, County Spar over Ballot Supply; Walker Cites Fraud Concerns; Barrett Cries Foul," *Milwaukee Journal Sentinel*, October 13, 2004, A1; Greg J. Borowski and Dave Umhoefer, "Walker-Barrett Ballot Dispute Heats Up More; County, City Accuse the Other of Trying to Make Election Day Controversy," *Milwaukee Journal Sentinel*, October 14, 2004, B1.

56. "Governor Sends Election Board into Milwaukee Ballot Fray," *Capital Times*, October 15, 2004, 4A; Dave Umhoefer and Steve Schultze, "Doyle Joins Rift over Ballot Supply; Governor Seeks State Inquiry; After Protest, Walker Agrees to Review City's Request," *Milwaukee Journal Sentinel*, October 15, 2004, A1.

57. Greg J. Borowski, "665,000 Unused Ballots Returned; Review Finds City's Original Allotment Would Have Been Sufficient," *Milwaukee Journal Sentinel*, November 25, 2004, B1.

58. Greg J. Borowski, "GOP Fails to Get 5,619 Names Removed from Voting Lists: City Commission Says Party Didn't Prove Case; Challenges Could Move to Polling Places," *Milwaukee Journal Sentinel*, October 29, 2004, A1.

59. Greg J. Borowski, "Vote Inquiry Sharpens Focus; Prosecutors Find Many Disputed Addresses Exist," *Milwaukee Journal Sentinel*, October 30, 2004, A1.

60. Greg J. Borowski, "Election 2004: GOP Demands IDs of 37,000 in City; City Attorney Calls New List of Bad Addresses 'Purely Political,'" *Milwaukee Journal Sentinel*, October 31, 2004, A1.

61. Ibid.

62. "Milwaukee Vote Deal Reached on Dubious Addresses," *Capital Times*, November 1, 2004, 5A.

63. Wisconsin allows election day registration. Same-day registration rules require new registrants to show some form of proof of residency; another registered voter may vouch for those lacking proof.

64. Greg J. Borowski, "Over 1,200 Voters Addresses Found Invalid; Some Mistakes Easily Explained, but Milwaukee Flaws Raise Concerns about Shoddy Record Keeping, Possible Fraud," *Milwaukee Journal Sentinel*, January 25, 2005, A1; Greg J. Borowski, "Fraud or Bumbling, Voter Problems Still Unnerving to Public," *Milwaukee Journal Sentinel*, January 30, 2005, A1.

65. "Widen Election Day Focus" [Editorial], *Milwaukee Journal Sentinel*, January 26, 2005, A14.

66. Of the 105 irregularities, 98 were identified as "felons who may have voted." See Wisconsin State Legislative Audit Bureau, "An Evaluation: Voter Registration," Report 05-12, Madison, September 16, 2005, 6.

67. "Felony Disfranchisement in Wisconsin," American Civil Liberties Union, n.d., available at http://www.aclu.org/pdfs/votingrights/wi_flyer.pdf.

68. Wis. Stats. 6.03.1b; disqualified from voting is "any person convicted of treason, felony or bribery, unless the person's right to vote is restored through a pardon or under s.304.078(3)."

69. "Felony Disfranchisement in Wisconsin."

70. Until recently, the Wisconsin voter registration application form did not clearly indicate that felons on probation or parole were ineligible to vote.

71. In an interview with the author on June 22, 2007, Steven Biskupic, the U.S. attorney for the Eastern District of Wisconsin which includes Milwaukee, offered a different explanation for why his district had more voter fraud indictments than almost any other. Biskupic said that he formed the federal-local task force in January 2005 at the request of E. Michael McCann, the Milwaukee district attorney after McCann failed to win convictions of the handful of people prosecuted for illegal felon voting following the 2000 election. Interview with Steven Biskupic, U.S. Courthouse, Milwaukee, Wisconsin, June 22, 2007. See also, Daniel Bice, "Biskupic Did Pursue Voter Fraud, Futilely," *Milwaukee Journal Sentinel JSOnline*, April 12, 2007, available at http://www.jsonline.com/news/wisconsin/29358809.html.

72. Interview with Craig Donsanto, director, Elections Crimes Branch, Public Integrity Section, U.S. Justice Department, January 13, 2006, in U.S. Elections Assistance Commission, "EAC Summary of Expert Interviews for Voting Fraud-Voter Intimidation Research," 2–4, available at http://www.eac.gov/program-areas/research-resources-and-reports/copy_of_docs/2006-election-crimes-appendix-3/attachment_download/file.

73. Ibid., 4.

74. The names have been changed to protect the privacy of those interviewed. In addition to the ten people charged with illegal felon voting, four more were charged with voting twice. All four of the latter group were acquitted or had their cases dismissed.

75. I also interviewed Nancy Joseph, the attorney who represented both Smalls and Robinson. Telephone interview with Nancy Joseph, April 4, 2007; Interview with Nancy Joseph, Milwaukee, Wis., June 22, 2007.

76. Gina Barton, "A Felon but Not a Fraud: No Charges for Voter with Prison I.D.," *Milwaukee Journal Sentinel*, March 17, 2006.

77. Telephone Interview with Tom Erickson, April 4, 2007. See also, Gregory Stanford, "Election Fraud Witch Hunt Disillusions Young Voter," *Milwaukee Journal Sentinel*, January 7, 2006.

78. In 2008, the conviction rate in federal cases relying on the "honest services" clause 18 U.S. 1346, an anti-fraud statute that was used in election fraud cases until 2006, was 92 percent. Lynne Marek, "DOJ May Rein in Use of 'Honest Services' Statute; Fraud Statute Up for Review Was Key to Many Convictions," *National Law Journal*, June 15, 2009; for a discussion of the "honest services" anti-fraud statute, see Craig C. Donsanto and Nancy L. Simmons, *Federal Prosecution of Election Offenses*, 7th ed., U.S. Department of Justice, Criminal Division, Public Integrity Section (Washington, D.C.: Government Printing Office, 2007), 77–78.

79. The final margin of victory of Christine Gregoire, the Democratic winner, was less than one-half of one one-thousandths of a point, or 0.0045 percentage points, the closest gubernatorial election in U.S. history. Gregoire finished with 1,373,361 votes (48.8730 percent) compared to her Republican opponent, Dino Rossi who received 1,373,228 votes (48.8684 percent).

80. A week before the election, Gregoire held a double-digit lead in the polls. Angela Galloway, "Governor's Race So Close, No Winner Likely for Days," *Seattle Post-Intelligencer*, November 4, 2004, A1.

81. W. Frank Mullen, John C. Pierce, Charles H. Sheldon, and Thor Swanson, eds., *The Government and Politics of Washington State* (Pullman: Washington State University Press, 1978).

82. Jim Camden, "Contest Hinges on Late Count; Statewide Provisional Ballots Still Remain to be Tabulated," (Spokane) *Spokesman Review*, November 4, 2004, 1.

83. Washington is one of only three states that allow absentee ballots to be postmarked as late as election day (the other states are Alaska and West Virginia). Mail-in ballots so postmarked may be received up to ten days after the election. U.S. General Accounting Office, "Elections: Perspectives on Activities and Challenges Across the Nation," Report to Congressional Requesters, GAO-02-3, October 2001, app. V, 390.

84. *Washington State Democratic Central Committee v. King County Records, Elections and Licensing Services Division*, Case No. 04-2-36048-0SEA (W.S.C., November 16, 2004). See Peggy Andersen, "Democrats Sue King County over Provisional Ballots," Associated Press State & Local Wire, November 12, 2004; Angela Galloway, "King County Faces Election Lawsuit; Democrats Object to Ballot Handling in Governor's Race," *Seattle Post-Intelligencer*, November 12, 2004, A1; Keith Ervin, "Governor Race May End Up in Court," *Seattle Times*, November 12, 2004.

85. King County issued approximately 31,700 provisional ballots, up from 17,081 issued in 2000 and more than three times more than any other county. Kenneth P. Vogel, "Vote Analysis Forecasts a Close Win for Rossi," (Tacoma) *News Tribune*, November 12, 2004, A01. Judge Dean Lum was persuaded by the Democrats' evidence that twenty-three of the thirty-nine Washington counties said they were notifying by phone or mail voters whose provisional ballots had problems and that twenty-four counties said they were making lists of problem provisional voters available to the public. Andersen, "Democrats Sue King County." According to the U.S. Elections Commission, this case was the first in the nation to test the HAVA provisional balloting rules. Kenneth P. Vogel, "Eyes on State Voting Law Case," (Tacoma) *News Tribune*, November 16, 2004, B01.

86. Peggy Andersen, "Judge Sides with Democrats in Ballot Dispute," Associated Press State & Local Wire, November 12, 2004; Jim Camden and Richard Roesler, "Rossi Leads by 19 Votes in Governor's Contest; Sides Scramble to Validate Ballots by Deadline," (Spokane) *Spokesman Review*, November 17, 2004, A1.

87. Quoted in Susan Gilmore, Andrew Garber, and Ralph Thomas, "Rossi Leading; Gregoire Allies Win in Court," *Seattle Times*, November 13, 2004, available at http://seattletimes.nwsource.com/html/localnews/2002089896_gov13m.html.

88. Quoted in Galloway, "King County Faces Election Lawsuit," A1.

89. Judge Lum's second memorandum opinion and order in this case noted that the plaintiff Washington State Democratic Central Committee "represented to the Court that its volunteers would try to contact *every* provisional voter on the list" (emphasis added). The plaintiff, however, did not say it would assist every voter on the list in correcting his or her provisional ballot.

90. Richard Roesler, "Gregoire Retakes Lead for Governor; Democrat Leads by 158 Votes with 22,000 Ballots to be Tallied," (Spokane) *Spokesman Review*, November 16, 2004.

91. Ultimately, the *Seattle Times* reported that the Democrats produced affidavits from 654 of the 929 problem provisional ballot voters that the Republicans countered with approximately 300 from Rossi voters, including 100 in King County. Ralph Thomas, Andrew Garber, Keith Ervin, Jim Brunner, and Mike Lindblom, "It's Rossi by 261; Recount Is Next," *Seattle Times*, November 18, 2004, A1.

92. Rebecca Cook, "Gregoire Edges Ahead, Boosted by King County," Associated Press State & Local Wire, November 15, 2004.

93. Stefan Sharkansky, "The 10,000 Magical Mystery Ballots," Sound Politics Blog, November 16, 2004, available at http://www.soundpolitics.com.

94. Rebecca Cook, "Bloggers Obsessively Track Votes in Governor's Race," Associated Press State & Local Wire, November 12, 2004.

95. In the week following the election, as the smaller counties began reporting their tallies and the number of uncounted ballots could be estimated, Sharkansky predicted a Rossi victory, updating his blog nine times in a single day. See the archives at http://www.soundpolitics.com, specifically, Stefan Sharkansky, "Still Calling the Governor's Race for Dino Ross," "Rossi Is Now in the Lead," and "Absentees Boost Rossi Gov. Bid," Sound Politics Blog, November 9, 2004. For a profile of Sharkansky, see Robert L. Jamieson Jr., "'The Shark' Uses his Blog to Take Bite out of Local Politics," *Seattle Post-Intelligencer*, January 12, 2005.

96. Stefan Sharkansky, "Vote Count Madness," Comment #1 by Jim King, Sound Politics Blog, November 15, 2004, available at http://www.soundpolitics.com.

97. Stefan Sharkansky, "Wednesday Vote Count," Sound Politics Blog, November 17, 2004, available at http://www.soundpolitics.com. The day before, Sharkansky included this report from a friend observing the King County count: "one explanation of the additional 10,000 count is gross mis-management of the County Elections office. Another . . . is that they were telling a lie. . . . I'd be very reluctant to allege explicitly organized fraud on the part of the election officials. On the other hand, this and other reports suggest that the process is sufficiently sloppy and disorganized to permit all kinds of fraudulent over-voting: individuals who vote multiple times, ballots of dubious validity that are aggressively accepted, ballots that are doubly counted, non-citizens who vote, etc. I have no specific evidence of any of these. But the sudden appearance of the 10,000 magical mystery ballots suggests a lack of proper oversight and controls that would inhibit the ordinary cheating that would tend to favor Democrats in King County." Sharkansky, "10,000 Magical Mystery Ballots."

98. When Grays Harbor County discovered an error in its computer calculations of the running totals—several batches of ballots appeared to have been loaded into the system twice—it decided to recount the county ballots, even though the ballots had not been mis-scanned. Elections officials could have simply fixed the program and recounted the totals. Instead, to enhance public confidence, they actually recounted the ballots, delaying their report until the last day of the deadline for counties to submit their certified results to the secretary of state. See Rebecca Cook, "Governor's Race: Rossi Back in Lead, Barely," Associated Press State & Local Wire, November 16, 2004.

99. Sharkansky reported more than 35,000 hits to his blog that day. See Stefan Sharkansky, "Gubernatorial Vote Count Post-Mortem," Sound Politics Blog, November 17, 2004, available at http://www.soundpolitics.com.

100. See Cook, "Bloggers Obsessively Track Votes." In reporting on the election, Goddard, whose blog was called "The Flag of the World" (http://www.timothygoddard.com/blog), often cross-posted on the Sound Politics Blog, where other bloggers with their own venues, such as Jim Miller, Brian Crouch, and Matt Rosenberg, also found a second home.

101. Stefan Sharkansky, "Voting Monkey Business," Sound Politics Blog, November 20, 2004, available at http://www.soundpolitics.com.

102. RCW 29A.64.021.

103. WAC 434-261-070.

104. Quoted in Steve Miletich and Brier Dudley, "GOP Files Suit over Recount; Governor's Race—King County Workers' Methods Called Improper," *Seattle Times*, November 21, 2004, B1.

105. WAC 434-261-120.

106. See comments by Mark Braden, Washington State Republican Party attorney, Transcript, Motion for Temporary Restraining Order before the Honorable Marsha J. Pechman (heard via conference call in Judge Pechman's Chambers), *Washington State Republican Party et al. v. Sam Reed, et al.*, Case No. C04-2350-RSM (W.D. WA, November 21, 2004), 6.

107. Complaint for Declaratory and Injunctive Relief, *Washington State Republican Party et al. v. Sam Reed, et al.*, U.S. District Court, Western District of Washington at Seattle, No. C04-2350-RSM (W.D. WA, November 20, 2004), 1–2. Blogger Sharkansky referred to these machine-rejected ballots as "haruspex" ballots—a *haruspex* was a diviner in ancient Rome who based his predictions on the entrails of sacrificial animals. Stefan Sharkansky, "Recount Follies," Sound Politics Blog, November 23, 2004, available at http://www.sound politics.com.

108. Quoted in Miletich and Dudley, "GOP Files Suit over Recount," B1.

109. Elizabeth M. Gillespie, "GOP Gets Court Date in Recount Lawsuit," Associated Press State & Local Wire, November 22, 2004. Attorneys for state and county elections officials argued that administrative rules required that "enhanced" or duplicated ballots be assigned unique control numbers that tied them back to the original ballots in the event that they needed to be retrieved later. They assured the court that the rules were uniform across the state and being followed in King County.

110. Transcript, Motion for Temporary Restraining Order Before the Honorable Marsha J. Pechman (heard via conference call in Judge Pechman's Chambers), *Washington State Republican Party et al. v. Sam Reed, et al.* See also, Lynn Thompson, "Judge Says No to GOP, Won't Halt Recount," *Seattle Times*, November 22, 2004, B1.

111. Chris McGann, "Rossi Picks Up Votes in Recount but Gregoire Hopes to Catch Up after King County Submits Total," *Seattle Post-Intelligencer*, November 23, 2004, B1.

112. Ralph Thomas, "All Eyes on State Recount," *Seattle Times*, November 23, 2004.

113. Quoted in Elizabeth Gillespie, "Judge Denies Request That Some King County Ballots Not Be Counted," Associated Press State & Local Wire, November 21, 2004.

114. Ibid. For details, see the November 21, 2004, Republican Party press release in response to Judge Pechman's order denying its request for a temporary restraining order, posted by Stefan Sharkansky, "Serious Problems in King County Election Department," Sound Politics Blog November 21, 2004, available at http://www.soundpolitics.com. See also, declarations filed by William Maurer, Tim Borders, Dan Brady, Richard Emmett Nollette, and Dalton L. Oldham in *Washington State Republican Party, et al. v. Sam Reed, et al.*, Case No. C04-2350-RSM (W.D. WA, November 22, 2004).

115. Gillespie, "Judge Denies Request."

116. King County Elections, Department of Executive Services, "2004 General Election Machine Recount," November 24, 2004, available at http://your.kingcounty.gov/elections/2004recount/results.htm.

117. Stefan Sharkansky, "Flash," Sound Politics Blog, November 24, 2004, available at http://www.soundpolitics.com.

118. Kenneth P. Vogel, "Reed Certifies Rossi's Win," (Tacoma) *News Tribune*, December 1, 2004, A01.

119. Stefan Sharkansky, "It's Seattle, Stupid," Sound Politics Blog, November 28, 2004, available at http://www.soundpolitics.com.

120. Susan Gilmore and David Postman, "Rossi Named Governor-Elect; Funds Flowing to Democrats for New Count," *Seattle Times*, December 1, 2004, A1.

121. Quoted in Chris McGann, "Reed to Certify Rossi as Winner; Democrats Struggle to Find Money for a Costly Hand Recount," *Seattle Post-Intelligencer*, November 30, 2004, A1.

122. John Carlson, "Note to Gregoire: Concede Already," *Seattle Post-Intelligencer*, December 2, 2004, B7.

123. Quoted in Peter Callaghan, "Gregoire Must Consider Costs of Staying in Race," (Tacoma) *News Tribune*, December 2, 2004, B01.

124. John Fund, "Florida Northwest: Will Democrats Steal the Washington Governorship?" *Wall Street Journal*, November 29, 2004.

125. Quoted in David Ammons, "Gregoire Seeks Manual Recount of All Governor Votes," Associated Press State & Local Wire, December 2, 2004.

126. Quoted in David Postman, "Gregoire Wants Full Recount—Or None," *Seattle Times*, December 3, 2004, A1.

127. The ballots questioned in that case were counted "and we still won, so it's moot now," Chris Vance, the state party chair, told the press. McGann, "Reed to Certify Rossi as Winner," A1.

128. Letter from David Burman to Sam Reed, December 1, 2004 [author files]. See also, McGann, "Gregoire Says She Wants Full Recount," A1. Republicans later saw the counting of formerly rejected ballots, which they characterized as changing the rules in the middle of the game, as evidence of potential fraud on the part of elections officials. Attorneys for the Democrats argued that Washington election laws required the recounting of all ballots cast, not just all ballots counted the first time (citing RCW 29A.64.021(1) and RCW 29A.64.050).

129. Chris McGann, "Governor Race Could Wind Up in Court; Justices Could Decide by Friday If They'll Intervene," *Seattle Post-Intelligencer*, December 7, 2004, B1. Of the 2,478 ballots rejected, 1,976 were ballots on which the signatures did not match those on file. David Postman and Andrew Garber, "Rejected Ballots Take Center Stage Governor's Race," *Seattle Times*, December 8, 2004, A1.

130. Postman, "Gregoire Wants Full Recount," A1.

131. Quoted in ibid.

132. Quoted in David Ammons, "It's On to a Third Count in Washington's Governor Race," Associated Press State & Local Wire, December 3, 2004.

133. David Ammons, "Democrats Will Finance Manual Recount of Governor Votes," Associated Press State & Local Wire, December 3, 2004.

134. *David McDonald, et al. v. Secretary of State Sam Reed, et al.,* "Petitioners' Amended Motion and Brief in Support of Emergency Partial Relief," Case No. 76321-6, Supreme Court of Washington, December 9, 2004.

135. In their lawsuits, the Democrats also claimed that ballots were inappropriately challenged, that county canvassing boards rejected qualified ballots and used different standards in judging whether absentee and provisional voters' signatures matched their registration records, and that voters were denied a meaningful notice of challenges to their ballots. See David Postman, "Suite Launches Battle over Ballots," *Seattle Times*, December 4, 2004, A16.

136. Andrew Garber and David Postman, "Democrats Will Finance a Statewide Hand Recount," *Seattle Times*, December 3, 2004.

137. Quoted in Richard Roesler, "Race Still Isn't Over; Gregoire Backers Hope Hand Recount Will Close Gap with Rossi," (Spokane) *Spokesman Review*, December 4, 2004, A1.

138. Quoted in Chris McGann, "Democrats Call for Statewide Recount; Election Drama Continues; Hand Tally Set to Start Next Week," *Seattle Post-Intelligencer*, December 4, 2004, A1.

139. Richard Roesler, "'Found' Votes May Tip Race; 561 Ballots Wrongly Tossed in Gregoire Stronghold," (Spokane) *Spokesman Review*, December 14, 2004, A1.

140. Quoted in ibid.

141. *David McDonald, et al. v. Secretary of State Sam Reed, et al.,* "Opinion Order," Case No. 76321-6, Supreme Court of Washington, December 14, 2004, 3.

142. Rebecca Cook, "Supreme Court Rejects Democrats' Recount Lawsuit," Associated Press State & Local Wire, December 14, 2004.

143. According to Bill Huennekens, King County superintendent of elections, the problem could be traced back to the decision by the county to implement a new voter registration system in August 2004, just three months before one of the highest turnout elections in state history. In the conversion of the old electronic voter registration system to the new one, several thousand signatures were dropped or missing. Because there was not enough time or resources to track down all the missing signatures in the division's paper files before the coming elections, administrators sent out letters asking voters to supply new signatures that could be scanned into the new system. Hundreds failed to return the form, which meant the field where their signature should have been was left blank in the county database. Absentee ballots were sent out to these voters, along with hundreds of thousands of others; when they came back, workers were instructed to code these files "no signature on file" and to take a second step in canvassing the ballots to look up signatures in the paper files. See Declaration of Bill Huennekens, *Washington State Republican Party et al., v. King County, et al.*, Case No. 04-2-14599-1, Superior Court of Washington for Pierce County, December 17, 2004. See also, Michelle Nicolosi and Phuong Cat Le, "New Election System Hit Glitches, Records Reveal," *Seattle Post-Intelligencer*, January 22, 2005.

144. Richard Roesler, "Recount Finds Errors; GOP's Rossi Widens Lead in Governor's Race," *(Spokane) Spokesman Review*, December 10, 2004, A1.

145. *Washington State Republican Party, et al. v. King County, et al.*, Case No. 04-2-14599-1, Superior Court of Washington for Pierce County, December 17, 2004.

146. Other critics of the election who were not party to the lawsuits developed their own lists of illegal ballots. These include the Evergreen Foundation, which formally requested a federal investigation, and the intrepid blogger Stefan Sharkansky. In a letter to U.S. Attorney General Alberto Gonzales, the Evergreen Foundation claimed that the election was marred by over 1,000 felon votes; at least 45 votes in the names of deceased voters; 15 double-voters; two noncitizen voters; more than 660 illegal provisional ballots; forged signatures collected by the Democrats to validate rejected ballots; 873 more absentee ballots counted than voters credited with voting; illegal enhancement of ballots for recounting; selective failure to count 93 absentee ballots, most of which came from one congressional district (suggesting deliberate malfeasance); illegal registration of voters at the King County Courthouse address; and illegal registration of voters at invalid addresses. Sharkansky's postelection round-up of irregularities included 170 known illegal provisional ballots that he said were counted on the instruction of Elections Superintendent Huennekens on behest of Project Vote; 32 provisional ballots from other unregistered voters; 113 federal write-in ballots from unregistered voters who had not requested ballots by the deadline; 30 absentee ballots that counted the same voter; 11 absentee and provisional ballots counted from the vote; and five absentee ballots postmarked after the deadline. Letter from Bob Williams to Alberto Gonzales, April 7, 2005 [author files]; Stefan Sharkansky, "No Evidence of Election Crimes?" Sound Politics Blog, March 13, 2007, available at http://www.soundpolitics.com; see also, Stefan Sharkansky, "Fatally Flawed: King County Knowingly Counted Hundreds of Ineligible Votes in 2004 Election," *Stranger*, October 12, 2005, available at http://www.thestranger.com/seattle/content?oid=23586.

147. The petitioners claimed that at least 2,820 illegal ballots had been counted.

148. "Final Judgment Dismissing Election Contest with Prejudice and Confirming Certification of Election of Christine Gregoire," *Timothy Borders et al. v. King County et al.*, Case No. 05-2-00027-3, Superior Court of the State of Washington for Chelan County, June 24, 2005, 3.

149. In 2005, the King County Prosecutor Norm Maleng (a Republican) prosecuted eight criminal cases of voter fraud in the 2004 election. Seven of the eight were charged with voting for a deceased spouse, partner, or other relative, and one person was charged with voting twice after registering twice, once under his real name and again under an alias. All eight pled guilty. See Letter to Jonathan Bechtle from Norm Maleng, January 31, 2007. Some of the voter fraud perpetrators were in their seventies and eighties. The lawyer for one, Doris McFarland, age eighty-three, said his client "simply did not know what to do with the absentee ballot after her husband of 63 years, Earl, passed away" in the month before the election, so she signed his

name and mailed the ballot. Another man, Robert Holmgren, age fifty-nine, told the judge for his case that "my wife died just before this election. My judgment was clouded by the grief, I'm really sorry for what I did." According to a news report, "The judge told each client the court was sorry for their losses and wished them luck." Gene Johnson, "Two Plead Guilty to Voting Twice in 2004 General Election," Associated Press State & Local Wire, June 2, 2005.

150. Ibid., 24.

151. Washington State Election Reform Task Force, "Report from the Election Reform Task Force," March 1, 2005, 5.

152. David Bowermaster, "Was McKay Ousted Over 2004 Election?" *Seattle Times*, February 16, 2007, available at http://seattletimes.newsource.com/html/localnews/2003574683_mckay/6m0.html; see also, David Bowermaster, Mike Carter and Alicia Mundy, "Hearing on U.S. Attorney's Ouster Reveals Hastings' Office Contacted McKay," *Seattle Times*, March 6, 2007, available at http://seattletimes.newsource.com/html/localnews/2003603490_webmckay06m.html.

153. U.S. Congress, House Committee on the Judiciary, Subcommittee on Commercial and Administrative Law, "Hearing on Restoring Checks and Balances in the Confirmation Process of United States Attorneys," 110th Cong., 1st Sess., March 6, 2007, 54.

154. Both Cassidy and Hastings insisted they did nothing improper. See Charles Pope, "McKay Tells of a GOP Call in 2004–5; Fired U.S. Attorney and 5 Others Appear before Congressional Panels," *Seattle Post-Intelligencer*, March 7, 2007, A1.

155. As a pro-business lobbying group, the BIAW opposes environmental regulations that raise costs to builders. Writing in their newsletter, Mark Musser, "Stormwater Field Representative," compared "extremist" environmentalists to Hitler's Nazis. Mark Musser, "Hitler's Nazi Party: They Were Eco Extremists," *Building Insight; Newsletter of the Building Industry Association of Washington*, March 2008, 8. The BIAW also argues that it is "orbital eccentricities of Earth and variations in the Sun's output" and not human activity or the greenhouse effect that is the main cause of global warming, that the world's wetlands produce more greenhouse gases annually than all human sources combined, and that without global warming the Earth would revert to an Ice Age (20, 22).

156. Quoted in Bowermaster, "Was McKay Ousted Over 2004 Election?" In July 2005, McCabe wrote a letter to Representative Hastings in which he urged Hastings to call on President Bush to fire McKay; Letter from Tom McCabe to The Honorable "Doc" Hastings, July 5, 2005 [author files]. McCabe claimed he gave McKay evidence of forged absentee ballots. That evidence was produced by the BIAW from a mailing sent to voters who had signed the Democrats' affidavits after the Washington state Superior Court ruled that rejected absentee ballots could be counted if the voters in question signed affidavits attesting to voting only once. The mailing included a home-ownership survey and a $10 check. To cash the checks, voters had to endorse them, sending copies of their signatures back to the BIAW. Thus, the BIAW surreptitiously and under false pretenses collected signatures from hundreds of Washington absentee ballot voters. It then hired a private handwriting expert to analyze 150 of the signatures for possible forgeries. The expert concluded that 23 of the signatures were forgeries. Memorandum from Arlen Storm to Craig Donsanto, "Subject: Election Fraud—Washington State," March 13, 2006 [author files]; letter from Bob Williams to the Honorable Alberto Gonzales, April 7, 2005. This was the evidence McCabe gave to McKay, to John Fund (see Fund's article, "Rating the 'Massacres' (of U.S. Attorneys)," *Hawaii Reporter*, March 14, 2007), and to Jonathan Bechtle at the Evergreen Freedom Foundation. That organization also petitioned the Justice Department for an "investigation" of McKay's alleged recalcitrance in investigating voter fraud in the 2004 Washington gubernatorial election. See Letter to Thomas F. McLaughlin from Bob Williams, May 20, 2005 [author files]. For his part, McKay said one of the first actions he took on the election controversy came in response to McCabe's allegations and evidence. McKay asked the FBI to review McCabe's alleged forged signatures and said, "it was not the conclusion of the FBI that they were forgeries." David Bowermaster, "McKay 'Stunned' by Report on Bush; President's Talk with Gonzales—Documents May Shed Light on Firings," *Seattle Times*, March 13, 2007. It is noteworthy that the Republicans and the Rossi campaign declined to present

McCabe's evidence at trial in the *Borders* case "due to the perceived unreliability of the handwriting analysis." Memorandum from Arlen Storm to Craig Donsanto, 3.

157. House Committee on the Judiciary, "Hearing on Restoring Checks and Balances," 54.

158. U.S. Department of Justice, "An Investigation Into the Removal of Nine U.S. Attorneys in 2006," Office of the Inspector General and Office of Professional Responsibility, September 2008, 266–67.

Chapter 7. Voter Fraud Allegations and Their Consequences

1. Richard L. Hasen, "Beyond the Margin of Litigation: Reforming U.S. Election Administration to Avoid Electoral Meltdown," *Washington & Lee Law Review* 62, no. 3 (2005): 937–99. See also Daniel P. Tokaji, "The New Vote Denial: Where Election Reform Meets the Voting Rights Act," *South Carolina Law Review* 57, no. 4 (2006): 689–733.

2. R. Michael Alvarez and Thad Hall, "Controlling Democracy: The Principal-Agent Problems in Election Administration," *Policy Studies Journal* 34, no. 4 (2006): 491–510.

3. Max Weber, *From Max Weber: Essays in Sociology*, ed. and trans. H. H. Gerth and C. Wright Mills (New York: Oxford University Press, 1946), 198.

4. C.R.S. § 1-7-110 (2008); see Election Reform Information Project, "What's Changed, What Hasn't and Why: Election Reform Since November 2000," Washington, D.C., October 22, 2001, 8.

5. Norman F. Kron, "Florida Fallout and Other Colorado Election Law Amendments of 2002," *Colorado Lawyer* 31, no. 8 (August 2002): 63–66.

6. With the exception of a brief interlude during the 2001 and 2002 legislative sessions, when the Democrats had a one seat advantage in the state senate, both houses of the Colorado legislature were controlled by the Republicans in 2000, 2003, and 2004. In 2004, the Democrats wrested control of both houses, held it, and expanded their margins through 2008. The Republicans held the governor's office from 2000 to 2006, when Bill Ritter, former Denver district attorney, was elected governor, the first Democrat to serve with a Democratic General Assembly in fifty years.

7. All references to the Colorado election code are current as of 2008.

8. C.R.S. § 1-8-113(3)(a) (2008).

9. C.R.S. § 1-8-113(3)(a)(I) (2008).

10. C.R.S. § 1-8-113(3)(f) (2008).

11. C.R.S. § 1-8.5-101(1) (2008).

12. Colorado counted 75.9 percent of provisional ballots cast. This in no way made it an outlier. See Kimball W. Brace and Michael P. McDonald, "Final Report of the 2004 Election Day Survey, Submitted to the U.S. Election Assistance Commission," EAC Survey Analysis Support, EAC 0524, September 27, 2005, pt. 2, "Provisional Ballots," 6–9 (data table). No reason is given for why a quarter of provisional ballots cast in Colorado were not counted.

13. C.R.S. § 1-8.5-101(3) (2008).

14. C.R.S. § 1-8.5-105(3)(a) (2008).

15. C.R.S. § 1-9-301(4) (2008) and C.E.R. 26.12(B).

16. Brace and McDonald, *Final Report*, pt. 2, "Absentee Ballots," 5–4 (data table). County-level data suggest the problem stems from missing or misreported data.

17. C.R.S. § 1-8.5-107(1) (2008).

18. C.R.S. § 1-8.5-108(1) (2008).

19. C.R.S. § 1-2-605(7) (2008). See also Ian Urbina, "States' Actions to Block Voters Appear Illegal," *New York Times*, October 9, 2008; Ian Urbina, "Colorado to Review How It Purges Voters' Names," *New York Times*, October 10, 2008. There should be some cause for concern here. A study by the U.S. Census Bureau of returned 2000 census questionnaires marked "undeliverable" by the U.S. Postal service found that 22 percent of those undeliverable addresses identified as "vacant housing units" were actually occupied. "Assuming that the final census status is valid, we conclude that the U.S. Postal Service correctly identifies vacant housing units about 50 percent of the time." See John Chestnut, "Study of the U.S.

Postal Service Reasons for Undeliverability of Census 2000 Mailout Questionnaires," Final Report, Census 2000 Evaluation A.6.b, U.S. Census Bureau, Decennial Statistical Studies Division, Washington, D.C., September 30, 2003, 10. Approximately 8.5 percent of the undeliverable mail was classified as "post office box" or "no mail receptacle," and it included people who do not receive mail at their place of residence but at a post office box (as in many rural areas) or those living in dilapidated apartment buildings where the mailboxes are broken. "These housing units were likely to be identified occupied through Nonresponse Followup" (11). Only 20.5 percent were later found to be addressed to vacant units. Of all of the undeliverable mail later found to belong to occupied units, 48.1 percent had been classified as "post office box" or "no mail receptacle" (11, table 7). (See also the app. for a table in Chestnut elaborating on the abbreviated definitions used to classify undeliverable mail.) Another study analyzed a Census Bureau–coordinated redelivery operation of the mail returned as "undeliverable." It includes some analysis of racial difference but does not use the same variables as the first study. Basically, this study finds that 12.7 percent of successfully delivered questionnaires went to black householders, but that black and other minority householders whose mail was returned were less likely to be reached on a second attempt than whites (black householders were 19.1 percent of the unsuccessful Census Bureau attempt at redelivery). The real bias, however, appears to be toward younger people, renters, and people living alone. The odds that those groups were reached by the U.S. Postal Service the first time were worse than for over-30-year-olds, homeowners, and people not living alone. Felipe Kohn, *The United States Postal Service Undeliverable Rates for Census 2000 MailOut Questionnaires*, Final Report, Census 2000 Evaluation A.6.a (Washington, D.C.: U.S. Census Bureau, Decennial Statistical Studies Division, April 10, 2003).

20. C.R.S. § 1-9-201 (2008).

21. "I do solemnly swear or affirm that I have fully and truthfully answered all questions that have been put to me concerning my place of residence and my qualifications as an eligible elector at this election. I further swear or affirm that I am a citizen of the United States of the age of eighteen years or older; that I have been a resident of this state and precinct for thirty days immediately preceding this election and have not maintained a home or domicile elsewhere; that I am a registered elector in this precinct; that I am eligible to vote at this election; and that I have not previously voted at this election." C.R.S. § 1-9-204(1) (2008).

22. C.R.S. § 1-9-204(1)(b) (2008).

23. C.R.S. § 1-13-715(1) (2008).

24. E. E. Schattschneider, *The Semisovereign People: A Realist's View of Democracy in America* (New York: Holt, Rinehart and Winston, 1960), 48.

25. For an elaboration of the argument that some electoral rules are a form of vote suppression, see Frances Fox Piven, Lorraine C. Minnite, and Margaret Groarke, *Keeping Down the Black Vote: Race and the Demobilization of American Voters* (New York: New Press, 2009).

26. Pub. L. No. 107–252 (42 U.S.C. § 15301).

27. According to Derek Willis and David Nather, conference negotiators on the final version of HAVA hailed the agreement as "the first civil rights legislation of the 21st century." Derek Willis and David Nather, "Conferees Strike Deal on Election Overhaul Bill," *CQ Monitor News*, October 4, 2002.

28. See Brief for the United States as Amicus Curiae Supporting Appellant and Urging Reversal, *The Sandusky County Democratic Party, et al. v. J. Kenneth Blackwell*, 387 F.3d 815 (6th Cir., 2004). The Justice Department took a similar position in *Florida Democratic Party v. Hood*, No. 04CV395 (N.D. Fla.), Memorandum, October 29, 2004, and in the consolidated cases *Bay County Democratic Party v. Land*, No. 04CV10257 (E.D. Mich.), and *Michigan State Conferences of NAACP Branches v. Land*, No. 04CV10267 (E.D. Mich.), Memorandum, October 18, 2004. There appears to be no consensus among legal scholars, however, that the Justice Department reasoning is sound.

29. Title I provides funds for replacing outdated voting machines and for poll worker education and training; Title II creates a new bipartisan federal agency, the U.S. Elections Assistance Commission, to serve as a clearinghouse for election administration research and information,

and to develop voluntary voting systems standards; Title III mandates provisional voting and the creation of computerized statewide voter registration lists; and Title IV includes provisions for improving absentee balloting for overseas military voters. Brian Kim, "Help America Vote Act," *Harvard Journal on Legislation* 40 (2003): 579–601. Kim thinks the HAVA is a balanced, bipartisan bill (and he was writing before major implementation problems surfaced). At the same time, he acknowledges that a similar reform bill adopted in Florida the year before, the $32 million Election Reform Act of 2001, "did not prevent some poll workers from being able to activate new touchscreen voting machines, other poll workers from failing to show up at voting stations, and still more workers from closing polling stations before their scheduled closing time. "The result," he concludes, "was the disenfranchisement of hundreds, if not thousands of voters [in the 2002 Florida Democratic gubernatorial primary]" (288).

30. The HAVA encouraged more privatization of the electoral process through its incentives to the states to computerize ballot marking and vote-counting functions. Without adequate federal assistance or guidelines, the states were forced to rely on private, for-profit corporations to supply electronic voting software and equipment. The outsourcing was not only another massive government boondoggle but a recipe for vote-rigging because private firms have so far used proprietary exclusions and intellectual property arguments to safeguard their voting technology from government oversight and to evade public accountability. The problem is not new. Stephanie Philips, "The Risks of Computerized Election Fraud: When Will Congress Rectify a 38-Year-Old Problem?," *Alabama Law Review* 57 (2005–2006): 1123–61. Writing in 2008, Jeffrey Toobin concluded that the HAVA "today ranks somewhere between a disappointment and a fiasco." Toobin, "Fraud Alert," *New Yorker*, January 14, 2008, 14.

31. By a margin of 362–63, the House of Representatives passed H.R. 3295, known (because of its two principal sponsors) as the "Ney-Hoyer" Help America Vote Act of 2001, on December 12, 2001. Eric A. Fischer and Kevin J. Coleman, "Election Reform Legislation: Comparison of House and Senate Versions of H.R. 3295," Report for Congress RL31417, Congressional Research Service, Washington, D.C., May 15, 2002.

32. Willis and Nather, "Conferees Strike Deal." On April 11, 2002, the Senate passed S. 565, known as the "Dodd-McConnell" Martin Luther King, Jr. Equal Protection of Voting Rights Act of 2002, after accepting forty-one amendments to the version passed in the Senate on November 28, 2001. Andrew Gumbel asserts it was a Justice Department official, Hans von Spakovsky, who got the identification requirement into the HAVA; Andrew Gumbel, "Bush Justice," *Nation*, October 20, 2008. But the congressional record of hearings on the HAVA as it wound its way through the legislative process is replete with testimony from Bond arguing for the identification requirement. And Bond was long on the record as an opponent and critic of the NVRA, which mandated that the states accept mail-in registration forms in the first place.

33. See chapter 6 for an analysis of the 2000 presidential election, which ignited Bond's long-held belief that Democrats win in Missouri only when they cheat. The defeat by a dead man of fellow Republican John Ashcroft, who was running for reelection to the Senate, must have been too much to take and appears to have triggered Bond's hysteria about nonexistent voter fraud. In addition to the HAVA voter identification requirement, Bond was responsible for a rule incorporated into federal law that requires any ballots cast during poll hours extended by court order to be provisional ballots. Here, Bond was nursing old wounds. He claimed that his opponent was able to defeat his own first bid for Missouri governor in 1972 by getting a court to keep the polls open in St. Louis for some period after their regular closing time. In a February 13, 2002, statement on the U.S. Senate floor, Bond said, "I am not a member of the rules committee. Nor, prior to last year, was I an expert on election reform. I first saw the corrosive effects of vote fraud in my 1972 election for governor of Missouri. My opponent engineered an effort to keep the polls open late in St. Louis. Now, fast forward 28 years. Same state, same city, same play called from the same fraud play-book. Again, I saw first-hand an effort to illegally steal an election."

34. For a sampling of Bond's allegations, see his various statements on the Senate floor (U.S. Congress, Senate Committee on Governmental Affairs, "Statement of U.S. Senator Christopher

"Kit" Bond," May 3, 2001; U.S. Congress, Senate, "Floor Statement of U.S. Senator Christopher "Kit" Bond on Election Fraud," August 2, 2001; "Floor Statement of U.S. Senator Christopher "Kit" Bond on Election Reform," February 13, 2002; "Floor Statement of U.S. Senator Christopher "Kit" Bond Responding to Claim Republicans Are Holding Up Vote Fraud Bill," February 28, 2002). See also Safir Ahmed, "Slimin' the City," *Riverfront Times*, November 15, 2000; Bruce Rushton, "Dead Man Voting," *Riverfront Times*, April 24, 2002. In 2005, the U.S. Senate Republican Policy Committee adopted Bond's view, issuing a press release that claimed voter fraud was reaching epidemic proportions in the United States.

35. The Caltech-MIT Voting Technology Project study concluded that some 300,000 votes were "lost," in other words, cast by eligible voters trying to vote but not counted due to system failure, in the 2000 presidential election because of punch-card technology. CalTech-MIT Voting Technology Project, "Voting: What Is, What Could Be," California Institute of Technology and the Massachusetts Institute of Technology Corporation, July 2001, 21, available at http://www.vote.caltech.edu.

36. U.S. Congress, Senate, "Floor Statement on Election Fraud," August 2, 2001.

37. For details on this episode, see the St. Louis, Missouri, case study in chapter 6.

38. Office of U.S. Senator Christopher Bond, "Bond Says Senate Passage of Election Reform Bill Will Make It 'Easier to Vote & Harder to Cheat,'" press release, April 11, 2002.

39. Ritzy Meckler's owners had listed her name instead of their own in the phone book to protect their privacy. Ritzy got registered in 1994 when someone copied her name on to a voter registration application during a voter registration drive paid for by business groups behind a ballot referendum to bring riverboat gambling to Missouri. If the City of St. Louis Elections Board had complied with the NVRA and attempted to verify Ritzy's registration, her name would have been stricken from the rolls. Ritzy never voted. But Bond loved this story and related it as often as he could as evidence of a voter fraud epidemic sweeping the country. Even after Ritzy was dead and gone, Bond continued to trot out the example of the registered St. Louis pooch, citing the story of poor Ritzy at a March 12, 2008, U.S. Senate hearing on "In-Person Voter Fraud: Myth and Trigger for Disenfranchisement?" Bond, who was not called to testify but obliged testimony as a courtesy, reiterated his call for strong photo identification laws, showing the committee a photograph of himself with Ritzy. "I'm the one on the right," he joked. A few months later, in May, when Missouri lawmakers tried to rush through a bill calling for a state constitutional amendment that would allow the legislature to mandate voters show photo identification at the polls, Bond chided opponents who claimed there was insufficient evidence of voter fraud: "I've got photos of Ritzy Meckler, the 13-year-old springer spaniel who was registered to vote in St. Louis," he told reporters. "This is what's happened. We know that vote fraud goes on." Quoted in Jason Rosenbaum, "Woman Decries Senate Committee's Vote on Photo ID," *Columbia Tribune*, May 13, 2008, available at http://archive.columbiatribune.com/2008/may/20080513News010asp.

40. The House report on the bill singled out state voter registration laws as contributing in significant ways to lower voter turnout in the United States. See H.R. Report No. 9, 103rd Cong. 1st sess. (1993). For an analysis of the history of voter registration laws and electoral turnout and an account of the successful twelve-year campaign to enact the NVRA by two of the principal organizers of the effort, see Frances Fox Piven and Richard A. Cloward, *Why Americans Still Don't Vote and Why Politicians Want It That Way* (New York: Beacon Press, 2000). For a detailed account of the legislative battle to pass the NVRA, and the Bush Justice Department's failure to properly enforce the law, see chapter 4 in Piven, Minnite, and Groarke, *Keeping Down the Black Vote.*

41. Bill McAllister, "President Vetoes 'Motor Voter' Legislation," *Washington Post*, July 3, 1992, A4.

42. Christopher S. (Kit) Bond, "'Motor Voter' Out of Control," *Washington Post,* June 27, 2001, A25.

43. U.S. Congress, Senate Committee on Rules and Administration, "Hearing on Election Reform," 107th Cong., 2nd sess., March 14, 2001, 99.

44. Ibid., 84.

45. Ibid., 34.

46. See editorials in the *Wall Street Journal*: "Blind To Voter Fraud," March 2, 2001, 10; "The Voter Fraud Iceberg," March 12, 2001, 22; "Manufacturing Votes," May 8, 2001, 26; "Too Easy To Steal," December 11, 2001, 18.

47. U.S. General Accounting Office, *Elections: Perspectives on Activities and Challenges Across the Nation*, Report to Congressional Requesters, GAO-02-3, October 2001, 75.

48. Ibid.

49. Ibid., 76.

50. Ibid., 84.

51. For example, according to the U.S. Federal Elections Commission, in 2000, registered voters exceeded the estimated number of voting-age residents in three states (Alaska, Maine, and Montana), and the District of Columbia. U.S. Federal Elections Commission, *The Impact of the National Voter Registration Act of 1993 on the Administration of Elections for Federal Office, 1999–2000* (Washington, D.C.: Government Printing Office, 2001), table 1.

52. According to the U.S. Census Bureau, nearly one in five Americans of voting age moves annually. Jason Schachter, *Geographical Mobility: Population Characteristics, March 1999 to March 2000*, Current Population Reports (Washington, D.C.: U.S. Department of Commerce, Economics and Statistics Administration, U.S. Census Bureau, May 2001), 1.

53. Steve Barber, Jim Halpert, Mimi Wright, and Frank Litwin, "The Purging of Empowerment: Voter Purge Laws and the Voting Rights Act," *Harvard Civil Rights-Civil Liberties Law Review* 23, no. 2 (1988), 499, app. A. The other states purging for failure to vote did so on an accelerated schedule, purging registered voters after two years of inactivity or for failure to vote in a single election.

54. The examples of this are too numerous to list. For one recent example, see the discussion of the 2000 election in St. Louis, Missouri in chap. 6, and the Justice Department consent order finding the St. Louis Board of Election Commissioners illegally purged 35,000 names from its voter rolls.

55. Those states are Alabama, Connecticut, Kentucky, Maine, Massachusetts, Missouri, Nebraska, and Texas.

56. U.S. Federal Elections Commission, *Impact of the National Voter Registration Act*, table 3. Kentucky, Maine, and Nebraska have yet to delete any names from their inactive lists.

57. These provisions apply to voters assigned to inactive lists for failure to respond to notices asking for address confirmation, and they are meant to secure the right of these voters to vote as long as they are eligible. Although the NVRA does not specifically require states to provide provisional ballots to voters disputing their denial to vote, the House Report on the Act recommended, "it would be appropriate, and in compliance with the requirements of this Act, to require that such a person vote by some form of provisional ballot." U.S. Congress, House Committee on House Administration, "National Voter Registration Act of 1993," 103rd Cong. 1st sess., February 2, 1993, H. Rept. 103-9, section 8. Moreover, a number of analyses of the 2000 election have concluded that reforms should seek to expand the use of provisional balloting given the documented level of error in list management contributing to an estimated 3 million eligible voters being denied their right to vote. These numbers are drawn from the U.S. Census Bureau Current Population Survey estimate that 7.4 percent of the 40 million non-voters in 2000 did not vote due to registration problems.

58. Kevin K. Green, "Note: A Vote Properly Cast? The Constitutionality of the National Voter Registration Act of 1993," *Journal of Legislation* 22, no. 1 (1996): 45–84.

59. See, *ACORN v. Miller*, 129 F.3d 833 (6th Cir. 1997); *ACORN v. Edgar*, 56 F.3d 791 (7th Cir. 1995); *Voting Rights Coalition v. Wilson*, 60 F.3d 1411 (9th Cir. 1995); *Condon v. Reno*, 913 F. Supp. 946 (D.S.C. 1995); Jonathan E. Davis, "The National Voter Registration Act of 1993: Debunking States' Rights Resistance and the Pretense of Voter Fraud," *Temple Political & Civil Rights Law Review* 6, no. 2 (1997), 119n. 20, citing Human Serve and ACORN, "Legal Obstructions to the Implementation of the National Voter Registration Act Including Constitutional Challenges: An Update," September 1995, 2–8.

60. See the congressional testimony of Hans von Spakovsky, who has criticized the NVRA on precisely these grounds. U.S. Congress, Senate Committee on Governmental Affairs, "Hearing on Federal Election Practices and Procedures, Part 2," 107th Cong., 2nd sess., May 9, 2001, 79.

61. U.S. Congress, House Committee on House Administration, "Hearings on Voter Registration," 103rd Cong., 1st sess., January 26, 1993, 135–36.

62. New York State has the second lowest rate of licensed drivers among all states after the District of Columbia (59.2 percent of the resident population in 2003, according to the U.S. Department of Transportation, Federal Highway Administration, *Highway Statistics 2003*, Washington, DC, 2004, table DL-1C, available at http://www.fhwa.dot.gov/policy/ohpi/hss/index.htm).

63. Quoted in Geoffrey Gray, "Schumer's Identity Politics," *Village Voice*, April 9, 2002, 42.

64. Ibid.

65. Emily Pierce, "Predicted Solution for Voter ID Dispute Fails to Surface," *CQ Monitor News*, March 7, 2002.

66. See 42 U.S.C.A. 15483(b)(2)(A)(i).

67. Kathy A. Gambrell, "Minority Groups Upset over Voting Reforms," United Press International, November 1, 2002. Other civil rights groups opposed the identification requirements. For example, the American Civil Liberties Union worried that "this legislative cure to the severe voting rights problems seen in the 2000 presidential election could be even worse than the disease," and that it threatened to roll "back many of the voting rights victories achieved over the past three decades through the Voting Rights Act of 1965 and the National Voter Registration Act of 1993." See Letter to Members of Congress from Laura W. Murphy, director, and LaShawn Y. Warren, Legislative Counsel, American Civil Liberties Union, Washington National Office, October 9, 2002.

68. Quoted in Robert Pear, "Rights Groups Say Voter Bill Erects Hurdles," *New York Times*, October 8, 2002, A1.

69. In 2006, the Missouri legislature passed and the governor signed Senate Bill 1014, the Missouri Voter Protection Act (codified at Mo. Rev. Stat. § 115.427) which imposed one of the nation's most restrictive voter photo identification laws. The law was invalidated, however, by the Missouri Supreme Court in *Weinschenk v. Missouri*, 203 S.W.3d 201 (2006).

70. For a discussion of this case, see Lorraine C. Minnite, "An Analysis of Voter Fraud in the United States" (New York: Demos, 2007), 9-11, available at http://www.demos.org/pubs/Analysis.pdf.

71. "Voter ID Problems in Florida" (Editorial), *New York Times*, September 7, 2004, A22.

72. Ibid.

73. Joseph P. Harris, *The Registration of Voters in the U.S.* (Baltimore: Lord Baltimore Press, 1929), 232–38.

74. For a fascinating analysis based on eye-witness accounts of how very unsacred the nineteenth-century polling place actually was, see Richard Franklin Bensel, *The American Ballot Box in the Mid-Nineteenth Century* (New York: Cambridge University Press, 2004). Inebriation at the polls, for example, was not uncommon. As Bensel notes, "Whiskey, it seems, bought as many, and perhaps far more, votes than the planks in party platforms" (295).

75. Survey research confirms high levels of public support for documentary identification requirements to vote.

76. Nine states, Colorado, Florida, Georgia, Indiana, Missouri, Montana, North Dakota, Ohio, and South Dakota all passed stricter voter identification laws under unified Republican Party control of state government. In Arizona and Michigan, Democratic governors opposed these laws, but Republicans and their allies were able to override potential executive vetoes through nonlegislative stratagems such as ballot initiatives (Proposition 200 in Arizona) and legal challenges that in Michigan lifted a ban imposed by the attorney general on a voter identification law passed by Republicans in 1996 (the court doing the lifting, the state's highest court, was dominated by Republican appointees). Alabama passed a moderate documentary voter identification law in 2003 when Democrats controlled both houses of the state legislature

and a Republican was governor. The law requires voters to show either a "current valid photo identification," or a copy of any number of other forms of identification showing the name and address of the voter, including a valid hunting or fishing license, or a Medicaid or food stamp benefit card. In only one of the thirteen states adopting stricter documentary voter identification laws since the passage of the HAVA—Washington—were Democrats in control of the governor's office and the state legislature. The story of the 2004 Washington governor's race is chronicled in chapter 6. It may be that the Washington voter identification law was the price that the Democrats were willing to pay bitterly angry Republicans for Christine Gregoire's 133-vote victory. In one other state where Democrats tightened up on voter identification laws after 2002, Louisiana, the change was minimal. Louisiana already had a polling place voter identification law. Democrats passed a law to make in-person absentee voting requirements conform to the polling place rules, presumably to the detriment of Republican voters.

77. Brief Amici Curiae of Historians and Other Scholars in Support of Petitioners, *Crawford v. Marion County Election Board*, 128 S.Ct. 1610 (2008).

78. Party control was split in the Texas legislature in 2002, with the Republicans dominating the senate over the 2002–2008 period and taking control of the house in 2003. The legislature meets only once every two years in odd number years and was not in session in 2002. In the 2007 legislative dispute over a proposed voter identification law, Texas state Senator Mario Gallegos Jr. emerged as a hero to those who opposed the bill. Gallegos was sick and still recovering from a liver transplant that he had received a few months before. Against his doctor's orders, he stayed in Austin, resting on a hospital bed in a room adjacent to the senate chamber so that he could be present to vote with his fellow Democrats against releasing the bill for a full vote on the senate floor. The Democrats defeated the bill, only to see it return in 2009. See Mark Lisheron, "Ill Senator Settles in for Voter ID Fight," *Austin American-Statesman*, May 22, 2007; Terrence Stutz, "Ailing Senator Helps Quash Voter ID Bill," *Dallas Morning News*, May 24, 2007.

79. Under the Aviation and Transportation Security Act, the transportation security administrator may promulgate security procedures at airports. As of 2008, these rules allowed for ticketed passengers lacking photo identification to board airplanes, subject to extra screening measures. Transportation Security Administration, "TSA Announces Enhancements to Airport ID Requirements to Increase Safety," *News and Happenings*, June 23, 2008, available at http://wwwtsa.ogv/pres/happeneings/enhance_ID_requirements.shtm.

80. Citing *Purcell v. Gonzalez*, 549 U.S. 1 (2006) at 7; *Reynolds v. Sims*, 377 U.S. 533 (1964); *Siegel v. LePore*, 234 F.3d 1163, 1199 (11th Cir. 2000).

81. This is the "broken windows" theory of crime control. James Q. Wilson and George L. Kelling, "The Police and Neighborhood Safety: Broken Windows," *Atlantic* 249, no. 3 (March 1982): 29–38.

82. Richard A. Posner, *Law and Literature*, rev. ed. (Cambridge, Mass.: Harvard University Press, 1998).

83. In at least one major U.S. city, New York City, the problem of littering and enforcement of antilittering laws is taken seriously. The 2007 Annual Report of the city Sanitation Department states that the seventy-four city sanitation police officers and 230 sanitation enforcement agents handed out 382,325 Notices of Violation. Supervisors in the Department's Bureau of Cleaning and Collection issued an additional 164,503 Notices of Violation, for a grand total of 546,828 tickets for violations of the city laws governing the maintenance of clean streets, illegal dumping, and the proper storage and disposal of waste and recyclable materials. The largest category of citations was "dirty sidewalk" violations (159,324 tickets issued). And littering penalties are now the second biggest source of all city revenue from fines, after parking violations. New York City Department of Sanitation, "Making New York Cleaner and Greener," Annual Report, 2007, 17, available http://www.nyc.gov/html/dsny/downloads/pdf/pubinfo/annual/ar2007 .pdf; Frank Greve, "Fewer People Trashing U.S. Roads, Beaches, Experts Say," McClatchy Newspapers, January 24, 2008.

84. Posner suggested that the motivation for the suit challenging the Indiana law on the part of the Democratic Party "is simply that the law may require the Democratic Party . . . to work

harder to get every last one of their supporters to the polls." *Crawford v. Marion County Election Board*, Nos. 06-2218, 06-2317, 484 F.3d 949 (7th Cir. 2007), January 4, 2007, 15.

85. Jeffrey Rosen, "The Dissenter," *New York Times Magazine*, September 23, 2007, available at http://www.nytimes.com/2007/09/23/magazine/23stevens-t.html.

86. Citing *Norman v. Reed* 502 U.S. 279 (1992). The other three justices in the majority, Scalia, Thomas, and Alito, rejected this framework, arguing, in effect, that the state did not need to justify the law as a deterrent to voter fraud. And they went further. Justice Scalia denied that the law presented an equal protection problem. "What petitioners view as the law's several light and heavy burdens," he opined, "are no more than the different *impacts* of the single burden that the law uniformly imposes on all votes" (emphasis in original). In other words, for Justice Scalia, an observable disparate impact is not an indicator of a law treating differently situated people differently.

87. M. R. Werner, *Tammany Hall* (New York: Greenwood Press, 1968 [1932]), 439.

88. Phuong Cat Le and Michelle Nicolosi, "Dead Voted in Governor's Race; King County Investigating 'Ghost Voter' Cases," *Seattle Post-Intelligencer*, January 7, 2005, A1.

89. For an attempt to quantify the harm, see Michael J. Pitts and Matthew D. Neumann, "Documenting Disenfranchisement: Voter Identification At Indiana's 2008 General Election," available at http://ssrn.com/abstract=1465529; and Michael J. Pitts, "Empirically Assessing the Impact of Photo Identification at the Polls, Through an Examination of Provisional Balloting," *Journal of Law and Politics* 24, no. 4 (2008): 475-527. Note, at press, the case was being heard on state constitutional grounds by the Indiana Supreme Court.

90. Robert S. Erikson and Lorraine C. Minnite, "Modeling Problems in the Voter ID-Voter Turnout Debate," *Election Law Journal*, 8, no. 2 (2009): 85–101.

91. The Supreme Court's reasoning in *Crawford* has preoccupied legal scholars and generated a vigorous debate about the meaning of the Court's rejection of a facial challenge in favor of an as-applied rule. For a sampling of views, see Demian A. Ordway, "Disenfranchisement and the Constitution: Finding A Standard That Works," *New York University Law Review* 82, no. 4 (2007): 1174-1209; Christopher S. Elmendorf, "Structuring Judicial Review of Electoral Mechanics: Explanations and Opportunities," *University of Pennsylvania Law Review* 156, no. 2 (2007): 313-94; Muhammad At-Tauhidi, "Access v. Integrity: Determining the Constitutionality of Voter ID Laws under *Anderson v. Celebrezze, Temple Politics and Civil Rights Law Review* 17, no. 1 (2007): 215-249; Ian McMullen, "Constitutional Burdens on the Right to Vote: *Crawford, v. Marion County Election Board,*" *Mercer Law Review* 60, no. 3 (2008): 1007-24; Andrew N. DeLaney, "Appearance Matters: Why the State Has an Interest in Preventing the Appearance of Voting Fraud," *New York University Law Review* 83, no. 3 (2008): 847-78; David L. Franklin, "Looking Through Both Ends of the Telescope: Facial Challenges and the Roberts Court," *Hastings Constitutional Law Quarterly* 36, no. 1 (2008-2009): 689-716; Maya Manian, "Rights, Remedies and Facial Challenges," *Hastings Constitutional Law Quarterly* 36, no. 1 (2008-2009): 611-30; Nathaniel Persily and Jennifer S. Rosenberg, "Defacing Democracy: The Changing Nature and Rising Importance of As-Applied Challenges in the Supreme Court's Recent Election Law Decisions, *Minnesota Law Review* 93, no. 5 (2009): 1644-79; Thomas Basile, "Inventing the Right to Vote in *Crawford v. Marion County Election Board*, 128 S.Ct. 1610, *Harvard Journal of Law and Public Policy* 32, no. 1 (2009): 431-50; Aaron J. Lyttle, "Constitutional Law – Get the Balance Right: The Supreme Court's Lopsided Balancing Test for Evaluating State Voter-Identification Laws; *Crawford v. Marion County Election Board,*" *Wyoming Law Review* 9, no. 1 (2009): 281-308; and Gillian E. Metzger, "Facial and as-Applied Challenges under the Roberts Court," *Fordham Urban Law Journal* 36, no. 4 (2009): 773-802.

92. For a useful discussion of why the asymmetrical balance between state and voter interests in these matters should have led the court in a different direction in settling disputes over voter fraud and voter identification, see Chad Flanders, "How to Think about Voter Fraud (and Why)," *Creighton Law Review* 41, no. 1 (2008): 93–154.

Appendix 2. Selected State Election Codes and Case Law Criminalizing Election Fraud in Twelve States

1. This appendix was compiled with significant assistance from Joshua Bardavid, to whom I am most grateful. Any errors are my responsibility.

2. Code of Ala. § 17-12-1.

3. Code of Ala. § 17-12-2.

4. Code of Ala. § 17-12-2. See *Williams v. Lide*, 628 So. 2d 531 (Ala. 1993).

5. Cal. Elec. Code § 16100.

6. See *Canales v. Alviso* 3 Cal 3d 118 (1970); and *Waite v. Brendlin* 26 Cal App 31 (1914). Both cases were decided on an older, but substantively similar, statute.

7. See *Patterson v. Hanley*, 136 Cal 265 (1902); *Keane v. Smith*, 4 Cal. 3d 932 (1971); *Escalante v. City of Hermosa Beach*, 195 Cal. App. 3d 1009 (1987); and *Scott v. Kenyon*, 16 Cal.2d 197 (1940).

8. For more details on this important case, see Lori Minnite and David Callahan, "Securing the Vote: An Analysis of Election Fraud," Report to Demos: A Network for Ideas and Action, New York, 2003, 39–40.

9. See *Peacock v. Wise*, 351 So. 2d 1134 (Fla. 1st DCA 1977); *Wald v. Shenkman*, 664 So. 2d 10 (Fla. 3d DCA 1995); *Gimbert v. Lamb*, 601 So. 2d 230 (Fla. 2d DCA 1992); *Bolden v. Potter*, 452 So. 2d 564 (Fla. 1984); *Boardman v. Esteva*, 323 So. 2d 259 (Fla. 1975); *McLean v. Bellamy*, 437 So. 2d 737 (Fla. 1st DCA 1983); *Spradley v. Bailey*, 292 So. 2d 27 (Fla. 1st DCA 1974); *Bolden v. Potter*, 452 So. 2d 564 (Fla. 1984). An excellent discussion of Florida election law and voter fraud can be found in William T. McCauley, "Florida Absentee Voter Fraud: Fashioning an Appropriate Judicial Remedy," *University of Miami Law Review* 54, no. 3 (2000): 625–64.

10. O.C.G.A. § 21-2-31 (5) (2000).

11. O.C.G.A. § 21-2-561 (2000).

12. O.C.G.A. § 21-2-570 (2000).

13. O.C.G.A. § 21-2-572 (2000).

14. O.C.G.A. § 21-2-575 (2000).

15. O.C.G.A. § 21-2-587 (2000). For a good discussion of what quantum of evidence is sufficient for a conviction under a former, but substantively the same, criminal statute, see *Lepinsky v. State*, 7 Ga. App. 285 (1910); *Cohen, Murrah & Pierce v. State*, 104 Ga. 734 (1898).

16. O.C.G.A. § 21-2-229 (c) (2000).

17. O.C.G.A. § 21-2-229 (d) (2000).

18. O.C.G.A. § 21-2-527 (2000).

19. See, for example, *Stiles v. Earnest*, 252 Ga. 260 (1984); *McCranie v. Mullis*, 267 Ga. 416 (1996); *Taggart v. Phillips*, 242 Ga. 454 (1978). For some other interesting recent cases, see *Streeter v. Paschal*, 267 Ga. 207 (1996); *Hendry v. Smith*, 270 Ga. 17 (1998); *Bailey v. Colwell*, 263 Ga. 111 (1993); *Hunt v. Crawford*, 270 Ga. 7 (1998).

20. 10 ILCS 5/1A-8 (7) (2001).

21. 10 ILCS 5/23-1.8b (2001).

22. 10 ILCS 5/23-26 (2001).

23. *Zahray v. Emricson*, 25 Ill. 2d 121(1962).

24. See, for example, *Hoffer v. School Dist. U-46*, 273 Ill. App. 3d 49 (1995) (noting that "it is incumbent on a petitioner in an election contest to plead specific facts indicating that the result of the election would be changed."); and *In re Contest*, 93 Ill. 2d 463 (1983) (noting the same).

25. Minn. Stat. § 201.195 (2000).

26. Minn. Stat. § 201.014 (3) (2000).

27. Minn. Stat. § 203B.03 (2000).

28. Minn. Stat. § 209.07 (2000).

29. Ibid.

30. Minn. Stat. § 209.12 (2000).

31. Miss. Code. Ann. § 23-15-923 (2001).
32. See *Manhattan State Citizens' Group, Inc. v. Bass,* 524 F. Supp. 1270 (1981 SD NY); and *Matter of Alamo v. Strohm,* 145 Misc 2d 810.
33. For examples, see *Leaks v. Gill* 123 Misc 2d 342 (1984); *Palla v. Suffolk County Board of Elections* 31 NY2d 36 (1972); *Vacco v. Spitzer,* 179 Misc. 2d 584 (1998).
34. *Vacco v. Spitzer,* 179 Misc. 2d 584 (1998).
35. *Matter of Kelly v. Villa,*176 AD2d 992 (1991).
36. For examples, see *Saxon v Fielding,* 614 F2d 78, *Bell v. Southwell,* 376 F2d 659; *Matter of DeSapio v. Koch,* 21 AD2d 20, 22, *Matter of McGuinness v. DeSapio,* 9 AD2d 65.
37. See *Combs v. Groener,* 256 Ore. 336 (1970); *Lessard v. Snell,* 155 Or 293 (1937).
38. ORS § 258.016 (1999).
39. ORS § 258.065 (1999).
40. See *Thomas v. Penfold,* 23 Or App 168, 171–72 (1975); *Stork v. Columbia River People's Utility Dist.,* 58 Ore. App. 51, 55 (1982).
41. 25 P.S. § 2642 (2001).
42. Ibid.
43. 25 P.S. § 3533 (2001).
44. 25 P.S. § 3312 (2001).
45. 25 P.S. § 3379 (2001).
46. 25 P.S. § 3405 (2001).
47. 25 P.S. §§ 3408 & 3409 (2001).
48. *In Re Williams,* 155 Pa. Commw. 494 (1993).
49. See, for example, *Wilkes-Barre Election Contest,* 400 Pa. 507, 513 (1960); *Winograd v. Coombs,* 342 Pa. 268 (1941); *Gollmar's Election Case,* 316 Pa. 560 (1934); *Ayre's Contested Election,* 287 Pa. 135 (1926); *Election of Tax Collector,* 41 Pa. D. & C.3d 37 (1986).
50. For an excellent discussion of illegal voting and election challenges, see Robert A. Junell, Curtis L. Seidlits, Jr., and Glen G. Shuffler, "Consideration Of Illegal Votes in Legislative Election Contests," *Texas Tech Law Review* 28, no. 4 (1997): 1095–60.
51. Tex. Elec. Code § 63.010 (2001).
52. *Fogo v. Talton: Hearings before the House Select Comm. on Election Contest-Hearing Testimony,* 73d Leg., R.S. (Feb. 3, 1993).
53. Wis. Stat. § 6.95 (2000).
54. Wis. Stat. § 12.60 (2000).
55. Wis. Stat. § 11.61 (2000).
56. *Carlson v. Oconto County Bd. of Canvassers,* 240 Wis. 2d 438, 444 (2000) (citing *McNally v. Tollander,* 100 Wis. 2d 490, 505 (1981).
57. Other examples of Wisconsin courts exercising significant power to either overturn an election or the Board of Canvassers decisions include *In re Hayden,* 105 Wis. 2d 468 (1981); *Lanser v. Koconis,* 62 Wis.2d 86 (1974); *Olson v. Lindberg,* 2 Wis. 2d 229 (1957); *Logerquist v. Board of Canvassers for Town of Nasewaupee,* 150 Wis. 2d 907 (1989).

Appendix 3. The Quest for Federal Data on Voter Fraud

1. Craig C. Donsanto, "Corruption of the Election Process under U.S. Federal Law," in *Election Fraud: Detecting and Deterring Electoral Manipulation,* ed. R. Michael Alvarez, Thad E. Hall, and Susan D. Hyde (Washington, D.C.: Brookings Institution, 2008), 34.
2. See letters to author from Amy McNulty, Office of the Attorney General, August 22, 2005; Daniel Metcalfe, Office of Information and Privacy, October 3, 2006, October 30, 2006, and December 28, 2006; Thomas J. McIntrye, Criminal Division, August 11, 2005; Nelson Hermilla, Civil Division, August 2, 2005, and August 2, 2006; Priscilla Jones, Civil Division, October 17, 2005, October 23, 2006, and November 1, 2006; Marie A. O'Rourke, Executive Office for U.S. Attorneys, August 17, 2005 and August 30, 2005; William Stewart, December 28, 2006 and January 31, 2007. In addition to these letters, I made numerous telephone calls to all four of the Justice Department agencies over the two-year period.

3. Letter from LCCR and sign-on groups to John D. Ashcroft, October 25, 2002 [author's files].

4. Ibid.

5. In 1980, the Elections Crime Branch was formerly established as a "national emphasis program" within the Public Integrity Section, itself created within the Criminal Division of the Justice Department just four years before. See Public Integrity Section, "Report to Congress on the Activities and Operations of the Public Integrity Section for 1980," U.S. Department of Justice, Criminal Division, n.d. The Public Integrity Section is charged with overseeing and coordinating the investigation and prosecution of official corruption at all levels of government and with training U.S. attorneys, FBI personnel, and other law enforcement officials and prosecutors in investigative and prosecutive techniques and effective prosecution theories for use against elected and appointive officials "who abuse the trusts bestowed on them by the public they serve." See Public Integrity Section, "Report to Congress on the Activities and Operations of the Public Integrity Section for 1978," U.S. Department of Justice, Criminal Division, n.d., 2.

6. Leadership Conference on Civil Rights, "Civil Rights Coalition Sues Ashcroft over Access to Election Fraud Policy Documents," Press Release, September 28, 2004, available at http://www.civilrights.org/press/2004/civil-rights-coalition-sues-ashcroft-over-access-to-election-fraud-policy-documents.html.

7. Complaint, *Leadership Conference on Civil Rights v. Gonzales et al.*, Civil Action No. 04-1664 (D.D.C. filed September 28, 2004), 404 F. Supp. 2d.

8. Little did David Iglesias, the New Mexico U.S. attorney, know that the eventual failure of his high-profile task force to find enough evidence to indict or prosecute a single case of fraud would later serve as probable cause for his firing. See David Iglesias, *In Justice: Inside the Scandal That Rocked the Bush Administration* (Hoboken: John Wiley & Sons, 2008).

9. Jo Becker and Dan Eggen, "Voter Probes Raise Partisan Suspicions," *Washington Post*, September 20, 2004, A5.

10. Ibid.

11. U.S. District Court for the District of Columbia, *Leadership Conference on Civil Rights v. Gonzales et al.*, Civil Action No. 04-1664, 404 F. Supp. 2d 246, 251; 2005 U.S. Dist. LEXIS 33158.

12. The Justice Department asked to be relieved of its disclosure obligations until August 2008; the judge ordered it to comply by October 2006.

13. See, for example, studies conducted by the inspector general and Office of Professional Responsibility of the U.S. Department of Justice, including "An Investigation of Allegations of Politicized Hiring and Other Improper Personnel Actions in the Civil Rights Division," July 2, 2008; "An Investigation of Allegations of Politicized Hiring by Monica Goodling and Other Staff in the Office of the Attorney General," July 28, 2008; and "An Investigation into the Removal of Nine U.S. Attorneys in 2006," September 2008. See also U.S. Congress, House of Representatives Committee on the Judiciary Majority Staff, "Reining in the Imperial Presidency: Lessons and Recommendations Relating to the Presidency of George W. Bush," Final Report to Chairman John Conyers Jr., March 2009, available at http://judiciary.house.gov/hearings/printers/111th/IPres090316.pdf.

14. See, for example, U.S. Congress, House of Representatives Committee on Government Reform, Minority Staff Special Investigations Division, "Secrecy in the Bush Administration," prepared for Rep. Henry A. Waxman, September 14, 2004, available at http://oversight.house.gov/features/secrecy_report/pdf/pdf_secrecy_report.pdf.

15. Memorandum and Order, *Leadership Conference on Civil Rights v. Gonzales*, Civil Action No. 04-1664 (RCL), (D.D.C. March 20, 2006).

16. Astutely, Coney suggested that the records could be found in the office of Hans von Spavoksky, who was then counsel to the assistant attorney general for the Civil Rights Division. See letter from Lillie Coney to Patricia D. Harris, Management Analyst, Justice Department, July 23, 2004 [author's files].

17. See letter faxed to Patricia D. Harris from Lillie Coney on August 11, 2004 [author's files].

18. But not before reviewing the materials disclosed to EPIC. After meeting Lillie Coney at an academic conference and finding out from her that EPIC had used FOIA to obtain BAVII records, I reviewed those documents at the EPIC offices in Washington, D.C., at her invitation. As it turned out, they were not fully responsive to my original request.

19. True to its promise to make documents procured through FOIA available to the public, the LCCR had already and generously made these documents available to me.

20. The LCCR was able to procure the disputed revised draft of the election crimes manual, but not other sorts of records on how final policy decisions were implemented.

21. Earlier versions of this document appear in the Justice Department "Vaughn Index" of withheld and exempt documents in the LCCR litigation.

22. U.S. Congress, House Committee on House Administration, Hearing on "'You Don't Need Papers to Vote?': Non-Citizen Voting and ID Requirements in U.S. Elections," 109th Congress, 2nd Sess., June 22, 2006, 245–54.

23. Interestingly, Chavez's testimony came a week before the House hearing on noncitizen voting. See U.S. Congress, Senate Judiciary Committee, Hearing on the "Continuing Need for Section 203's Provisions for Limited English Proficient Voters," 109th Cong., 2nd Sess., June 13, 2006, 346-55.

24. Lori Minnite and David Callahan, "Securing the Vote: An Analysis of Voter Fraud," Demos: A Network for Ideas & Action, New York, 2003, available at http://www.demos.org/pubs/EDR_-_Securing_the_Vote.pdf; U.S. Election Assistance Commission, "Election Crimes: An Initial Review and Recommendations for Future Study," available at http://www.eac.gov/clearinghouse/docs/reports-and-surveys-2006electioncrimes.pdf/attachment_download/file; Delia Bailey, "Caught in the Act: Recent Federal Election Fraud Cases," in *Election Fraud: Detecting and Deterring Electoral Manipulation,* ed. R. Michael Alvarez, Thad E. Hall, and Susan D. Hyde (Washington, D.C.: Brookings Institution, 2008), 89–98.

25. Lexis-Nexis is also a dynamic database with changing content. This cuts down on the reliability of any search as a measure of the universe of all possible cases of a thing. A search string used at one time might not produce the same number of cases or "hits" when used at another point in time.

26. U.S. Elections Assistance Commission, "Election Crimes: An Initial Review and Recommendations for Future Study," app. 4, December 2006. The final report states, "Very few of the identified cases were applicable to this study," and refers readers to an appendix listing just under two hundred cases reviewed by the researchers (10). Wang and Serebrov's research mandate was broader than the scope of the Minnite and Callahan and the Bailey studies, including in its scope a review of case law on voter intimidation.

27. Cross calls the FFCID "by far the most prominent" database used by legal scholars for statistical analysis of case outcomes. Frank B. Cross, "Comparative Judicial Databases," *Judicature* 83, no. 5 (2000), 248–49.

28. The Administrative Office of the U.S. Courts (AO) data purports to cover every case filed in the federal courts. Theodore Eisenberg and Margo Schlanger observe that "it seems more than likely that this is indeed its coverage. Cases get entered into the database on filing, and there is a built-in check because they get entered again, on termination." Theodore Eisenberg and Margo Schlanger, "The Reliability of the Administrative Office of the U.S. Courts Database: An Empirical Analysis," *Notre Dame Law Review* 78, no. 5 (2003), 1463.

29. Administrative Office of the United States Courts, "United States Title and Code Criminal Offense Citations," 7th ed., August 1988, iv.

30. PACER was designed by the Administrative Office of the U.S. Courts and serves the U.S. Judiciary to provide easy electronic public access to court information.

31. U.S. Department of Justice, "Department of Justice to Hold Ballot Access and Voting Integrity Symposium," Press Release, August 2, 2005; U.S. Department of Justice, "Fact Sheet: Protecting Voting Rights and Preventing Election Fraud," Press Release, November 7, 2005; U.S. Department of Justice, "Justice Department Holds Fifth Annual Symposium on Ballot Access and Voting Integrity Initiative," Press Release, July 26, 2006.

Appendix 4. Steps in Extracting Voter Fraud Records from the Federal Court Cases Integrated Database

1. The FCCID includes district, office, docket, and defendant numbers for each defendant. For cases involving multiple defendants, the defendant numbers run sequentially within a docket number (keyed to a district and office). This information is also included in the federal courts' PACER system. To draw out more case detail, court documents and docket sheets for all ninety-five defendants on the Justice Department case list were examined, and the docket and defendant numbers matched against the PACER system records. Three of the Justice Department's ninety-five defendants were coded correctly by docket number, but clearly miscoded by defendant number in the FCCID.

2. The AO provides coding guidance to docket clerks responsible for keying in court data. See Administrative Office of the United States Courts, "United States Title and Code Criminal Offense Citations," 7th ed. Statistical Analysis and Reports Division, Criminal Branch, Washington, D.C., August 1988.

3. E-mail communication to author from Mark Motivans, statistician, U.S. Department of Justice, Bureau of Justice Statistics, May 24, 2007.

4. The Justice Department BAVII case list includes only five defendants docketed for this case. This may be a department error because defendants 6 and 7 were indicted during fiscal year 2005 and are (probably) included in the FCCID.

5. This finding stands in contrast to that of Eisenberg and Schlanger, who examined the reliability of the FCCID data for two large categories of civil cases, torts and inmate civil rights, using a similar method that compared the FCCID records to docket sheet data. On the one hand, my findings challenge Eisenberg and Schlanger's conclusions. Although they did not systematically examine the AO citation code, they write that "the most basic code for researchers' use of the AO data—the case category, which identifies cases as pertaining to a specified subject matter—appears, from the limited research already done, to be highly accurate." Theodore Eisenberg and Margo Schlanger, "The Reliability of the Administrative Office of the U.S. Courts Database: An Empirical Analysis," *Notre Dame Law Review* 78, no. 5 (October 2003), 1463. The inaccuracies that I found in similar codes used in the criminal files should be important to election law scholars because criminal election law cases cannot be distinguished in the FCCID data any other way. If we rely on the AO citation code to overcome the fact that election law cases cannot be accurately identified by charge data alone, we may still miss upward of one-third of all cases that should otherwise be included. To be sure, Eisenberg and Schlanger investigated civil not criminal cases and were interested in qualitatively different variables, primarily the reliability of judgment and award data. They found anomalies, but these were limited to types of cases that occur infrequently (i.e., cases in which the plaintiff is the victor but the data report a judgment for "both" parties), leading them to conclude that small errors do not undermine the usability of the data. In contrast, my analysis concludes that additional information is required to keep at least some of the criminal data usable. That said, my findings support Eisenberg and Schlanger's more general findings about data reliability. Their research showed that errors were confined to the types of cases that occur infrequently. Similarly, election law cases are cases that occur infrequently compared to the volume of criminal cases coming through the federal courts (an annual average of about 150,000 cases over the ten-year study period ending in FY2005). If the problems coding election law cases are to be explained by their exotic character (and perhaps by the unfamiliarity with election law cases among the court clerks who prepare the documents that are the basis for the AO data, leading to coding errors), these errors should be of little concern to researchers using the FCCID data for other purposes. For studies questioning different aspects of the reliability of the FCCID (or AO) data, see Thomas E. Willging, Laural L. Hooper, and Robert J. Niemic, "Empirical Study of Class Actions in Four Federal District Courts: Final Report to the Advisory Committee on Civil Rules," 1996, 197–200, available at Federal Judicial Center, http://www.fjc.gov/library/fjc_catalog.nsf/autoframepage!openform&url=/; Margo Schlanger, "Inmate Litigation," *Harvard Law Review* 116, no. 6 (2003), 1555–1706; Kimberly A. Moore,

"Judges, Juries, and Patent Cases—An Empirical Peek inside the Black Box," *Michigan Law Review* 99, no. 2 (2000): 365–409.

6. This, too, stands in contrast to studies that have considered the accuracy of the case category data. Eisenberg and Schlanger found that the case codes used for tort and inmate cases "are not terribly *over*inclusive." Eisenberg and Schlanger, "Reliability of the Administrative Office," 1463. And Eisenberg, in an earlier study of a single district court, found very few civil rights cases had been inaccurately classified, suggesting problems with underinclusiveness were minimal; Theodore Eisenberg, "Section 1983: Doctrinal Foundations and an Empirical Study," *Cornell Law Review* 67, no. 3 (1982): 482–556.

Index

Index

Beck, Glenn, 10
Bensel, Richard Franklin, 282n74
Berendt, Paul, 114
Biskupic, Steven, 270n71
Black, Bert, 261n8
Black's Law Dictionary, fraud defined by, 26
Bloggers, role in Washington's 2004
    gubernatorial election, 115–16,
    272nn95,97, 275n146
Blunt, Matt, 101–2
Boardman v. Esteva, 203, 206
Bond, Christopher "Kit," 99, 101
    identification requirements and, 95–96,
    135, 136, 139, 140, 279n33, 280n39
    registration procedures and, 8
Bradbury, Bill, 264n45
Bridges, John, 125
Brost, Kirsten, 121
Bryce, James, 16
Buckno, Norma, 72–73
Building Industry Association of Washington
    (BIAW), 126, 276nn155–156
Burke, Chip, 112
Burman, Dave, 119
Burmeister, Sue, 92
Burnham, Walter Dean, 38, 39, 43–45,
    257n32
Bush, George H. W., 49, 136
Bush, George W. *See* 2000 presidential
    election; 2004 presidential election
Bush v. Gore, 92, 118, 119

Calculus of voting model. *See* Rational
    choice theory
California
    absentee ballots, 55–56, 61, 260n70
    complaint data, 57–61
    election codes and case law, 203–4
    registration laws, 5, 42
    September 11 hijackers and, 9
Callahan, David, 224, 225
Campbell, Tracy, 38
Cantwell, Maria, 113, 121
Carlson, John, 121
*Carlson v. Oconto County Bd. of
    Canvassers*, 217
Cassidy, Ed, 126
Chaudhary, Usman Ali, 33–34, 254n45
Chavez, Linda, 224
Chertoff, Michael, 7
Civil rights issues
    dynamics of electoral competition and,
    87–89
    federal enforcement of voting rights, 27

identification requirements, 139–40,
    282n67
incorporation of African Americans into
    party system, 87–89
registration laws, 24–25
Clay, William Lacy Jr., 100
Clinton, Bill, 8, 136
Clinton, Hillary Rodham, 140
Coleman, Norm, 263n35
Colorado
    absentee ballots in, 132–33
    allegations of voter fraud in ACVR report,
    164–67
    election day registration, 5
    election laws, 132–33, 277n6
    identification requirements, 148, 282n76
    2002 election and, 2
Coney, Lillie, 221–22
Connecticut, identification requirements,
    143
Consequences of allegations of voter fraud,
    129–58
    HAVA and identification requirements,
    134–35, 139–41, 150–53, 278n29,
    279n30
    myth of fraud and voter exclusion,
    153–58
    NVRA and corruption versus inefficiency,
    136–39
    unwieldy election laws and Colorado,
    130–34
    see also Partisan allegations of voter fraud
Contemporary evidence of U.S. election
    vulnerability, 45–56
    federal government prosecutions, 45–48,
    258nn37,46,47
    Forty-Sixth Congressional District in 1996
    election, 49–56, 259nn61,64, 260n71
Converse, Philip E., 39, 40, 44
Conyers, John, 126
Costa Rica, 251n7
Covode v. Foster, 15–16, 250n44
Cox, Gary, 86, 87
Crawford v. Marion County Election Board,
    154–58, 284nn84,86

Daschle, Tom, 3, 139
"Deadwood," weeding from voter
    registration lists, 138–39
Delaware
    identification requirements, 143
    registration laws, 41
Demeo, Marisa J., 140
Democracy, ideology of myth and, 90–92